World War II Survivors
Lessons in Resilience

Glenn R. Schiraldi, Ph.D.

World War II Survivors

Lessons in Resilience

© 2007 Glenn Schiraldi
Published by Chevron Publishing Corp.
5018 Dorsey Hall Drive, Suite 104
Ellicott City, MD 21042

Cover design by Peggy Johnson
Edited by Diane Gwin
Layout design by Peggy Johnson

All rights reserved.
No part of this book may be reproduced, translated, stored in a retrieval system, or transmitted, in any form or by any means, electronic, mechanical, photocopying, microfilming, recording, or otherwise, without written permission from the Publisher.

Excerpts from *The Life Story of John Winston Downs*, unpublished autobiography by J. W. Downs. Copyright © 1966 by J. W. Downs. Reprinted by permission.

"Give Me a Man," poem by John R. Giles, III, reprinted from *No Regrets: The Autobiography of Brigadier General Don Rue Hickman, U.S. Army*, unpublished autobiography by D. R. Hickman. Copyright © 2000 by D. R. Hickman. Reprinted by permission.

Printed in the United States of America.
This book is printed on acid-free paper.

Library of Congress Card Catalog Number
Application in process
ISBN-1-883581-23-0
ISBN-978-1883581-23-7

CHEVRON
PUBLISHING CORPORATION
5018 Dorsey Hall Drive, Suite 104
Ellicott City, MD 21042 USA
Telephone: (410) 740-0065
Fax: (410) 740-9213
office@chevronpublishing.com
www.chevronpublishing.com

Dedication

To the individuals in this book and the comrades with whom they served, we, the younger generations, salute you. We, whose freedoms you have preserved, express our profound gratitude—for your service and the examples that you have set for us.

Forward

World War II gave birth to many things of great wonder. We unleashed the power of the atom. The jet propulsion engine was developed. Great advances were seen in military medicine. And we saw emerge a generation of individuals who were special in many ways...so special that they have been referred to as "the greatest generation." One attribute that they clearly showed was that of resilience.

Dr. Glenn Schiraldi has compiled an amazing collection of stories...personal accounts of resilience in the face of great adversity. Dr. Schiraldi takes the most important step toward answering the question, "What made the greatest generation great?" Is it resilience?

Resilience may be thought of as the ability to rebound in the face of adversity. Perhaps it is more, perhaps it is a form of immunity to distress associated with adversity. Whatever it is, it appears to be an essential life skill. So how does one learn to be resilient? Clearly, one source is to study those who have shown the attribute to an extraordinary magnitude. Dr. Schiraldi has given us a highly unique and personal glimpse into the nature of resilience.

This book is not only informative, but it is entertaining...the stuff from which movies are made. The lessons learned from these 41 personal examples of resilience are lessons that we all can benefit from. They are lessons that we should endeavor to teach our children.

They are lessons from which, in our darkest moments, we can learn. They are lessons of life, of joy, of sorrow. There is something for everyone in this book

George S. Everly, Jr., Ph.D.
Johns Hopkins Center for Public Health Preparedness, and
Johns Hopkins University School of Medicine

Table of Contents

Dedication iii
Foreword iv
Introduction vii

PART I: EARLY YEARS 1
Chapter 1. Irene Gut Opdyke, *Polish Partisan* 3
Chapter 2. Captain Joseph Knefler Taussig, Jr., *Pearl Harbor* 13
Chapter 3. Leonard Lee Robinson, *Bataan Death March* 21
Chapter 4. Earnest Benjamin "Benny" Dunn, *Burma-Thailand Death Railway* ... 31

PART II: EUROPEAN THEATER OF OPERATIONS 41
Chapter 5. Thomas E. Vail, *B-17 Bombardier* 43
Chapter 6. John Winston Downs, *B-17 Down* 51
Chapter 7. Vernon J. Tipton, *Down over France* 59
Chapter 8. Colonel Charles Edward McGee, *Tuskegee Airman* 67
Chapter 9. Carl Douglas "Chubby" Proffitt, Jr., *Omaha Beach* 75
Chapter 10. Jerry N. Markham, *Navy Frogman, Omaha Beach* 83
Chapter 11. Alfred A. Alvarez, *Omaha Beach* 93
Chapter 12. Quentin C. Aanenson, *Fighter Pilot* 103
Chapter 13. Kenneth John Sawyer, *Gold Beach* 111
Chapter 14. Amos E. Small, *With the Band of Brothers* 117
Chapter 15. Russell Dunham, *Medal of Honor* 125
Chapter 16. Roy A. Freitag, *Tank Commander* 133
Chapter 17. Colonel Douglas Clark Dillard, *Battle of the Bulge* 139
Chapter 18. Robert R. Vanover, *Infantryman on the Western Front* 149
Chapter 19. Seymour D. Selzer, *Standing Against Hitler* 155
Chapter 20. Brigadier General Don Rue Hickman. *Rifle Company Commander* ... 163
Chapter 21. Michael DeMarco, *Footsoldier* 171
Chapter 22. Glenn Howard Hamm, *193rd Glider Infantry Regiment* 179
Chapter 23. Lin H. Johnson, *Scout Corporal* 187
Chapter 24. Jackson Brownell Vail, *Infantry Squad Leader* 193
Chapter 25. Joseph Robert Curcio, *Surrounded and Wounded* 199
Chapter 26. Robert B. Jacobs, *Supporting the 9th Army* 205
Chapter 27. George S. Everly, *Signal Corps* 215

Chapter 28. John David Blumgart, *Captured at Inden* 221
Chapter 29. Colonel Robert "Butch" Carroll Kendrick, *Paratrooper* 227

PART III: PACIFIC THEATER OF OPERATIONS 237
Chapter 30. Troy Dempsey Sullivan, *USS* St. Louis 239
Chapter 31. Emil Paul Kauffmann, *Platoon Sergeant* 247
Chapter 32. Milo Louis Ballinger, *USS* Rocky Mount 253
Chapter 33. Karl J. Nielson, *USS California* 263
Chapter 34. Colonel Thomas McCoy Fields, *Iwo Jima* 271
Chapter 35. Luther Carl "Juke" Crabtree, *Iwo Jima* 279
Chapter 36. Robert Davis, *Bougainville and Iwo Jima* 291
Chapter 37. Dr. Samuel William Billison, *Navajo Code Talker* 295
Chapter 38. George M. Nash, *Navy Frogman* 303
Chapter 39. Frank Albert Tinker, *Pilot in Japanese Prison Camps* 311
Chapter 40. Byron Stanley Harris, *Abandon Ship!* 323
Chapter 41. Brigadier General Oscar Esko Davis, *Serving in Three Wars* 331
Chapter 42. Epilogue: *Portrait of Resilience* 339

APPENDICES 343
Appendix 1: Key Dates 345
Appendix 2: References and Resources 348
About the Author 349
Photo Credits 350

Introduction

Following the outbreak of WWII, America and her allies sent forth a uniquely prepared generation to defend the cause of freedom. They generally served honorably, endured their trials courageously, and returned to live productive lives. In this turbulent post-9/11era, our hearts again turn to this remarkable generation, seeking the timeless lessons about resilience that they must *still* reveal to us. What strengths of mind and character enabled them to cope under duress? How did they survive the cauldron of war? What made them strong? How might their experiences help us to navigate *our* perilous challenges ahead?

Here forty-one survivors of WWII combat, all but two American-born, tell their stories — how they endured war and returned to live fruitful lives. Their backgrounds ranged from dire to privileged. They hailed from the coal mining regions of West Virginia to the farms of the heartland, ranches of the West, and cities of the Northeast. Their accounts cover far-ranging aspects of the war, including Hitler's invasion of Poland, Pearl Harbor, the Bataan Death March, the Burma-Thailand Death Railway, D-Day, Bastogne, Iwo Jima, and Stalag Luft III — the prison camp made famous by the movie *The Great Escape*. They represent and evoke the proud names of Tuskegee Airmen, Navajo Code Talkers, Infantrymen, Airmen, Sailors, and Marines. Despite their diverse backgrounds, they shared certain commonalities: All were united by a common cause. All overcame enormous adversity and came home well adjusted. All learned and shared powerful lessons on coping which are vitally relevant today.

Over a five-year period, I traveled the country to interview the forty-one individuals, almost always in their homes. They were located in nearly all cases by word of mouth. That is, I asked people to identify people whom they knew to be (1) survivors of combat, (2) well-adjusted, and (3) well married — an enduring marriage being one indicator of good psychological adjustment. The interviews typically lasted several hours, and sometimes spanned several days. The average interviewee was just over eighty years of age at the time of the interview.

In order to put their insights into context, the survivors first described their pre-war lives, and then their war experiences. I explained the symptoms of post-traumatic stress disorder (PTSD),* which can afflict combat survivors, and ruled out its occurrence as another indication of good adjustment.

Then we discussed the strengths of mind and character that enabled these individuals to function well under duress and live satisfying lives, despite the wartime strains that have historically caused many to break psychologically. I started with an open-ended question ("What helped you to cope?") and then asked specifically about the attributes identified in the scientific and historical literature as factors that protect against PTSD. The attributes that I specifically inquired about were:

- Calm under pressure
- Rational thought process

- Social support

- Comfort with emotions

- Self-esteem

- Active, creative (or flexible) coping

- Spiritual/philosophical strengths—which included beliefs in divinity, meaning and purpose, morality, love/altruism, optimism, humor, and the long view of suffering.

- Maintaining balanced living—which included recreational interests and health practices.

Finally, I asked what advice they would wish to pass on to benefit younger generations. I generally called and/or revisited the individuals to check or clarify facts, and returned the manuscripts for review and corrections.

What have resulted are profiles of resilience—those strengths of mind and character found in hardy survivors. As these stories make clear, resilience does not simply emerge during crisis, but is cultivated over a lifetime. Once acquired, resilience facilitates performance under pressure, protects against mental illness, speeds recovery in those who psychologically stumble, and promotes growth and well-being across the lifespan. We have learned from the study of public health problems that preventing illnesses by strengthening individuals is far more effective than trying to treat illnesses that have already occurred. Since approximately half of American adults will suffer from stress-related mental illnesses (including post-traumatic stress disorder, anxiety, depression, problem anger, and substance abuse), the vital importance of understanding and developing resilience becomes very clear.

Because these survivors' strengths were forged in the crucible of personal experience, their lessons are credible and beneficial to all of us who are coping with stressors large and small—from everyday overload to war and terrorism. This book might especially interest those whose work puts them in the path of traumatic stressors and thus places them at higher risk for stress-related disorders. These include firefighters, police officers, military service personnel, rescue and disaster workers, emergency medical service providers, doctors, nurses, and other emergency responders. Because it vividly describes the nature of war, *WWII Survivors* will likely interest active duty service men and women, military personnel in training, and veterans who all must make sense of combat. Since resilience is also vital to the recovery process, survivors of any trauma, including rape and abuse, could greatly benefit from the universal lessons found herein. Families, friends, and health professionals who care about vulnerable or afflicted individuals might also find this book important. Because no one in today's volatile climate is immune to stress, parents, teachers, youth leaders, managers, counselors, and clergy might also find this book to be a valuable resource.

A few observations about the process of compiling the book seem fitting. First, I was impressed at the recall accuracy of the interviewees. I checked as many historical details as feasible. However, I was primarily interested in personal perspectives, rather than historical precision. If certain historical details miss the mark precisely, I hope that this does not detract from the primary purpose of this book.

Second, although I tried to be detached and objective in my role as a researcher, this was indeed challenging at times. This was, after all, the generation of my parents, aunts, and uncles. My admiration for these people and the sacrifices that they made for their country was undoubtedly apparent. On not a few occasions both the interviewed and the interviewer fought tears as the survivors related their poignant stories. In becoming acquainted with them and in calling or revisiting to check aspects of the interview, I indeed felt like I was speaking to respected friends and family, and genuinely felt interested in their lives. It was not unusual to hear comments as I departed, such as, "It feels like you're family." In every case I left feeling profound gratitude for their service, for the examples of their lives, and for the privilege of being in their company. I tried to let them know of my gratitude, and the gratitude of the younger generations, for both their wartime sacrifices and their life examples. One career soldier said, "God bless you, old soldier." I felt that he was speaking for all his contemporaries in conveying their love of country and their profound connections to the younger generations.

Third, I continue to be impressed by the many ways in which these survivors' lives edify us. Their lessons transcend simply coping with war. After all, they have endured not only WWII and the Great Depression, but also the challenges of living a long life—including marriage and family, work and retirement, death and illnesses of loved ones, and personal illness. War is a metaphor for other forms of stress, and their lives indeed provide sublime insights into surviving many forms of adversity across the lifespan. Perhaps their greatest legacy is their strength of character and examples. It also seems to me that each individual expressed at least one crucial lesson on coping in a uniquely powerful way. Even their glimpses of pre-war America and Europe, of a time when life was simpler and perhaps happier, seem instructive.

As you read these stories, you will meet ordinary people who often served in extraordinary ways—human beings at their courageous best. Their accounts are poignant, heartwarming, and often humorous. They instruct, inspire, and empower, for their stories reveal more than just history, but what was in their minds and hearts.

NOTE: PTSD was formally named following the Vietnam War to describe a complex of symptoms that can result from exposure to an extremely distressing event or series of events, such as combat, terrorism, rape, abuse, torture, tornadoes, or industrial or traffic accidents. The disorder significantly disrupts the victim's life and includes symptoms from the following three areas: (1) Re-experiencing the event in distressing ways—haunting memories at unwanted times, recurrent nightmares, or flashbacks; (2) Arousal—difficulties sleeping or concentrating, angry outbursts or irritability, being easily startled, and/or being constantly on the lookout for danger; (3) Emotional numbing—avoiding any reminders of the trauma, forgetting aspects of the trauma, withdrawing from people or formerly pleasant activities, feeling different from others, and/or difficulty feeling tender or happy feelings.

Part I
Early Years

Chapter 1

Irene Gut Opdyke
Polish Partisan

Irene Gut Opdyke was in nursing school in Radom, Poland, when Hitler's forces invaded her country in 1939. She fled to the Ukraine with the Polish army. Returning to Poland, this young Catholic girl risked her life to save Jews and serve in the resistance movement. Her story is one of extraordinary courage and compassion.

Mrs. Opdyke now lives in beautiful Yorba Linda, California. Her walls are filled with awards and recognitions, including the Righteous Among the Nations Award. This award, which Oskar Schindler also received, is given by the Israeli Holocaust Commission to people who risked their lives to aid Jews during the Holocaust.

She also received Israel's highest honor, the Israel Medal of Honor, and a special commendation from the Vatican.

A diminutive, elegant woman with warm, radiant blue eyes and delicate features, she is one of the kindest, most loving women I have encountered. She reminds one of Mother Teresa. As she spoke I often found myself choking back tears. She says, "I try to bring the love to children." As we parted, she gave me a kiss and a hug, saying, "You are like a son, I love you" — words I will always cherish.

We were five girls in my family. I was the oldest—born May 5, 1922, in Kozienice, eastern Poland. The others came about every two years and were born in different cities in Poland, as father moved for his work. Father was a builder, an architect and chemist, who made ceramic parts for factories.

I had wonderful parents. They taught us to help humans in need. There was always someone we had to help with food. For holidays like Christmas, we always had two or three chairs for invited guests. We helped gypsies in the forest, animals, anyone who needed help we were taught to help. All my sisters are wonderful, wonderful people. We brought every animal home that needed help—cats, dogs, birds. Mother ministered to sick gypsies and called the doctor if needed. She had a talent for animals. She rehabilitated birds and could get them to come to the window to be fed. She provided whatever old people needed—food, drink, or encouragement.

We were a happy and close family. We loved our parents very much. There was always music and singing in our house. Father loved to play the piano and guitar. We all loved to sing and had beautiful voices. Mother taught us cooking, baking, and cleaning. I baked very beautiful tortes. We went to church regularly and dressed nicely.

My parents taught us right and wrong. There were rules. We had to be nice to people. When we did wrong, father would correct us kindly and talk to us about being good human beings. Mother said you can marry a millionaire, but you must still learn to work. We had a maid, yet we had to scrub our wooden floor and mother checked.

Father and Mother did not distinguish among their friends—Jews, Germans, Poles—and neither did we. My parents were happy that we had many friends of different backgrounds.

We were well-to-do, not rich, but we had no worry about money. You might say we were upper echelon, Polish intelligentsia. We had a maid from the village. They gladly came to learn how to serve.

When I was a teen, we were living near the German border. Hitler was already screaming over the radio. My father had no son, but I thought I'd be a nurse to help in the defense of Poland. I left my family at the age of sixteen to study nursing in Radom, an industrial center in central Poland.

WORLD WAR II SURVIVORS - LESSONS IN RESILIENCE

The Invasion

Poland was taken from both sides by the Germans and the Russians. The Luftwaffe bombed Radom on September 1, 1939, as I was walking to the hospital. The city was on fire, and the wounded were everywhere. I had tended the wounded at the hospital for several days when the Polish army officers asked for volunteers to go with them. I, three other young nursing students, and other nurses and doctors joined them as we fled eastward. But a Polish general said the war was over because of the German/Russian pact. So we ran to the forest in the Polish Ukraine. We had little food, and would go to the villages to barter for food. A Russian patrol truck came and I was standing watch alone. I had time to yell a warning to my friends, and then tried to run to the woods. Three soldiers got hold of me and violated me, beat me, and left me in the snow to die. Someone found me and brought me to a Russian hospital in Ternopol. After recovering, I was put to work as a nurse. There I met Dr. David, a Ukrainian Pole, who helped me to escape after the hospital administrator tried to rape me. I had hit the administrator with a bottle with all my might and was scared that I had killed him. I told Dr. David, and he helped me to escape eastward to the Russian village of Svetlana. I stayed there a year with a woman doctor who had gone to medical school with Dr. David. I believe that Dr. David was Jewish.

Exchange

In January of 1941, I learned that Poles could now return to their families by going back through Ternopol for processing. I wanted to go home so I took a train to Ternopol, where somebody recognized me from the hospital. I was arrested and repeatedly interrogated with threats of Siberia and torture. The hospital administrator had accused me of being a dangerous Polish partisan and spy. I hid my train ticket in my bra. They tried to discover the identity of my friends who helped me escape from the hospital and hide. I escaped from a guard and ran through back alleys and yards back to the train station. The time was now past for my train to leave. However, I learned that the train had been delayed for two days and I boarded it. Crossing into German-held Poland, the passengers were placed in a quarantine camp. I was suffering from influenza. A German guard thought I was German because of my blond hair and blue eyes, my German-sounding name, and the fact that I spoke German. That helped me. He got the doctor. At last I recovered and continued on to Radom, where my aunt lived.

Radom

By now, my shoes were falling apart and my coat was to the floor. I could not find my way in the ruined city with new German street names. A man in a buggy took pity on me. He said he had four daughters and didn't mind that I couldn't pay him. After traveling for some time, I recognized the house. When I got off I found that all my family was now at my aunt's house. My father had left everything in Oberschlesien, ousted by the Germans. Now he was making black market slippers. I told my father about my experience at the hands of the Russian soldiers. He said, "Child, that should not ruin your life. During war, men are animals. You didn't freeze in the forest. Someone found you. That means God has something for you to do."

Soon thereafter, the Gestapo picked up my father because they needed to make changes in the machinery in a factory that he'd built in Oberschlesien. We had no way to make a life. Pretty girls were put in soldiers' casinos and brothels there. So Mother decided to take the three young girls and go be with Father. Janina and I, the oldest, stayed in Radom. We cried for loneliness. Later I learned that the youngest girls became slaves in the clay mines.

One Sunday at church, the doors opened and we found that the church was surrounded by the Gestapo and Wehrmacht. They took the young boys and girls. I was sent to work in the ammunition factory. I was weak from malnutrition and anemia and fainted at my station. When the Major Rügemer came to inspect, he saw me and yelled at the soldiers for using sick people. He asked me my name. I answered in German. He asked if I was German. I said, "No, I am Polish and Catholic." He said I spoke good German. I said I had learned it in high school as a second language since we lived near the German border. He said he would assign me to serve meals to officers and secretaries who were quartered in a large hotel in town. I was assigned to work with the cook named Schulz. He was Wehrmacht, a good man. When we were introduced, he said I was skinny, and gave me food to eat.

Once I was setting tables in an upstairs ballroom of the hotel. There were heavy velvet drapes. I heard shooting, dogs barking, and screaming. I opened the curtains to look. I saw the Gestapo running after people in the Jewish ghetto, dogs biting, dead bodies. I stood paralyzed with my mouth opened. I asked Schulz, "What is happening? Why are they doing that?" He put his hand over my mouth, and said, "Shhhhhh. Don't let the officers know that you feel sorry."

There was a small space between the hotel and the Jewish ghetto. The ghetto was surrounded by a fence with barbed wire on top. I dug a hole under the fence with a spoon. I filled a metal box with bread, butter, meat, and whatever other food I could steal and placed the box under the fence. The next day the box was empty. That was the first thing I did to help. I continued to do that each day.

I asked Schulz if my sister Janina could come to work in the hotel because I wanted to be near her. I asked him for a job away from the German soldiers, working as a secretary. The Major approved this. By this time the Germans were fighting the Russians. Ironically, the whole plant moved east to Ternopol! Before we left Radom, the Jewish ghetto was bulldozed.

In Ternopol, I again prepared food and served officers quartered in a hotel. I saw hangings. As we walked by, the Gestapo would force us to watch. I saw the killing of men, women, and babies.

I believed in God. I had been taught by my parents. But there I threw a tantrum against my Maker. I said, "I don't believe in you. How could you not help? They were little angels." I cried in my bed with visions of these children in my soul. I awoke with an answer in my heart that "I am your God and will help; I will be with you always." I asked Him to help me to help. I said I am still young. I don't know much. I believed so strongly that God said to me that he would be with me always, and that's what I felt.

I was also put in charge of a laundry facility. Twelve Jewish men and woman from the local work camp were brought by truck each day to work there. I had asked Schultz to bring them, pretending that I needed the help. They were afraid of me because they thought I was German. I wanted them to understand that I was their friend. Every day after dinner I put leftovers in a clean towel in a laundry basket. Pretty soon they realized I was a friend. From then on I took care of them. When it was cold and they were freezing, I asked Schulz for a few blankets for my sister and me. Schulz gave me many. I felt that he knew what I was doing, but didn't want it known that he knew. We made a hiding place behind the shelves in the laundry room in anticipation of a time it would be needed.

The Villa

One of the men I served food to was an icy SS battalion commander, Sturmbannführer Rokita—the head of the Gestapo. He was always bragging of liquidating the ghettos and the killings in the concentration camp. He said that soon there would be no Jews left in Ternopol, which I told my friends in the laundry room.

The Major wanted to commandeer a big villa to entertain officers from Berlin, and he wanted me to be the housekeeper. My Jewish friends knew that the villa had been built by a Jewish architect. There was a rumor that it had a secret hiding place. The Major sent Schulz and me to see it. I saw that it had servants' quarters in the basement. I told my friends in the laundry room that we would hide them under the Germans' noses, and that with God's blessings this would be possible. In the meantime, Rokita is doing the liquidation. I took six of the 12 in the laundry room to the forest by hiding them in a hay wagon. I left them in the forest. I felt like a bad mother to leave them there.

They lived in a hole under a tree. The summer was not too bad because there were berries and mushrooms, and I brought supplies as often as I could.

While serving dinner, I overheard Rokita tell the Major that this was the week when Ternopol would be free of Jews. The Major protested that he needed the workers. When the Gestapo came with a wagon to pick up the workers, I hid them behind the shelves and told the soldier that they had left to sleep in their homes. He looked in the laundry room and did not see them. That night there was a big party in the hotel. Fearing that the Gestapo would return and search more thoroughly the next day, I brought all six to the Major's apartment. I hid them in an air vent above the bathtub. The idea to use that vent as a hiding place had come to me that day all of a sudden when I needed a solution. I was cleaning the Major's room when light from a window shined on the vent that I had never before noticed.

The next day the Ukrainian family that was staying in the villa moved out, so I could now move my six Jewish friends there. That night the Major retired early because he had a headache from the previous night's party. He took a sleeping pill and was snoring. I entered his room and let my friends out from the air vent. I stole his keys and opened the hotel doors, permitting them to escape into the night. They found the villa and entered through the coal chute.

The next day I ran to the villa. I went downstairs and saw my six friends plus four others whom I hadn't met before. Now there were ten people in my keeping.

I learned that the Major would paint the villa that day, so I hid them in the attic until I could safely return them to the basement. Altogether, they stayed safely in the basement more than seven months. I also smuggled another with pneumonia back from the forest along with her husband.

A married couple, Ida and Lazar Haller, discovered that she was pregnant. They decided they must end the pregnancy to save everyone from being discovered. I asked them not to do this. In the forest, I spoke to a Polish freedom fighter named Zygmunt. He told me to bring her to his house in the forest. There he had a hidden room, from which he communicated by radio with England. I took valuables from the villa and smuggled them to Zygmunt, along with other supplies. My excuse to the German soldiers was that I was going to visit my cousin in the forest.

One day, returning from the warehouse, SS men were hanging a Jewish family and the Polish family that had been hiding them. The SS made us watch. I stumbled back to the villa. I was so stunned that I did not lock the door behind me as usual. I could not tell my friends what I'd seen, but they knew something was terribly wrong and were comforting me. Just then, the Major came in. He was furious as I pleaded with him to spare their lives. Eventually he said that he would keep my secret if I gave myself willingly to him. I could not tell my friends about this.

Escape

The Russians were approaching now. The Major said that rumors were spreading and that I must get rid of my friends. I smuggled them out to the forest in a wagon at night, dressing one of the men in the Major's uniform. Then the Germans retreated westward to Kielce. There I escaped from the Major. Zygmunt had given me the address of a partisan couple. I went there and said the code word, Mercedes-Benz. I joined the partisans. I met their son Janek, who was very handsome. That was the first time I fell in love. The parents were very happy and we were so happy. As partisans, we had to plan to marry in the forest. His mother was making my wedding dress and I was full of pins when he walked in and took me in his arms to dance. He said, "You are so beautiful. I love you." I was counting on the wedding. He was going that day to ambush a German transport that had much-needed ammunition. I begged him not to go, but he said he was the leader. That night I heard a knock on the door. I knew Janek was dead. I felt like taking poison to join him.

Now I had no fear of death. I knew that God was looking over me and helping me. I was a messenger girl for the partisans. I carried money dropped from planes from England. I hid messages in my hair when I talked face to face with German guards. My excuse was that I was taking my bike to see my family. I became very sick with pneumonia from living in the forest, and stayed with Janek's parents. They wanted me to stay, but the war was ending and I wanted to find my family. I was twenty-three and feeling so old and exhausted. As I was traveling homeward, I first went to Kraków to see if I could find my Jewish friends from the villa. I had heard that many Jews from Ternopol had gone there. Through the temples and synagogues I located many of them. I learned that Ida Haller had borne a son, Roman, at Zygmunt's home. I thanked God for "my baby." As I was walking to the Haller's, two Soviet military policemen arrested me. I was known as a partisan, and was suspected of being a leader. I was interrogated for days. Because I was so thin, I was able to squeeze through the bars of a window and escape. From the Jewish underground, I learned that my father had been killed by the Nazis. I was being hunted by the Russians. After being arrested because of me, my mother and sisters had been released and were now in hiding.

Repatriation

I could only flee the country. My Jewish friends died my hair black and smuggled me to a Jewish repatriation camp in Germany. I contracted diphtheria there. I was there three years when in 1949 a United Nation's delegate came to interview me. His name was William Opdyke and he was American. We spoke through a translator. He was moved by my story, and said that he would be glad to help me come to the U.S.

I came to the U.S. without a family. The second day I found work in a factory. I learned English. I was grateful to be in the U.S. and felt entitled to nothing. It was hard and lonely without a family. I was a citizen when I met Bill again in a coffee shop in 1956. He asked me to dinner, and six weeks later we married. A year later we had a little daughter. God gave me a family of my own.

In the 1970s, friends in a Jewish organization went to Poland. I learned that my mother died of a stroke shortly after the Nazis killed my father. But my sisters were still alive. My sister Janina wrote, "Come, I am waiting for you." Although I was afraid of the Russians, I flew to Poland because my desire to see my family was so great. I have been three times now to Poland.

We raised our daughter in Yorba Linda. We had orchards. My daughter has two children and lives on a horse farm in Washington. I have been talking all over the world for the last twenty years.

The Hallers never knew what I did to help them. How could I tell them? After the war, they lived in Munich. They went to see Major Rügemer, who had become fond of my friends in the villa. His two sons were Gestapo, so he had been ostracized and had no home. The Hallers helped him to get a home. Roman, the Haller's son, played with him. I met Roman when I went to Israel in 1982 to receive an award.

PTSD Symptoms?

I did not have PTSD. I made it my mission in life to help. I kept busy and filled up my time. I had no time to be distressed. Thank God everything passed away. Sometimes in dreams you can see things. It is still hard to discuss some things and I still want to cry. You can not help this. I'm a good speaker because I speak from my heart. I don't use notes. I've been in thousands of places.

What Helped You Cope?

I am very thankful to God for the opportunity to save lives. What could be better than that? There's no time to feel sorry for myself.

Our parents taught us to be self-reliant. When Mother took the youngest sisters on vacation, Janina and I were left to take care of Daddy. We learned responsibility.

CALM UNDER PRESSURE

I could not be influenced by pressure if I was to be helpful. I was afraid not for myself but for my friends in the villa. I felt anger at Rokita and wanted to hit him with a tray, but I had to keep it under control because I was responsible for others.

When the Russians interrogated me, I had to stay calm. They asked for the names of the friends who had sheltered me. I said, "I don't remember." "You don't look that stupid," they said. I said, "There is a war, and I'm without my family." I gave them my dog's name.

I hate Hitler with all my heart and soul, but in a way to be able to speak as I do you must forgive, too. Without forgiveness I cannot live. Schulz made it difficult to hate the Germans. He showed me pictures of his wife and children. He knew what I was doing. When I escaped from the Major I had already forgiven him. The Major was an old man, quiet. I never expected him to want me. But like my father said, war makes people animals. He allowed my sister to come to work at the hotel and then go back home when Rokita became interested. He was good to my friends in the villa. I couldn't speak and love children if I held grudges. Forgiving was a decision, even though it was difficult to do. It was the only way I could stay alive.

RATIONAL THOUGHT PROCESSES

In Svetlana, there was a beautiful Christmas tree. I'd remember the good things. I'd focus on the good things, and not the bad. Despite the terrible things people did, there were also so many people who were good and brave.

Prayer helped me through. I asked God for help: "I am so young, and don't know much and I want to help." I had the feeling that He always put me in the right place at the right time.

I get upset when people blame others in an over-general way. For example, a young rabbi once blamed all of Poland for mistreating the Jews. I kindly corrected him. I had the courage to explain that that was true of some, but not all.

When times are tough, I have to do what I *can* do. In the war I did what I could do. In the U.S., I found a job in a factory making bras and corsets.

For my mistakes in the war, I can't feel sorry because I was trying to help. Today when I speak I don't worry that I make mistakes in the language. I know people will understand.

SOCIAL SUPPORT

I have no enemies. People, especially children and youth, like me. They hug me. On the streets after I speak to them they come after me for another hug because I love them and they feel that. American children are hungry for love—the love of parents and grandparents. Parents must set time to talk, to know them. Children are running off most of the time. They don't come home from school. Young people will listen when they feel love.

People are just people—not Jews or Germans. If not taught to love, they hate. I feel sorry for those who hate because they are not happy. I have many Jewish and Christian friends today. It makes no difference. I love them all.

The love of my family was very important and sustaining. Since the war, family has been very important. I was to go this Christmas to Poland to spend it with my sisters, but the doctor said no. Instead, my youngest sister came here to take care of me.

I loved my husband very much.

I have kept contact with and reunited with several of the people I helped. I gave one a ticket from New York to California so that she could stay with me in my home. I helped collect money for Israel. The Haller's baby was born in 1944. Even though I wanted to see my family, I first saw my friends and their baby. I am still in contact. They called just a few days ago to wish me Happy New Year.

COMFORT WITH EMOTIONS

I am not afraid to show emotions if they come naturally. I *am* emotional when I speak. The pictures are before my eyes and heart like a kaleidoscope, so how can you be unemotional? I allow feelings to come out. I tell young people, "I am here because I love you. I want you to understand that the future is in your hands and you must love and help each other. Hate accomplishes nothing. It ruins your lives, your families, and your country. We all belong to one human family." I still can cry. I have the feeling.

I wrote my book so that we wouldn't forget and so that young people would know what war was like. I am happy with the book. In a very personal way it makes the Holocaust live. It puts names to people. I cried many times in writing my book, but afterward felt better.

SELF-ESTEEM

I always felt I had something to contribute. As a youth, I studied to be the best to make my parents proud. I didn't date or go to movies while in nursing school. I felt I had something to accomplish. I didn't know what, except to be a nurse to help people defend against Hitler.

I wrote my book because I wanted to share my life with young people. Even though I am getting old, there is time to do things before I die. I am not afraid to die, but I want to accomplish as long as possible to speak and have my movie come out. Not for money or for glory, but to encourage people not to be afraid to love, help, and learn.

ACTIVE, ADAPTIVE COPING

I could not be passive and help. I am determined. What you start you must finish. Rokita had said that Ternopol would be Jew-free. But I had to take action to ensure that it was not, that my friends lived. Shuffling my friends around the hotel was very hard; there were Gestapo living there. I had help from the Almighty.

I knew I was young and couldn't shoot, so I asked God for strength to help me to help. Then I kept thinking up ways to help. I told Schulz that we needed more help and obtained Jewish workers from the ghetto. Once when a worker in the laundry did not return, I feared an SS raid. So I told Major Rügemer that the worker had taken some of the secretaries' dresses to the ghetto to work on a special sewing machine. He gave me a pass to go to the ghetto, where I found her hiding, and brought her back. The SS had raided her home and taken her family.

When the Russians were asking me all those questions, I kept my mind on an injured stork that we had nursed as children. The stork was formidable, it fought back although it was captured and weak. Then it flew away at the first opportunity. Thinking of that image gave me courage. It gave me a way to find words and not reveal names of the partisans. When I saw the first chance, I escaped, too.

I saw a German soldier throw what looked like a fat bird into the air and shoot it. It was not a bird. It was a child. That was a haunting vision. Later, with the help of Jennifer Armstrong, who helped me write my book, I actively changed that vision; I came to view it as a bird flying away, in freedom.

Rokita was taken with Janina. She was very beautiful, statuesque. Finally, I had the courage to talk to the Major. I told him I didn't want him to take advantage of her. I asked if he would allow her to leave. So he wrote a permit for her to go to Radom. In the hall, Rokita asked me where my sister went. It came to me to tell him that she had tuberculosis

The war was awful and difficult, but I was there to help, even if I should lose my life. If you witness what I witnessed you must be moved to action.

SPIRITUAL AND PHILOSOPHICAL STRENGTHS

God

God is someone who is for me and for everybody. He loves us all. When you pray and ask with a clear heart, you will be helped. I believe in that very much. When I cried, "Why did you not help?" I awoke with the knowledge in my heart that "I am God. There is evil." I prayed constantly and just asked to find a way to help, and did. I went to church during the war, and still go now.

After I had to give myself to the Major I felt very, very bad . In a church there was a young priest. He said I had to let all my friends go and leave the Major myself. He didn't understand. There was a war and I couldn't, so I did not, and he didn't give me absolution. In the U.S., after I was married, I told a priest my story. I was crying. The priest said, "My child, you were very young. There is no guilt in you because you did what you did to save others." That has helped me to this day.

Meaning and Purpose

I felt from a young age that my life had a purpose. As a baby, our dog saved me from falling into a river by biting onto my diapers. The priest told my mother that God had a purpose, a plan for me. After the Russians mistreated me, Father told me that I had survived for a purpose, to accomplish something. I knew as a teenager that I was destined to save lives.

In the war, I knew that my purpose was to save my friends and the unborn baby. Standing on a balcony of the villa, I spoke to God. "I don't know much. Should I feel guilty that I gave myself up to save the lives of my friends and an unborn baby?" A peace came over me. I knew that I was not alone. I depended on God. I also knew that my purpose was to disrupt the Germans as much as I could, and return to my family. If I had to die I hoped to do so with the least possible pain.

Morality

I was raised to be honest, but I had to deceive and cheat in order to survive and save others. I told the Major and Schulz that it is not right to kill innocent people in war. Maybe because of that they trusted me. I feel bad that I violated their trust, but I had to in order to save my friends from the concentration camp. I decided to do right, even though it was difficult.

I think morality means to be good to others, to help others, and to live virtuously. If married, you have one husband and are faithful. In Poland it was taken for granted that girls married before living with boys. After the war, morals haven't improved. Television does not put wholesome images before children. They see stories about witches, not angels.

Love

I am very comfortable loving. Most of all, my life is to love children. If I could just convince everyone that there is goodness, that they should not hate each other, I will accomplish much. That's what I pray I might do if I can live.

Optimism

I am not sitting. When you speak to kids and see their young faces, they have so much before them. I tell them: "I believe in you. You can be what you want to be. Learn, study, stay together. Don't fight. Fighting brings hate, war, and persecution."

Even though I saw much cruelty, I also think there is much good in the world. In the war I knew, in spite of all the troubles, that we would survive. Now, I am not afraid to die. We pick up our crown up there.

Humor

We all laughed at times. For a big party at the villa, I told the Major that my mother was a great entertainer, and asked him to put me in charge. So I went with Schulz and bought all the food needed, plus more for the people in the forest. There was a secret tunnel from the basement of the villa to a bunker under the gazebo. During the party, my friends were hiding under the gazebo when Rokita took a fräulein there. I was scared he'd hear Ida cough. I took a tray with glasses of wine and hors d'oeuvres and yelled, "I have something for you and the lady." He was so mad. He was improperly dressed. The people below could hear this and were laughing. Later they told me I had interrupted something.

It was farcical, almost funny, to think of hiding my friends under the commandant's nose, and feeding them with his food. To escape the Russians, I was disguised as a Jew, the only Catholic in a Jewish camp.

I use humor when I speak. Sometimes you must break up the heaviness. For example, I mention that my husband and I spoke six languages when we first met, but had none in common.

Long View of Suffering

Knowing all I went through, people ask if I would do it again. Yes, without even thinking about it. It is such a wonderful feeling to know I helped to save lives. It makes me happy inside. I saw my mission through to completion. Now Roman's son is a lawyer in England. I am sorry the war happened; it was horrible. But I am thankful to God that he helped me to help. I learned to depend on him. I am thankful for my life in the U.S.

Maintaining Balanced Living

I never drank in my life or smoked. If I had, I would not be alive today. I always exercised. I loved to swim. I like lots of milk, cheeses, bread, fruit, and vegetables. The thing I like least is meat. Normally, I have gotten ten hours of sleep; early to bed and early to rise.

I now balance between speaking and home, but speaking is my life. I travel and speak often. I've been too busy to realize that I'm getting old, until I look in the mirror. I speak to people of many different religions. I don't see any difference. I speak to many organizations around the world—schools, temples, churches, Holocaust Museum. I love to speak. I speak from my heart, never with prepared notes. I love the people I speak to. I love young people and would do anything for them. I am hugging them and they chase me and ask for another hug. They are hungry for love.

I read many books. I became, without formal training, an interior decorator, to help with bills. But I would play hooky and take my grandsons to the beach. I enjoyed them. I had a breast removed in 1984. I forgot about the surgery and caught a grandson falling out of a tree, and that was painful.

When my husband was alive I cooked and had parties. When my husband was ill with Alzheimer's, Jewish friends took him into a nursing home without charge, to repay me. He was the only non-Jew in the home.

Advice to Younger Generations

First of all, be a friend. Try to understand that we all belong to one family. We have only one God; no matter what language you speak, he will understand. Love, don't hate, because hate brings disaster—war, persecution, Holocaust. The world is so beautiful. If people love each other it will look better, more beautiful, warm. So love each other. There is a goodness in people. We must work hard to try to love and speak to everyone, explaining to people that hate will ruin you, your family, and your country. The most important thing is to love and stay together. Discuss things before trouble starts.

Listen to your heart. Youth can make a difference, fighting evil. You can accomplish most wonderful things if you learn and study—you can be anything you want to be if you are honest and aware of others, and if you draw strength from God and people's goodness.

William and Irene Opdyke

Irene at home in Yorba Linda, California

Still fearing the Russians, Irene, lower left, returns to Poland to reunite with her sisters, circa 1984

Chapter 2

Captain Joseph Knefler Taussig, Jr.
Pearl Harbor

Joe and Betty Taussig reside in Annapolis, Maryland, near his beloved U.S. Naval Academy. They designed their comfortable house, which overlooks the serene Severn River. Joe was among the Americans who saw the first action of WWII, the Japanese attack on Pearl Harbor. He was the officer of the deck of the USS Nevada, the only battleship to move under its own power during the attack. He lost a leg as a result of that action, and was awarded the Navy Cross for his performance on that day. Sturdy and hale, he exhibits a most agreeable blend of charm, good humor, and confidence. His wife describes him as fun-loving and exuberant, with an inner joy and contagious enthusiasm, "full of charge and crash." She adds that if he is in a room of one hundred people, they will all remember him.

I graduated from the United States Naval Academy (USNA) in 1941. My grandfather was an admiral, USNA class of 1867. Dad was a rear admiral, USNA class of 1899. Because my Dad was a Naval officer during the Great Depression, I was relatively privileged, though I didn't realize it. My parents never gave me money so I wouldn't think I was better off than the other kids. I sold magazines door to door.

There was no dysfunction in my family. Neither parent was ever heard to raise their voice, blaspheme, or swear. We enjoyed a sense of fun at home, although there were not many jokes. Father was gentle, quiet, and calm. He read a book every night after supper to us kids. (I was the youngest of three; I had two older sisters and was especially close to the middle sister who was near my age.) After we were nine or ten, mother broke out the card table and we played hearts and other card games. I had a very high IQ, yet no academic problems or achievements. My parents didn't pressure me ever. They were much more interested that I was well rounded and played. When I asked my parents about that once, they said, "Well, we discussed it, but we didn't get straight A's either." My family was very close. Dad and I cruised all summer in 1931 on his Navy ship. Dad issued orders to others in an absolute calm voice.

No matter where we lived, people took care of each other. Nobody starved. Without federal welfare, people locally provided for each other through the Salvation Army, soup kitchens, or volunteers helping each other whenever we could. Financial security was foreign to my generation, yet we were survivors — independent, self confident, and self-reliant. We had no feelings that we'd fail. At age 13 or 14 we had to take care of ourselves; my Boy Scout troop was led by two young men because the adult leader was injured. The boys were dirt poor, but had initiative. I became aware of the resiliency of the underprivileged and learned from them.

We didn't feel different if we wore an old uniform for the Washington High School Cadet Corps. There was pride in a passed-on uniform. Our military drill and discipline led to lower death rates in later combat. I learned respect for superiors and subordinates. I had all the self-confidence in the world. I knew I could do it because all the other kids succeeded, each community taking care of itself. Everyone on welfare got the same treatment. Everyone was in the same boat. We sank or swam together. Today there are special services and welfare.

Divorce rates were low then. It was almost non-existent among my classmates, because we mixed very much at dances and got a broader exposure to a wide range of people. By the time Betty and I were engaged, I'd probably dated 50 girls and danced with 450. Because of the general rule of not dating the same person more than twice in a row you didn't get stuck going steady. At eighteen I was sure I wanted to marry Betty. But I had to wait by law until age 23 to marry. The Navy had a rule requiring Naval Academy graduates to wait two years after graduating to marry. This rule was rescinded in 1942.

At 8:00 a.m. on December 7, 1941, Pearl Harbor was attacked. As officer of the deck of the battleship USS *Nevada*, I was in charge of the ship routine during the four-hour watch from 8:00 a.m. to 12:00 noon.

In the first wave, Japanese torpedo planes targeted us, but Marines shot down three with machine guns. A torpedo hit the port side of our ship. Japanese bombers scored two hits on the antiaircraft deck, then returned to strafe. On the second pass, a strafing bullet from a dive bomber broke my leg, and my foot ended up under my arm pit.

During the lull before the second wave of attacks, I gave the order to get under way, in agreement with the chief petty officer. Ours was the only battleship to do so, even though we had a 40'X20' hole in the port side. After we were underway, the entire second wave of Japanese planes tried to sink us because we were the largest ship underway. Bombs hit the forecastle and lit off aviation gasoline and paint. The ship was sinking, so the Admiral ordered it aground.

I saw approximately sixty men killed and one hundred wounded on deck. Dead bodies and pieces of men were scattered on the deck. A friend with his eye hanging out appeared dead. Many were badly burned from fires.

My leg was amputated in April, 1946, after 52 months in the hospital and 19 major operations. I came out of the hospital in good physical condition, just from using crutches.

From 1946 to 1948 I went to law school in the Navy, and worked in JAG part-time. In 1949 I returned to Honolulu as an aid to the commanding officer of the Naval base. In 1952 I returned to Annapolis to teach military law and administration at the USNA.

Because of my injury, I retired as the youngest captain in the Navy in 1954, but continued working as a civilian until 1992. I became the Secretary Treasurer of the Naval Institute for two years. I was a senior engineer for Westinghouse, the Washington representative for companies such as Joy Manufacturing and Raytheon, and formed my own consulting business.

I received a political appointment as Deputy Assistant Secretary of the Navy for Civilian Personnel Policy and Equal Employment Opportunity from 1981until 1985, with 400,000 people working under me. In 1985 I assumed a new position as special Deputy Assistant Under Secretary of the Navy for Safety and Survivability. *[This office explored ways to enhance the safety of our Sailors and Marines on the front lines or in training. Captain Taussig drew from his experience of fighting fires aboard the USS* Nevada*].*

Betty and I married in 1943. I had met Betty at a junior Army-Navy dancing school. We were thirteen. We met again at a little party outside the gates of USNA when I was a youngster (sophomore). Our courtship was fun. After our first date my stomach hurt from laughing so much. We were engaged after Pearl Harbor. On April 1, 1942, I sent a news clipping stating that the ban on marrying within two years from graduation was lifted. On the clipping I wrote, "Well?" Betty sent an ad back, which said, "She's lovely, she's engaged, and she uses Ponds (soap)." She sent a silly picture of her climbing over a fence, rear view. So I never proposed and she never accepted. I wrote her father, Admiral Carney, who was then at war as Admiral Halsey's Chief of Staff *[and who would later become Chief of Naval Operations, the top job in the Navy]*, asking for her hand. He replied, "If my daughter's hand is all you want, perhaps we had better review this whole courtship."

PTSD Symptoms?

I had no PTSD because I had no anticipation. There were no vivid feelings or sad recollections and I used no drugs aside from painkiller for the excruciating phantom pain during recovery. I was almost able to look at it objectively, as though it happened to someone else.

I did feel depressed for a time. On December 17, 1941, I was evacuated by ship from Pearl Harbor without enough medicine. I arrived on Christmas day in San Francisco in a tiny hospital room. My only Christmas present was a lollipop, a toothbrush, and tooth paste from a first grader. I cried.

What Helped You Cope?

CALM UNDER PRESSURE

In sky control, I was on my back with my foot under my armpit. I was still giving orders; I refused to be evacuated. I was in physical shock, but I felt no pain; I knew exactly what I was doing.

Our job was to kill the enemy. We had a job to do. I did not feel badly toward the Japanese professionals. They were just doing their job. I think I would have hated the decision makers, but I held no animosity toward the Japanese people.

RATIONAL THOUGHT PROCESSES

My injury was just a remote fact—I don't pity myself or catastrophize. It was just part of the job. I'd visualize a rope with injured people. I was never at the bottom. There were always people who were worse off than I. I never felt I was bottom man on the totem pole.

Dad wrote me, when I was a plebe, regarding Navy stupidity: "The best philosophy: a few fleas are good for a dog because it keeps you from brooding about being a dog." In other words, fleas are just pests, not catastrophes.

My daughter once said, "You're the most well-adjusted underachiever I've ever known." I knew I wanted to be Chief of Naval Operations. Yet I'm an 80%er. In this country we have this zero defect attitude. I had to pass calculus and chemistry, which I knew I would never need to use. Valence in chemistry is something wives hang curtains on. I got by, but saved my energy for the naval courses.

SOCIAL SUPPORT

We were always close as a family. My family was very supportive. After I was wounded, my mother came out to California to stay with me for a long time, until things were settled. After I returned to the east, Betty and both mothers would keep me entertained with mahjong after dinner every night. In rehabilitation, I had more angels taking care of me, and made friends with my music. We also felt 100% support form the citizens of our country during the war. There were no Jane Fondas.

I always got along with people irrespective of their station in life. I was very respectful of my juniors, whom I have remained friendly with. When sixteen years of age, my father took me to the Arlington Cemetery and said, "Son, look at 20 or 30 grave markers for me. When I asked why, he said: "In war the people who get killed are young."

The U.S. Navy was a much firmer fraternity than the Army, since all Navy officers before the war came from the USNA. I've been to many annual reunions of the USS *Nevada* Association, and have socialized with my classmates on a regular basis since the war.

COMFORTABLE WITH EMOTIONS

I am not uncomfortable thinking of lost sailors. I weep when they play the Navy Hymn ("Eternal Father Strong to Save"), thinking of so many friends who didn't come home. However, I didn't grieve long or with abnormal difficulty. I talked about the war with Betty and my colleagues.

SELF-ESTEEM

I had very good self-esteem. From growing up in a good family and watching people succeed during the Depression, I had all the confidence in the world.

ACTIVE, CREATIVE COPING

I was resourceful. I was put in charge of rehabilitation in the Chelsea Naval Hospital in Boston. I set up a rehabilitation program on my own as I was recuperating. I learned accounting, air conditioning, and metal tools and taught these skills to the other sailors.

I learned to play the accordion while bedridden in the hospital. I played it and others all down the hall joined in and learned to play it, too. I made friends, and felt no self-pity. I found it hard to turn out the light in the hospital at 2:00 a.m. because I was engaged in stamp collecting, writing articles, and studying business.

SPIRITUAL AND PHILOSOPHICAL STRENGTHS

God

I believed in God. I knew I depended upon God. My beliefs gave me my moral compass.

Meaning & purpose

I knew that we were protecting our home, family, and freedom. I would have served even without pay. I did my job as best I could. I was proud of my crew. No one ducked—we were too defiant.

Betty and the kids were my joy. Betty was a traditional Navy stay-at-home wife who really made home life peaceful and fun for everybody. She made me feel glad to come home. Even when the children were little, we'd find time to go off alone together.

Morality

Our parents were products of the Victorian era and had very strict morals. Even after high school, Betty couldn't date the same fellow twice in a row. Some of their rules were a backlash from the flapper age. My parents never discussed morality. It was just there, in the society. Most of us went to church. I went to church all through my teens. My father felt obligated, as a leader, to attend the churches under his command, so sometimes he went several times on a Sunday. Mother was Presbyterian; Dad mostly Episcopalian. There was a strict sense of morality back then. We knew there were limits. Kissing was fine, but beyond that certain barriers were not violated very often. I guess 80% to 95% of women were virgins at marriage, 75% to 85% of men. There was absolutely no use of drugs. Drinking to excess in Navy officer circles was out (social drinking was acceptable but being drunk in uniform was a kick-out offense), and most colleges were straight laced. The honor code at the Naval Academy was totally straightforward: Midshipmen did not lie, cheat, or steal. It was not formalized, but it was important for the class of 1941 to bond inseparably since we'd be fighting shoulder to shoulder. Loyalty demanded honor. Someone who lied was silenced by his classmates.

Love

I had genuine affection for the crew. The USS *Nevada* was called the "Cheer-up Ship"—we were the cheeriest bunch in the Navy, a bunch of happy guys. In the Navy I learned to respect and trust non-commissioned officers. As young officers we had wonderful rapport with the sailors.

Optimism

We always said, 'Look over the forecastle instead of the stern." In other words, look forward.

Humor

Wife Betty notes that he has a wonderful, waggish sense of humor. "If he didn't give me 30 chuckles a day it was a bad day. Every day he was fun to be with."

I honed my sense of humor at the Naval Academy. As plebes we had to constantly entertain the upper classmen. We made up jokes, like: What is a bollard? A cross between a boll weevil and a mallard? When upperclassmen asked what are you famous for, we might reply: "For sawing toilet seats in half for half-assed SOB's like you, sir." Sunday night was happy hour; plebes put on a show for the upperclassman. I played harmonica while a buddy sang hilarious songs. There was almost a game with some officers to see who could outwit the others. Exchange officers got it bad. At a rally before an Army-Navy football game, the brigade commander smashed an Army exchange officer's car with a sledge hammer. He passed the sledge hammer on down the chain of command until the car was reduced to rubble, then they handed the Army officer keys to a new car that the brigade had chipped in on. I used to joke that at Annapolis I never studied, so my eyes were excellent.

A major concern was not to take life too seriously. Certainly things, like your family's security, are serious; most other things don't warrant worry.

[Since I am a West Pointer, he felt obligated to tell me the following jokes, which are typical of his playful, affectionate nature: "How do you get a West Pointer off your porch? Pay him for the pizza." " What does a West Pointer say to a Naval Academy grad? 'Welcome to MacDonald's.'"]

My father-in-law, Admiral Carney, was once asked to deliver a speech to the USS *Missouri* Association. His health was failing so he asked me to do it. When I addressed them, I said, "Admiral Carney asked me to speak. I called up Admiral Carey's daughter. We drove down yesterday and spent the night together." Then I introduced my wife. My father-in-law set a great example for humor. Once he was concerned with the excessive use of foul language among his crew. Rather than issue a stern and useless order, he simply tacked an amusing note to the bulletin board. In it he noted that the pointless reference to the malodorous residue of digestive assimilation or to illegitimate and depraved shipmates of canine descent on the distaff side — and other unimaginative attempts to be forceful — added little to clarity of expression. The crew loved it. When the admiral was around he heard a crew member describe another as "malodorous intestinal residue."

Long View of Suffering

I am very happy with my life. If I hadn't lost my leg I may have been less happy — my life might have been different. So I see my adversity as a blessing, not a curse. I have found a soul-deep satisfaction working for the Safety and Survivability Office of the Navy and finding the means to save hundreds of lives. One device permitted pilots downed at sea to breathe underwater. That device alone has saved scores of lives.

Maintaining Balanced Living

We've had three regular meals daily. We were raised that way. We had a very healthy diet, with as much fresh food as possible. I liked fresh fruits. I swam regularly for exercise. I have generally retired by 9 p.m. and arisen between 6:00 and 7:00 a.m. I didn't drink except for a very rare cocktail.

For recreation, I loved to visit with my classmates. The Navy was our community, my purpose and mission. We'd invite friends for dinner, playing games, and they'd invite us. We got together nearly every weekend. I also love to stay in touch with friends by email.

We have a beautiful porch. My wife and I enjoy sitting there. I tell her that traveling wouldn't be any better than being here. I like to watch football games on TV and go to Navy football games.

Since I was a boy, I've been an avid stamp collector, and got my son and grandson collecting.

I've written many articles for the Naval Institute about various aspects of naval operations. Some were humorous with an important point. For instance, one article called "Toilet Paper Procurement" described the ridiculous steps needed to procure needed equipment.

Advice to Younger Generations

You can't predict the future, and your goals may not always unfold the way you planned, but you can always serve your country and others in an excellent manner; then how you do it will come to you day by day. Take advantage of what's before you every day.

Joe and Betty at Ring Dance, USNA, 1940

Arriving at Pearl Harbor for reassignment, with Betty and children Susan and Joseph III, 1949

At his retirement as Deputy Assistant Undersecretary of the Navy for Safety and Survivability, 1992. Joe proudly wears his most precious possession, the "Captain's uniform," given to him by the Navy chiefs who tested life saving equipment for ships. He said he wants to be buried in that coat.

Joe, right, with Betty, receiving second Distinguished Public Service award, the highest civilian service award, presented by Chief of Naval Operations, Admiral Frank B. Kelso II, 1991. Joe thought he was the only one to receive this award twice.

Chapter 3

Leonard Lee Robinson
Bataan Death March

Within hours of the Japanese attack on Pearl Harbor, Japanese planes attacked Clark Field in Luzon, the principal island of the Philippines, effectively crippling the U.S. Far East Air Force. Three weeks later, Japanese amphibious forces landed on Luzon with complete air superiority. Ill-equipped, ill-trained, and malnourished, 11,796 Americans and about 66,000 Philippine soldiers retreated southward to the peninsula of Bataan. On January 10, 1942, up to 200,000 Japanese attacked our forces on Bataan. On February 22, President Roosevelt ordered General MacArthur to Australia, leaving General Jonathan Wainwright in command. A heroic defense caused the Japanese to bring in reinforcements from the East Indies, which may have prevented a Japanese invasion of Australia. Starving, ravaged by disease, and short of supplies, the forces on Bataan were surrendered to prevent a slaughter on April 9, 1942. The American and Filipino forces had held out far longer than expected, buying valuable time for America to prepare for the war in the southwest Pacific and upsetting the Japanese timetable there. In the infamous Bataan Death March, the Japanese marched captured forces 65 miles or more (depending upon the place of surrender) northward to be imprisoned at Camp O'Donnell. Stragglers were beaten, shot, bayoneted, or beheaded. By mid-May, dozens of men were dying each day in Camp O'Donnell. On June 1, 1942, the POWs were taken to Cabanatuan, the biggest POW camp in the Philippines. In September, 1943, many survivors, including Leonard Lee Robinson, were shipped to Japan.

Leonard Lee Robinson now lives in a comfortable, yellow ranch house in Casper, Wyoming, a town that originally served as a military outpost to protect settlers. He is a learned, friendly gentleman, standing 6'2" tall. He spent three and one half years as a Japanese POW.

I was born July 30, 1919, in Englewood, Arapaho County, Colorado, near Denver—an only child. We had a very close family, very wonderful, very supportive. Both parents were very firm and fair. If they said something they meant it. I was disciplined and appreciated the discipline I had. If I deserved a spanking, I got one; and I got a few.

Dad said, "I don't want you to lie to me and I'll back you as long as you don't." Dad was a wonderful person. He was quiet, soft-spoken person. He walked so silently that he'd walk up on you and you never knew it. He'd follow me when I played tournament golf, but he'd stay back and never interfered. He died in 1943, while I was a POW, from inhaling chlorine gas while repairing a chimney on a defense plant building.

Mother was a very wonderful homemaker, quiet and firm. She was excellent in her duties as a wife and mother. She was all positive. After Dad died she went to work as a seamstress fitting shirts in a shirt department.

Dad opened a tire shop. Then he worked as a carpenter for a contractor. At one time during the worst of the Depression, only three homes were being built in Denver. During the Depression, you didn't realize how much your parents were going through. Many people had to borrow and then pay back with interest. Making meals was tight. In the spring of 1938, things began to ease up, and contractors built a lot of cheaply-built homes. Dad built two at a time and would sell them himself on speculation. Dad wouldn't just throw together a home and for a year and a half he had no business. He enjoyed animals. He was the boss and they responded well to him. We raised Rhode Island red chickens to show; then in 1935 started raising greyhounds.

During the Depression, we stayed home at nights, listening to the radio. We played checkers and dominoes. Sometimes we went to the mountains to relax. We worked together on the chickens at several fairs, and in training the dogs. Dad walked them four to five miles each morning and sometimes I helped him rub them down. He was strict with his training rules. We'd also hunt with the grey hounds. We went regularly as a family to church (if I was working I'd go by myself in the evenings), and prayed together at meals. We talked about current events and our beliefs and how they related.

I graduated from East Denver High school. I played on the golf team. At age eleven, I began caddying. At age twelve, I was invited by Ralph Smith, a famous golf pro from Scotland, to come into the shop to repair clubs and sell golf balls. I made $1.00 per day working from 6:00 a.m. to 6:00 p.m. A lot of men would have gladly had that pay, and few caddies earned that much. With that dollar, I bought clothes and other needed items.

After high school, I completed one year at the Colorado School of Mines and then attended Colorado University for a year. Before entering the service I drove a sand truck, worked summers as a laborer on the golf course, or helped my father on the houses.

I went into the Army in March of 1941, training in El Paso, Texas, with the 200th Coast Artillery (Anti-Aircraft), Battery E. At first, I was one of only five who were not from New Mexico. We sailed from San Francisco in September of 1941, on the USS *Calvin Coolidge*. We arrived in Manila, and then were sent to Ft. Stotsenburg, next to Clark Field in the Philippines.

On December 8, 1941 (December 7 in Hawaii on the other side of the International Date Line), I had heard about the attack on Pearl Harbor. Because I had pulled the last watch on guard duty, I went to sleep shortly before noon—the first time I ever remember sleeping during the daytime as an adult. My two buddies let me sleep as they left on a truck for noonday chow. I heard them driving off and yelled for them to stop but they didn't hear me. We were bombed by the Japanese shortly thereafter, and my buddies' truck was hit; they were probably the first to be killed in the Philippines. I shouldn't have survived the first day, but for the grace of God. The Japanese caught nearly all of our Air Force on the ground.

On New Year's Eve we were guarding the bridge to the Bataan Peninsula at Calumpit, as our forces were pulling back. Then we were moved to defend the Bataan Air Field. Near the airfield there was a banana plantation. I made friends with the plantation owner. He would sell me bananas for a half cent apiece and I'd sell them to members of my platoon for the same price. He showed me what we could eat or could not eat in the jungle, which was helpful in surviving because the Army cut our rations in half. By February, they were cut in half again. We ate cashews, bananas, papayas, mangoes and other fruits, mules and horses, wild chicken, monkeys, and lizards.

The Japanese were supposed to have conquered Luzon by January, but we kept them from advancing. Only 23% of our shells, which were WWI vintage, exploded. The others were duds. We were running out of food and ammunition. Nevertheless, the Japanese had to bring in their crack troops from the East Indies. This stiff defense of Bataan and Corregidor spared Australia from being attacked.

My position was dive bombed 10 times on the day before we surrendered. At one point a bomb blew up six feet in front of my foxhole. I felt something hot against my chest. It was shrapnel. The New Testament that I carried in my pocket saved me from serious injury. I also found bullet holes in the ground a couple of inches above my head after one raid. Our communications were destroyed. I was sent through the jungle to find out orders, because I knew the jungle. We buried essential parts of our guns so they couldn't be used by the Japanese.

General Edward King disobeyed orders from MacArthur and Wainright and surrendered Bataan on April 9, 1942. I was in the first group to be captured, and was in the original group to be marched out of Bataan. The Japanese searched us and took what they wanted. I was spit on and hit with clubs, sticks, and rocks. We marched from noon until 4:00 a.m. the next morning. At one point a Japanese non-commissioned officer lined a group of us over a bluff to have a firing squad shoot us. They had raised their rifles to fire, when a Japanese officer shouted at them to stop. Thousands of the already weakened Americans and Filipinos died on the march.

At San Fernando, we were herded, 100 to a railroad boxcar. Those who were sick or dying with malaria and dysentery couldn't even fall to the floor. We then marched again to Camp O'Donnell, arriving on April 13, 1941. Camp O'Donnell has been compared to the worst prison camp in the Civil War. About 7000 Americans went there. A quarter of these died in the first six weeks. Most of the time we were burying our own dead. The camp commander told us that he'd rather kill us than have the burden of caring for us. POWs found with traded Japanese coins or the like were executed because it was assumed that they were obtained from dead Japanese soldiers.

On June 1, 1942 we were moved to Camp Cabanatuan. We worked there on details, building airfields or roads, farming, burying the dead, etc. Sometimes we would dig out hibernating cobras from seven foot ant hills for the guards to eat. I was ill most of the time. I contracted diphtheria from a corpse that I was carrying that fell on my face. I was sent to a diphtheria ward. Only five of us out of about 150 walked out of that ward. There was no medicine to treat us. I had a paralysis in my feet, hands, and throat. I couldn't drink or eat for ten days without most of it coming out my nose. I was in a coma for 17 days from a heart attack. A doctor in the states said that no one could live through that. At various points I also had malaria with a 107.5 degree temperature, scurvy, pellagra, dry and wet beriberi, yellow jaundice, boils, and dengue fever. (In Japan I also had bone infection and pneumonia.) Again, if there be a survivor, by the grace of God, I'd be it. I had many close calls. We were starving, barely being kept alive. We ate soupy rice, maybe a five-gallon bucket for 100 men. They would bring in whatever they could find, once in a great while there was meat in it. We grew some vegetables and potato leaves (like a poor spinach) on a farm. About 2600 men died at Cabanatuan.

I left the Philippines in September, 1943, bound for Japan in the hull of a hellship with 850 POWs crammed below. One POW needed an appendectomy. The guards refused our doctor's pleas for help, and told him to operate in the crowded hull of the ship. He did so as we watched, using only a razor blade, borrowed spoons, and a needle and thread. The man lived and became our medic. They wouldn't allow chaplains to go to Japan. In El Paso I had been too young to be a chaplain, but I was asked to act as the chaplain because it was known that I had an interest in the ministry. Despite several air raids, we made it safely to Japan, although several other POW ships were bombed or torpedoed because the Japanese did not mark the ships as being POW ships.

In the port city of Niigata, Japan, I worked as a stevedore. Others worked in the coal yard or steel mills. On New Years Eve, 1944, the building we were sleeping in fell down on top of us. Several died in that collapse. The first year I loaded pig iron from the ground to boxcars. Each of us had to move 15 tons a day. The second year we did this and also carried 198 pound bags of soy beans or other goods from a ship to boxcars.

Some guards would be good to us and then beat us for no reason. One guard took a liking to me and told me to help coolie workers one day. There were two men and twenty women moving bags of beans to the box car. I simply had to point where they should drop the bags and count the number of bags stacked. It showed their view of women. Once, while I was carrying a bag of beans to the warehouse, a guard took a long hook and tried to rip me open. If I hadn't rolled with the blow he would have succeeded. Instead, he scraped my body and tore my shirt. Sometimes we would reach into the bags we were carrying as we unloaded them and try to steal a carrot, orange, or apple. One fellow was hit with a crowbar for doing that and had his nose broken. When he came to fifteen minutes later, they made him go back to work.

My ankle swelled up with a bone infection. When the dock guard saw my ankle he told me to take my shoe off and do some lighter clean up. When the camp guard saw me doing this, he took my shoe and hit my ankle two dozen times as hard as he could. I had to be carried into camp that night. Our doctor who was visiting our camp took a canteen cup of pus out of the ankle. I was back out working in three week's time, although a British doctor said I shouldn't be able to stand, let alone work on that ankle.

We were still starving, getting only about two-thirds of a pound of food per day, mostly barley or cane seed (which was usually used for chicken feed). We were served grasshoppers boiled in soy oil, and we supplemented our food with whatever we could catch, including cats and dogs. We also had seaweed and potato leaves.

American planes started dropping mines into the harbor in June of 1945. In July Niigata was attacked by the first dive bombers. In August, we knew something big had happened. The guards got antsy any time that a single American plane flew over. We learned later that if Nagasaki had been covered by clouds, our port would have been the target for the A-bomb, since it was the only open port in Japan.

In late July, 1945, our camp commander, who graduated with high honors from the University of California, Berkeley, had used a POW for bayonet practice. We learned that on August 29, all POWs were to be killed. However, the A-bomb saved us. In mid-August, the Emperor spoke to end the war. When we were carrying wood in on August 16, a Japanese guard, an escaped prisoner of the Chinese who'd had half of his fingers and toes amputated, told us the war was over. He asked us if he'd done anything unfair to us, and told us that we could punish him if he had. We said he hadn't, that he had been a good guard.

On August 18, 1945, negotiations for peace began, and all the old Japanese guards disappeared. Within four to five days, Navy and Air Force pilots began dropping food to us.

I was liberated September 5, 1945, and was flown to Okinawa. General Stillwell met our plane in Okinawa and would not return our salute. He said that with what we went through we shouldn't salute anyone, by his order. On the next flight, a typhoon was heading toward Okinawa. Our B-24 had engine trouble. The pilot said we could parachute into the water or pancake with the plane. I chose to stay with the plane, which landed safely in the Philippines. On the troop transport carrier ship with approximately 125 other POWs, we were allowed to go through the chow lines repeatedly. I gained 47 pounds in six weeks. I estimate that my weight had dropped from 190 or 195 pounds to 95 pounds at one time. I reached San Francisco in October of 1945 and drove with two friends to Fitzsimmons Hospital in Denver. I met my wife while there. She was stationed there as a WAC. We had gone to the same church as teenagers in Colorado, but didn't know each other then. We corresponded and we married in June of 1951. I had been discharged in March of 1946.

In the fall of 1946 I attended the University of Colorado, and graduated in 1948 with a degree in architectural engineering. I played on the golf team. I had wanted to play on the basketball team, but as a POW I had lost the spring in my legs. Then I attended Northwestern Seminary in Minneapolis for three years, earning a bachelor's of theology. I played basketball and baseball and started a golf team.

I took a pastorate in North Bonneville, Washington, from 1951 to 1955, and then returned to Denver when my son became ill and the family's help was needed to care for him. We moved to a pastorate in Iowa in 1956, then moved in 1959 to Minnesota. Over the years I had earned Masters and Doctoral degrees in theology. After additional pastorates in Nebraska and Colorado, we came to Casper in 1973, retiring in 1990. I still serve from time to time when the pastor is on vacation.

We have three children, a nurse, a financial planner, and a manager of auditing for the state. We're very close. I talk to the children a minimum of once a week, and sometimes two or three times a week. And they visit regularly.

PTSD Symptoms?

I don't feel that I had any PTSD symptoms whatsoever. I was keyed up. I had so much energy. Yet I could fall asleep as quickly as anyone. The first night back in the U.S. at Letterman Army Hospital I got out of bed and slept on the floor. Thereafter, I could sleep in a bed. I went back to the golf course and played golf while at Fitzsimmons. Within a week's time, I was playing par golf. I had no problem getting among people. I never had nightmares. I counseled Vietnam vets who did have PTSD. I let them talk. Most won't talk, so they're eaten alive inside. They told me that they improved 100% once they got it out.

What Helped You Cope?

My faith. The Lord was with me. I look back and see so many times that I could have died, but didn't.

Since coming back, I've not held the enmity that so many held. I've not held any grudges. Who does enmity hurt? Me, not them. When back in Iowa, a friend introduced me to a Japanese physician who had finished his training in Philadelphia. My friend introduced me as a POW. The doctor froze, but was told that I held no grudges. The doctor asked me if I remembered the kids at the docks at Niigata who spat at the POWs, called them names, and threw rocks. He admitted that he was one of them. I went to his home and visited with him and his wife, who enjoyed my attempts to converse in broken Japanese.

I've talked about it and gotten things out. I've spoken at Boys' State for the last thirteen or fourteen years, and at high schools and junior high schools. I notice that the ones who talk about it didn't have the problems. Many of those who didn't talk about it drowned their problems with alcohol or drugs.

We could find the funny side of it. You even turned getting a beating into comedy. The Japanese would slap you and you'd start smiling and nodding your head, saying something like, "If you had a brain in your head it would be lonesome." The Japanese would read our facial expressions. Anger would only bring on a worse beating.

On the Bataan Death March, sometimes the Filipinos smuggled food to us, at the risk of their lives.

The Depression toughened all WWII veterans. You learned to get by with what you had. You'd eat what was in front of you. Some fellas in camp gave up, saying they couldn't eat the rice. Since we were at the margin of starvation, they would die shortly thereafter. I had a good friend who was giving up like that. I took out a piece of paper and asked him his wife's name and address. He asked the reason. I told him that I was going to tell her that he didn't have guts enough to come through. He got mad. It kindled his fighting spirit. He said, "You can't do that to me."

The discipline and hardship of basic training also helped prepare us for the difficulties ahead.

CALM UNDER PRESSURE

In combat you don't realize the danger or think of the fear until it's over. Afterward you think, "Hey, that was close." Such was the case when I had to tell the lieutenant when to commence firing on the diving planes. After the raid was over I noticed the holes near my head and realized how close the danger had been.

As a prisoner, if you fought back that would have been it. Maybe you would have been tied out in the cold to freeze and get gangrene, or you'd be starved, or given raw rice and then water. The rice would swell and your stomach would burst.

You knew that in order to get through you could not carry the hatred. You had to roll with the punches. There was no need to hate them and allow yourself to get worked up. You were under their captivity. You tried to sabotage them if you could. But you knew not to carry the enmity.

RATIONAL THOUGHT PROCESSES

It would be depressing to think too negatively about the past, present, or future. You had to forget the past regarding the defeat and imprisonment or ask forgiveness for mistakes and then go on. If we confess mistakes to God, we're forgiven. We had to look beyond the realities of the present and focus on the prospect of the far distant future. We'd think, "Golden Gate in Forty-eight. I may be late but that can wait." If others made mistakes you had to be forgiving. If someone made a mistake I'd advise him to go to the person and apologize. Make restitution if possible. Say you ate an orange that you didn't realize belonged to someone else. When you learned it belonged to someone else, you should take responsibility and try to replace it.

SOCIAL SUPPORT

No one would have made it back if someone didn't help him with food, medicine, encouragement, etc. True friends were more precious than gold. On the march, one major received some eggs, which he shared with me and two other enlisted men. Whenever one friend caught some food, we shared it with the others. When I got sick, a friend got me food and made me eat a little. When I had pneumonia in Japan, another friend smuggled coal into the hospital and built a small fire.

Friendship meant so much. Most of the soldiers in my unit had grown up together, known each other since grade school. Those of us who were not from there had our friends too. I tried to be friendly to all. I had two especially close friends. One was with me from El Paso through Japan. We are still corresponding. I found that as friends were separated from each other, people became less willing to share.

We were very close. We'd do anything we could to help our friends and they would do the same for us. Even in the hospital, guys in my battery came to talk.

When war broke out in December, 1941, my captain called me and another in. Each of us made a roster of the battery. I carried the roster and wrote down the dates of all who died. I hid it in the hollowed boards in the floor at the head of my bed, and tried to contact the families of those who died.

I only received six letters from family and friends. My mother wrote weekly, but I only got four of her letters. They cheered me up a lot. After the war ended, a U.S. plane that was dropping us supplies accidentally dropped the pilot's duffel bag with all of his love letters from his wife. That made interesting reading for us.

COMFORTABLE WITH EMOTIONS

As a POW, you had to control your emotions. My childhood training helped. Neither of my parents showed strong emotions. When I was a little kid—a lot of kids are afraid of the dark—my folks would send me into the house first in a rather natural way. I got used to not being afraid. When someone died at camp, you grieved but were not overwhelmed. Death is the hope of eternity. I felt it was God's prerogative as to who lived and who was brought home. There was the believers' comfort about meeting those who died again.

My children got after me to write about my experiences, so I wrote a book in 1987. Those of us who have spoken about it have come through better.

SELF-ESTEEM

My self-esteem hasn't changed too much. I hadn't changed so why should my attitude toward myself change? You live one day at a time and do your best. I had good self-esteem. I had confidence from childhood, developed from home training and discipline over the years. My Dad said, "If there's a Robinson, there's a way." I never played a game in tournament golf that I didn't think I could do my best to beat my opponent. In fact, I beat a golf pro at the age of 15. My golf pro set up the match. Only after beating him, did my golf pro allow me to compete against others. The reason for this was so that I would play my own game and not be influenced by my opponent.

ACTIVE, CREATIVE COPING

An active person is a people person. He tries to deal with people. A passive person withdraws from crowds. An active person is competitive. The passive person doesn't care if he gets beat. The active person has a determination to survive. Faith gave me that determination. Faith has no room for quit.

On the march, after facing the firing squad, I was searched. My New Testament was thrown to the ground. I dusted it off and put it back in my pocket. I looked my guard in the eye. Fortunately, no one else was there to see him lose face and he walked away after hitting me. I might have been shot—a lot of guys lost their lives for less than that—but I retained my New Testament.

On the docks I stole some paper. I counted the number of steps from the front gate to the docks, railroad tracks, warehouses and other buildings, and I recorded their dimensions. I had a hiding place located. That's a way I kept my mind going.

We played twenty questions, guessing games, and made a two-week menu for our return. We had heated arguments about where the Americans were and how we knew that based upon bits of information we'd gleaned from stolen Japanese newspapers.

We always tried to do something special for birthdays. In the Philippines, a family friend gave me some ingredients, obtained on the black market, for a cake. We took rice and ground it into flour. We added two duck eggs, a moldy coconut, an overripe pineapple, and two bicarbonate of soda tablets to make it rise a little. Our frosting consisted of an overripe banana and some mashed peanuts. Even the little things helped to keep the spirits up.

I noticed that an oldest child seemed to fare better in prison camp than the youngest, or only children. The oldest was used to making decisions, rather than having them made for them, and could accept stresses better. There were, of course, exceptions to this rule.

SPIRITUAL AND PHILOSOPHICAL STRENGTHS

God

I think and thought that God is a personal God, interested in every individual. You have a personal relationship with Him.

As a child I'd memorized a number of scriptures that strengthened and comforted me during those dark times. For example, "Casting all your care upon Him, for He careth for you." Psalm 23 was fulfilled to the letter. I tried to read from the New Testament each day. It helped me get through the day and kept me thinking.

I found no straddling of the fence in prison camp. Either people thought, "God doesn't care and I don't care about Him," or the opposite. I figured he cared for me and all I had to do was look back and see what He'd done to bring me through.

Sometimes I'd remind people who were losing hope of a certain verse. They didn't seem to resent or resist this. One Japanese camp commander allowed us to hold a funeral. I spoke of the hope in the resurrection, which others told me they appreciated.

Meaning & Purpose

Basically, my faith gave me a direction. From the time I was 14, I knew I'd be a minister. I looked forward to returning to the states, seeing family and friends, going to school. I looked forward to all of life, even if I didn't know exactly the details. Take this little stone oil lamp. It was found by an archeologist. It's 2000 years old. That lamp gives you just enough light to see the next step. As a POW, there was just enough light to look ahead one step. You might not see the whole picture, but just the next step. Down the road you might have hopes of having a family, but often our hope was the next step, to be liberated. Then you thought about flying home, etc. So you had an overall big picture, but you accepted what happened and focused on your next step.

Morality

As a POW, the only thing on your mind was food. Our diet was so close to starvation. I'm one of the biggest soldiers who survived. The average survivor was probably 5'6" or 5'7". All we talked about was food. Some guys stole from each other. Most didn't. I never recall taking anything that didn't belong to me. It didn't enter my mind. If it was theirs, it was theirs. You traded or shared. Some guys would trade their food for cigarettes. The soldiers who gave away their food died within two days. So I never traded cigarettes for their food, even though I didn't want my cigarettes. When I was sick, a Navajo offered to give me his milk. I told him that he needed it, but he said he was allergic to it. So I traded so he'd have something in return. I made friends with a lot of Navajos.

I've also believed in being true to each other when married. It's part of my faith and childhood training to be loyal, honest, pure, and not cheat. Dad kept himself under the speed limit when driving. He never asked me to see if a cop was following us. That carries over. This may seem comical, but my folks never told me to believe in Santa Claus—it might cause me to doubt their credibility in other things. A lot of survival goes back to childhood training. I figured I basically lived the principles my folks had instilled in me.

Love

We were interested in people getting through, and helped one another. There is a love and mutual respect among survivors of the Japanese POW camps, but there is a special bond among the survivors of the Bataan march and Camp O'Donnell. Sometimes compassion was all we could give each other.

Optimism

I was an optimist. If you were pessimistic, thinking this would go on forever, you didn't come back. You lived for the prospect of the future, to return to the states, to family, loved ones. We believed things were going to get better.

Humor

Every night we had roll call and had to stand at attention on the dirt floor. Ernie was sitting down in the back row, thinking he wouldn't be noticed, but he was. The guard told our group leader to humiliate Ernie. So our leader went over to Ernie and said with the harshest gestures and tone of voice, "Ernie, as far as I'm concerned you can sit there any time you want to." Ernie and the rest of us started snickering. The perplexed guard ran out of the barracks and we didn't see him again.

Whenever a guard came into the barracks and we had contraband out, we'd yell "Air Raid." Once the guard, thinking we'd named him Air Raid, came in and announced himself as Air Raid. We'd laugh to ourselves after he left.

Most of the Red Cross boxes ended up in the hands of the Japanese. One guard was washing his clothes, grousing about the American soap. One of the POWs asked if he' like to trade it for a bar of Japanese soap. He agreed. Afterward, the American cut off the edges of the American "soap," and ate it. It was really cheese.

Once in Niigata, a fellow from Georgia bounced out of bed in the middle of the night and said it was time to go to work. We teased him about that.

One group working with butter would reach down and put it into their mouths. One guard tried to protect them, slapping them and saying it was no good to eat. We'd laugh at this, because butter was so nourishing to us.

Long View of Suffering

I've been very fortunate. Perhaps it's partly my attitude, but the doctors always said I was in the best shape of any survivor they'd examined. I was told that the POW experience would take twenty to twenty-five years off my life. Many died around between 50 and 60 years of age. Physically, many of us had problems; some lost some of our lifespan. I still get a fever when I'm in the sun for just a few minutes, and the pleurisy I had in Japan causes me to shut down when I get a cold. So physically things are not the same and we've had to adjust. Spiritually, though, I gained strength.

I think I've been able to help others because of the POW experience—for example, speaking at Boys State and schools, and counseling other vets. Perhaps my experience helped me relate to others and helped them gain perspectives. I encourage people to keep their bodies healthy (which enabled me to survive), establish life goals (planning toward the future), and go to college. All of our children have graduated from college.

Maintaining Balanced Living

I believe in exercise. I ride a stationary bike daily and walk the mall. I've played golf regularly. I shot my age or better between the ages of 65 and 75. I have umpired baseball and refereed basketball. I've set up sports programs for youth. I sleep so soundly that six hours is all that I've required down through the years. Lately, I sleep 6½ hours, including a nap. I've eaten balanced meals, three times a day, including a couple of glasses of milk a day. I eat fruits and vegetables, and like many raw vegetables better than cooked.

I never smoked or drank before, during, or after the war. A doctor in the Philippines told me that the only reason I was alive was because I never smoked or drank. I was in good physical shape when I went into the service.

I was very interested in youth camps at the various places I lived, either as director or serving on the board. In Casper, I am Chaplain of the United Veterans Council, and have served as state chaplain of the Disabled American Veterans. I have served as the chaplain to law enforcement for eleven years.

I do lots of reading for recreation. I have a library of 2000 books. I like Biblical archeology, theology, and current events. I also like to watch travel tapes.

My wife was a school teacher. When she was well (she has been a semi-invalid for the last five or six years), we liked to go for a malted together. We set aside Tuesday nights for family night, unless there was an emergency. We'd go with the children on a picnic, bowl, or play board games. We'd try to go to their sports games on Friday nights. I talk to our children at least once a week and often 2 to 3 times per week. They visit us regularly.

Advice to Younger Generations

Do whatever you have to do to the best of your ability, whether it is sports, hobbies, the military, or school. Make the best of it. It's like playing checkers—a careless move early on can determine if you win or lose. Don't go to college to play around. Try your best. Don't assume you can skim along, as you did in high school. Many valedictorians fail out of college. Try to get along with whatever peers you have.

If you are in the military and are captured, you're under your captors' rules. Try to live up to these rules as best as you can. Give only the information you have to give, no more. If you can get away with it, try a little sabotage.

In short, live day by day, to the best of your ability.

Erma and Leonard Lee Robinson, marrying in 1951

Home in Casper, Wyoming

Note: Photo on chapter title page taken while Robinson was a POW in Niigata, Japan, 1943 [with permission from Robinson, L. L. (1987). *Forgotten Men*, Victoria, Columbia: Trafford, p. 85]

Chapter 4

Earnest Benjamin "Benny" Dunn
Burma-Thailand Death Railway

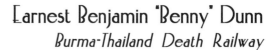

A young school teacher before the war, Earnest Benjamin Dunn spent three and one half years as a prisoner of war of the Japanese, including the year of 1943 working on the Death Railway, made famous by the movie "The Bridge On the River Kwai." Thousands of American, Australian, British, Dutch, and Indian POWs as well as Asian civilians died constructing the 260 miles of railroad through the jungles and mountains of Burma and Thailand. The Japanese wanted the railroad to bring men and supplies between Bangkok, Thailand, and Rangoon, Burma, to facilitate their conquest of Burma and possibly India. The land route would be faster and safer than the sea routes, which were vulnerable to Allied airplanes and submarines. In addition to being beaten, starved, and exhausted, the POWs suffered dysentery, malaria, beriberi and other tropical diseases because the Japanese withheld needed Red Cross foods, medicines, and clothing.

"Benny" lives in an immaculate, well-kept rambler in Murphysboro, IL. Genuinely warm, friendly, patient, and without the slightest trace of pretense, he stands at 5'8" and still has arms of granite.

I was born in Gorham, Illinois, a town of 600 people that now has about 250, February 17, 1917. There were six children, and two grandparents also lived with us. Growing up was very pleasant. I liked baseball. I could eat breakfast on summer mornings and then go to the baseball diamond when it was cool. In the afternoon we'd swim in a swimming hole whose owner charged ten cents a day. We'd go there nearly every day. Everybody in town knew me. If I got out of line some of them told my parents. I never got into trouble really.

My grandfather, an engineer, built drainage ditches along the Mississippi and built a levee to help keep the land dry. My Dad was one of the founders of the high school and grade school, and laid out half the town. He was an engineer, superintendent of highways for the county. He always had a job and we never went hungry. We had a garden, pigs, two horses, and a milk cow. We never worried about food, but my friends did. My best friend's dad was killed in the tornado of 1925 and the family had a difficult time. We rode my horses together. When coal cars came through Gorham, I got on and threw off coal for him. I never thought of it as stealing. We measured time by tornadoes and floods. The 1925 tornado was the worst to hit the U.S. It killed my older brother, and injured two other siblings. It killed 37 people in my little town. I can just about name every one of them.

My Dad was loud, but his bark was worse than his bite. When supper time came, he blew reveille on the bugle. You could hear it all over town. And when he blew it all the Dunn kids would run from all directions going home. A lot of people thought he was stricter than he really was, especially my three sisters, but he had a heart of gold. He'd help anybody. During the Depression he sold lots and gave some away. My dad let a family with 13 kids build a one-room house on one of his lots. For a hobby, he collected and rebuilt old guns.

My Mom was perfect, just a good person. Dad taught her to be a draftsman for bridges and everything else that he worked on. Dad had his office in the house so she was home with us. She could sew, and made all our clothes. She was an artist who painted pictures. She could cut out a horse from a piece of paper without sketching it first, and it would be in perfect proportion. We were a very close family. At meal times everyone ate together.

My Mom sent groceries home with my friends and made clothes for the neighbors. Following the tornado of 1925, the Red Cross gave bats, balls, and gloves to the boys. A team came to Gorham to play our boys. Well, our kids didn't have uniforms like the other team. So Mom made every kid a uniform that fit, with their names on the back. When neighbors came by to gossip, she'd tell me not to repeat a word and I wouldn't. We sure loved our mother. She had more willpower and courage than anybody I knew.

When I was 14, in the summer I took my two horses and worked for a man, plowing corn. He'd pay $1 per day plus feed for the horses. I took care of the horses and sometimes milked the cow with my brother. We had chores at home, such as mowing the yard. We were about the first people to start mowing grass in Gorham. In 1937 we got one of the first gas mowers.

In high school I played baseball (catcher), basketball, and ran track. The most the school ever had was 180 students. My older brother and I were especially close. We played on the same baseball team and would go into St. Louis to see the ball game. You could get a reserved seat for $1.10.

Every so often, Dad would take Mom and a child or two on a trip to survey the county roads. He'd sing as he drove.

After high school I attended Southern Illinois University. They didn't have a baseball team, so I boxed on the boxing team. Eventually, I was credentialed to teach. I taught two years of grade school.

In June, 1941, I enlisted in the Army. In July, I went to Camp Roberts, California, for artillery basic training. It was a new camp, so we spent half our time building streets. We shipped out for the Philippine Islands to bolster our defenses there, stopping at Pearl Harbor for a peaceful overnight stop. We left there on December 1, 1941. As we were traveling, we learned of the Japanese attack on Pearl Harbor and the Philippines, and were diverted to Australia, becoming the first American troops in Australia in WWII. We arrived there two days before Christmas. Something rather amusing happened in Australia. At a big dance hall, I asked an Australian woman to dance. She said that she'd like to but she was all knocked up. I didn't know that that phrase did not mean pregnant, but worn out.

We took a five-day trip on a Dutch ship to the island of Java in the Netherland East Indies—Indonesia today. We landed on January 11, 1942. On a Dutch airbase there were 13 of our B-17 bombers that had escaped the Japanese destruction of the Philippines. I became a ground crewman for a B-17, loading 500-pound bombs on the famous "Swoose"—bearing the Walt Disney figure with the same name. Seventeen of us from Camp Roberts were transferred to the 2nd Battalion of the 131st Field Artillery, a National Guard unit out of Camp Bowie, Texas. We would develop many good friendships that would be so necessary later in helping us survive. We were each given five rounds for our rifles. Not knowing if the rifles would fire or not, my friend Fred Grass and I decided to go into the jungle to fire a round. Satisfied that our rifles worked, we immediately headed back for camp. Soon after reaching the trail, a captain hurried down the trail and asked us if we had seen anybody shooting. Thinking quickly, Grass said, "Yes, sir, there were two men in the draw shooting." The captain raced in the direction we had pointed, and we made it safely back to camp.

In March 1, 1942, the Japanese invaded Java with tens of thousands of troops after bombing and strafing us several times. They had already captured 100,000 British Empire troops in Singapore with a force of 30,000, and then kept coming for Java. They easily overwhelmed our defenses and we were given the order to surrender. We were imprisoned near the port, what is Jakarta today, and the beatings started. We were on pins and needles all the time, because they would bash us if we didn't understand them. If you made a mistake counting off in Japanese, you were slapped or hit with a rifle butt. Sometimes they beat everyone if someone did something wrong. The Japanese soldiers lived by Bushido, the Samurai code that required them to die fighting or else to commit suicide. They couldn't understand why we surrendered, and considered us as already dead. We worked in the rubber company, or sorting automobile parts, or on the docks. We had to stand at attention as they beat us. Sometimes you would kneel for hours with a two by four behind the knees, cutting off the circulation. They would kick you, especially in the shins with their hob-nail shoes. And we knew it was going to get tougher. However, at the time, we were allowed to have a basketball team and a boxing team. I was in charge of the American boxing team. We boxed the Australians and New Zealanders. The Texans pinned the name "Dynamite" on me after watching me box. We also played volleyball, touch football, and basketball. We enjoyed the friendly rivalry and the chance to let off steam. Sports also helped those of us who participated to make new friends. These ties would prove invaluable later. A year later, when we were working on the railroad and I was very sick, my New Zealand opponent brought me food that I vitally needed and gave me a visit that buoyed my spirits.

In October, 1942, they started moving us out; 450 of us were loaded on a Japanese prison ship, a hell ship, bound for Singapore. It was a stinking hole. You couldn't lie down for four days. We received only rice and weak tea twice a day. We arrived in Singapore in November 1, 1942, at a place called Camp Changi. We couldn't believe the number of prisoners there—British, Scots, Gurkhas, Indians, Australians, Americans, Dutch, and Javanese. We were being starved to death. Some were starting to get diseases: malaria, beriberi, and pellagra. These would intensify in the coming months.

In early January, 1943, we were herded into a freight train to Georgetown, and then we were shipped by way of the Bay of Bengal to Burma, where we were to help build a railroad to move Japanese troops and supplies. By now our bombs were sinking Japanese ships. On January 15, 1943, American bombers struck our unmarked ship, but didn't damage it seriously, although seven Australians died. With picks and shovels, 60,000 POWs and several hundred thousand natives were to build 260 miles of railroad in a year's time. There were no machines and no wheelbarrows. No one knows how many died working on that railroad. They say that as many as 16,000 prisoners of war died within a year, and more than 100,000 native Asians. In fact, one camp commandant said the railroad would be built on time, over the dead bodies of the POWs if necessary. You dug dirt and carried it. You built fells in low areas or cut down high areas. Some broke up rocks for the railroad beds, and sometimes you cut wood for fuel. Sometimes the Japanese set off charges of dynamite, paying no mind to whether or not laborers were in the area. As privates, we had the hardest jobs. Lieutenants supervised the work details, but the other officers did not have to work on the railroad.

Most men wore only loin cloths or shorts and many went barefoot. You knew every day you'd probably get beaten. You were starved, getting only rice and a little water every day. We ate snakes, anything that moved. During the monsoons, May to October, 1943, it rained all the time. You worked in slosh. If you got a scratch you were likely to get a tropical ulcer. The English and Australian doctors amputated legs. There were two Dutch doctors who had lived in the tropics. They would gouge out the rotten flesh and helped many to live without amputation. Bedbugs and body lice were abundant.

I got dysentery, malaria, beriberi, and hookworms, dropping from 175 lbs. to 100 lbs. The amoebic dysentery that I had was the more severe type. You felt like you had to defecate often, but only blood and pus from the ulcerated colon was excreted. It was incredibly painful. Most of the time, I was required to work anyway.

We cheated if we could. Sometimes we would move the stakes they'd set out so we didn't have to move so much dirt. If we were caught, we had to line up and slap each other. You got a rifle butt in the back of the head if we didn't hit each other hard enough. It wasn't uncommon for people to be beaten to death. If you tried to escape, you'd be executed. So you didn't try. There was no way out of the jungle anyway. I don't know how many times I was beaten. One guard didn't like blue eyes, freckles, or red hair. When I was slapped, I stared at his eyes until an Aussie told me not to do that, to look down.

If you were too sick to work on the railroad, you were moved into a death camp where many died from disease or starvation. I was so sick at one point that I was sent there for two months. At least sixty percent of our men died there within three months. I was the only one who could walk. I was able to pick through the garbage and sometimes find some discarded tubers that the Japanese considered too small to eat. I found that if I lay in the sun, it provided the only relief from the pain. Visiting with friends and talking about everything boosted my spirits, and I began to recover.

Eventually, they moved us to another camp. Then we moved by train to Thailand in January, 1944. We were in a camp right next to the Bridge on the River Kwai. The bridge was technically on a tributary of the river, for there were no bridges over the Kwai itself, although the railroad followed the Kwai river valley. We stayed there for four months. I was sick. Sometimes friendly bombers missed the bridge and dropped bombs on us, killing several prisoners. The Japanese never gave us Red Cross supplies. The English and Australians assembled quite a good little band. When it came by my malaria ward, the English would plead, "Play 'Colonel Bogey March.'" It was appropriate that that song was chosen as the theme song for the movie, "The Bridge On The River Kwai."

In a hospital camp in April, I was getting better. My weight was up to 110 pounds. We were put to work digging a moat around the camp, ostensibly to keep prisoners from escaping. We understood that the prisoners would be executed and buried in that ditch if the Japanese were to lose the war.

We took the Death Railroad to enlarge an airfield south of Bangkok, Thailand, for five weeks. A couple of our guys escaped and were helped by friendly Thais, who were independent and brave people. By now our B-17s were flying overhead, which made us both elated and edgy.

On July 4, 1945, we walked 20 kilometers to board a train to Bangkok. We then took a barge to a warehouse, and then got on another train to the town of Nakon Nayot. We marched 25 miles barefoot through a swampy area to a new prison camp where we were to work. We helped the Japanese dig in for their last stand and acted as pack mules for their ammunition. The Korean guards told us that the war was ending and the Japanese were going to kill us.

We sensed that the Japanese knew the war was ending. Three of us were on detail. A burly friend went into a Japanese tent filled with officers and boldly asked for three cigarettes for each of us. Instead of beating us, they gave us the cigarettes. An officer then told me to pick up a 220-pound bag of sugar. Even in good shape I couldn't have lifted that and we both knew it, so I said, "Pick it up and carry it yourself, you SOB." He said in perfect English, "Don't call me an SOB," and bashed me in the head with a bamboo pole. My burly friend took the pole away from him. Ordinarily that would have gotten us all shot, but the officer went back into the tent.

The next morning, August 17, 1945, our sergeant major announced that the war was over. That was the happiest day of my life. The English started singing "God Save the Queen." The Dutch sang their national anthem. The Aussies sang "Waltzin' Matilda," and we sang, "God Bless America," which seemed to capture our feelings. Everyone raised their national flags, except us—we didn't have one. So we scrounged materials and sewed one that waved proudly. On August 27, 1945, the Americans were evacuated from Thailand. It was a thrill to fly over the Statue of Liberty, as if the United States was saying, "Welcome Home."

I went back to Southern Illinois University and was captain of the baseball team. My appetite started to return and I was gaining weight fast, back to about 150 pounds. I graduated and taught history in high school in Gorham. I went to dances every night. Two years later, at a dance, I saw my future wife. She had been a senior during the first year I taught. She was mature and I married her. She died a year ago. It was the best 52 years I ever spent in my life. I knew it wasn't wrong. We have two fine boys who have done well. I spent several more years teaching and then became principal and superintendent.

PTSD Symptoms?

I had dreams after the war; still do. I needed to have the light on when sleeping for 6 to 8 months. I dreamed of breaking out. I frequently dreamed I was home and had to get back to camp or be beaten, or dreamed of rescuing kids who were POWs. I didn't want to be picked on and had a chip on my shoulder for awhile. I told myself in camp no one would ever run over me again. But I had no drinking problems and functioned well. I wanted to see my friends and went to dances every night.

What Helped You Cope?

Because I'd been active in athletics all of my life, I was a good competitor. My friend said, "I knew by the way you played baseball that you weren't going to give up. There was no quit in you." One of the guys just gave up and died. There was nothing wrong with him. But I wanted to get home to my family.

Even when I was sick, I'd read. A Navy lieutenant loaned me H. G. Wells' *Outline of History*. It was 1000 pages long. I read it three times. When I went back to college I was a step ahead of the professor.

During the Depression, the Work Projects Administration paid the unemployed $50 per month to work 100 hours. My buddy, the one who I stole coal for, and I worked on the railroad pulling and tamping ties for half of that because the other boys were doing it. The hard work toughened me up.

CALM UNDER PRESSURE

I liked the native Asians. I felt hatred for my captors because they were so inhumane to the prisoners; most believed they were superior. I don't hate the young ones that don't know any better, and I never took out my anger on my captors. You learned that survival demanded that you control your anger—even the most hot-tempered learned that. There were a few that were decent to us, though. I remember them. One took us to the Japanese kitchen and got us good food. He could speak some English and was interested in talking about farming. After the war, but before the treaty was signed, some of my buddies ran into one particularly mean guard. They stole his jeep when he was in a store, and ran him over when he came out. I wouldn't have killed anyone, nor would I have hurt any that surrendered. I also felt bad to see the way the Japanese officers mistreated the Japanese soldiers, almost as badly as we were treated. Degradation is unpleasant regardless of the victim.

RATIONAL THOUGHT PROCESSES

I had blind faith in the United States. I never gave up or thought pessimistically. Most that lived never did. I just looked one day ahead. A lot of those that got sick just gave up.

When someone died and we heard about it there would be deathly silence. Some would shed a tear, but rarely did anyone break down and cry.

SOCIAL SUPPORT

A number of things motivated us to survive, including the desire to return home. But one's friends were probably the most important element for survival. You have to have a clan. We were like a family. Seventeen of us from Camp Roberts left Java with the Texas unit. Most of us stayed close. When we got home, they were part of my family as far as I was concerned. We visited each other. I wrote letters to them. To this day, I and one other are still living. I took my whole family to California to see one friend, Fred Grass. Just before he died he wrote, "Never does a day go by that I don't think about you" *(tears)*. I'm the same way about him. He was the one that gave me his money to buy food, when I was sent to the death camp to die. He thought I would need it more than he would. It troubled me to learn later that he almost starved to death and went totally deaf and partially blind.

Your buddies would goad you, maybe tell you that you had no guts when you complained or were homesick. When I got sick and was complaining, one friend said, "Aw, shut up, you SOB, you're not worth living anyway." Something like that would motivate you—stop you from wanting to give up. When I was too sick to eat, one buddy kept riding me, telling me that I had to eat that white rice or I would die and never go home. I determined that once I got stronger I would give him a licking. I got mad and told him, "If one SOB gets home, it's gonna be me." Friends cared enough to bug you that way. Being nice made it easier to die. But make you mad, and you wanted to fight.

After I got too sick to work, an illiterate man from Texas, when he returned from working, would sit on my bunk and whistle Mexican songs to break the monotony and relax me.

My mother sent letters all the time. I got a few in the late camps. I saved all kinds of them. It was wonderful. We shared our letters with each other. I got some that were two or three or four years old.

I also made it my business to become acquainted with soldiers from the other countries—Australia, England, Scotland, Ireland, and India, and usually found them friendly and pleasant. Intermingling helped to relieve the boredom.

COMFORTABLE WITH EMOTIONS

Every time our bugler played "Taps" we knew that one of our friends was being left in the jungle. Even today, when I hear "Taps," I think of those guys and tears come to my eyes.

I was scared many times. You talked about anything with your buddies, especially with those that were really close. One buddy, that I slept side by side with, was a boxer in Java with me. A tough, tough guy. We shared all our experiences. We'd argue, but never fight. I visited him, too, with my wife. We both admitted we wanted to whip each other at times but were both afraid we'd lose. My wife and I visited him on his farm in Nebraska, and boy was he glad to see me.

You really got close to your buddies. I knew things about some that I wouldn't know about my brother, things that worked on your mind. Within your clan, nothing was held back. If you were a loner, your chances went way down. I believe that. The guys who lay down and died were loners.

I've found it helpful to express negative experiences. In the hospital in India, shortly after I was liberated, I started writing down everything about my experience. I eventually turned these notes into a book. Writing the book helped me, and I also felt good that people read it and benefited from it. I learned fifteen or twenty years ago that writing about my dreams seemed to help. It helped them to stop. I started that on my own. I've also gone to a meeting of POWs nearly every month for the last ten years. We just talk and that is helpful.

SELF-ESTEEM

My self-esteem was pretty good. Even when I was very sick, I thought I would make it and was confident in myself. There was only one night that I wasn't. I had an attack of malaria. There was intense pain down my spine with each heart beat. The guy next to me was dying. There was nothing I could do. I hoped that if I died, they'd bury me and put my name on a cross. We'd do that for everyone. When the war was over, our government exhumed those who died and buried them in well-marked graves, mostly in Hawaii.

ACTIVE, ADAPTIVE COPING

It was futile to resist or try to escape. You had to accept the Japanese as your temporary master and concentrate on staying alive.

I kept my mind active reading. I also would visualize my home town and try to remember each person and where everybody lived.

We had a school in a couple of camps. I used to try to remember all I could about U.S. history. I taught others, before the Japs put an end to it. The Aussies and Americans also competed to see who could put on the finest stage shows. The Americans put on an excellent original musical comedy and the Aussies a famous mystery that buoyed our spirits. However, as a punishment for something trivial, the camp commandant put an end to all classes and entertainment.

I learned a lot about Australians. I made good friends with some English. We swapped books. I obtained a volume of the encyclopedia in Singapore. It was Volume XXIII, TEXT-VASC, and thus had the U.S. in it. I carried it with me into the jungle. I also had a *Student's History of England* and laboriously memorized the kings of England. I'm sure my books helped to keep me alive.

Early on, when we had the strength, the long-legged Americans and Australians would step up the pace when marching. It was funny to watch the shorter Japanese guards try to keep up. They didn't want to lose face by ordering us to slow down.

The Japanese had a chain of command, and if the officer slapped the sergeant, the sergeant slapped the guard, and the guard would slap us. Once, a buddy and I tried to convince a guard to strike the sergeant back. We even demonstrated. The guard liked the idea, although he wouldn't try it. It was worth the try just for the thought of a guard striking back.

Having scissors and a couple of needles, I fell into the hobby of being a tailor. I made shorts for people out of scrounged material.

Horse racing was a tradition in Australia on Boxing Day. So the two lightest guys mounted up on the two biggest and everyone cheered, forgetting for a time that they were prisoners.

We had a fighting spirit. The English soldiers could be arrogant at times. Once when we were building the moat, one said our officers weren't any good and they had to put the English officers in charge of ours. He said that twice. I said, "You're just a lying SOB. If you don't think an American will fight, just step up and I'll knock your teeth down your throat." Well, he said it again, and I did. I really felt bad about that.

SPIRITUAL AND PHILOSOPHICAL STRENGTHS

God

When I started getting sick, I had a little Bible from a Texan who'd died. I memorized the 23rd psalm. I'd also recite the Lord's prayer. They gave me comfort. Every night I'd repeat them lying in the dark. I prayed to God. My beliefs became stronger. Something kept me going.

In some camps we had church. One Scotsman was an agnostic. As he came close to death, he was read the Bible. His friends wouldn't let him die. When he returned home to Scotland, he became a minister. Then he became the Dean of the Chapel at Princeton University.

Meaning & Purpose

I wanted to get home to my family. I knew it would be devastating to my parents if I didn't make it. I wanted a family.

One thing I knew I would do was go back to college and get a degree to teach history. I just liked history. I wanted to tell people about the war, what they did to us. I'm glad I taught history. I knew that, even before the war, the Japanese indoctrinated the Asian natives to believe that they'd be better off if they'd get rid of the Europeans. And of course, the people in Indo-China turned against the French after WWII. I believed in the U.S. and the just cause we were fighting for.

After coming home, I had a couple of thousand dollars in back pay. Gorham had no baseball team. I approached the fellow I had plowed corn for and said, "Nick, what would you charge to build a diamond on you property?" He said, "If you put up a fence to keep the cows in, you can have the land." So I used my money to build a diamond. I gathered the best team of ex-GIs in southern Illinois and we played other teams for five years. It meant a lot to many of us.

Morality

It was honorable to steal from the Japanese, but I never stole from my buddies and they didn't steal from me, and we didn't tolerate those who did. The Australians had an unwritten code. You might get beaten to death if caught stealing from another Australian. Once, a buddy and I were delivering a load of materials to our guards. I smelled something good. It was a boiled duck. I reached in and we helped ourselves to it. We dropped the load and left quickly before they discovered that their dinner was missing.

The prison camp was full of vulgar, foul language. You never heard such swearing in all your life. I tried to keep myself from using all the foul language, from letting myself go and losing my pride. I didn't use the f-word and still don't. I'd call someone an SOB when mad. That's about the worst.

In the clan, if I got something extra to eat out of the jungle, I shared it with them. I always had close buddies, and it never occurred to me to not share. That was very important.

I got upset with people who shot prisoners. I never thought that right. To kill a man who is not armed or causing problems is wrong.

You'd listen to your buddies brag about some really bad things they did when they were younger. I was glad I hadn't done those things.

WORLD WAR II SURVIVORS - LESSONS IN RESILIENCE

Love

We stuck together. Slim Chambers got into an argument with someone. He couldn't fight a lick, but he looked at me and read my mind. I told Slim later that he would have been beaten up. He said, "I knew you'd help me."

As I said, we were as close as any family. My buddies saw that I ate and encouraged me when sick, helped me face my fears. Without them, I wouldn't have survived.

I'm so glad my wife and I married. Our kids said they never worried about our getting divorced. She was perfect. I sure miss her.

Optimism

When the war ended I wasn't surprised. I knew we were going to win. Some guys said we'd be there for ten years. I never thought it would be more than a year. I kept thinking the Americans would get in there and get us out.

Humor

We saw something funny in the prison camp all the time. The Japs couldn't understand how we could laugh. One Marine was a cartoonist. One of his cartoons showed the mangy POWs lined up for chow. The sign said: Menu: rice, rice, and rice. We even laughed at each other when we were made to shave our heads.

A close friend was Slim Chambers. He had a dry sense of humor; no matter how bad things were he'd have something funny to say. He always had stories and made jokes about us (Ol' Dunn this, and Ol' Dunn that). Taking baths in a creek after working, I called his attention to the big ringworms on the English soldiers' backs. He said that he thought they were regimental insignia, because they all had them. Even in the death camp, Slim joked every day. But, he knew when to quit, too. When the end of the war was announced, we were slapping each other on the back and celebrating. He said, "Oh hell, Dunn, I'll get home just in time to pick cotton."

We gave names to the guards, like Hollywood (he was good looking and neat), Liver Lips, and Dillinger (he was the one who beat me because I had blue eyes).

In Java the sailors and Marines put on a stage show that was one of the funniest things I ever saw. It contained homemade jokes that the Japanese wouldn't understand. The English put on a play in one camp. A soldier said that, when he got home, the first thing he was going to do was spend all his back pay on his beautiful wife. The second thing he'd do was take his pack off his back. That was typical English wit. I couldn't think up jokes, but I appreciated humor.

Long View of Suffering

I often thought about what might have happened if I hadn't been a POW. Maybe I'd have gotten shot in battle. I didn't feel unlucky.

Being a prisoner helped me to control my temper. We learned that patience in the face of provocation meant survival. When the Japanese slapped us, I wanted to hit them, but didn't. If you could bear up, you could do a lot of things you didn't think you could. When I got to college I would dig down and do well. I got a bachelors and masters degree on the GI bill. I had more confidence and purpose.

Being a prisoner helped me be a better parent. I've been a good parent. I can understand the points of view of children for doing things. If they were not good, I'd straighten them out with more self-control and patience. It also helped me coach. We had to follow rules.

In spite of the suffering, we also had many pleasant memories, mostly of true friendships and people we encountered. It seems that most of the survivors were motivated to succeed more than the average person. I could study for hours after the war, but never before. I was motivated. I'd stay up until 2:00 or 3:00 in the morning. I wanted to do well. I wanted to make up for missed years.

Maintaining Balanced Living

I never smoked as a POW. All my friends did, but not me. I drank very little, five or six beers the entire time I was in the service. In India, after we were released, you could get beer or coke. I'd take the beer and swap it for two cokes. My dad didn't drink. No one in my home ever did. My coaches discouraged smoking and drinking. I wanted to play sports. In the sixth grade on the doors to our room, a poster showed young men whose health deteriorated the more they smoked. So I decided I wouldn't smoke or drink. My wife saw that I got the right food—plenty of vegetables and fruits, and three meals a day. I usually go to bed between 10:30 and 11:00 p.m. and get up between 6:30 and 7:00 a.m.

My wife and I danced all the time, dances from before the war, every week until I got new hip joints. We went swimming every day together. I played baseball and basketball after the war. I always had a punching bag and would also jump rope every night.

I participated in the Senior Olympics between the ages of 60 and 75. I swam and could still sink 23 of 25 free throws. I still feel good.

My wife and I enjoyed parties. We socialized, mostly with other teachers, coaches, and their wives. We went to movies, if they were good movies.

I'm still active in church. I go nearly every Sunday. My wife was very active, too.

I attend our reunions yearly.

Advice to Younger Generations

Always be proud of serving honorably, irrespective of the branch of service. Do a good job at whatever you do. Do it right, and you'll be proud afterwards.

Don't be captured if possible. If I'd known it would have been so tough, I would have tried to escape in Java despite our orders to surrender. If you do get captured, try to learn the language of your captors so you will know what's going on and can understand orders. Know the local culture. For example, some of our buddies escaped because they knew they could trust the local Thais who were friends to Americans. Make friends and stick together. That's the most important part of being a POW. Your chances are almost nothing if you are a loner. Know who you can trust. You must have those you can trust in your group.

"Benny" Dunn, right, back in the States, November 28, 1945.
(Photo courtesy of *South Bend Tribune,* South Bend, Indiana)

"Benny" Dunn at home in Murphysboro, Illinois.

Part II
European Theater of Operations

Chapter 5

Thomas E. Vail
B-17 Bombardier

Nestled in pine trees of Kennebunk, Maine, the home of Tom and Betty Vail is a cheery grey ranch with blue-grey shudders, a bay window, and neatly manicured shrubs and roses. I visited them on a grey and stormy Maine day. Tom and Betty are the parents of three children, including a son who served in Vietnam, and have six grandchildren. Betty cites among her husband's best strengths his honesty, loyalty, and strong desires to be fair with people and to encourage schooling for young people. Tom and all three of his brothers served in the Armed Forces during WWII, including one who was shot down in Europe after seventeen B-17 bombing missions. Tom's 301st Bomb Group of the 15th Air Force received the Presidential Unit Citation.

I was born in Burlington, Vermont, in March 9, 1919, the second of four boys. My family moved to Massachusetts, and then to Maine in 1929.

We were happy kids in a close family. I had wonderful parents. My father grew up on a farm in Pomfert, Vermont, a very small place, and went to a rural school. There was no high school there, so the family moved to Randolph, Vermont, and left the farm to my uncle. Father was an outstanding athlete in every sport. He went to Middlebury College and was an outstanding pitcher who signed with the Red Sox. There was not much money in professional ball in those days, so my mother decided he should do something else. His uncle set him up in a hardware store. He was a wonderful, outgoing guy and everybody liked him, but he never really made it in business, although he'd invented an oil burning stove for heavy duty cooking for hospitals, college cafeterias, big restaurants, and hotels. He left Randolph and went to Boston, and then came to Maine in 1929, operating his business on a shoestring. He was always optimistic, saying that in another two or three years we'd take some great trips together, but the Depression was getting bad. He loved to hunt and fish, and had fly rods, shot guns, and bird dogs. He was very good to my mother in so many ways, but she never knew where the next meal was coming from.

Mom was very beautiful, an ideal mother. Of course, I'm prejudiced. Unlike my father, she was very quiet and reserved. Because my father traveled a great deal, she was left at home with the four scrappy boys. It was tough for her. We all know that now. She worshipped my father. He could do no wrong, but he couldn't provide a good income. She really raised us. She gave us a hug every time we went to school. We couldn't do any wrong either. We fought and did things that boys did, but she was so forgiving, so proud of her boys (*he said this with tears*). She was also very cultured. She was a very good artist, and before marrying she had taught art in the elementary school. She was good at spelling and grammar, and sat down with me to help me learn my multiplication tables. She insisted that we go to an inexpensive dancing school in town because she wanted us to learn some of the finer things in life. She could also be very protective. Once, a policeman came to our home because some kids had shot out the windows of summer homes along the shore with BB guns. She set that guy straight, saying, "I'll have you know that my husband has taught our sons how to handle guns and they would never do anything like that."

When my father did come home, he always got a warm welcome. He'd play ball with us, and take us fishing and hunting. We ate what we caught or shot—partridge and woodcock mostly. We'd go on picnics out in the country, maybe to a pasture, and play a ball game.

We didn't even know there was a Depression as kids, but we knew we didn't have much. We had salt pork quite often, dried beef gravy, and potatoes and vegetables from our garden. Mom was hard working. She darned our socks and mended clothes in the evening. We wore old patched up clothes. There were very few treats. I don't look back on it as suffering or a hardship. We knew we were all in the same boat.

Christmas was always a wonderful time. The kids hung up their stockings. There just wasn't any money to buy presents to speak of, but my father had a good friend in Portland, a kind Jewish man, who had a store with everything in it—from hardware to clothing. One year, he dug up some old toys from out of the cellar. So that one year we had some presents.

We all worked. I mowed lawns early, then worked for contractors some summers. I loaded gravel trucks by hand, using a shovel, which was tough work. I also loaded soup and vegetable cans for a can company. I learned to work hard from a rough stone mason, mixing cement and carrying bricks in buckets up a ladder.

My high school was very small. I played all sports, but basketball was my best sport. I played three years on the varsity basketball team. I also played baseball and track, and skated in winters—pick-up hockey games just for fun. All my brothers were good athletes as well. Our parents took a keen interest in our school life. They supported us by their encouragement and attendance at all sports events and school activities.

I graduated in 1938 and went to state teachers college for three years in Gorham, Maine. I had saved enough for tuition, which was about $100 a year. My folks paid for a room in a rooming house, which was $2 a week. I made the varsity basketball team as a freshman.

In 1940-1941 I had seen advertising to join the Air Corps. It seemed so glamorous. I decided I could finish my degree after the war, so I joined in 1941. I trained at Ellington Field, Houston, Texas, for three months. Then another three months of training as a B-17 Flying Fortress bombardier in Albuquerque, New Mexico. The new secret Norden Bombsite was a miraculous and very complicated instrument. It actually flew the plane, and was a great contribution to victory. Every correction I put in that bomb site meant that the plane would make an adjustment in course. I was commissioned in 1942, and then went to crew training in Sebring, Florida. My B-17 crew consisted of myself (the bombardier), the pilot and co-pilot, navigator, radio operator, engineer, and four gunners (ball turret, tail, and two waist gunners). These were the men I would live with for the rest of the war, if they survived. It was a very close-knit group. We had all sorts of training. We made practice runs over the Gulf of Mexico in preparation for over-water flights, and nine-hour training missions to western states. At the end of December 1942, my crew flew overseas. We were almost all kids in our teens or early twenties, and here we were given responsibility for this very expensive plane. We left West Palm Beach and began our journey to the coast of Africa. We were one of many crews that were sent individually to either England or North Africa. Our orders directed us to fly a southern route to Gambia (a British base on the west coast of Africa). This route took us to Trinidad, Bellum, and Natal. We left South America on a non-stop flight to Africa, and we hit the western coast of Africa right on the nose.

At that time, the Germans under General Rommel were fighting the British and French in North Africa. The job of my 301st Bomb Group was to bomb docks, railroad yards, and supply ships crossing the Mediterranean to deprive Rommel of needed supplies. As an experiment we also bombed German troops with fragmentation bombs, not a very nice thing to do, until Rommel's army was defeated. Then we began over-water missions, bombing big ports and cities in Italy, Sicily, and Sardinia.

Occasionally, we had fighter escort support from experienced British pilots in Spitfires, but many times we had no escorts. We were hit by German aircraft, attacking our formations over Africa and Italy. There was also great danger flying those long missions over water. There was no oxygen at 30,000 feet. We carried our own oxygen, and if that went out you were sunk. If you were hit, there was no friendly territory. We also met heavy anti-aircraft opposition over the cities of Italy. We were hit by a lot by flak. It was very difficult to return to home base with a crew of friends missing, which happened several times.

Having completed 50 combat missions in 1943, I was among the first "war heroes" (I use that term loosely) to return from the war. I married my high school sweetheart, Betty, in August 1943. We were sent to Midland, Texas. We stayed at the training field there until the war ended. I was a squadron commander in charge of a training and operations squadron. My wife loved it and we made lots of friends. It was a wonderful time for us. We had our first child there.

I went back to finish college, and then we settled in Kennebunk in 1946. I taught industrial arts at Kennebunk High School for ten years and coached baseball before becoming the principal of junior high schools in Kennebunk and later in Scarborough, Maine. I retired in 1975, working for two years at my old college as executive director of planning for vocational teacher education for all of New England. Then I spent ten years in charge of maintenance and grounds for the town's first real nursing home. I enjoyed every minute of that.

PTSD Symptoms?

When I returned to Texas, I had some apprehension of flying for a time, but no other symptoms, and eventually I overcame that apprehension. Malaria flared up upon my return to the states. The doctors said it was due to relief from tension.

What Helped You Cope?

We didn't have much fear of work, having worked hard growing up. I had a very fine upbringing, with a loving family.

My mother would write to me oversees, even if she had nothing to write about she would write anyway. Although less frequently, my father also wrote wonderful letters, and gave me great encouragement.

We were very well treated upon our return. The reception for military people was worth mentioning. The home town people were most kind. We were treated as heroes. Compared to Vietnam, WWII was a popularly supported war. People—women, the workers, everyone— really got behind us and were united. It was a great age. My father did such things as man a post on the coast looking for approaching submarines.

CALM UNDER PRESSURE
The plane's engineer, a six striper and the oldest man in the crew, had run a garage in Colorado. He had been a good mechanic until we started flying combat missions. After three missions, he said to the pilot, "I can't stand this." So he was sent to a psychologist and was taken off combat. He lost his six stripes—although he eventually earned most of them back on the ground. In another squadron, when enemy fighters attacked, one man left his gun position, and curled up behind the armor plate behind the pilot. He almost died of fear. They took him off combat. For me, the most dangerous time of all was on the bomb run. I couldn't be looking around at flak flying or at enemy planes. That was a time I had to concentrate and do the very best job I could. I was grateful for that, for at that dangerous time I was concentrating as best as I could to do a good job. Even though looking through the site I could see flak, it was helpful because I was needed and busy, and had to be at my best at a dangerous time.

I had a great deal of respect for the Germans' flying ability and their planes. Despite the propaganda against Hitler and Mussolini, I never had any real bad feeling toward the Germans. I just felt we had a job to do. It was important and we did it.

RATIONAL THOUGHT PROCESSES

Everybody makes mistakes. We had sympathy for the engineer who couldn't stand it. Sometimes even the top brass made mistakes. I disapproved of a raid against Palermo, Sicily, which was scheduled on Mother's Day. It just didn't seem appropriate to do this. Americans have a lot of respect for their mothers.

We never had dissention among our crew. We didn't make a lot of mistakes, but there was very little criticism among the crew. We respected each other. There was a good feeling.

My wife and I have three wonderful children, who have all done well. They care for us and we see them frequently. When we worried over them, we found family discussions helpful. As a kid, I had run with some wild guys, so I could empathize when my kids gave us trouble. I let them know I cared for them and accepted them. I could never understand families that kick their kids out.

SOCIAL SUPPORT

Betty was very loyal. We wrote a lot. I still have a lot of her letters. My brothers and I wrote each other. I wasn't the greatest writer, but I wrote. We were very close. Those letters meant a lot then.

COMFORTABLE WITH EMOTIONS

I was as scared as the rest of them. No question about that. There was nobody who wasn't scared. We had a tough job to do, but when we got back from a mission we were on safe ground. We had good meals and were generally safe. There were ball gloves and horseshoes to play with. These kinds of things helped. Except, at rest camp on the coast, a German fighter dive bombed us on the beach. I ended up in a little bathhouse with two chaplains diving for cover. They were just as scared as I was. I'm not sure how much protection those bathhouses would have provided. I could explain my fears in my letters to my folks, but said that I wanted to do my job as best I could and asked them to pray for me to have more courage so I could do my job well.

SELF-ESTEEM

I really do think my self-esteem was good. I felt secure. I thought I was a pretty hot kid who could win the war all by himself. I think we all were maybe a bit cocky. We had espirit de corps, nothing to be ashamed of. We were confident, which I attributed to the group I was in. We were a select group. You had to have had two years of college, be physically perfect almost, and have good reflexes. We were well trained. We had good instructors and worked hard. That kind of training builds confidence.

ACTIVE, CREATIVE COPING

The military trained us in leadership, and not just the officers. You were expected to take the initiative and lead. My military experience helped me in my civilian life. I observed leaders. I had the tendency to be more like the type of leaders I most admired.

Those of us in the Air Corps were thought of as fly boys, perhaps less disciplined compared to infantry soldiers. So when we got overseas to our bivouac areas, we could set up our pup tents without restrictions. You should have seen some of the innovations. The American has ingenuity. We took advantage of empty gas cans to wash clothes and found a use for just about anything else we found to make life easier. If we couldn't make what we needed, we'd go into town and scrounge or barter for it. When we asked a Frenchman to do our laundry, he said he had no soap. We scrounged up soap and pretty soon he was doing laundry for everyone in the outfit.

SPIRITUAL AND PHILOSOPHICAL STRENGTHS

God

Guys that never prayed prayed in the war. I prayed before the war. If you don't know if you're going to live the next day or not and you like life, you're going to pray. I believe everybody does it. Some more than others. Some had good backgrounds in religious training. I think my beliefs helped me face the battle with greater ease. As kids, we went to Sunday school. My mother sang in the choir and set a great example. We prayed in our house. My father, on special occasions, was excellent at praying. I never thought of God as punitive, but kind.

Meaning & Purpose

WWII had a real purpose; some other wars since then have not seemed so clear cut. We knew what we were fighting for. We just knew that Hitler was out to conquer the world. We knew of his hatred for the Jewish people. He never kept his word. He was a bad, bad man. It might have been propaganda, but we believed it. I still do. We wanted to free the world. There was no question that freedom was worth fighting for.

Morality

As far as my family went, we were highly moral. We were not loose about our beliefs. We were raised to know what was right and not right. If something was morally wrong, you didn't do it. I don't think there is so much of that today. Not all of the guys in WWII were moral, but I think there was a tendency to be moral. It was there and you just did the right thing. I was never unfaithful to my wife.

Love

I do believe we felt it was very important to work as a team. We worked at it. We made an effort to include all members of the crews in our wins and our losses and the good times and bad. There were differences in our backgrounds, but our training unified us. For the good of each individual it was important to know that the person on your right and your left was your friend, and a helper when needed. If a crew had a good leader, this was easier, but we were trained anyway to accept that philosophy, and in most cases that's the way it worked out.

Optimism

We had confidence we would get work, get married, and raise a family after the war. Most young men and women looked forward to that. We had great faith that everything was going to be alright after the war. We lived without fear.

Humor

Some of the crew were more entertaining than others, but most of us were willing to have a good laugh or enjoy a joke. On the long flight to Africa, we were nearly out of fuel as we got near the African shore. We still couldn't see land at that point. Over the intercom, the pilot tried to make light of it, asking how many of us guys could swim, and how good a swimmer we were. He and the co-pilot were worried, but they tried to prepare us in a friendly way for a very serious situation. He eventually said, "This may be it, it's going to be touch and go," but he made light of it.

Long View of Suffering

Within the crew, we weren't perfect and probably made mistakes. Sometimes that could be inspiring. For example, the radio operator, a big red-headed coal miner from Pennsylvania named Red Springer, had a special room in the bomber. He had to remove the overhead plexiglass canopy in a hurry in order to fire his 50 caliber machine gun at German fighters. He had never done the maneuver in combat, only in training. When he did it in combat for the first time, the wind almost swept it away. He was such a gutsy guy. He held on to it with all his might and pulled it in. He scraped his hands. It was a bloody sight, but he got the gun in operation. It was a mistake, but he compensated by sheer guts and determination to make it right.

It was a great honor to have earned a commission. In high school, I thought I could do most anything without any fear. I could hunt in the woods alone. I had made every team I had tried out for. But when I came back, I was even more confident. I had done something big. There was no question that my experience helped me.

Maintaining Balanced Living

I usually have slept 7 to 8 hours regularly, and was usually in bed by 10:00 p.m. I could get along with less, but if it was convenient, I got regular sleep. Of course when you get older you don't sleep quite as well as you used to.

I've been pretty active most of my life. I am an avid tennis player, playing at least once a week. I still use the treadmill and stationary bike, and do calisthenics regularly.

I am and have been a moderate eater. I don't like to feast. I'd rather have a small steak than a big one. Both my wife and I eat a lot of fruits and vegetables. Usually I have cantaloupe, a few prunes, a banana on my cereal, orange juice, and so forth.

I have never been a heavy drinker. My wife and I enjoy a cocktail before dinner or sometimes wine with dinner. I gave up smoking over twenty years ago. I think of the money I wasted on cigarettes. It's terrible for people to smoke. I feel strongly about that, and I was among the most guilty.

I like outdoor work, gardening and painting. We enjoy living in our modest home. I made most of the living room furniture, and other pieces throughout the house. I have a well-equipped shop in the basement.

Robins made a nest in our planter, right on top of the flowers. My wife calls the robin "Rosey the Robin." We have fun watching it from the kitchen window.

For recreation, I follow sports on television. I'm a Red Sox fan, and enjoy watching tennis and golf.

We go to church— that's part of our life. I'm quite active in church. My wife has played a big role in Sunday school. We've supported our church financially without fail over the years. I take pride in that. I wish more people would support a church, even if they don't attend. Our freedom of religion is so necessary, part of our country's way of living. Once you start to support a church, you realize you are doing something for posterity. Just going to church occasionally is better than nothing, but true religion should be supported; to support it you have to make a commitment. I also feel that supporting the schools is vital.

Advice to Younger Generations

Don't just think of yourself and your money, but be a good citizen. There is no reason we can't all be good citizens. Become familiar with government—local, state, and national. You'll be a better, more successful person in all ways, not just at making money.

There is so much more to learn today and there are so many opportunities, so pay attention, set your goals, work hard. Don't just take a job. My father taught us, no matter whom you go to work for, even if it's just sweeping a floor, do it right.

Kids can't do it alone. The younger generations need love and encouragement. Home plays such a big role today, as always. Kids also need good teachers and good schools.

Thomas and Betty Vail, Kennebunk, Maine

The Vail brothers: Jackson, Ted, Robert, and Tom, circa 1943

Ted, Jackson, Tom, Robert, 2000

Chapter 6

John Winston Downs
B-17 Down

At a trim 6'4" John W. Downs possesses an heir of quiet, thoughtful dignity. He and his wife live in a pleasant home in the suburbs of Washington, D.C. He was a navigator on a B-17 Bomber with the Eighth Air Force, at a time when bombers did not have fighter protection. He was shot down over Germany and spent nineteen months as a POW in Germany. He and his wife, Jean, have two sons and a daughter. His family describes him as a man of character and honesty, a stoic who did not complain, and a caring parent.

I was born in 1916 into a close-knit, religious home, a family of eight. We operated a fruit farm in the Rocky Mountains, where we worked hard and that gave us a sense of pride. We had no hired hand or machines. All work was done by hand and one horse. We hoed weeds, dug irrigation ditches, cut and pitched hay, and of course, picked strawberries, cherries, raspberries, cherries, apricots, peaches, pears, apples, and tomatoes. I also milked the cow and fed the horse, pigs, and chickens. Days were long. Only the kitchen was heated, so we shivered when we got out of bed on cold winter mornings. Fresh fruits and vegetables back then were only available from peddlers. Sometimes I'd accompany my dad on peddling trips into the city, where we sold mostly door to door. The Depression coincided with a drought, which caused us to be even more frugal. Although we were poor, there was a joy in working on the farm. It taught us humility, and respect for nature and the rights of others. We saw beauty around us. We had lots of good neighbors to play with, and wearing no shoes in summer gave a wonderful sense of freedom.

I earned my bachelors degree in chemistry. I was called to serve as a navigator in the Army Air Corps. I was assigned to a heavy bombardment group (the newly organized 100th Bombardment Group Heavy, 350th Squadron) and sent to England to fly combat missions over Germany and its occupied territories with the Eighth Air Force. My plane was a B-17 bomber, the Flying Fortress. It had a crew of ten men and was fortified with eleven 50 caliber machine guns, two of which were my responsibility. We bombed cities in Norway, France, and Germany. We usually lost two or three planes from our group on each mission to enemy fighter planes or anti-aircraft fire from the ground. You had to harden your feelings toward losing your friends.

Toward mid-August, 1943, we were ordered to bomb the Messerschmidt Aircraft factory at Regensburg, deep inside of Germany and well fortified. My plane was in a group of 21 B-17's. As we crossed the English Channel, we were picked up almost immediately by German fighters at the French coast, attacking furiously from all directions. The sky was full of our 50 caliber bullets and the Germans cannon shells and bullets. German transport planes flying above us dropped long steel cables through our formation. This continued for the full two hours to the target and was emotionally exhausting. I saw many planes on both sides burst into flames and explode. Several times we had to pull up sharply to avoid head on collisions with German fighters. One by one we were being picked off. By the time we reached Regensburg, only two of the 21 planes in my group were left. The co-pilot on the other plane went berserk from the emotional strain and had to be restrained for the rest of the trip. I had already fired 5000 rounds of ammunition, completely ruining the barrels of my two guns. We straggled individually across the Mediterranean Sea to land in North Africa. My prayer was answered.

My plane was downed during the bombing of Bremen, Germany, on October 8, 1943. I was then a POW from 1943 to 1945, mostly in Stalag Luft III prison camp in East Germany, near the small town of Sagan. Our compound consisted of single story wood buildings on about five acres of land, surrounded by barbed wire fences, with guard towers at the corners. The guard towers had machine guns and searchlights. The Germans gave us a ration of barley soup and bread, supplemented by some Red Cross parcels. As the number of POWs increased, the rations decreased in size. During that time, my weight shrunk to just over 100 pounds.

On January 29, 1945, as the conflict with Russia on the Eastern front became very intense, we were forced to march west. We gathered our warmest clothes, some food, and left camp. It was thirty degrees below zero, snow was falling, and a stiff wind was blowing. The march—some called it a death march— ended ten days later at Spremburg, Germany, and we were then transported to Moosburg, Germany—near Munich and the Dachau concentration camp. It was brutally cold. I think hell is not fire, but cold, hunger, fear, and loneliness. At Moosburg, we were crowded, underfed, and had no cooking facililties.

Early one morning in April of 1945, I walked outdoors, and as I looked in the direction of Moosburg, I saw the American flag flying over the steeple of the village church. That is without doubt the most beautiful sight I have ever witnessed. Tears came to my eyes and I stood transfixed as I thought of the words of the Stars Spangled Banner. Later that day, General Patton walked down through our camp, followed by a tank escort and a group of GIs. So it was that I regained my freedom that I will always cherish. A few days later we were flown to Reims, France. There I was deloused, given a new uniform, and placed on a diet of eggnog until I could again eat regular food. I finally got back to the USA in June of 1945.

I met Miss Jean Huff while training at Gowen Field, Boise, Idaho. We married after the war. After retiring from a career in the Air Force, I became a Physical Science Administrator with the U.S. Naval Radiological Defense Laboratory, San Francisco, California. I then worked at the Naval Ordnance Laboratory, Silver Spring, Maryland, in the Nuclear Program Office.

PTSD Symptoms?

I still don't like to be hungry or cold. It reminds me of the prison camp, but I don't think that I suffered from PTSD.

What Helped You Cope?

I felt I could do what I was trained to do. I learned this on the farm.

CALM UNDER PRESSURE

On the day my crew was shot down, October 8, 1943, I was a B-17 navigator and gunner in the lead plane in a bombing raid of Bremen, Germany. We had no fighter protection. There was awesome anti-aircraft fire from both the ground and German fighters. In a span of only a few minutes, one by one, the U.S. planes were being shot out of sky too fast to count, until mine was the only remaining of 21 bombers. I was struck in the leg by a 30 caliber machine gun bullet from a diving German ME109 fighter. Other bullets were stopped by the experimental flak vest that I was wearing for the first time on this mission. Then my plane was shot down by 20 millimeter cannon shells from the fighters.

This was indeed a greater concentration of destruction than I had heretofore witnessed. This was the closest I have ever been to being killed. Oddly enough, however, I felt composed. My mind worked clearly, and I hadn't the least fear or panic. Perhaps we just fear death or pain from a distance. I have heard others speak much the same way, that when death was most imminent they had no fear.

I noticed that the altimeter said 22,000 feet and the time was 1500 hours as I jumped from the plane. Despite the chaos, flak, and fighter fire, I was not afraid; I was too busy thinking.

I decided not to pull the ripcord until I stopped spinning so as not to entangle my wounded leg. Knowing that I had plenty of altitude, in curiosity I experimented. I found that I'd stop spinning if I stretched my legs out, but if I crossed them I'd roll over on my stomach.

I was about to pull my ripcord when I noticed two German fighters, so I waited.

I started thinking about my bleeding leg, and how I'd land. It is remarkable how clearly one thinks under such circumstances.

I landed near a small country village. A group of villagers, mostly women and children were watching me. One of the women could see that I couldn't walk so she brought a bicycle for me to lean on. I was honored with the foremost position in front of the parade to town and the entire village fell in behind. I was brought to the town hall in the village. As I entered the door, the first thing I saw was a large Nazi flag covering the entire wall. I joined the rest of my crew and was soon taken by train to Frankfurt for three days of interrogation, and then sent to the first POW camp in East Germany.

Though I was thankful to be alive, I was depressed and more than a little scared and very lonely. I felt lucky that I was the only injured member of my crew, and that I was game.

Our commanders taught us to hate the enemy, but I never did have personal animosity. I thought that they were in the same position as we were. On a flying mission you have a job to do. You have to keep your head.

RATIONAL THOUGHT PROCESSES

I sometimes think of the worst thing that could happen under the circumstances, then reconcile myself to that situation. This helps me to stop worrying and the result is usually less than I anticipated. So when I was engaged in combat day after day, I reconciled myself to the loss of my comrades and accepted the fact that death could likely happen to me.

Complaining was minimized by realizing how much worse off other prisoners were. For example, we knew two Jewish soldiers who were captured and imprisoned in Buchenwald before they convinced their captors that they were GIs. So we heard about those camps.

SOCIAL SUPPORT

In the prison camps we formed combines of friends. We played chess, read books, formed a theatre group, and did many other things to help each other get through. On a 10-day forced march in the winter to elude the Russians, five friends in my combine stayed together. We shared our food with no selfishness.

While I tended to be a bit of a loner by nature, I've kept good friends from the war. For example, my co-pilot calls on the anniversary of our being shot down, on my birthday, and some holidays.

COMFORTABLE WITH EMOTIONS

I was aware of my feelings, but did not feel much need to talk about them. However, my daughter once asked about my experiences and I discussed them. It spurred me to write my autobiography, which has been healing.

Nobody is strong at all times. You need to minimize your weaknesses and depression. For example, I was depressed at times during captivity, but I pressed on.

I have no problem recalling the most stressful experiences, because they were always resolved in a wonderful way. So I look back, not in horror, but in joy, as I count my blessings one by one and am reminded of the wonderful thing the Lord has done for me.

SELF-ESTEEM

I was rather cocksure of myself during the war. Today I am, hopefully, more humble and wiser.

ACTIVE, CREATIVE COPING

In our combine we pooled our resources. We'd plan a menu and took turns cooking. For Thanksgiving we fashioned a "turkey" out of SPAM furnished by the Red Cross. We made an iron to iron clothes by melting a lead pitcher given to us by the Germans. We fashioned a sort of washing machine from a big can with a plunger made from a smaller can. We tried to exercise together.

We were always planning some form of escape or helping someone with his plans. Although some made it out of the compound, none made it out of Germany. The Germans would punish us when someone escaped, but no one complained because we felt we were doing our duty as soldiers by actively planning escapes.

SPIRITUAL AND PHILOSOPHICAL STRENGTHS

God

The war experiences strengthened my beliefs when I think of the times my life was spared and my prayers were answered. Prayer works. In fact, I can not think of a single instance when it didn't work. Not always as I would have thought, but always in a way that was best for me. Prayer is my medicine for anxiety and stress. Each time I was faced with a traumatic situation, I'd have a prayer. I have learned to expect an answer.

A very stressful experience occurred at Wendover, Utah, on Christmas day of 1942. We had almost completed a scheduled six-hour bombing and air-to-ground gunnery training mission in our B-17 when we were directed to land immediately because of an approaching snowstorm. We were about 20 minutes from the field when we received the order, so by the time we had entered the landing pattern, snow flurries blocked our vision but the visibility was still adequate for landing. We were within a half-minute from touchdown when the blinding force of the snowstorm struck. All objects on the ground and in the air disappeared. Even the wings were blurred to my vision. Benny Demarco, the pilot, immediately put the plane into a steep climb and banked sharply in a direction away from the mountains. We reported our condition to the tower and were advised to climb on course toward Salt Lake City. Five minutes later an advisory from the tower indicated that Cheyenne, Wyoming, was the nearest open field. Our predicament was now precarious. Cheyenne was almost four hours away over one of the highest and most rugged portions of the Rocky Mountains and we had less than two hours of fuel remaining. Benny called for a course heading to Salt Lake City, which I had already computed and was able to give him immediately. However, giving him an estimated time of arrival was something else again due to the severity of the storm. The falling snow was so dense that our wing tips were not visible from my window. I bowed my head and said a prayer for our safety. I tried to maintain an estimate of our course and position, although I knew it would be unreliable because of the turbulence of the storm and our rapid climb. We broke out on top of the clouds at 31,000 feet, which was above the ceiling altitude for a B-17. A sea of clouds lay about us in all directions as far as the eye could see. I estimated our position, and gave it to Benny, as being near Salt Lake City. We circled a couple of times and talked over what we should do. Our prerogatives were to bail out or try to stretch our limited gas supply to reach Cheyenne. The first presented the hazard of descending by parachute through the 30,000 feet of snowstorm to an uncertain landing that might well be in the snow-covered mountains. It also meant being without sufficient oxygen for at least 20,000 to 25,000 feet of that fall. The second, using our high altitude to advantage and leaning out our carburetor mixture, offered an almost equally remote chance of reaching Cheyenne. Neither alternative was safe to try. We were still debating when I spotted what appeared to be an opening in the clouds some distance to our right. I described its position to Benny and he turned the plane to investigate. It was an opening in that vast sea of clouds and as we flew over it, we looked down at, of all things, the runways of an airport. A miracle had been performed for us and I thought of my prayer and I knew that it had been answered. We spiraled 30,000 feet down through the opening to the Salt Lake City airport below and, as we descended, the clouds above closed over us. When we landed, the sky was again an unbroken overcast.

Every time I said a prayer, I saw it answered. So the next time I was more assured that I'd be given a way to get through it. I got so I depended on prayer. I still depend on it. As I reflect back on it, I saw that problems were solved. I am still strengthened by prayer. I was raised with prayer. Even today, I pray when faced with special problems. I'm confident I'll get an answer that will turn out the best for me.

In 1975, my Nuclear Program Office was studying the effects of a nuclear explosion on Naval communications. Transistors were vulnerable to radiation, but no one knew how vulnerable. After one year, a working group had no conclusions to report. I was invited to join the group, thinking that an additional mind might be helpful. My boss gave me an electronics book to read. I was not an electrical engineer. So I said a prayer, asking for guidance. Although I was lost as I perused the book, my mind was drawn to one paragraph and equation. I read it 100 times until I understood the paragraph. I was able to change the equation to compute the vulnerability of each of the Navy's 800 transistors, a report that eventually was used by many experts around the country. That was the only positive result to emerge from the working group.

If I doubt my capability, I turn to prayer. For me, I find praying first is the most surefire way to combat worry. I even recognize that some answers started out years before. Prayer gave me courage that I could do my job well. I attribute my protection from PTSD to prayer, which erased all negatives.

Meaning & Purpose

In the prison camps we were preoccupied with getting along. In a way, it was just like being on the farm. Perhaps we take our freedom for granted and never come to a full realization of just how precious it is until it is taken away. I knew that it was the German leaders' purpose to rule the world, yet their actions toward even their own people showed how unfit they were to do so.

Morality

I have a sense of right and wrong. It's important to be true to yourself even if no one else knows. I wouldn't steal a pencil from the government and take it home. I've been faithful to my wife.

Love

The members of my crew — they were our family. We trained together. We were disciplined. We felt a pride in our crew.

Optimism

I had optimism and it increased in the war. I'd think, "I got through that OK. I can make it through this one, too."

Humor

John Downs has a subtle sense of humor. For instance, giving a talk on the preciousness of freedom, he began by saying that the listeners could exercise their freedom and take a nap while he spoke if they wanted to. In his autobiography, he notes that he could see the logic of turning off the refrigerator during the Depression. "Food requiring chilling would have kept just as well in my bedroom." After landing his plane in Wendover, members of his crew kissed Old Terra Firma, and he agreed with the statement, "the more firma, the less terra."

His son Drew notes that he loved to tease and tickle his wife. Daughter Diana says that he has a very wry, low key, hilarious sense of humor and, because of his brilliant mind, makes witty twists on words.

Long View of Suffering

The war taught me much. I learned from first hand experience the great blessing of freedom. My faith grew stronger. And I'll never complain about our bread or heating.

Maintaining Balanced Living

In the prison camp, I spent much of my free time reading books provided by the Salvation Army. I also played chess and walked around the perimeter. Since the war, I've loved to read. I've read the Harvard classics, about nine feet of books by the old philosophers and classic authors, like Shakespeare. I liked to come home each day from work and do the crossword puzzle in the paper, then take a short nap before dinner. As an adult, I found it relaxing to play the violin, guitar, mandolin, and banjo, which I learned to play as a youth. I was a Scoutmaster and camped with my sons. I liked to work with my hands. I gardened and whittled. Maybe I'd have been a good surgeon.

Jean and I enjoyed attending the national symphony concerts and the opera. We also enjoyed touring the historic sights around the Nation's Capitol.

Jean always prepared nutritious, balanced meals with vegetables, salads, and meat. I'm not a smoker or drinker. I generally slept easily eight hours a night, usually from about 10:00 p.m. to 6:00 a.m. I attend church every week.

Advice to Younger Generations

Keep your head when you have a job to do. Don't hate or retain bitterness. It keeps you from thinking clearly. Go to church to keep your mind on the fact that there is a God.

John and Jean Downs

John and Jean Downs

Chapter 7

Vernon J. Tipton
Down over France

Vernon J. Tipton lives in a bright, immaculate home surrounded by a redwood fence at the foot of the Wasatch Mountains, in Utah. He was a member of the 450th Bomb Group ("The Cottontails") 15th Air Force, and was a prisoner of war for a year after being shot down over France. His time as a prisoner included nine months at Stalag Luft III, probably the most famous of the German POW camps, which the movie The Great Escape *made famous. Tall and dignified, he presents a commanding presence.*

I was born in Springville, Utah, in 1920. My father died in 1927 at the age of 42, when I was six years old. I had three brothers and three sisters; I was next to youngest. Times were tough. The Depression, because of Dad's death, came early for us, and eroded our finances completely. We never owned a home or car before Dad died. Then, after he died, we were even poorer. The second oldest brother dropped out of school to be the breadwinner. Mother, of course, worked.

I went to college for two quarters, ran out of money, and went to Torrance, California, to earn money working at a steel mill. Then the war broke out. I met my wife there in Torrance and married her in 1943. Our oldest daughter was born while I was serving in Italy.

In May 1942, I entered the Army Air Corps and became a bombardier on a B-24 bomber. I flew twenty-five actual missions out of Italy. On nearly every mission we encountered German fighters, as well as fire from the ground. A plaque, a Presidential Citation at the U.S. Air Force Academy for our bombing group, indicates that we bombed Regensberg, Germany, the site of the Messerschmidt factory, and the Ploesti oil fields in Romania, probably the principal energy source for the German war machine. Those sites were among the most heavily defended targets in Europe. In those two raids in February and April of 1944, we lost 1505 men, either killed or missing.

On the last raid, April 29, 1944, we went to Toulon, France, near Marseille. After those brutal missions in Regensberg and the oil fields, this was to be a relatively safe mission. We were second in the formation, and were shot down by a battleship. The plane went down in flames; we bailed out. As I descended, the air was turbulent from bombs bursting on the ground and flak bursting in the air. Tracer bullets were all around me, so close that I felt I could reach out and touch them. The navigator and two crewmen died; seven of us survived. I landed in the harbor. Germans in a tugboat pulled me out with a grappling hook. I was struggling for my life and couldn't get myself free from my parachute. Their first words were, "For you der var is ofer." I was stripped of my clothing. Norma, my wife, received a telegram only stating that I was missing in action. Later, a letter from a member of my squadron who'd witnessed my bomber going down indicated that he'd seen parachutes. That gave her some hope.

I was in solitary confinement for three days of interrogation in a place near Frankfurt. A German Major said that he couldn't guarantee that I would be alive the next day if I did not provide the information he wanted. I eventually joined hundreds of other prisoners in a large compound guarded by ferocious German Shepherds. Then I was sent to the first of three prison camps, Stalag Luft III. The camp was in Sagan, near Breslau, Poland, and I was there from April 1944 to January 1945.

In January 1945, we were moved from our compound westward because the Russians were approaching and the Germans didn't want to lose potential hostages. We walked 75 miles in three days and nights. It was a difficult journey because the worst blizzard in 80 years swept across that part of Europe. Even some of the older German guards died from exposure.

We were sent by rail to the final prison camp. At least 51 airmen plus German guards were crammed into a boxcar that normally would fit 40 men. There was only room to stand. Many men were sick, vomiting, or had diarrhea. We spent three days on that train, so the stench was beyond belief. We were fed a little cheese and bread only twice. During my imprisonment, I went from 185 pounds to 130 pounds on a 6' 2" frame. I was liberated on a beautiful day in April of 1945. After a battle for the nearby town, General George Patton entered our compound with his pearl-handled revolvers, swagger stick, and air of absolute confidence. My friend was busy giving another prisoner a haircut. General Patton asked if he could be next in line. When the German swastika was replaced by the Stars and Stripes, macho men sank to their knees and gave thanks with many tears.

After the war, I came home and completed my bachelors and masters degrees. In 1949 I accepted a commission in the Army for the second time and was assigned to the Walter Reed Army Medical Center. (A Major promised me that if I came and worked with him he'd see that I'd get my Ph.D. through the Army). Six months later I was put on a research team and sent to Malaysia to work on a disease called Scrub Typhus. I returned and was assigned to Madagascar to work on controlling the plague. Then I went on to Berkeley for my Ph.D. in parasitology with an emphasis in medical entomology.

I went to Korea after the war as the commander of a preventive medicine company. At that time there was a very severe disease called epidemic hemorhagic fever, which we tried to prevent/control. We also were responsible for malaria control and disease control in general.

Subsequently, my assignments included: the 5th Army Medical Lab in St. Louis; Panama, in charge of malaria control for the Canal Zone; San Antonio, Texas, for four years, teaching in the medical school in the Preventive Medicine Department; and the 406th Medical Laboratory in Japan, involved in the control and prevention of several diseases in Japan, Korea, and the Okinawa chain of islands.

I retired early in 1968 as a Lieutenant Colonel, because I was invited to teach zoology at a large univeristy, which I did until 1983, ultimately becoming a full professor.

PTSD Symptoms?

I was probably like most. I had dreams of being a POW, or of being in combat. I had initial difficulty going to war movies and preferred not to be there. Otherwise, I was fairly free from any of those problems associated with PTSD.

What Helped You Cope?

Without question, anyone who went through the Depression was better equipped to handle the pressures of the war. Being poor, we struggled for everything we got, and I learned how to work when I was young. I believe the Depression helped in the formation of a value system, which was a great strength to me as I attempted to cope with the realities of war. Those values distinguished my generation from those of the Korea and Vietnam periods. My family was so close. We supported each other and worked together. We had assigned chores. We accepted responsibility; we were accountable. Today's kids have whatever they want, and they don't have to do anything for it. I think if we had another war we'd be worse off than we were in Vietnam or Korea. I believe one of the key words would be sacrifice; I think it came natural to those who went through the Depression. We weren't any greater than any other generation, except for the great preparation that came from the Depression.

CALM UNDER PRESSURE

As the gunnery officer, it was my job, after bombs were dropped, to put my head in the plexiglass bubble up near the nose of the plane, and announce the position of German fighter planes to our gunners. Of course we were excited. This was an adrenaline moment, when fighters were trying to shoot you down, but we didn't panic. We did pretty well. I don't remember ever having great bursts of anger after coming home, or ever being violent.

I never dissociated (mentally escaped from combat)— you couldn't afford to. Directing fire and using the bombsite was probably the highest form of concentration I've experienced. Our lives were hanging in the balance. You couldn't allow your mind to wander.

We were taught to hate the enemy but it didn't persist. I had no harsh feelings for the Germans. I don't remember any of my fellow airmen wanting to kill for killing's sake. We just had a mission to perform. I escaped from the death march with a friend of mine. In the countryside, we talked with the Germans. They wanted the war to be over and I could see they were just like us, and were victims of poor leadership. Today I drive a VW while my German friend, who was a POW in the U.S., drives a Buick. We've put those feelings behind us.

On the death march, we had walked more than fifty miles on blistered and frostbitten feet with little food or rest. As we passed through a village, an old German woman walked beside me and slipped a potato in my pocket. She was "the enemy" and probably had meager rations herself. Her kindness still warms my heart.

RATIONAL THOUGHT PROCESSES

My circumstances were similar to others. There were 10,000 others in camps, and many others being shot at. I didn't feel that I was singled out. There was a feeling that we were all in this together.

We were told at an airfield in Texas by General Hap Arnold that one third of us wouldn't come back. We didn't have high expectations of survival, which served as a form of immunization, so that each time we landed safely we felt lucky. In general we also didn't make mountains out of molehills.

SOCIAL SUPPORT

Without question, my wife was a part of my ability to cope. I can't say enough about her support. When we were first married we used Sweetheart soap which had a singular aroma. She sent me a bar and I kept it; didn't use it to wash with. I just kept it under my pillow. It was really of tremendous value in that it was a reminder of home and my obligation to family—kind of a link. The thoughts of going home to a family were a sustaining influence that is difficult to measure.

My mother was a wonderful angel; so were my family members. I couldn't ask for better support. They had confidence in me. They showed love and encouragement. I could not ignore their expectations. They expected me to be and do my best to handle things well. The ambiance of our growing up was great expectations.

Walking around the perimeter of the prison camp, I talked with friends of home and family. We buoyed each other up. Being in the same kettle and seeing others do their best were examples. Some men were especially great examples; they earned the respect of others.

When I saw my disfigured buddies, I felt gratitude. The courage they showed in handling their adversity inspired me. I thought, "If they can cope in going home without a nose or with some terrible disfigurement, I can do the same." I felt too fortunate to complain.

COMFORTABLE WITH EMOTIONS

One of the most difficult times was when my navigator, a good friend of mine, was shot while parachuting, then he drowned. Of course, I felt animosity. It is impossible to feel good toward those who take the lives of friends. But there was no residual hate. Anger was natural and normal.

SELF-ESTEEM

Even though we were poor and struggling, my mother kept telling us we were as good as anyone. But I never thought I was anything more than average. In the service, though, I discovered I could do most anything most anyone else could, maybe better, whether math, physical training, or Morse Code. I don't say this to boast but to indicate that my experiences in the military service provided a greater perspective and helped to build self-esteem.

ACTIVE, CREATIVE COPING

I read over 100 books in camp and read the Bible all the way through for the first time. We tried to better ourselves, and offered classes to each other. We had people offering classes in architecture, agronomy, and math. I tried to teach myself calculus. My association with these skilled people inspired my desire to continue my education.

To occupy my mind, I compiled a book of my buddies' favorite recipes, and made a cover from a tin can. We said we would send each other ingredients when we got home, like pecans from Texas or oranges.

There was never enough fuel for cooking or for heat. However, there were many tree stumps where the forest had been cleared to make room for the prison camp. Six or eight men would sit around a tree stump and dig it out with teaspoons and tin cans. While we worked we shared our fondest aspirations and stories. With determination and persistence we eventually accomplished our seemingly impossible task, and gave a great cheer. More importantly, we lifted each other through the process of sharing our innermost thoughts. One of my buddies in this group was trained in the use of codes. He received a deck of playing cards. Bits of a map were hidden on the backs of some of the cards. When assembled, the map became a useful escape tool. He also smuggled in camouflaged radio parts that enabled us to hear the war news.

When the opportunity arose, my buddy and I did escape from the death march by rolling over an embankment. We traveled at night, but were eventually recaptured.

SPIRITUAL AND PHILOSOPHICAL STRENGTHS

God

One of the worst days of my prison experience was shortly after I was captured. However, as I made my way around the compound, I saw a British chaplain, who quoted a Biblical passage (*Not one sparrow "shall fall to the ground without your Father."*). He said, "a bomber is bigger than a sparrow. Don't you think your Father saw your plane fall to the ground?" That lifted me from the depths of despair and I suddenly realized I was not alone and without hope.

I had the sense then that I do now, that God is very kind and loving, and concerned about me. My faith was important. It motivated me to survive and do the best I could while I was in the prison camp.

The nineteen fellows of my faith in my west compound at Stalag Luft III held services on our own every Sunday without fail. There was a bonding, a comraderie that was special among us. We didn't smoke. We exercised well in prison. We traded our cigarettes and coffee for chocolate. We didn't drink (some others made potato peelings into vodka). So, when we went on the death march in 1945, we were in pretty good shape.

The human body is fairly well equipped to deal with one insult at a time, but it is more difficult emotionally and physically when multiple insults occur simultaneously. Many of the prisoners were coping with multiple insults: malnutrition, Dear John letters, lack of support from home, and intangibles, including dormant faith.

My wife and I made marriage promises to each other and we believe we'll be together forever. It is hard to put into words how important and motivating that was to make the most of my time in the prison camp.

Meaning & purpose

I was determined to do something with my life and not squander the opportunities. I wrote to my wife from Italy that when I returned we would try ever so hard to make this a better world to live in. My family was my number one priority.

Morality

It was very important to be moral. The prison camp was a test. We were all hungry; it would have been easy to take advantage of others when cooking, but we didn't. Integrity was strengthened by the war. We didn't steal, though with eighteen men in a crowded room, this would have been easy to do.

Long View of Suffering

Overall, the war strengthened me—no question. I'm a better person because of being a POW. Although it was the most difficult period of my life, I think, "If I can handle that, I can handle anything." That experience makes peacetime stressors seem insignificant by comparison.

I was asked to be assistant librarian with another fellow for the books we received through the Red Cross. So I read over 100 books in camp. It was there that I decided I'd go as far as I could with my education. Being a prisoner wasn't all negative.

It may sound strange, but my year in German prison camps was probably the most liberating experience of my life. I was stripped of my clothes (literally) and my outer choices, yet I could concentrate on the choices that really count and on possibilities that had before only been dim and vague. For example, I overcame my bias about Germans. I committed more strongly to living a good and healthy life so that I would always be satisfied with my choices.

Optimism

I never blamed the war for any of my problems. Nothing but great things have happened to me. Even the Depression and being a POW were great blessings. I am so grateful to the Army for my Ph.D. And as I said before, talking about our hopes and dreams buoyed each other up.

Humor

There was a lot of humor. We made fun of the guards, pigeonholing them because of their appearance and the way they crawled around under the barracks checking for tunnels. And we tricked them. We got pleasure by building a radio, listening to BBC, and outsmarting them. The guards counted the slats on our beds. We found it humorous that we could shave down the slats on our beds and use the shavings for fires. As long as the Germans could count the slats, it didn't matter how thin they were.

Maintaining Balanced Living

I live a fairly normal and active life. I walk about two miles daily, mow the lawn, and garden. I'm not a couch potato. I have been a good eater. I have a good appetite, and eat lots of vegetables and little meat. I sleep well and regularly, from 10:30 p.m. to 6:00 a.m. I have never had a problem with alcohol or tobacco.

For fun, I play rook. I'm writing my memoirs and a column for the local weekly newspaper. I like to visit my children, but I'm kind of a homebody. My wife and I go for rides and an occasional movie. We watch TV together, and listen to good music.

My basic philosophy includes service to others. I have served others in various church capacities in different countries and with different peoples, and am now helping to organize prison ministries in Central Utah.

Advice to Younger Generations

People who know how to work, I mean really work by the sweat of their brow and try their muscles, and have the capacity to stick to it, can cope better than those who have not disciplined themselves to work mentally and physically. We condition ourselves to cope, just as physical exercise conditions the body to withstand vigorous demands. Mental activity is important as well. We played mental games at the dinner table raising our children. I think it's been good for them. We have two doctors, a computer engineer, an editor, and our youngest daughter teaches part time at a major university where her husband is an assistant dean.

Home life helps kids become successful and learn to work. Our children were pushed. They weren't lazy physically or mentally. Such people don't cope well. We need to instill a love of work in our young people, to see the rewards and satisfactions from working. Work is an antidote for many problems. I wasn't satisfied to lie on the bunk, but read and worked in the library or dug up stumps for firewood with teaspoons and tin cans.

Everyone needs a family support system. I can't imagine anyone coping with insults from one's surroundings without such support.

One needs an idea of where one is going, a direction. A lot of this comes from home life—parents who talk with their kids about things that are important, a value system. My granddaughter, eighteen years old, already has a "game plan" which comes from being around people who have goals in mind. She'll have no problem coping with failure because she has a wonderful view of life, where she's going.

Bombardier on B-24 bomber, top right

Norma in Mesa, Arizona, during the war.

Vernon and Norma Tipton

Chapter 8

Colonel Charles Edward McGee
Tuskegee Airman

Thoughtful, soft-spoken, warm, and an authentic gentleman, COL McGee is a trim 175 pounds, the same as he weighed in high school. He stands at 5' 8", but looks much taller. He trims the beautiful shrubs and flowers of the red brick split level home near the Naval Hospital in Maryland.

COL McGee is a member of the famed Tuskegee Airmen. He flew more combined fighter combat missions in WWII, Korea, and Vietnam than any other pilot, and is highly decorated. His 332nd Fighter Group had the unprecedented distinction of never losing a bomber to German fighters in 200 escort missions.

He fought two wars simultaneously: WWII and segregation, and did so with nobility and grace. In 1948 President Harry Truman's Executive Order No. 9981 directed equality of treatment and opportunity in all of the U.S. Armed Forces.

Known as a loving and dedicated family man, he has three children, ten grandchildren, and six great grandchildren. His children include an Emmy Award winning editor (Yvonne), a college administrator and professor (Charlene), and an Air Force and commercial airline pilot (Ronald). He presently serves as president of Tuskegee Airman, Inc., which he helped found in 1972. The association is dedicated to preserving the history of black aviators and motivating young men and women to fly and to participate in a democratic society. He is still active in air shows and speaks around the country.

After his wife Frances died, his daughter Yvonne reflected: "When we moved in together, I thought I'd find he was different, but he's always kind and the same."

I was born December 7, 1919, in Cleveland, Ohio, the second of three children. I had an older brother, and my mother died shortly after giving birth to my sister when I was one year old.

Dad was a minister and a social worker, and also did some college teaching. He always ensured that we were well taken care of. He was not a hard disciplinarian—always very light, pleasant to be around, but with expectations. He was not extremely talkative, but I remember lessons learned. Once my brother and I were in the yard, playing and throwing stones at a ground hog. He lectured us on being good to animals. From that time on, I never took a gun to shoot deer or had an inclination to hurt animals.

We visited my grandparents in the summer. Dad would put us on the train in Cleveland. He gave the porter our lunch. Of course, people don't do that anymore. Grandmother met us in West Virginia. They lived in a town with unpaved streets. I remember gathering firewood for the stove and grandmother making hot gingerbread. With a father and grandfather who were ministers, I played church, standing on an old coke bottle box for a pulpit. I'm told that I once said, "Now it's time to sing one more song and get out of here."

Dad moved to Chicago for employment in 1929, and the kids were housed with the Harris family in St. Charles, a small town west of Chicago, from my third grade year to my first year in high school. Those were good years. The Harris's were like my parents. Mr. Harris was hard working and very conscientious; Mrs. Harris was very kind and jovial. But, if we misbehaved, we had to get a switch, and if we got one too small, she sent us back for one of the proper size. We had a good life with them. They were attentive to how we were doing in school, and saw that we had a right balance of work and play. We had regular chores and good manners were required. Schools in Ohio were segregated then, but not in St. Charles. Perhaps that is why my father settled us there. There were only a couple of black families in the city. Although the school was integrated, blacks had to sit in the balcony of the theatre and couldn't eat in restaurants. I played on the Fox River. We couldn't afford skates but played hockey when the river froze over, using sticks we made from a tree limb. I sold newspapers, and finally got a bicycle from money I earned.

Mr. Harris worked at the Moline Malleable Iron Company. He took me on some Saturdays to see how to make molds and burnish chain links. We didn't have a car, and walking to the plant kids sometimes called names, but fortunately there were enough good people so that my growing up years were not too adversely affected.

We didn't have a lot, but we were able to keep our clothes clean and be presentable enough. There wasn't money to freely buy things during the depression. I put newspapers in the soles of my shoes to keep the cold out. But we always had food on the table and were protected from the elements. We were aware that we had enough, no different from anyone else, because everyone was struggling in the Depression.

In Chicago, Dad took a job in social services and had an active ministry. He taught in a college in Florida for a year. He took a church in Keokuk, Iowa, and my brother and I joined him in 1935 for 2½ years. Those were good years because the Iowa schools were excellent. Then he took a church in south Chicago, and I finished high school there, graduating in 1938.

I always enjoyed school and participated in musicals, chorus, basketball, football, and debates. Once a classmate in Iowa told me that I would have won a debate had I not been a Negro. But, along the way, there were always good and inspiring teachers who didn't let prejudice get in the way and keep you back.

Prejudice was not really a dominant theme in my younger years. Boy Scouting was open to my participation, and was an important influence. My Scouting experience and scout camp went well. I went all the way to Eagle Scout. While there were some places you might not be really welcomed, I was never turned away or denied. Part of that is that I might have stayed away from certain activities that might have been awkward.

In high school, I realized the value of education. I determined I'd go to college, but had to work a year to earn money to go. In 1939 I worked with the Civilian Conservation Corps, and learned surveying and contour farming engineering in Northern Illinois.

In 1940, I started at the University of Illinois, which was open to black students, and studied engineering. In my second year, Dad took a church in Gary, Indiana. During the summer I worked there in the labor force for a steel company, making enough to pay for school.

I met my wife on campus. We started going together in 1941 and married in October, 1942. One week later I was called to training. In 1942, at the university, I had been taking Army ROTC, and was a member of the Pershing Rifles. At that time there was negotiations to get blacks in Army aviation. I applied to be a pilot in the Army Air Corps Aviation, and was accepted in April 1942. I finished the semester and summer work in Gary, and was called up in October, 1942.

What was then Tuskegee Institute in Alabama was one of six black colleges that trained students to be civilian pilots. As an experiment, they then built the Tuskegee Army Airfield for training fighter pilots beginning July 1941. The first group of combat pilots went to combat a few months after I started training there.[*The first aviation cadet class included Benjamin O. Davis, Jr., a West Point graduate. His father was the nation's first black general.*] I arrived in Italy in January, 1944, as a member of a segregated group assigned to harbor and coastal patrol. We flew from our own base and could not take rest camp with the other pilots.

In April of 1944, my 332nd fighter group was picked to escort B-17 and B-24 bombers out of Italy to Germany with the P-47 Thunderbolt. In early July of 1944 these were replaced by the P-51 Mustangs, which could fly longer and at higher altitudes. I named mine "Kitten" after my wife, and also because the engine purred like a kitten. We had great leadership in Ben Davis, Jr. We respected him as a West Pointer and what he represented. He imposed great discipline that resulted in our not losing a bomber under escort to German fighters. We abided by his leadership. Out of our respect for him, the end result was that we probably flew closer and tighter formations than some other groups. We stayed with stragglers to protect them and probably saved a number of lives. We were forbidden to leave our assigned post to go after German fighters in hopes of a kill when they were not attacking the bombers we were escorting. This was called "Happy Hunting," and would have left our bombers vulnerable.

I fell in love with flying. I remained in the service for 30 years, actively flying for 27, which is not the norm, including Korea and Vietnam. I had a great experience. After WWII, I returned to Tuskegee as a replacement for the white instructors that taught us.

The Air Force really led the country in integration. In 1949, I went to my first integrated assignment in Salina, Kansas. Although I couldn't bring my family because a black family couldn't rent a home in town, I got along fine on base, because the Air Force used people based on their skill, not their color.

I couldn't have sat down and written a script for better career opportunities and experiences. After flying in Korea, I became Commander of the 44th Fighter Bomber Squadron for two years, flying F-80 jets in the Philippines. Many other great assignments, including command, followed.

I retired in 1972. In Kansas City, I went through real estate school and became director of real estate and purchasing for a large company. I finished a degree in business administration and had various jobs in public administration and management. Then I began to do various kinds of volunteer work.

PTSD Symptoms?

I don't recall feeling frightened or having feelings of remorse, because we realized that our actions were protecting our forces.

What Helped You Cope?

I carried the attitude that you treated people as you would want to be treated. Doing anything else isn't going to make life any better or change things. Some of the attitudes that I got out of Scouting—to do my best, to do my duty to God and country and my fellow men—dominated my thinking and sustained me.

I also felt it was important to carry yourself in a bearing that you wouldn't regret and could hope this would gain respect of those you came in contact with.

Both the Depression and the war galvanized our nation. The war united the country around a common cause of supporting our allies in Europe. That block of experience did something for us that was unique and influential. It was also a more innocent time. You had the sense of security then. When it got hot you could take the whole family out to the park and sleep. Everyone was glad to share. Now we don't do that. It's not as safe. Things have changed.

Moving around broadens your perspective compared to staying in one place. Along the way, individual teachers helped broaden my focus, to like history, the arts, in a way that stayed with me.

Three institutions kept me in the path of not looking at negatives: Scouting, Church, and the Alpha Fraternity at the University of Illinois, which held the principles of education and helping others.

Somewhere along the way, I learned the principle of not fighting back even if provoked, realizing that little is gained by fighting over mistakes that perhaps aren't that important in life. Focus on what life you'd like and live to help bring that about rather than one that has no merit.

I'm not a religious fanatic, but I grew up believing in turning the other cheek. Words won't hurt me. I let them roll of my back. Fighting back over insults doesn't gain respect. By WWII, I was very cognizant of circumstances. On the train going south, we had to move to the front, closest to the coal car. *("Back of the bus, front of train," he said with a soft laugh.).* But my father had passed along his vision of a world where all people treated each other as they'd wish to be treated. That ideal was my guide.

He had taught me that all people are truly equal, created in God's image. I had learned that if you bear humiliation with dignity, you might later earn the person's respect. I believe in the promise of America.

CALM UNDER PRESSURE

In WWII, we were completely immersed in the situation at hand. I had the expression, "If I think I know everything there is about flying, I'd better do something else," because flying is a constant learning experience that causes one to focus. One must be attentive to each circumstance. Our training, which had some superior elements, helped us keep that focus. There was never any doubt about our abilities. In fact, it was just the opposite. If it's called for, I've got the training and equipment to do it. We had confidence in our team. There were no doubts about the maintenance guy or anyone else doing the job right, so we could keep our focus on the mission without worrying about the engine not running right.

There was no hatred there at all for the Germans. We had our assigned tasks related to winning the war. I've always had some empathy/understanding for other persons, believing that we're all individuals who didn't have a choice in our circumstances. So, I've never had a disrespect for that other person regardless of background, nationality, etc. Part of my early training that I mentioned, I never liked the idea, "Oh they're gooks, or they're wops." We didn't need to put that type of marker on folks. We need to be accepting people for, as Martin Luther King said, the content of their character and what they do, not their happenstance of birth. Monikers on folks set them apart. I never had the feeling of them being an enemy to hate or dislike. It was more that they had a point of view, a different perspective, and a loyalty to country and to upholding the rules of the country they represented.

RATIONAL THOUGHT PROCESSES

I always looked on the positive side of things and kept a positive attitude, because the negatives don't help your thinking or planning. Not that you don't take into consideration the "what ifs," but I didn't dwell on negatives.

If I messed up, I'd ask, "Did I do my best? Was I properly prepared and using the equipment properly? I have to do better next time. Wake up and do it right." On the personal side, if I said something that hurt someone, I'd be big enough to say "I'm sorry" and do better the next time. It doesn't hurt to pause a moment before you open your mouth.

When others made mistakes, I never liked labels, like "dummy," for others or myself. Labeling is negative, not positive. We don't help ourselves or others using labels. I had no problem being straightforward, regarding what should be done, but I tried to do it without labeling or belittling. That doesn't help them or me. I'd try to get them to think, "Are you doing your best? If not, do it right." I'd try to get them to think in positive terms to improve themselves and their performance.

SOCIAL SUPPORT

This was very important. Being lonely can be tough on keeping a focus. I had a very supportive wife and family— thumbs up, as we would say in aviation. The Harris's died when I was in the war. So my wife was my home place. We wrote regularly. It was my support to have and know I had loved ones who were thinking about me and writing regularly. It was sustaining. My sister was in the WACS, my brother was in the Pacific, and my father had served in WWI and again in WWII as a chaplain. So there were letters and communication. But I also knew the foibles of the mail, so I wasn't devastated if I didn't get a letter at mail call.

From our Tuskagee experience, from those years from 1941 to 1949, when we were together and not mixed, we developed a comraderie and support that no other unit could claim, because we were together for so long. We got to know nicknames. We all trained, were in combat, married young, and had families—all of this association gave us a bond that had a bearing on our performance that was difficult to measure. We had not just a couple of buddies, but we had numbers. This bolstered pride to keep you walking tall. I wasn't a smoker or much of a drinker so I didn't participate in some aspects. But I was friendly with everybody. I didn't hold myself aloof but I also maintained an independence.

Spending a lifetime in the field of aviation, I believe there's something that sets aviators apart from the others, like a fraternal group that shares common experience and knowledge. I like being around people that are interested in aviation. I still enjoy air shows, being with people whose common interests transcend the focus on race.

COMFORTABLE WITH EMOTIONS

I didn't give much thought to fear. I slept well. I was ready to face another day with thanks for good health. I don't recall having a case of pessimism, fearing what might happen.

I always believed in prayer. I said thanks at the end of a day, and prayed to keep me through the night and to face another day.

SELF-ESTEEM

My focus was hoping I'm doing something that can be respected, that I'm not doing something against you as an individual, that we can both walk down the sidewalk with our shoulders back and heads up, able to look you in the eye because I've not done anything that needs to be hidden. I'd like your respect and I give mine.

Thinking about that, I was walking down the street in Rome one day with a squadron mate who was white. Perhaps he was thinking of prejudice, for he said, "Why don't you say you're Egyptian?" I thought for a moment and said, "I'm American. I don't need to be Egyptian." It never crossed my mind that I needed to be somebody or something different. Don't try to be something you aren't. I was comfortable with who I was and what I'd accomplished, walking upright, hopefully, before God. I didn't need to be something else to please a few. A lot of people do a lot of stumbling trying to be something they're not.

ACTIVE, CREATIVE COPING

I just tried to keep focused and responsive. I had learned, early on, to participate, do my best, carry myself worthy of whatever accolades that might come.

Acceptance of what you can't control comes with doing something positive. As a captain at Tuskegee after the war, I was traveling to Florida for gunnery training with a group of airmen. As the senior man, I had the ticket form for train travel. Since I had some whites and blacks in the group, I started to approach the main window, rather than go to the blacks' ticket window. Immediately there were objections. I chose to give the voucher to the white staff sergeant and left the station, leaving it to him to get the tickets. Soon the sheriff drove up and I stayed removed from the station until the train came and I got on it. There was nothing I could do. Protesting would have only brought a confrontation that I could see there was no way I could win.

SPIRITUAL AND PHILOSOPHICAL STRENGTHS

God

I do believe we are a small speck in the mighty universe and someone above is the master of this universe. I see God evidenced in the beauty of flowers or birds in fabulous colors, eating at the feeder. When I'd fly at sunset and see the canopy of stars come out overhead, it was rather humbling. Somebody's in control. It helps to keep in a positive mode to realize that there is a being there somewhere that keeps the scorebook.

There were times when my faith was helpful. I don't recall asking for special protection on a specific mission, but more in terms of being at peace with myself—a calming effect that I felt I could commune and know I'd been heard, and felt I was important, knowing there is a merciful God.

Meaning & Purpose

WWII was a declared war, so the military was in harmony with the nation. The military was subordinate to civilian rule. I understood that and wouldn't want it any other way. Yet, the military's hands were not tied, so we could be capable.

I had taken an oath of allegiance and was part of a unit that was directed to participate in the war. We were fighting to give people a political freedom — freedom from fascist rule and from the military's overrunning adjacent countries. Basically, I saw the war as about freedom of choice.

Morality

Ethics and morals are most important in all aspects of being a soldier because without these you have no respect. Without ethics you will do anything to get by. And you begin to fall into non-positive thoughts. I don't think I'd ever make a politician, because politics requires compromise. Morality added to unit cohesiveness and morale. During the war people were probably more amenable to following the law.

Morality includes how you relate to others and the opposite sex. Morality goes beyond honesty. It includes how you think and look at others, how you treat them, regardless of circumstance. It includes not using degrading monikers and put downs (e.g., slut). People who think that way are anti-social, separating rather than bringing people together and focusing on things that would be uplifting and noble in cause. Going into overseas areas you weren't seen as a black man, but as another person; and until you did something unethical, you were accepted.

Love

We had a great sense of togetherness because we were forced together. We knew each other's weaknesses and strengths.

Optimism

I'd call myself an optimist because I like to think that things are going to come out all right. But we have to do right, then the chances are much better that things will come out right. I don't think I go around with my head up above the clouds without seeing things that are going on around me.

Humor

I wasn't so much a humorist. But there was lots of humor that lifted the level of everyone's feelings, particularly in the early years when we were operating in a segregated environment. Many times the humor could lessen bad situations and help us deal with them more positively. For instance, we had affectionate nicknames, like Jelly Butt Walker, Smirkin Smith. I was Maggilicutty. We kidded each other. A couple of folks were very talkative and kept things going. Spontaneous things lightened things up—not in the combat environment but in many other situations. After the war, my wife and I were amused when our daughter avoided a drug store displaying a sign that said, "We serve Whites Ice Cream." Whites was a brand name.

Long View of Suffering

Suffering for a good cause, when suffering had a good impact, was worthwhile. As I was traveling with my family, motels would have signs flashing vacancy. We'd stop and I'd go in. My oldest daughter said she could always tell what took place inside by my mood, whether we'd stay or drive down the road. I guess in all of those circumstances I carried myself in a way that made it worthwhile, based on how my children came out. The fact that there has been some progress in equity, equality, and opportunities made it worth facing. I wouldn't opt to do it any other way. I never focused on 'what ifs' or 'whys' (what if mother hadn't died). The real question is how I conducted myself and how things actually came out. It was worthwhile if suffering resulted in a better life not only for me but from a total social viewpoint. The same was true of the war. War gained freedom. I didn't want war, but I hope the world came out a little bit better as a result. You'd like this to happen without war.

Maintaining Balanced Living

I've always liked the out of doors—tennis, golf, sailing, picnics. I like to take in opera and symphony a couple of times a year. I like all music. I've had stamp and coin collections. I still read a lot. I participate actively in church, and sang in the choir until recently.

I've always done a little exercise. I still do an exercise program of pushups, situps, and stretching on most days, and resting on weekends. I used to run, but walk now. I've been a regular sleeper, from about 11:00 to 6:00. I told my kids, when you wake up get up. I sleep well. I lie down and I'm out. I've eaten fairly wisely and kept my weight fairly constant. I never smoked, and only drink occasionally, never binged.

Advice to Younger Generations

I tell youngsters, whatever you do, always do your best, whatever it is—in school or out. Think positively.

Don't be afraid of helping others. It's important to consider being helpful; for older folks to look back and help someone who is behind, to give back. Don't think you did it all on your own. We've all been helped by others along the way. Sometimes it's just a good word from somebody when you least expected it, or a helping hand.

You don't need to toot your own horn. If you're doing things right, the sound will be heard.

Wing and Base Commander,
June 1972

Charles and Frances McGee at Tuskegee
Airmen Convention, 1993

Charles, daughter Yvonne, and Frances

Chapter 9

Carl Douglas 'Chubby' Proffitt, Jr.
Omaha Beach

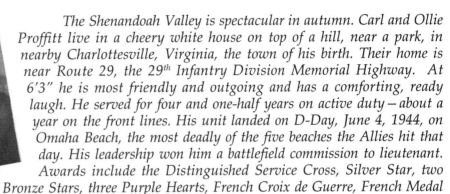

The Shenandoah Valley is spectacular in autumn. Carl and Ollie Proffitt live in a cheery white house on top of a hill, near a park, in nearby Charlottesville, Virginia, the town of his birth. Their home is near Route 29, the 29th Infantry Division Memorial Highway. At 6'3" he is most friendly and outgoing and has a comforting, ready laugh. He served for four and one-half years on active duty — about a year on the front lines. His unit landed on D-Day, June 4, 1944, on Omaha Beach, the most deadly of the five beaches the Allies hit that day. His leadership won him a battlefield commission to lieutenant. Awards include the Distinguished Service Cross, Silver Star, two Bronze Stars, three Purple Hearts, French Croix de Guerre, French Medal of Freedom, State of Virginia Distinguished Service Award, and others.

I was born November 23, 1918, the third of six children. During WWII, four of us, including my one sister, were in the service, and the two oldest brothers worked in the Naval Yard near Washington, D.C.

It was tough going during the '30s. Dad made fairly good money as a mechanic with the Southern Railroad, working nights. Mom worked for a shirt factory for a short period of time during the Depression. Dad was a good provider. I dropped out of school in my senior year to help provide for the family.

We were very closely knit. My sister played ball with us boys and we are still all close. We had to make fun for ourselves. There was no transportation. We skated or walked to school or rode a scooter, about three miles to elementary school and four to high school. I carried papers after school from grammar school up through the 7th grade. In high school I cut grass and worked at a service station.

We had a happy childhood. For fun, I loved all kinds of sports, mainly baseball, softball, basketball, and football. As kids, we played games at night, kick the can and tag, and liked to play pranks on Halloween. We'd damn a creek to make a swimming hole, and went sleigh riding in winter. As a family we visited relatives nearby, and had extended family gatherings and picnics.

Generally, we had meals together, except when Dad was working. We always had three meals a day. Mother and Dad were both excellent cooks. Good old home cooked meals might be fried chicken, gravy, mashed potatoes, green beans, macaroni and cheese, corn on the cob, cornbread, salad, and buttermilk. Mom would fry fish we caught and also frog legs.

Dad had a great personality. He loved to tease and tell jokes and pull pranks. He worshipped his wife, and was very warm and loving. Mother was sort of a homebody. She loved to invite her sisters to play cards. She was calm, easy going, dignified. She made all her clothes. She lived for her family, like most mothers those days.

There was real good discipline because Dad cracked the whip. He was firm, but good. When he said something he really meant it, and you knew you'd better take him at his word. He didn't attend church regularly because he worked seven days a week. He worked four to midnight for the railroad, walked two miles home and slept. At 6:30 he woke up to go to work at the University of Virginia as a carpenter. He was one of a kind. Everyone liked him. He had good morals, and was friendly to everyone. There were crowds and crowds of people when he passed away.

I met Ollie in 1940 at a dance hall near where she was raised, 15 miles from where we now live. I was in the National Guard. At first, she wanted nothing to do with me. She was at a dance with a fellow in the band. She worked at a department store in town. I was working for a trucking company, delivering goods to her store. We dated for a year and a half. We married in May 1942, while I was on active duty.

In terms of my military service, I joined the Monticello National Guard in 1939. I was a member of K Company, 116th Infantry Regiment, 29th Infantry Division. On February 3, 1941, the unit was activated for what we thought would be one year. About ninety men left Charlottesville. Only three of us are still in Charlottesville. One lost his right arm. We trained at Ft. Meade, Maryland. We were on our way back from maneuvers in North Carolina, when we learned that the Japanese had bombed Pearl Harbor.

In September 1942, I was shipped to England on the *Queen Mary*, which held practically all of my division—about 17,000 men. We almost didn't make it. When we got into German U-boat waters, we picked up an escort to protect us—destroyers and cruisers and those types of ships. A British corvette with a crew of about 400 cut in front of us and was sliced in half. All 400 were lost. Had we hit the ship's ammo magazine, both ships might have gone down. We had to slow way down thereafter because of a hole in our hull that was larger than my house. We landed in Scotland. The bag pipers were playing "Carry Me Back to Ol' Virginny" and "Dixie."

We went to Tidworth Barracks in England to train for the invasion. I was platoon sergeant by then. I had been promoted from private, to PFC, corporal, sergeant, staff sergeant, and then tech sergeant. We trained for D-Day in bangalore torpedoes, flame throwers, and demolition TNT. My unit had not been in combat before. We were landing beside a unit from the 1st Division that had been in combat in North Africa.

My unit was in the first wave to land at Omaha beach. It was about 7:15 a.m., although who'd look at watches with all that was going on. We landed about one mile left of the intended landing. That might have helped my boat team get to the sea wall without casualties. A boat team was a 30-man fighting unit consisting of riflemen, bazooka teams, a BAR team, a mortar and machine gun team, wire cutters, and a flame thrower team. I was second in command to the platoon leader. Some guys threw their bodies over barbed wire and we ran over them. In our regimental combat team of about 1200, we lost pretty close to 900 wounded or killed in action before we cleared the beach by about 8:30 or 9:00 a.m. How we survived, how we crossed that 300 yards of beach, I'll never know. That whole day we fought Germans. The next morning we withdrew back to the beach to reorganize. You talk about a sight there. The tide had washed debris and bodies to the seawall. It was gruesome. Bodies were mangled, blown in half, sometimes bodies stacked 8 to 10 feet high. There were rifles, helmets, and equipment everywhere. It was the most gruesome sight that I've ever seen in my life.

On June 8, we got orders to help the Ranger battalion, who'd scaled the cliffs of Pointe du Hoc, attack Grandcamp. The Rangers were pinned down outside Grandcamp. Coming over the knoll, near where the Rangers were pinned down, we had to stay on the road because the Germans had flooded the low lands. They'd set up heavy fire to cover that road. When we came up over the knoll, I could see a U.S. tank in the road. A land mine had blown off its track. Shells were bursting everywhere. Bullets were flying. Now we were pinned down, too. I spotted the source of the German machine gun fire, but the tank was blocking our advance. The first sergeant asked me what I was doing as I took my pack off. I said, "I hope I'll do something. Watch and see." I ran to the tank, jumped up onto it and jumped down inside the turret. I told the tank commander where the machine gun was. Bullets were ricocheting off that tank like you wouldn't believe. I directed him to swivel the turret. He knocked out the machine gun. That action led to my receiving the Distinguished Service Cross, the nation's second highest decoration for bravery. We moved into Grandcamp and took it shortly thereafter. (We went back there for the 55th reunion. When I was laying a wreath, some of those old Rangers saw my 29th Division insignia. They hugged me for helping them when they were pinned down. That meant a lot to me).

We continued toward St. Lô. There were many skirmishes among the hedgerows. I was offered a battlefield commission before St. Lô. This was after my lieutenant had been killed on a night patrol I'd been on. I went back to find his body. They couldn't guarantee that I would stay with my unit, so

I refused the offer then. On D+22 (June 28), I was wounded in hot fighting near St. Lô, and was sent back to England. I had taken shrapnel in my leg, which required five or six weeks to heal. I headed back to rejoin my unit, refusing a direct order to go to a different company. My unit was sent to fight across the Siegfried Line in Germany. I was again offered a commission in August of 1944. This time I was guaranteed I'd stay with my unit, so I accepted. (I once heard war historian Stephen Ambrose say that a battlefield commission means more than an award for bravery because such awards are earned for single acts, whereas a commission is earned for sustained leadership.) I was wounded again in the fall. After 1½ weeks I was back to the front. The Germans were only 200 to 300 yards from us when I was given the commission. We had set up the platoon command post in the basement of a row of houses. My platoon had the biggest feast to celebrate my promotion. They killed a cow and we had steak. They ran stovepipes throughout the row of houses so as not to attract German artillery.

We attacked all the way to Koslar. Digging a fox hole, I was told to report to the company command post. While I was gone, German artillery shelled the area, and a shell landed plumb in the center of that hole. Fate saved me. I could have been blown to smithereens.

At Hasenfeld Gut on December 5, 1944, we were attacking a heavily defended position. The adjacent platoon advanced ahead of us and got cut off. It was 5:00 a.m. and pitch black. My platoon was ordered to relieve them. We did. As we withdrew, some of my people were pinned down in a minefield by machine gun and artillery. I went into the minefield to help administer first aid and evacuate the wounded. Some of my guys had legs blown off by mines. I was wounded again, and went back to England for five or six weeks. I received the Silver Star for that action. I was on my way back to the unit for the fourth time when the war ended. I was still in K Company. I still have shrapnel in my leg from my first wound, a mortar shell.

None of the WWII guys came back complaining, feeling sorry for themselves. One neighbor has one arm, and never complains. He helps people, and never gives the impression of feeling sorry for himself. I told him the only reason they let him pass the plate at church is that he doesn't have a second hand to take the money out. He's been my best friend since the '30s.

After the war I drove a bus for two years. Friends, fellas I was raised with, invited me to work at their wholesale candy business. I stayed with them 37 years. I managed the company and retired in 1983.

Wife Ollie adds: We had 11 children in my family. We grew and raised all our food. Our parents were strict and fair. My parents fed a whole community of people without food, black and white. My dad died at eighty-two with all his teeth except one, which he had pulled himself. He loved to polka and two step. During the war a group of about fifteen servicemen's wives got together regularly to share our letters and news. My faith and my friends at church also helped me get through the war. After the war, we felt like we'd gotten through it and defeated the enemy and we could defeat anything else.

PTSD Symptoms?

The first year I had some symptoms. I was nervous, a bit jumpy. My wife said I had nightmares, although I didn't realize it. I still went to dances and parties. After that year, I was fine.

What Helped You Cope?

I think the WWII generation learned to cope with life more quickly. They had to fend for themselves, hustle for jobs, help their families. As kids we learned to take care of ourselves. Today the parents do it for the younger generations.

Athletics, going to work at an early age of 17, working as a laborer in construction, and then working in a warehouse and delivery developed my body and kept it in good physical shape.

CALM UNDER PRESSURE

The war was something we had to get done in order to get home. I was married and wanted to come home to my wife. I felt killing was a duty to my comrades and to myself for survival. We were a close-knit unit. There were ninety from the Charlottesville area that I'd been raised with. To see those boys get mangled is bound to effect you and spur you on, but I didn't hate the enemy. I didn't hate the German people.

Being a leader, a lot of the guys looked up to you to lead. That urges you on, if you're any kind of a person. I felt a sense of obligation to my men. I felt that the better I trained them, the more apt they were to survive.

If you hesitated and thought too much, you probably wouldn't do some things that need to be done. But you can be cautious and brave and do something on the spur of the moment, without being a daredevil. This is part of leadership training. Before running to the tank, I surveyed the situation. I saw that the tank was lined up with the machine gun position and the lid was up, and knew that the tank would give me some protection as I ran. I knew something had to be done. Rescuing my troops had to be done. I had to think quickly. In the darkness at Hasenfeld, I put tourniquets on legs. I had no chance to think at all.

RATIONAL THOUGHT PROCESSES

I'd just think of ways to get out of the predicament. Some guys just went to pieces. I had to think of something, especially being a leader. In real life, you have to think the same way.

I was successful in the service, but I wasn't a perfectionist because I knew I made mistakes also. I've always liked to take care of things, like the car or yard. But there is no point in expecting perfection. Instead, I try for excellence, to do things right. I've always been clear on that.

Regarding mistakes, the time to correct a mistake is when it is made. The only person who doesn't make mistakes is the person who doesn't do anything. Correct the mistake on the spot. The worst thing is to punish someone for making a mistake. Teach them why they are wrong. In the service, you don't want a person to obey from fear, but from respect. If they respect the leader, people will obey to help the leader and will go the extra mile.

I wasn't hard on people. I've never told someone to do something that I wouldn't do myself. I tried to lead by example—with my two sons and grandsons, too. I was patient with people. I never flew off the handle.

I had limits. One of my squad leaders was a constant complainer. We'd take three twenty-five mile hikes a week in England. He kept complaining. I told him several times to knock it off for everybody's good. I finally told him to shut his mouth or I'd knock his helmet off. Four miles later I did.

SOCIAL SUPPORT

My unit was a great big family. People helped each other because our unit was so closely knit. There was a lot of comraderie in the boys in our company. We had many friends in the unit.

The first time I was wounded and was in the hospital, the first sergeant wrote me a letter, telling me to hurry back, because I had a great following in my unit. My brother went to see me in Germany, but I was in the hospital. After the war, he told me that the guys told him I'd have no problem getting guys to volunteer to go on patrol. Everyone wanted to be in my platoon.

I had lots of friends in the service. You had to create a lot of friends to help with your survival. You looked out for each other. I thought I was good at making friends. I still go down the street and people speak to me. We have a lot of close friends now. Only three of us from my unit are left in town.

Support from home meant everything. We got supplies from home. In England we wrote to each other continuously. After combat began, letters were few and far between. Getting a letter from my wife was always great, getting updated on everyone back home and the community.

All the wives back home helped each other and shared news, like one big family.

COMFORTABLE WITH EMOTIONS

I think I was comfortable with my emotions. I'm a pretty softhearted guy, tenderhearted—mostly since I came back from overseas. I cried lots of times when my buddies were lost. It sort of made me angry at times too. I still get emotional when I see something sad on television. Tears stream down my face. In the war I was absolutely afraid. If you're not, you're crazy or a damn fool, if I can use such a word. The first night after D-Day, I was shaking. I wasn't shaking on the landing, but I was afterwards. I was never much of a talker about it, yet it never bothered me to talk about it when people asked, even when I first came home. I've been to a lot of schools to talk about the war, and about twenty school kids have interviewed me for papers. I didn't write about it in letters, because you didn't want to worry the folks back home.

SELF-ESTEEM

I always felt I had a good following. I know the boys in my platoon trusted me. I didn't feel better than anyone. I never bragged. I felt like I did my duty and helped the country. I felt absolutely confident, because I'd been well trained and I'd worked hard.

ACTIVE, CREATIVE COPING

I think I'm an active person, not only in the service but in civilian life. I was never one to lounge around much. At the seawall, I was active. I was running about trying to lead guys on and not let them get immobilized. Things were so loud I had to kick people to do things. Of course, when the tank was blocking our advance I was active.

You had to solve problems with perseverance. Near Koslar, Germany, on the attack, the Germans had dug trenches across the brow of a hill. I told my platoon sergeant to put boards over the top of the trenches to get the men out of the rain. We went to sleep, and the pouring rain caused the trench to cave in on top of us. I felt close to suffocation. I was muscular. I kept twisting until I broke loose and then dug him out. I saved his life. One boy was lost in a nearby trench.

After the war, I stayed active. I went back to fast pitch softball until I got too old to run. I coached little league and American Legion baseball for at least twenty years altogether. I also umpired after I was too old to play, did yard work and gardening, and painted my house.

SPIRITUAL AND PHILOSOPHICAL STRENGTHS

God

I believed in God then and now. I see him as my protector, spiritual leader, the Almighty. He doesn't single out any one particular person based on color or creed. You need spiritual guidance when going into a conflict, when you're facing death every minute. I remember one attack in a wooded area and shells were hitting the top of trees, and shrapnel was spraying down like rain. I got down on my knees by a big tree and prayed, it was that bad. I prayed quite often. I am a regular church attender now. I go every Sunday. We raised both our boys in church. Part of spirituality is to not judge someone quickly. I've never been quick to judge. I like to be around a person before I make a decision about him.

Meaning & Purpose

You need to set goals in order to get through, even though you might not meet them all. My first goal was to come home to my wife and have children. I wanted to come back to my hometown and have my own home, which fortunately I've attained, and get a good job. I always wanted to be a railroad man, like Dad, though I didn't do that.

I was fighting for freedom, to have the type of life we have in this country today. When I signed up and volunteered, I felt it was my obligation to do my part.

Morality

A moral person has the respect of his peers and family. I don't think there's any question about it. I'd like to be thought of as a good, decent person. I'd hate to have people talking about me because of certain things I'd do, so I try not to do things I'd be criticized for.

I've believed in being faithful, absolutely, to family and friends, and to my church. *(Ollie adds, "He's been a faithful husband and good protector and provider. We raised two good children on account of him. He taught them right from wrong. I told him I expect him to never run out on me and never hit me. And he's always lived up to both of those promises.")*

I could never understand why a soldier would kill civilians or rape.

When we won the European Theatre baseball championship, we got seven-day passes. We were in a bar in London, the only place you could go for a cold beer. The bar brought in streetwalkers. Our shortstop, who was married, wouldn't even look at another girl over there. One of the guys sicked a girl on him, knowing exactly the kind of person he was. He said, "Leave me alone. I don't want anything to do with you." We respected him.

Honesty is one of the main qualities a person should have. It is an absolute must to be honest about everything, regardless of what it is. If you do something you shouldn't do, don't lie about it. *(Ollie: "Honesty is one of his best traits.")*

Love

I'd call it more of a close-knit feeling for my comrades, rather than love. You showed altruism to them by training them well. I helped lots of guys who were wounded, bandaging their wounds.

I love all of my family, even though you don't get along with all equally. I feel love for mother, wife, and my children. All are different but important, and show love in different ways. My grandchildren hug me when they come in.

I received the Rotarian Award for service to my community. We used to help neighbors all the time, visiting, playing croquet. It's a different life style now; everyone is inside watching television.

Optimism

I try to be optimistic about things. It helps you obtain your goals. I thought without question we'd win the war except for the first day. I thought we'd lost it and were going to be driven right back into the channel. As soon as we got in and got going I knew positively we'd win. We were too strong and had too much support from the homeland. It was something we had to do. Just think of what the country would be like if we hadn't gotten rid of that dictator.

Humor

(Smiling) Humor has to be a big part of your life. It keeps you loose and happy go lucky. I felt that I was in the same mold as my Dad. There's nothing I like better than a good joke.

Long View of Suffering

The hardest part of the war was being away from home, and seeing my buddies lose their lives. Faith enters into enduring suffering. You have to be physically sound. But the war strengthened me in some ways. It taught me perseverance. It made me appreciate life and peace, seeing how some people suffered.

I would not take one million dollars to repeat the war, ever, but it gained us freedom, and greater love for family, country, and friends. It taught me to love life more.

I've always said Germany is one of the most beautiful countries in the world. I sure noticed that beauty. I liked the cleanliness and order.

Maintaining Balanced Living

I've stayed active in sports. I played first base on a team that won the European Theater of Operations Championship in England. We won 33 straight games without a loss. Now I like to play golf. We love to go dancing, and go every month—country, electric slide, big band. We met dancing and have been dancing ever since, almost 61 years. I think that's one of the reasons we've lasted physically as well as we have.

For recreation, I also like gardening, yard work, painting the house. I like sports on television. My wife thinks our television only shows sports. We used to play a lot of bridge. We vacation and travel together. I went back to Europe for the 55th reunion. We raise a garden every year—you name it, we raise it. I cut grass. Spiritually, we like going to church and are always there on Sundays.

I've always been a good sleeper. I'm in bed every night by 10:00, up by 7:00. I eat three meals a day— a good breakfast, light lunch, and a sit-down dinner. Lots of fruits and vegetables, and fish. Cereals, bananas, occasionally steak. We don't eat fast foods.

I've used alcohol some, not much. Maybe a drink at a party. Occasionally a drink before dinner, not more than twice a month. I was never a heavy drinker. I smoked until 1960. A pack lasted three days.

The family visits at least once a week for big meals. Both sons live within 15 miles. Both sons were in the service—Army and Navy. We have Christmas together.

Advice to Younger Generations

Never turn your back on a problem. Always try to find a solution. There's a solution for every problem.

Develop a good wholesome way of life. Try to attain the goals you set for yourself and don't be dependent on others. A friend has been a sergeant on the police force for 40 years. He said he admires more than anything else a man whose name is never on the docket at a police station.

Participation in sports, above all, teaches strong discipline to do the best you can. You very seldom see youngsters who occupy themselves with sports get into trouble.

The service matures people and teaches discipline. Service was good for each of our boys. They came back independent and self-reliant. I was a strong disciplinarian with my kids. I set guidelines. Even in the Army I always adhered to the rules and regulations. It paid off.

Be involved and help people out. In the service they told us that, as a rule, when you volunteer you get yourself in trouble. But I was a person who loved to help people one way or another to rectify their problem. I'd try to help people who would appreciate what you were trying to do for them. In the service I tried to help by leading by example, by loaning money, or making budgets for enlisted men. I've always been pretty easy to get along with. I help anyone I can. If anybody asks me to help with needs, I never turn them down. I work hard in several organizations that I belong to. I've been chairman of a local club to recognize outstanding athletes and academic achievements. I've also been a member of the Masonic Order, Elks Lodge, Falcon Club, Moose Lodge, American Legion, Disabled American Veterans, and VFW. I've been very community minded. I do business with local businessmen. It helps my community. *Ollie adds. "I'm very proud of his accomplishments for the U.S., Virginia, and Charlottesville, because he's done a lot for all of them."*

The secret of a long marriage is to do everything your wife tells you *(chuckling)*.

"Chubby" and Ollie Proffitt, Charlottesville, NC

Chapter 10

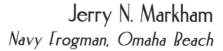

Jerry N. Markham
Navy Frogman, Omaha Beach

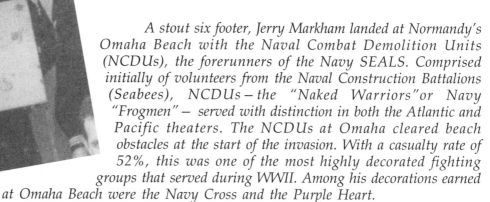

A stout six footer, Jerry Markham landed at Normandy's Omaha Beach with the Naval Combat Demolition Units (NCDUs), the forerunners of the Navy SEALS. Comprised initially of volunteers from the Naval Construction Battalions (Seabees), NCDUs – the "Naked Warriors" or Navy "Frogmen" – served with distinction in both the Atlantic and Pacific theaters. The NCDUs at Omaha cleared beach obstacles at the start of the invasion. With a casualty rate of 52%, this was one of the most highly decorated fighting groups that served during WWII. Among his decorations earned at Omaha Beach were the Navy Cross and the Purple Heart.

Chief Petty Officer Markham was an original NCDU member. He was active in researching and raising money for plaques to recognize those who served at Omaha and Utah beaches for the UDT/SEAL Museum in Fort Pierce, Florida.

I was born in New Orleans in 1918, an only child. My father died in the flu epidemic of 1918 right after I was born. My mother and I joked about raising each other because she was only 17 when I was born. I was a street-wise kid, raised in the French Quarter of New Orleans. I was mature for my age. The French Quarter was a small melting pot. It was heavily populated with Irish, Italians, Arcadian French, South American Indians, and a strong migration of Filipinos. New Orleans had a peculiar brand of its own language, a combination of accents. I can pick it out. My first schooling was at a Catholic school. I was an altar boy until they found out I wasn't a Catholic. Then I attended public school. My mother left me to decide on the religious question. She exposed me to all, but never asked me to join, letting me make up my own mind in my own time and my own way. I worked after school selling papers, and at grocery and poultry stores. I'd get five cents a week allowance and went to the silent pictures at the movie house. I'd put the money I earned in the pot. My mother and I shared and shared alike.

Most of my playmates had large families. I'd pick up slang words and get disciplined by adults in the neighborhood. Once in the backyard of an Italian family, the mother said "eat." And I cursed in Italian without knowing it. She pulled her apron up and came down the stairs and boxed me in the ear.

My greatest form of recreation was athletics. As kids, we'd go down to the Mississippi River to the paddle wheel ferries. We'd get down under the docks behind the ferries and tie a rope to the railing around the paddle wheel. When the ferry took off across the river we'd jump in the water and grab the rope to see who could go the farthest before letting go and swimming back to shore. I went out too far and got caught in the current and came out on the other side of the river, three miles down. My buddies thought I'd drowned. They went and told my mother. I hopped a ferry and came home 1½ hours later. She grabbed me and screamed in tears of joy, scaring me to death. She congratulated me and told me not to do that again.

I had a thing for reading. I'd play hooky from school and go to the library. Although I was recruited to play high school and junior college football, and to box and swim, I never graduated high school.

My mother and I came to Jacksonville, Florida, in 1935, in the middle of the Depression in an old Hutmobile. There were very few paved roads back then, so one of my jobs was to take care of the tires and keep the inner tubes inflated. I was a big, strong, husky kid. I got a job as a lifeguard for the summer. When that ran out, I worked as a carpenter's helper for 35 cents an hour, which wasn't bad pay back then. Meanwhile, my mother had finished her visit in Jacksonville and headed to New York. I decided to stay. After the carpenter's helper job ran out, I found I could get work with construction companies, if I were willing to travel. So I hit the road, traveling from one job to another. When a job ran out in South Carolina, I drove a truck, making local deliveries for a building supply company. That ran into another construction job and I was invited to be a pipe fitter helper. After working around the country on several pipe fitting jobs, I landed back in Jacksonville, working on the construction of a big new paper mill. Prior to the opening of the mill, I asked the new plant engineer who was coming on board for a job. He hired me to help him conduct cold water tests on all the water lines and different piping systems, since I knew where they were. When that was done, I went to the mill's power department as a fireman. Shortly thereafter, I became foreman of the boiler room. I took a course in steam electrical engineering, and in a few years I was promoted to shift engineer in charge of the turbo-electrical generators and the whole power department.

In the Fall of 1942, I volunteered to be a Seabee, although I was exempt from the draft. After basic training, I was sent to a water purification school. I saw a notice on the board calling for volunteers for dangerous and hazardous work. You had to be a good swimmer and experienced with small boats. Thus, I began my career as a Naval Combat Demolition man.

There were 90 volunteers in the first group, which was trained at Camp Peary, Virginia. We were turned over to the Marines for induction training, which was a modification of the Marine Raider program. It was very strenuous, and primarily physical disciplinary training. They'd push us to the limits of our endurance to see how we would react under duress. By the end of six weeks, only 30 of us were left. You could leave whenever you wanted.

At the end of six weeks, six of us were held back to go through with the next group of volunteers. They wanted me to lead the training for shallow water diving, which meant I had to go through the training again. It didn't bother me because I was particularly fit. We were trained in small boat handling, knife fighting, navigation, deep sea diving, physical training, small weapons, and combat jujitsu, plus the usual obstacle courses and close order drill. We developed a close order drill unit so good that we put on exhibitions for the base.

We then went to Ft. Pierce, Florida, for advanced training. It was similar to the Raider training, but it included the famous Hell Week. You went seven days and nights through different training phases without any sleep or food to speak of, running out to the ocean and in small boats over rocks and jetties and through the swamp, using high explosives. This went on day after day. If you made it through that, you were in. About half of the guys couldn't make it. The officers took the training shoulder to shoulder with the men. At the end, the basic units of the NCDU (Naval Combat Demolitions Units) — an officer and five enlisted men — were formed. This was the only democratic process I ever saw in the Navy. The officers got together and they individually picked their number one man from our group. That man would be second in command in the unit of six. We were asked if we wanted to serve. If the answer was yes, you and the officer picked four more and asked each one if that were agreeable. The reason for this process was that everyone in the unit had to want to be together. You had to know and like each other. This impressed me. You developed a tremendous espirit de corps. You knew what the guy next to you had been through and you could trust him implicitly. I'd never seen such unity, such coordination, and espirit de corps in a group of men as I found in the NCDUs. Once formed, we trained again as individual NCDU units. We learned reconnaissance in small rubber boats and demolitions — blowing up underwater obstacles.

I helped to put together a team for the landing at Omaha. I was the senior petty officer of the team, in charge of all enlisted men. Rank meant nothing. The only saluting or calling officers "sir" was for public display. Yet we had a strong, healthy respect for each other. No one took advantage of anybody. We were in constant support of each other.

In December of 1943, we were shipped to Plymouth, England, in the first batch of 11 NCDUs. We trained for D-Day. We had no idea where or when we'd land so we trained on different sections of the coast. In Wales, we took cold water training. We were housed with Army combat engineers who specialized in demolition work. We taught them how to blow the underwater beach obstacles.

The English Channel has 26-foot tides. The beach's gradients were anywhere from 300 to 400 yards wide at mean low tide. The Germans had placed mined obstacles in rows at different tide levels to make sure the incoming boats would hit one. Our job would be to blow a 50-yard path at Omaha Beach and mark it with buoys so that our landing craft could make it through.

Just prior to the invasion, our intelligence showed us that we were totally undermanned for our mission. Five men and an officer couldn't blow a 50-yard path through a 300-yard beach. So we closed ranks with the Army combat engineers. We added five Army combat engineers and three Navy volunteers to our NCDUs. So now we were a 14-man unit for our 50-yard path. To this was added an Army combat engineering team of 26 men. This Gap Team would go in together at H-Hour in the same landing craft. The NCDUs would blow the obstacles from the low water mark, The engineers would go about half way up the path and blow the obstacles and then open the minefields into the ravine exits. So we taught them about our underwater training and we learned from them about bangalore torpedoes.

After five weeks of intensive joint training, we went to the embarkation point at South Hampton. The LCT *[landing craft, tank – a 110 foot flat-bottomed craft]* was originally designed for four tanks and a jeep or two. They put two tanks and a Gap Team on it, plus a jeep. The tanks were going to land with us to give us fire support. Each NCDU and engineering team also had a rubber boat, in which to carry explosives. We spent three days and nights on the LCT, waiting to go. Men were wet, hungry, and deadly seasick from going out and returning.

H-Hour was 6:30 a.m. At 5:00 a.m. we could just see the outline of the Normandy coast. We towed an fifty-foot LCVP *[landing craft, vehicle and personnel – or Higgins boats, named after it's New Orleans builder, Andrew Higgins]* behind us. This is what the Gap Team was going to use to go on the beach with, ahead of the tanks and the LCT.

The LCT started sinking at 5:00 a.m. I went up to the young captain of the LCT and told him that he was pretty low in the water. So we went down to look in the engine room and it was nearly flooded. We signaled the LCVP to come up. We unloaded everybody onto it, along with the explosives. The LCT went down two minutes later, with the tanks. We unloaded all but the Gap Team personnel to a transport ship and got back on line for the invasion, and made the beach in time for the first wave.

Omaha beach was slightly crescent shaped, about five miles long. H-hour was at mean low tide, which meant, as I said, that the beach was 300-plus yards wide to the high water mark. The beach, which had been zeroed in for direct and crossfire, was fronted by sheer cliffs 100 to 150 feet high. There were five heavily-mined exit-type ravines. Our 16 Gap Teams were to blow 16 paths, each 50 yards wide and about 200 yards apart from each other, through the mined obstacles, and mark the paths

The pre-invasion plan was that the Air force would bomb the imbedded concrete gun emplacements on top of the cliffs. Thousands of rockets from the Navy rocket ships were to destroy the booby traps and mine fields at the base of the cliffs. The Navy big guns were to blast gun positions for two hours prior. But the Air Force dropped its bombs too far inland. The German gun emplacements were impervious to our shells. The rockets were mostly duds, short of the targets on the cliffs. The Germans had tunneled underground at the cliff and would cross fire at us on the beaches.

When we landed we dropped our ramp. Immediately, many of the 26-man Army team was killed by machine gun and mortar fire. In my 14-man unit, five were killed the minute we stepped out of the boat. My officer and two others in my original unit were killed. Two of the five Army engineers were killed. The other three joined the Army unit ahead of them. Mortars had also blown up our explosives. Then I was with about six men left. You had to hide behind obstacles to escape machine gun or mortar fire.

The tide was advancing one foot every eight minutes. We'd been given 30 minutes to blow a path. The second wave was due in at 7:00; then, every 30 minutes another wave was due. We blew five paths and three partial paths. The enemy fire was devastating. So, about two hours after H-hour, we'd bunched up. Very few were out of the water on the high water mark. The NCDU to my right was caught in a swift current and came to my area. I pulled them together with their explosives and blew a partial path. At about H+4 hours we got to the high water mark, what was left of us. What should have taken 30 minutes took four hours.

Later I learned that General Omar Bradley was watching this. At 9:00 a.m. the beach master called off landing vehicles because everything was jammed up and more couldn't get ashore. Bradley was getting ready to divert everything to the British beach called Sword when, and I watched this, four destroyers "laid their keels on the bottom" to fire point blank at the machine guns and mortar positions in the ravines. Then our guys got off the beach and up the cliff and the enemy eventually surrendered. You can thank the four Navy destroyers for putting themselves in harms way to do that.

I was lying at the high water mark. I'd been caught in several explosions and had a severe concussion, but shook it off. Three soldiers had dug a deep foxhole in the sand. A mortar caused it to cave in on them. Without thinking, I jumped up and dug their heads out while under fire. This was witnessed by others, and I was awarded the Navy Cross.

I had to take command and organized two partial units. Over the next two days we cleared out 85% of the mine obstacles. We commandeered bulldozers from the Seabees and stole explosives from the engineers. That pretty much completed our mission there. We had 52% casualties in the 16 units of the NDCU men. It was a very highly decorated group: eight Navy Crosses, Silver Stars, Purple Hearts, Presidential Unit Citation, and others. Lieutenant Walter Cooper was the task commander for the east side of Omaha Beach. He was in the command boat behind the units going in. His job was to see who needed help the most. He had five relief boats. He saw more of what happened to the different units. When he talked to me on D+1 or two and told me of the casualties, he became very emotional, choked up.

Those who were left, went back to England and made sure all of our wounded got their records to the hospitals where they were located. Then we were shipped back to Ft. Pierce. Each man was given the option of going somewhere else in the service. They could become part of an Underwater Demolition Team (UDT), which was being organized for the Pacific Theatre. They had found, through experience in Europe, that the units were too small and should not be used in combat like British commandos behind the lines, but should be used in reconnaissance and demolition work in opening up potential invasion beachheads. So they went to the UDT concept. The team comprised 100 men in four combat squads of 15 men and officers. The other 40 were officers, signal men, medics, and four small boat crews. The team commander could be a lieutenant, lieutenant commander, or commander. Ensigns and warrant officers led the squads.

Lieutenant Cooper asked me if I'd be his senior chief petty officer to form a team of 100 men. In the Fall of 1944, we put together UDT #25, with an advanced training base in Maui, Hawaii. We were assigned to a destroyer, and trained to recon different islands with different types of explosives, using only face masks and fins. Seventeen destroyers assembled off Ocean Beach, California, with 17 UDT teams or 1700 men, going up the coast of California to take cold water training because the Japanese landing sights were similar to northern California and Washington. We were learning to use rubberized suits because of the cold water, preparing for the invasion of Japan. The A-bomb saved us from what, in my opinion, would have been much bloodier than Normandy.

Two days after Japan sued for surrender, I went up to now Lieutenant Commander Cooper and said, "Walter, I want you to shake hands with #1 American citizen." He said, "Aren't you going to help me go to Japan to occupy?" As far as I was concerned the war was over. The Navy Cross gave me extra points, so I separated in San Diego. Admiral Kauffman hung the Croix de Guerre on me there. He was the father of the SEALS/Demolition Units. He was the first guy I met at Camp Peary when I'd joined the NCDUs. I was out by the Fall of 1945.

I went back to work, and was active in the union movement from 1946 to 1955 with the International Brotherhood of Paper Makers. At first I negotiated labor contracts. The Navy had trained me to be fearless. I went to school on the GI bill. In 1946, I married a lovely girl, who became a serious diabetic (I was widowed in 1974). In 1949 I went to Harvard, completing a year in advanced management in 13 weeks. Between 1955 and 1968 I managed labor and industrial relations for two manufacturing companies. Starting in 1968, I worked in upper management, ultimately becoming president and chairman of the board of directors of a large graphics company.

PTSD Symptoms?

I was blessed and fortunate that, with the experiences at Omaha, I'd have had PTSD if I had been the least susceptible. I've seen some of our guys have it. One 17-year-old had tears and was trembling. I had to slap him out of it. I've had bad dreams at times, but I took it in stride.

What Helped You Cope?

It was a matter of the discipline I learned or acquired in training. We were pushed to the utmost of physical limits with great discipline. You had no fear of the unknown because you felt you'd already been there. That training stays with me even today. When I finished fourteen weeks at Harvard, I came away equipped, feeling there wasn't anything I couldn't learn if I wanted to. I'm pretty self-contained emotionally.

CALM UNDER PRESSURE

In the heat of serious combat or the stress of training, you had two fears—the fear of being killed or hurt and the fear of not doing your job. If you gave into fear of being killed, it was over. You take five men and an officer depending on each other totally to do the job and protect each other as best they can under any circumstances—it was comaraderie, loyalty, espirit de corps that kept me going through it all. I wanted to do my job and help those I was with.

In my experience, we were trained and indoctrinated to prove you should be there mentally, physically, and emotionally. And you had a purpose to clear the way for combat forces to invade the beach and occupy and engage the enemy. So our job, ultimately, was to save lives. That was our motivation. I had a healthy respect for the reputation of the German soldiers at the war's beginning. They were fearsome. But I had no blood thirst. I didn't blame the German soldiers for the concentration camps, but Hitler and his characters.

RATIONAL THOUGHT PROCESSES

At the risk of being immodest, I respond well mentally and emotionally under stress. I look around me. If others are involved, I have a "take charge" instinct. I feel that someone has to do something. I might get shook up afterwards, thinking about how bad it could have been, but at the time I rise to the occasion. I always have. I think about the fear and my job, but I discipline myself to think that the job is more important than the fear.

If I see a person screw up something and I feel he didn't intentionally do that but didn't know better, I'd be inclined to teach him better. Maybe reprimand him for not thinking or asking questions, but then teach him to do better. After the war, when I was a corporate vice-president, I trained three men (who later became vice presidents in large corporations) in the field of industrial relations, by telling them, "Don't make stupid mistakes because you don't ask questions of me." That's the way you train men. You earn their confidence that you're not going to demean them or hold it against them.

When I made mistakes, I mentally kicked my own ass, but I never denied mistakes. I have no problem making mistakes. I did a lot of homework on my job. I was self-taught. Most of my learning came from experience, not books. So I knew how easy it was to take a bad reading and make mistakes, but I'd tell my guys, "I don't mind first mistakes, but if you repeat it, I'll kick your ass, because it's clear you're not learning anything."

Training with my UDT #25 at Ft. Pierce, we were out in the beach and I had given a young Seaman three caps to explode demolitions. I told him to sit on the dune line until I was ready for caps. Out in the surf, loading these obstacles with live explosives, I turned around and here's this kid standing there with the caps. I had to kick out the Seaman because he could have killed every man in that group. That was the only time I severely reprimanded someone. In explosives you can't afford to make that kind of mistake.

SOCIAL SUPPORT

In England, I got economy mail regularly from my mother and other members of my family, and I wrote back. Under the circumstances—the strains and stress of getting ready to go into a big invasion—it was a great source of comfort to hear from loved ones. My mother and I corresponded more in that year than in the other fifty years.

COMFORTABLE WITH EMOTIONS

We were all fearful. We could all be wiped out in one explosion. We'd be strong, then fear came afterward. We'd talk it out or sometimes play-act it. In the NCDU, if we took a crazy risk, we'd go back over it and figure a better way to do it next time. I didn't talk about it after the service.

Once, coming home at 10:00 p.m. to my driveway, another car pulled up. Two guys walked up. One had a gun, the other went to the side of me with a hammer. The guy with the gun said, "Give me your wallet or I'll blow your brains out." I remember saying, "Look, you want my wallet; get this crazy SOB with the hammer away from me. I want my driver's license and medical card." They took my wallet and drove off. It was like pulling the three soldiers out of the sand, done by instinct, not bravery. Afterwards, I thought about it and the fear came. But again, after being put through the limits of your endurance in training, if you were going to crack, you would have cracked. You were equipped for any reality. You weren't completely immune, but the majority of our guys didn't crack.

The only time I ever got into an emotional state was when I lost my temper about something. My anger would sometime cloud my judgement and I'd get all worked up. But somehow I'd find something humorous to relieve it—that's my best antidote. I'd tell myself things like "Even a blind pig gets an acorn once in awhile." If I felt sorry for myself, which was rare, I'd kid, "If it wasn't for bad luck I'd have none at all." Or there's Murphy's Law—if something can go wrong, it will. In other words, it isn't always your will or brains that wins out. Sometimes it's luck or things you can't control, and maybe I'll get lucky sometime.

SELF-ESTEEM

I had a lot of self-respect. I was never ashamed of anything I did. I was conditioned by hard work before the war, going in four years from a drop out in school to sanding cars for 20 cents an hour to a top job in a power department. My boss had to help me with the trigonometry, which I didn't know a thing about, to pass the qualifying test. I figured I had a right to be proud of myself.

I am very proud of myself and the men I was with in the Navy. This pride came from qualifying for the NCDU, and then being picked #2 for the unit, and then being made chief before the Normandy invasion. There was mutual respect between the men and officers in the close-knit group. We had a lot of pride in our unit and never took advantage of the leeway we had.

ACTIVE, CREATIVE COPING

If I caught a guy hanging back, dragging his feet or shirking his duties, I'd go up and say, "What are you, a spectator? You gonna sit this dance out or are you going to join the rest of us and do something?" That was sufficient most of the time. I was a doer and achiever. I was part of life. In industrial relations, I was in a joint industry meeting. There was a big celebrity basketball player who had a job for this large dominating corporation. He was a glad-hand, smiling guy, but in a crisis he was always looking out the window, fiddling with something else. So I spoke up and said, "Let's stop this discussion for the time being. We have five companies sitting here and one company has the power to make the decision, to set the pattern, to call the shot. But the SOB is a spectator looking out the window." We started to laugh.

We had a warrant officer in the UDT team in the ships company in charge of the small craft motor crew mechanics and coxswain. I was senior chief over all non-commissioned personnel. I only had direct authority over them when they were not performing under the jurisdiction of their officer. The warrant officer was an ambitious politician who disliked my authority. I unintentionally countermanded some of his instructions to his mechanics. He reported me to Cooper for deliberate countermanding. Cooper called me in to talk in his presence, which I thought was a mistake. But he gave me a tip that saved my butt. He said, "Chief, I'm going to ask you questions and I want nothing but the answers, no explanations, no opinions, no ad libs. Did you countermand his orders?" I said that I did. When he asked me why I didn't ask the warrant officer's permission, I replied that I'm not in the habit of asking permission to give instructions to people I have authority over." In other words, I don't exceed my authority, and they knew that that was true. I knew my limits and didn't exceed them.

SPIRITUAL AND PHILOSOPHICAL STRENGTHS

God

I allow for the possibility of God's existence. I don't know the answer, and don't worry about it. I live by the Golden Rule. I strive constantly to do that and taught my children to live by it, to guide their life by it, and freedom in their choice of religion (one is a devout Catholic). I think God wouldn't ask for more and would accept me based on my living that way.

Meaning & Purpose

I was a student of the war in Spain when the Germans and Italians abused that country. I read a great deal about what was going on in Europe under Hitler, taking Poland and bombing England. I was not a spectator. I was a reader all my life. I knew why I went into the service—to do something constructive, to win a war that needed to be won, because our way of life would have been in serious jeopardy if Hitler had won. I was a great admirer of President Roosevelt. And don't forget, the anti-war forces in our country at the time were very powerful. That's why FDR created the Lend-Lease program to keep England alive with loans. Then the Japanese took us off the hook by destroying Pearl Harbor.

I also wanted to prove I was a self-reliant, responsible, independent person who could be successful. That was my motivation prior to and during the service. By age 24, I was chief petty officer. Some guys spent 20 years before making chief.

Morality

I'm a pretty tolerant guy, but my sense of morality tells me that people should not take advantage of one another or abuse others' weaknesses by criticism, bad humor, or any other way. I think parents, and adults in general, should always strive to show good examples to the children in regard to behavior and values. Children need to be taught simple, honest values in order to have a decent morality. I feel very strongly about this and will openly criticize those I see violating those concepts.

Abusive language in front of children, drunkenness, whoring around with women, criticizing people, and denigrating them with racial bigotry—those kinds of things upset me.

I can't tolerate deliberate or malicious lies and mistakes. I've always tried to be honest with my men, even if it made me look bad.

If you get married, you should be loyal to those vows. As a widower, I won't touch a married woman.

Love

I had an extra feeling of regard for my military buddies because of what we went through together. We had a tremendous comaraderie, mutual respect, and espirit, even moreso than I would for everyday acquaintances. I knew the fiber of the guys, and I'd have done anything for them within the sphere of good taste and needs.

Optimism

If you don't plan and do things to make things happen, then the worst will happen, and it will be your fault. If I work hard and do all I can within my means to accomplish it, I'm optimistic that it will work. But if I don't do those things, then I have no right to be optimistic. Optimism to me is like the weather. Everybody talks about it, but few do much about it. Optimism is wishing for the best, expecting the best, predicated on your own inner sense of judgement and values. It's not just wishful thinking. I think of two boys sitting on the curb. One says, "I wish I had 1000 lollipops." The other asks, "Would you give me one?" The first says, "Hell, no. You're too lazy to wish for your own." Is that optimism, or what?

Humor

Who could live without it? It is probably the most forceful tool I've had in my life—the ability to laugh at myself and make others laugh too. You don't have to be a big comedian to have a sense of humor. To me, if used properly, humor opens your mind to hidden meaning. There's an element of humor I call tragic humor. People will laugh when someone like Jackie Gleason stumbles and falls. What's funny about that? It provokes the sudden thought that it could have happened to me but it didn't; how fortunate I am generally. It's a relief to laugh.

Humor very often helped in the service. One character in our quarters used to march in and holler at the top of his lungs, "We just got the word. The war is over but the SOBs won't tell us." We were all worn out from being on the beach, but everybody would break up and start laughing like schoolboys from a silly little crack.

I had a mustache then, as I do now. At Ft. Pierce, one of the men with a good sense of humor approached me and said, "Chief, can I ask you a question? Why do you grow something on your lip that grows wild in the crack of my ass?" I had to laugh and couldn't get angry. He put me down without getting offensive. We also had a kid from Brooklyn who loved to sleep. He wouldn't get up when the bugler blew, so I turned his bunk over. He got up bruised and sputtering, "Chief, you go ahead and knock me down and kiss my ass and see if I get mad about it." He told me to kiss his ass and got away with it because of his humor.

I often used humor to relieve tension in difficult situations in industrial relations.

Long View of Suffering

The service made me a better person in my mind, because I was able to prove something that I always wanted to prove, that I was as good as any other man—physically, mentally, or otherwise. I could do what the best of them could do and learn things as difficult as they learned. This gave me great personal satisfaction. That's probably why I got promoted so often. I was always showing a good example, but I wasn't a show-off. I always helped the other guys to do the best they could. I'd demonstrate the idea of doing as I do, not as I say. The discipline I learned absolutely helped throughout my career.

Maintaining Balanced Living

I've gone to health clubs to work out to keep my weight down. In recent years I've played golf three times a week. I walk three miles five times a week. I stretch every morning with weights. My pulse is 60 beats per minute. It used to be 45. I keep my blood pressure down with exercise and diet. I watch my diet. I've cut out starches and decreased my quantities. I won't go too far too long from a balanced diet.

I usually averaged seven or eight hours of sleep per night. Over the last 20 years about five hours a night is adequate. I have the ability to completely relax and get rehabilitated. The doctor says I'm lucky.

I stopped smoking in 1984 when I retired. Prior, I had smoked a pack or two a day. I drink only moderately, maybe a glass of wine in the evening, plus an occasional additional drink.

I like lots of reading—mostly historical novels and detective stories. Music is one of my passions—big bands and old standards. I make my own concerts on the computer. My wife and I liked plays, eating out two or three times a month, and card clubs. I attend reunions every year, and have kept in contact with a couple of my buddies.

Advice to Younger Generations

If parents and children could learn the simple values of living together with people it would be a better world. They shouldn't learn their values from TV or movies, but learn the Golden Rule. Learn to respect the system we live under— the freedoms we have and how we fought like hell to get them and fought like hell to keep them. Learn to appreciate those freedoms and those who got these for them. Exert yourself and your values. Take charge of your life. Help others to help themselves. My mother told me as a boy that the best way to avoid criticism is to do, say, and be nothing.

I notice that kids today have no concept of simple monetary, material, and moral values. Everything is taken for granted. Parents have to demonstrate values by example and action. TV does everything for kids, including telling them what to think. The media is the worst teacher. It leads people to think our country is going to hell in a basket. It is not.

Modern warfare is changing. You can sometimes win a war in a matter of days with combined combat arms now. There are fewer over-the-top soldiers and more specialists. But you don't all have to fire guns. Look upon serving your country in the military in a number of specialist ways. You are just as valuable working behind the lines. There are no second class citizens.

If you are trained for combat, you'd better forget about the glamour and concentrate on the teamwork and learn how to perform all your functions in a manner that is effective and protective of one another.

When you lead, make sure you can and would do what you ask others to do. Make others feel that you know what you are talking about and that you'll help them succeed.

Jerry Markham, top row, center, with NCDU #46 at graduation, Ft. Pierce, Florida, 1943

Jerry, center, in Maui to prepare for invasion of Japan, early 1945

Admiral Draper L. Kauffman, left, who organized the first NCDUs, presents the Croix de Guerre award to Markham at San Diego separation center.

Jerry in Jacksonville, Florida

Chapter II

Alfred A. Alvarez
Omaha Beach

Al and Florence Alvarez live in a brick home with a wrought iron balcony. Old Glory was out as I drove up. Al is a youthful, cheery, well-spoken 80-year-old man, who is quick-witted and sharp as a tack. He was on the front lines in Europe for nearly a year, from Normandy to Czechoslovakia. Florence describes him as "a very strong, good, cheerful, and moral man. He is a great parent. He taught the children what they should and shouldn't do. They followed that counsel and turned out great. The boys treat their wives well. They're all crazy about their father." He stands 5'6" tall. His awards include two Legions of Merit and two Bronze Stars.

My life started in Chelsea, Massachusetts, north of Boston, in April of 1924. I was a Depression baby. My father passed away when I was about four years old. My older brother was 14 years older and became the father. I also had an older sister. I always wondered how we survived the Depression without a father's income. My brother worked as a truck driver. I was a shoe shine and paper boy, earning a dollar a week. I brought that money back to the house and thought that was the most natural thing to do. I'd ferry to Boston, which cost one cent. I charged five cents for the first shoe; the other one was free. We rented a home in the French, Italian, Irish Catholic neighborhood. We were the only Spanish family that I remember there. There was a rich Protestant area on the hill, and a Jewish area at the other end of town. We called my older brother "Infallible Freddy" because he never made a mistake. We didn't eat until he got home. He was the man of the family. He disciplined me; more than once he smacked me across the head. He was an amateur boxer. I watched him fight. He was very good. You didn't win money, but received watch fobs (a leather tab for a pocket watch, which was kept in the little pocket that people today think is for change). He became production supervisor in a factory and years later had his own set of factories.

We had no green grass or parks. We ran across the tops of buildings for fun, and played ball on the roofs. Mom yelled when she heard the footsteps on the ceiling. Everyone carried a jackknife then. We'd carve chunks of tar from the street and chew it or stab ice from ice wagons. This was an innocent time. I was in the Boy Scouts for many years, and reached Star Scout. Swimming stopped me from advancing, because there was no place to swim. There was a minor correlation between Scouting and life with the Army in the field.

Mother was very strong, very proud, and a firm disciplinarian. She was a great cook and the center of our universe. She demanded that I attend school and earn good marks, which I did. She made me a smart person. Before I went to school I could read, write, and do numbers. She sat me by the window. I'd write down the numbers of the street cars and the time they passed by. (After I left for the Army, my mother took in a young foster child. He didn't know how to eat and was a poor student, but she changed him around.) I was jumped from fifth to seventh grade, but couldn't afford college. So I joined the Army at age 18 in 1942. I must have had high marks in the various tests because I was sent to different communication schools, starting at Ft. Monmouth, New Jersey. Finally I went to radar school, which was new then, and I became an expert early on. I was sent overseas in January of 1944 as a replacement for the 1st Infantry Division, the oldest division in the Army and the only assault division in England that had seen combat in Africa and Sicily. I was assigned to land on D-Day with the 7th Field Artillery Battalion, 16th Regimental Combat Team, 1st Infantry Division. I was a radio operator for the forward observer. The forward observer, an officer, called in artillery fire for the infantry. I would echo his instructions over the radio. As a PFC, I drew $50 a month. They took $22 away and gave it to Mom, and then gave her another $28.

We assaulted Omaha Beach at D-Day, landing about 6:30 in the morning. All I could see was five feet on each side of me. I was in a team of seven—two lieutenants, a sergeant, and a number of us as drivers and radio operators. The two lieutenants and the driver were in the jeep; the rest of us trudged along behind. The water where we landed was up to my nose and there were also runnells, or deep depressions, beneath us. Because we were an experienced outfit, old timers taught us things that kept us alive. For example, one taught us to put our gas masks under our chins, which kept our heads above water when we inflated the life preservers around our waists. When we landed, the lieutenants and the driver had disappeared. The sergeant found us another lieutenant who was hit as we got to the top of the bluff. Because we were out front, the German artillery was firing behind us on the beach and the American rounds were landing in front of us, but snipers were firing around us. Bodies were everywhere. Most of our guns had been destroyed, but by about 4:00 p.m. we had seven of our guns in position on the beach and firing. As we were sitting on top of the hill, a single German plane came toward us strafing everybody. Everybody started firing at the plane, and the fire was coming toward us, so we had to find a hole and hide.

The next day I was told to go back in the surf to bring back food. I brought back long cans of spam that I found. Equipment was strewn all over the place. The surf coming in and going out buried the bodies of the dead. A good 30% to 40% of my regimental combat team were casualties. In my battalion, sixty people were missing as amphibious trucks sank. A month later some of these were still finding their way to our unit.

We continued through Normandy for about thirty days. We had been well prepared except that no one told us about the hedgerows. Five hundred years earlier farmers had built them as boundaries for their farms and to block the harsh winds. They were now up to twenty feet tall and ten feet wide. The only way to move was in the sunken, single lanes through them. The Germans had machine guns sited on those lanes. So we lost many people and this delayed our advance. An enterprising engineer, Sergeant Culin, figured out how to take the tank barriers from the beach, slice them with an acetylene torch, and weld them in front of our tanks, to be used as rams to break through the hedgerows. Culin received the Legion of Merit for that invention.

As I lugged the radio, I saw five of my lieutenants become casualties over the next few months. Finally, we broke through in Operation Cobra and were bombed three times. First we were bombed by American bombers. It felt like clothes were being pressed to our bodies. We jumped in holes, the world vibrated, and we came off the ground. There were hundreds and hundreds of casualties all around us. The next day it happened again. The next night, the Germans bombed us. They hit us bad. Our battalion commander lost an arm, and the S-3 was killed. All unit commanders and sergeants were wounded or killed since the artillery battalion command group had gone forward to plan the artillery fire.

After breaking though and leaving the hedgerows, we went through the flatlands of France toward Germany for two weeks, and hit Belgium. In Mons, Belgium, we crossed a German division that was retreating. That night was a madhouse, with two divisions shooting at each other. We took our vehicles and circled the wagons. We captured the division.

We entered Germany at the town of Roetgen, and were one of the first units to fire on German ground. Then we encountered the fortified Siegfried line. We ran out of gas literally and figuratively as the Germans fought to protect their Fatherland, so we sat there for months.

We hit a town called Stolberg, which was difficult, and we finally arrived at the largest town in that portion of Germany called Aachen, the holy city of Charlemagne's time. There we spent a month with a lot of casualties. When you realize that a division has 15,000 men, and we ended up the war having had 50,000 men, so there were about 35,000 casualties. That's a lot of people. Most of these casualties were from the Battle of the Bulge.

In November, 1944, my four-man team entered Hamich, which had been taken in fierce house-to-house fighting. The Germans were counterattacking. Our job was to take out a strategic nearby hill. A one-day job turned into three weeks with many casualties. As we were moving out one day, we got hit by mortars. As I was sitting with my back against a tree, my fingers stung, burned, and vibrated, much like the feeling of having a firecracker go off in my hand when I was a kid. People in my vicinity were killed or wounded. Most people were throwing up, defecating, or urinating. The medics were running around fixing everybody. My lieutenant was sprawled out. I moved him and blood came out of his sleeves. I lugged him back to the jeep and got him to the medics. Now a good, experienced corporal was in charge. We were there in the town for about a week. Most of the buildings were made of stone. We were getting violent headaches and nosebleeds from the dust in the air from the German artillery. They were matching us round for round. At the time I learned that the captain and half of the two hundred soldiers in one unit were casualties. We learned that there was a time-on-target planned on the town to repulse the German counterattack. That is, all units would plan to hit the town at a certain pre-arranged time. We hid under a stone staircase leading to a cellar and put mattresses over us when it happened. The whole town was leveled. Then German tanks came into the town and fired rounds into the cellars. We fired down at them from the second floor with bazookas. There were about 400 casualties out of the five hundred Americans in the town. We eventually secured the town and advanced to Heisten to the northeast.

At nearby Merode, two companies in our sister regiment were captured. On December 10, 1944, we were told to go back 30 miles to set up a town for R&R. We took over a school house. Then the Battle of the Bulge started. My four-man forward observation team joined the hastily organized Task Force Davisson, which had engineers, tanks, tank destroyers, and recon troops. It was to be a tank-killing reaction force, designed to counter the German tank penetration.

At Weimes, Germans entered the town and captured a hospital. We showed up and they left. I realized this was the forward edge. At this time, a bunch of Germans in American vehicles entered the town and killed Americans. We learned about it and opened up on them as they drove through town. We captured a German officer. He looked like he was right out of Hollywood. He was immaculate and spoke perfect English. One of our guys smacked him with a rifle butt, because his friend had been killed. Through interrogation, we learned that the German officer was in charge of photographing the Germans in their penetration, the Bulge. Now everyone began searching the snow around the German's jeep for the film. We eventually found it, and today, when you see the classic pictures of victorious Germans in the Battle of the Bulge, they come from this event.

We successfully directed fire on the approaching Germans. This went on for 30 days. It was cold and the snow was deep. GIs put straw around their feet and wrapped their feet with blankets. We were called the Frankenstein Brigade because of our monstrous feet. We wore as many layers of clothes as we could and then took bed sheets from houses for camouflage.

January, now we were pushing back. I had a sled that I used to carry a radio and food. It took a month to return to the beginning lines in February of 1945. Finally, we broke out and the weather cleared and we got to the Rhine. The 9th Armor Division took Remagen bridge and we rode over it. We rolled over the plains of Germany going as fast as we could. Still every town was being fought over.

Eventually, we moved to Bavaria and then Czechoslovakia to fight anticipated terror wolves after the war was over. As the war ended, May 7, 1945, we were in Cheb, waiting for the Russians.

After the war, I remained in the Army reserves. I drove a sedan for a colonel. An innocent conversation changed my life. He said, "You're too smart for this. Why don't you go to Officer Candidate School?" I told him that I didn't know how to balance a teacup, which I thought was needed to be an officer. He sent me to OCS in Kansas for six months, and then I spent three more training as an artillery officer. I qualified as a parachutist and served two combat tours in Korea with the 187th Parachute Infantry Regiment. I was an artillery forward observer in the war.

In a subsequent assignment, I was sent to Buenos Aires, Argentina, as part of a team that included a general, colonel, lieutenant colonel, and me—now a major. Our job was to sell weapons to the host nation. In 1965, I went for 18 months to the Dominican Republic with the 82nd Airborne to stabilize the uprising. There I knew Butch Kendrick *[See Chapter 29]*, who was a regimental commander. I later joined the Special Forces at Ft. Bragg, was promoted to lieutenant colonel, and worked with COL Bull Simons, who led famous rescue operations in Iraq and Vietnam. I finished college while there. With the Special Forces, I went to Bolivia, where Che Guevara and his Cuban terrorists were. Since I spoke Spanish and had lived in South America, we trained teams to chase him around. One of the teams captured him.

After serving in Vietnam, I retired in 1974. I took over the Department of Human Resources for North Carolina, was a county planner, and then supervised retail merchandising for department stores. I became a military teacher at Ft. Bragg for 10 years, and ran a radio show called "Military Matters" for five years. Now I write stories for military magazines. I wrote an article, for example, summarizing the many unforgettable moments of Army life that will live forever with me.

In the 1980s, we became interested in putting together an airborne museum downtown. We finally got four million dollars in seed money for the Airborne/Special Operations Museum in Fayetteville, North Carolina. I organized the two hundred docents and now volunteer twice a week as a docent.

I met my wife in 1948. We had joined a minstrel show. Florence worked for the telephone company. She was in the chorus. We went on a double date set up by friends. We dated a year and a half and married in June 1949 before I went to OCS. We have four children— two served in the Navy—and nine grandchildren.

PTSD Symptoms?

I sleep like a *bear*. I have a fantastic memory for WWII details, but am not troubled by any PTSD symptoms.

What Helped You Cope?

There was a sense of pride. I came from a proud family and have always been in proud units. It was unheard of to do something that would hurt your family or your unit. I think there is a point there.

I had a desire to succeed, determination. That desire still keeps me exercising, because of the good that it does. Perhaps the Depression gave inner strength. In the service I saw men work for a nickel or dime at tasks like ironing clothes. One of my friends, we called him Mumma, ironed our uniforms for a nickel.

CALM UNDER PRESSURE

I never "lost it." I wasn't one to get mad and smash phones. Not that I couldn't raise my voice and pound the table to get what I wanted if necessary, but I didn't lose control.

I was very fortunate to join a unit that was so experienced, and I had six months with them in England. They were harsh and demanding. They'd been in war for a year or more. For example, anytime you did or did not do something, you told three people about it, like going to the bathroom. With that little requirement, chaos was less likely. We were required to dig a hole anytime we stopped. We'd cover up the wheels and radiator of the jeep with sandbags to protect the jeep. So my team never lost a jeep at Normandy.

If someone was wounded, I left and let the medics do their job, since I had no business with treating them—we had another mission. After Normandy was bombed at the breakthrough, we buried Germans all day long for several days. I was so young, though, that it had no impact on me.

I was happy when we hit our targets, but I didn't feel animosity toward the Germans or wish ill toward the individuals. Once, we captured two German PFCs on a snow-covered hill. We were all in a room cooking food. The lieutenant told me (also a PFC) to take them and go out to repair a break in a wire. We three PFCs knew each other and knew the world was against us. As we walked through the snow, I fell down and my pistol flew into the snow. The three of us were looking for it. A German found it, blew off the snow, handed it back, and raised his hands to surrender again. We were snow buddies!

When the war was over in Czechoslovakia, I was standing in a crossroads to separate armed German soldiers from the civilians and have the soldiers dump their weapons in a pile. I wasn't frightened. They weren't going to bother me. I gave water from my canteen to a soldier even though the civilians couldn't believe I'd do that. He was a fellow soldier who was thirsty. The look he exchanged with me said, "You've been there too." And he went on his way.

I write to a German man in Merode. His father was there in Hamich. It is amazing to hear his perspective of the battle.

RATIONAL THOUGHT PROCESSES

Mother taught us that someone complained about only having bananas to eat until he turned around and saw someone eating the peels that he was dropping. So we were taught never to complain, because we were fortunate to have what we had.

When you're a private and everything is going wrong, you feel dumped on and wonder why the world is dumping on you. But you laugh. Later as an officer, I'd wonder why those guys were so stupid and unable to complete what I had so intelligently devised. I'd think of the old Army saying, "If I'd wanted to send a stupid SOB, I'd have gone myself."

You make a mistake, you learn, and you shake it off. In the '60s, I was a lieutenant colonel, G-1 of a corps. A G-1 gets people, uses them, and gets rid of them. There were riots in Detroit, Baltimore, and Washington, D.C. Thousands of soldiers descended to quell the disturbance. This was our first experience with a domestic disturbance. I met with the chiefs of police in Detroit. There was martial law and I was the boss, although the chiefs had no respect for me. They told me we had 5,000 prisoners, or "detainees" as the Army called it. They said they had been in street cars and buses for two days. In desperation, I told them to put them in gyms and public schools, arraign and jail the felons and release the others on their own recognizance. One of the chiefs of police told me I wasn't as stupid as I looked. There was still much looting in the streets, and we had 40,000 troops in the streets. I told the chiefs of police that we wouldn't shoot the looters. So first, I told them to seize the loot, which I thought of as gas, weapons, etc. But our soldiers would grab milk from grandmothers who were taking it for their families. That wasn't good. The newspapers destroyed us. Then I decided we'd try to manage the loot areas. We tear-gassed stores. Well, looters were taking furniture, appliances, and furs, and the tear gas would settle to the basement where more furs were stored. They're still trying to get the tear gas out of those furs. Then I saw the stupidity of my decision and changed it. Everyone was making so many mistakes. We had never been in the street, fighting civilians before. This was our first time through—we learned. In Baltimore, we'd learned lessons and were much better.

SOCIAL SUPPORT

After being in the service a number of years, there's a small group of guys you know and care bout and you run into them within parachute units for twenty or thirty years.

I wrote all the girls in my hometown and they answered. I got more mail than anyone. The most enjoyable part of being in the field was being told that you had mail.

My brother worked in a paint factory and would send a box filled with sawdust and two bottles of beer. When that came in, that was the biggest thing and everybody knew what it was. I drank one and shared the other with buddies. My mother sent boxes with pepperoni. It took months to get there and the pepperoni had turned green. We'd scrape it off and make sandwiches.

A wonderful corporal, a section leader, was a fine, fine man. He saved my beer, pepperoni, and mail when I was gone on a mission. A couple of times when I was gone and feared to be a casualty, he personally saved my things and prevented guys from taking stuff from the so-called "lucky bag," which held the goods of dead soldiers. Forty years later I found his address and called him. I've seen all of the guys at reunions.

In England I was a FNG (Funny New Guy) and was treated like a rookie. Once, I got lost in an English town. I was wandering down the road when a jeep passed by me with an officer in it. Apparently the driver recognized me, because the jeep stopped and backed up. The driver said, "Jump in, Al." I realized he knew me by name. That was the first time I wasn't "Hey, you." Recognition is the main drive of humans, to be known. I've told the driver this story at a reunion.

By the end of the war I felt very close to my unit. I enjoy saying I'm from "Big Red One – 1st Division." The division made three invasions in WWII and went through eight campaigns, and took thousands of casualties.

Usually, there were only four of us in the team assigned to a company of 200 others. So I didn't know the 200, but I knew if one of the four were wounded or killed. I remember the names of our team who got killed and their replacements and can tell you anything you want to know about them. This wasn't necessarily true of the lieutenants. One New Year's eve, a lieutenant got liquor and didn't share it or offer us a drink. I said I'd be different if I were ever an officer.

I think I was good at making friends. When I went to work teaching at the post, we were all old friends and even now we still meet several times a week. It's old home week. We walk two or three miles in groups of four or five. My group has three command sergeants major. They are the toughest people in the Army, and funny. They tell me things I never knew about the goings on of people like myself. We've got to be such friends.

COMFORTABLE WITH EMOTIONS

I wasn't afraid. It was a tremendous adventure. I was 18 years old. After six months of digging holes and learning weapons in England, I was well trained. I knew my job. I became a survivor.

Humor helped. Once during shelling, when I was in a hole packed with 20 people in a space that was meant for four, someone from Louisiana said, "This reminds me of Mardi Gras" – with all the noise and fireworks. There was always tomfoolery.

Although the *Saving Private Ryan* movie captured the sensations of D-Day, it didn't capture the smells of vomit, diesel fuel, defecation, urination, death. I admit that watching the movie made me uncomfortable. However, it would be weakness to tell your loved ones of your fears back then.

The only distractions or beauty I could think of were the girls in Europe. They were pretty, voluptuous, and unobtainable. I was also a pretty good drinker. Growing up, we had wine and occasionally liquor. My father had produced wine, which was kept in the cellar. So we drank at meals. I enjoyed wine in Europe and could drink sensibly.

SELF-ESTEEM

I had self-esteem, 110%. I always thought I defecated chocolate ice cream. No matter what it was, I was going to do it and I did. Like parachute school. It's a difficult thing to get 1200 feet up in the air and throw yourself out of an airplane. As a GI, I felt I was smarter than the average guy, bright as a son of a gun. I liked who I was as a person and still do.

ACTIVE, CREATIVE COPING

In communications, no one had to tell me when there was a dead phone to replace the wire after an explosion. I'd always think of a different route, though, so it wouldn't get broken again. The unit needed that communication. From all my prestigious communication schools, I knew how to enhance the capabilities of radios and did everything possible to get good reception, such as orienting the jeep or putting a light bulb at the top of an antenna to make sure reception was maximized. If we were stopped long enough, the jeep would be below the ground from digging. During the Battle of the Bulge, we were in a church steeple as forward observers, and noticed that the counterfire was getting closer. We were smart enough to leave just before it was blown away by the Germans.

My cohorts, who were veterans of North Africa and Sicily, had experienced all manner of common communication breakdowns. They taught me to always have alternate routings in anticipation of outages caused by the enemy. I followed this advice and laid redundant wire lines, and it paid off. When we were under heavy enemy bombardments, at least one line of communication was usually available.

SPIRITUAL AND PHILOSOPHICAL STRENGTHS

God

Mother was a churchgoer. I went with her. Later I went with the guys. In the service, I went all the time. At Normandy, it was emotional to see strong GIs leave their helmets and weapons at the door and go into the church. The French priest explained that the Germans did this, and we must too. I still go to church. It was a good feeling to go. There has to be a God who produces good and bad. He should have given pets more time to live, though. We've gone through ten dogs, and it's a killer. And I wonder how He allows some of the terrible things that happen.

Meaning & Purpose

My first purpose was not to shame my Mother, and then the unit, and now my family. Mother said, "Come back with your shield or on your shield." In other words, don't shame your family name. You and I are so fortunate for what we have. Somewhere, someone with 27 cents said, "Let's go to America." That guy put us in the position we are in now. So we shouldn't do anything to ruin that. Mother had difficulty speaking English. My brother never completed junior high and told me to be the first one to complete college. My sister got hospitalized, so I was the only one in the family with the potential for bigger and better things, and I shouldn't screw it up. So my goals were to get an education and be a success in the Army and make my family proud. It took me 25 years to get my college degree, one class at a time, which showed the determination I had.

We've been to so many countries and saw the terribleness of it and you appreciate this country more. In Argentina, they had a saying, "First me, second me, and third nobody." The kids there during WWII went back to fight for the country of their descent, be it German or French. In the U.S., American youth fought for America. If their families were from Italy, they didn't go fight for Italy. They belonged to America.

Morality

My unit was composed of young guys from New England, brought up in nice families. Raping and assaulting young ladies was unheard of. The term rape wasn't even used. We chased girls but I knew of no such cases.

I'm a prude. I dislike anything that's dirty, filthy, morally wrong, and my kids know it. Hollywood foists on us certain standards that we don't have, such as cruelty to or assaults on women or violence to animals. Viewers become conditioned to think that's natural.

When I was a commander, my troops said, "Don't fool with Al." They knew that I felt that if they'd cheat on their wives, they could easily cheat on me — when I needed an honest count, for instance. I'd get rid of such people. I once got rid of someone who had "misplaced" money.

Morality is almost black and white. If it's wrong, it's wrong. I took my grandson to return a quarter to a neighbor. For the rest of his life, he'll remember that quarter and won't steal 25 million dollars. My wife knows I'd never cheat on her. We've been married 54 years.

In war, certain people are mean. Now someone gives them a gun and now they're deadly mean, and they're the ones who kill prisoners. I hated that as a private and changed it when I was an officer. During the Battle of the Bulge, a medic killed a badly wounded German so the other GIs wouldn't have to take him to be detained. I thought that was a rotten thing to do. I remember it to this moment. As an officer in combat, if I sensed a meanness in guards, I'd replace them.

I wouldn't take watches or rings off of prisoners. I saw cases of dead Germans whose teeth had been knocked out or fingers cut off to remove the rings, but I didn't do that. I don't know how you live with something like that.

Love

In Korea, I was a platoon leader of 40 guys. I was the experienced lieutenant. I was concerned for them, and saw that they had what they needed, and hopefully they noticed.

Every May, we have a reunion on post for members of old airborne units. It's a three-day affair. All those 80-year-old guys wear tuxedos and ribbons and really look good. I still feel close to those guys. I feel guilty to still have a wife. General Yarborough, the centenarian who started the airborne units, showed up last year.

Working at the museum, I often see many of the old-timers. The first Saturday of the month, I go to an artillery breakfast. The old soldiers see my writings in the magazines and write to me, and I write them back.

Optimism

I am an optimist. I seek the harder right rather than the easier wrong. I know the sun will come up in the east every morning. Things aren't as bad as they say.

Humor

I saw humor in everything going on. I still do. When I give tours at the museum, I'll slip a wrong word in my sing-songy little speeches. For example, I'll say that the founder of the airborne first took "Forty *stupid* guys and threw them out of an airplane and if they survived then we had a new program."

On the beach at D-Day, everything was being fired at us. Next to me, there was a Black-American barrage balloon unit. Every ship had one, to keep German planes from strafing us. Essentially, there was a large balloon attached by a thick cable to something looking like a stretcher. Now, for some reason, these people had brought balloons ashore amidst us. Someone shoots the balloon, which collapses and falls to the ground, so now these men have no job. So a black GI next to me is furiously digging a foxhole. Sand is flying everyplace as he's trying to dig his way to China. He looks at me and says, "Lazy men don't live long around here, do they?" The stupidity of that balloon at that particular moment plus those words struck me as funny. Sometimes, when people asked what unit you were in, you'd say an "underground barrage balloon unit."

When we were under the stairs with mattresses over us, the heavens opened up. People were losing control of their body functions. Amidst the noise, the dust, and the stench, someone said, "That sure clears out my sinuses." Everyone laughed. It broke the tension of the moment.

Humor is a relaxation, seeing the idiocy in things that other people take as serious. Humor is making games of the serious. My children all have my humor and it gives us great rapport. My mother would ask me questions from the newspapers. At supper I did this with my kids. Everyone tried to outdo each other. Now we compete in Jeopardy. At Christmas, the kids would hold back and try to be the one who opened up the last present. One on my kids held back a present and opened it in June. My whole family has humor that many people don't understand. For example, on the phone with my youngest son, I said that it was raining so hard that the animals were lining up two by two. Or I'd say that someone was as unlucky as the third monkey on Noah's gangplank. We try to catch each other. My son has a paper manufacturing company. I've said, "Hey, that's my right hand man, Lefty." He likes that and uses it in the factory and makes them all laugh.

I learned to laugh at everyday things that seemed so foolish. In Aachen, I was getting food for others, because I was a private. I had five layers of clothes on and straw in my boots because it was so cold, and I was carrying four or five weapons along with all this food. Music was playing. I had the runs and was dehydrated. As I turned the corner, I ran into two Germans, literally, and was about to faint, when they surrendered. I reached in and found a weapon and dumped them off somewhere, and realized then that I no longer had to go to the bathroom.

One guy told me I was lucky to have a last name beginning with an "A." That way my name would be at the top of a war memorial, so high that the dogs couldn't pee on it.

My nickname is "Smilin' Al, the soldier's pal." I smile and laugh a lot, although I am firm as well.

Long View of Suffering

To me the war was a great adventure. I worked hard and did well under stress and came out unscathed. It certainly made me better. I often think that my best friend was Adolph Hitler. If he hadn't caused the war, I'd be working as the younger brother in my brother's paint business, never achieving his standard. The Army let me be successful in my own right. Throughout the discomfort, you learned to laugh, and wondered how you could accomplish anything with so little knowledge. What I didn't realize was that I was gaining a heck of a lot of experience.

Maintaining Balanced Living

I walk every day a couple of miles. I swim two nights a week, and take Tai Chi twice a week. I walk around the museum. And I always kept active while in the service.

We have soup and salad every afternoon. Florence counts my calories and slaps my hand if I go for seconds. We rarely have meat. We have fish three times a week. (If I go to a steak place, I order filet of sole.) We have lots of fruits and vegetables. At breakfast today, we had bananas and strawberries. We even feed the dog fruit.

I sleep like a horse. We're in bed by 10:00 p.m., and usually fall asleep before the news (we set the timer). I'm up by 6:45 every morning.

In the '50s and '60s, we had happy hour once a week and drank. In the last 30 years, I have a glass of wine at dinner. For special family occasions I might have two or three glasses.

I might have smoked during the war, but never since. Smoking was pushed on us. Free packages were in our rations or were given out at USO dances. Once I didn't need them, I stopped.

Florence and I travel. We recently took a wonderful 16-day boat trip from Vienna up the Danube to the Rhine to Amsterdam. We've traveled to other countries as well. I went back to France for a fifty-year reunion. I saw an obelisk with the many names of those who died. That had quite an impact.

I loved being on the radio. I did my radio show for five years until we ran out of stories. I like to watch "Lawrence Welk" and "Are You Being Served?" about British retailers on television. I attend church with my wife. We either talk to or see my children at least once a week.

Advice to Younger Generations

Do the right thing even if you fear the consequences. If you conduct yourself well you can pass the toughest test and look in the mirror without shame. Then you'll be a hero. "Take the harder right, rather than the easier wrong" applies to so many life situations.

Punctuality is one of the most important things. Always prepare ahead. *[When I arrived at his home, he had prepared and labeled a folder with his photographs and notes prepared for the interview.]* The Boy Scouts taught us that. I go on a recon the day before I must go somewhere to give a talk, to see how long it takes to get there. Get there on time. On time, to me, is five minutes early!

In England, before the Normandy invasion, 1944

Al and Florence Alvarez

At a WWII Commemoration, Ft. Bragg, NC, 1994

Al and Florence at home in Fayetteville, NC

Chapter 12

Quentin C. Aanenson
Fighter Pilot

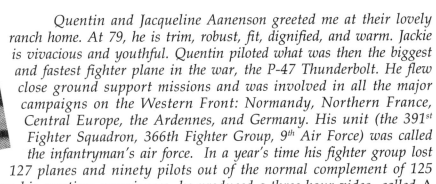

Quentin and Jacqueline Aanenson greeted me at their lovely ranch home. At 79, he is trim, robust, fit, dignified, and warm. Jackie is vivacious and youthful. Quentin piloted what was then the biggest and fastest fighter plane in the war, the P-47 Thunderbolt. He flew close ground support missions and was involved in all the major campaigns on the Western Front: Normandy, Northern France, Central Europe, the Ardennes, and Germany. His unit (the 391st Fighter Squadron, 366th Fighter Group, 9th Air Force) was called the infantryman's air force. In a year's time his fighter group lost 127 planes and ninety pilots out of the normal complement of 125 pilots. Based on his wartime experiences, he produced a three-hour video, called A Fighter Pilot's Story. *The project was begun in response to his family's repeated requests to share his experiences with them. It then became a nationally broadcast film for public television, and has been repeated on three occasions. A love story in one sense, the film has touched many viewers, for Quentin and Jackie have received 35,000 personal letters. Sometimes the video explained to families why some who returned from the war had such difficulty adjusting.*

My birthplace was a farm in Rock County, prairie country in southwestern Minnesota. I was born in 1921, the fifth of six children, and spent my first 18 years on the farm. My family was close. We were somewhat isolated on the farm. Except for when I was in school, I usually only saw my family. My father was not well schooled, but was unusually competent at expressing himself and conversing with just about anybody. He was a hard-working, wonderful man. My mother had the flare for life about her. She was very bright, read about society, and had the heart and soul of an artist. She was a wonderful mother. Usually farm kids went only to grade school at that time. She said, "All of our children will go to high school." Our home was hard working and happy. During the Depression everyone was poor, so we felt the same as everyone else. But things were extremely difficult; I could recognize the stress on my parents, who were trying to keep us kids in high school. We walked to country school, but when we entered high school, my dad had to drive us to school every day in our clunker of a car. There were no school buses back then. But we had the advantage of living on a farm where we raised our own food.

We all had chores. As we grew older, we assumed greater responsibilities, and I had no hesitation in meeting my responsibilities. We worked with the cattle — the milking, the feeding, the pasturing. We farmed the land, which was labor intensive. We learned a work ethic.

It was a spiritual home. All of us were confirmed in the Lutheran church. We believed in God and went to church get-togethers. The sense of integrity and responsibility that came down from my parents was my guiding light.

I was the first of the children to go to college. I left college to enlist in the Army Air Corps after the Japanese attacked Pearl Harbor. I was trained as a fighter pilot, and fought in all the major campaigns on the Western Front. We flew close ground support missions, strafing and dive bombing targets on the ground. With the exception of the grunts, the GIs fighting on the ground, we probably had as bad a war as there was. Except for company grade officers in infantry outfits, we had the highest casualty rates. We were shot at nearly every mission. It took me a while to figure out that, when I heard cracking noises outside of my canopy, it was the sound of bullets breaking the sound barrier, within inches of my canopy. I seemed to have a knack for picking up flak damage to my plane. In my first 10 missions, I had battle damage on three occasions and had to crash land once. Near Omaha Beach in Normandy, our mission was to strafe German troop positions, two to three hundred yards inland from Pointe du Hoc. If we fired short we would hit the American troops below the cliffs. If we went too far, we could hit our airborne troops. In the days and weeks after the invasion, we fired at anything that moved behind the lines on the ground: troops, tanks, trucks, gun positions, trains. Flak was our biggest danger. Often the sides of boxcars would drop suddenly and flak would come at us from moving trains. Certain memories especially stand out. I remember my friend waving at me the moment before he crashed; in that instant he knew he was dead. I saw another friend's body bounce off the ground when his chute didn't open. I saw planes hit by flak and pilots burned to cinders. When I was coordinating ground support in front of the 8th Infantry Division during the Battle of the Roer River crossing, a German artillery shell blew the brain tissue and blood of an enlisted man all over me and the maps I was using. During the time I was directing the close air support in front of the VII Corps, I saw the horrors of the war up close on the ground. It was as though I had a ringside seat on the edge of hell.

Jackie and I married on April 17, 1945, when I came home on leave near war's end. She was 22, and I was about to turn 24. We had met and committed to each other when I was training at Harding Field in Baton Rouge, Louisiana, before I went overseas. One of my best buddies while I was in combat, Suitcase Simpson, a West Point graduate, was my best man. After the war ended, I attended Louisiana State University, taking 27 credits my last semester while working full time at a radio station. During this time, I was receiving biweekly injections for severe pain as the result of a head injury suffered in a crash landing after being hit by flak. I studied management and ultimately became a sales manager for a major national company.

PTSD Symptoms?

I don't remember giving much thought to it. I remained gregarious and didn't go into a shell after the war. My children thought I was a very good father, and still do. But, I remember there were times, in the early years after the war, when I occasionally found little things distressing; for example, when a baby could not be comforted. This was internal stress, nothing external. While I had vivid, haunting memories, I encapsulated them in my mind during the daytime. But the nights were different; the demons came back. Jackie was only 22 when we married, and I never told her much about my combat experiences. There was no way I could find the words to describe them, and there was no possible way she could understand what I was saying. When we lost a buddy in combat, we went through his footlocker that night to make sure that nothing inappropriate would go home to his family. Then we rarely ever talked about him again. It was a way to try to cope with our circumstances. To protect ourselves emotionally, we quit making new friends.

What Helped You Cope?

In Normandy, Suitcase Simpson and I went for a walk in the apple orchards near our base on a beautiful summer evening after an unusually bad mission. We talked about our situation and the likelihood of our being killed. We discussed it openly and came to the conclusion that, since we would likely die, we wanted to make sure it would count for something. From then on I had less fear, and dealt with it through mental discipline. My thought was, "Let me do my job, so mine isn't a wasted life." I was in my most effective "warrior" mode after that decision. We both made it through the war, but he was killed two years after the war ended, in a peacetime flying accident. That was one of my most difficult losses. I was brought up in a very stable, well-anchored family. There was such a comfortable and loving family relationship. I do not remember there ever being an argument in our home. Because of being raised on a farm, when I went to war I was conditioned to having responsibility. Farming also taught discipline to do everything that was required. In war, we did everything just as we had been trained to do. Also, I had a couple of years experience in the National Guard while in school.

CALM UNDER PRESSURE

I had fear on the ground and after the mission, but I never went into combat with fear. It was gone. During a mission, I was automatic. I knew the ritual, my reflexes were there, and I could see acutely. I knew what to do and did it with speed, delivering death in the middle of death. I had mental discipline. I didn't dissociate. You had to be constantly aware of everything going on around you. While in war, you just tried to deal with the day in front of you. Tomorrow was a fog and yesterday's memories were distant.

It was apparently harder for me to kill than for most of my buddies. I became sick and nauseated the first time after I knew I had killed men. The Germans still depended on horses to move much of their army. On my first strafing run of horses pulling artillery pieces, I couldn't squeeze the trigger. I remembered our horses on the farm. Through unusual circumstances, in two missions about a week apart, I killed a very large number of the enemy. In both circumstances, there were massive concentrations of German troops. I caught 100 to 125 of them in double tandem trucks with no warning to them. Then we encountered Germans hurriedly retreating from Patton across the Seine River on barges and flat boats in the daytime. Four of us pilots made repeated strafing passes. It was hard to watch it. I had no personal animosity for the Germans. I only killed the enemy to save the lives of our guys on the ground.

When Patton was just breaking out of the beachhead in Normandy near St. Lô, there was a German tiger tank in the hedgerows that had destroyed several American tanks, and was holding up an entire column. We tried to bomb it. Four multiple 20-mm. flak guns were firing at us. I was so close to the ground that I could clearly see the faces of the guys shooting at me. When I saw them I thought, "I'm dead if I can t get out of this crossfire." In determined anger, I made a tight turn and dived and fired directly at them as they fired directly at me. They had much greater firepower, but my bullets struck first and killed all eight or nine soldiers manning the guns. We destroyed the tank, which enabled our tanks to charge ahead. The next day my buddy, Johnny Bathurst, and I returned to the position to see the tank and flak guns we had helped destroy. This was the only time I saw from the ground, up close, the men I had killed. It was a horrible scene. I felt shock and wondered, "Why did I come up here to see this?" A young German, killed by my guns, had a photo of his wife or girlfriend sticking out of the pocket of his uniform. I put it in my pocket, along with the next 20-mm shell from his belt of ammo thinking, "If I hadn't killed them, this shell might have killed me." I have kept the photo, and it still bothers me. I came to realize early on that most of these were just young guys fighting for their country, not fanatical Nazis. I wonder how many family lines I ended. I've since met several of the top German aces. We felt no animosity toward each other; we were just men who had shared a difficult time in our young lives.

RATIONAL THOUGHT PROCESSES

It is impossible to execute everything just right in a combat situation. There are too many variables. You know that if you get sloppy and careless you increase the chances of dying real fast. I made my share of boners on missions, but I had confidence that I was a good pilot. I was not the perfect man, warrior, or pilot, but I never had the feeling that I was slacking off. I never aborted a mission or turned back because of engine noise or engine trouble, or something like that.

SOCIAL SUPPORT

My mother and siblings wrote to me regularly. Jackie wrote to me every day. We exchanged 700 letters while I was overseas. I felt so sorry for the guys in my outfit that seldom received letters. They seemed so alone.

I had a ritual. As I was swinging into the cockpit, I'd whistle the first bar of the Air Corps song and kiss the ring Jackie had given me just before I left to go overseas.

Some of the most moving moments of the war for me occurred on our airfield in Normandy. My crew chief, a father figure, was older than I by perhaps fifteen years. Before each mission he would help me get strapped in and check all the instruments and controls. Just before I taxied out for takeoff, he would pat me on the shoulder and say, "Good luck, Sir" then step down off the wing. At times I would see tears in his eyes before he stepped down. Later I found out that as soon as he got off the wing, he knelt under the wing and prayed for me. From then on I had an even closer respect and bond with him.

You got close to a few buddies, although after so many died, you isolated yourself from the new pilots. I kept in touch with Johnny Bathurst after the war; he and I were the sole survivors from our tent. Before his death in 1999, he had asked me to write the eulogy for his funeral.

COMFORTABLE WITH EMOTIONS

I experienced fear, yes, and told Jackie so. We all experienced fear at times, especially as we saw more and more of our buddies getting killed. Some fellas were worse than others. But once we got airborne on a mission, any fear we had seemed to disappear.

During the war, and after, I encapsulated my emotions in order to cope. Yet, producing the video (*A Fight Pilot's Story*) was therapeutic; it took the monkey off my back. It forced me to read all the letters, mission reports, casualty lists, etc., and pass on information to the families and children. My being forced to go into it was more traumatic than when I returned from the war, but it unlocked the demons. I finished the video for my family. Three generations of my family watched it together in my daughter's home in Schaumburg, Illinois. It was very emotional for all of us.

During a particularly brutal time during combat, I wrote a letter to Jackie in which I tried to vividly describe what my world of war was really like. But I never mailed it. But it probably helped me just to write it.

SELF-ESTEEM

My parents convinced me that I had qualities that should help me be successful in life. As I progressed in school, I knew I could compete. I found out that I had good communications skills in speaking and writing. By the time I graduated from high school, in my mind I could do anything. This feeling of confidence helped me compete in the rigorous selection process and training to become a fighter pilot.

ACTIVE, CREATIVE COPING

I'd go through my mental checklist before a mission. I'd check my maps, anticipate emergencies, walk out to my plane before the mission and check instruments and equipment, talk to my crew chief, etc. To this day, I still run through a mental checklist when I get into my car.

In combat, you had to do something or you'd die. Deciding to turn into the flak guns near St. Lô is perhaps an example of how decisive action, rather than passivity, might have saved my own life. The Germans were tremendous soldiers, but didn't improvise as rapidly as Americans. The orders had to come from above.

SPIRITUAL AND PHILOSOPHICAL STRENGTHS

God

Once on a dangerous mission flying into Germany under radio silence, one of the pilots in our Group had either inadvertently or deliberately pressed his radio transmitter button, and was reciting the 23rd Psalm. We probably all recited it along with him, silently. When we landed, we couldn't guess who the voice was, although we usually could identify a pilot by his voice. That mission, we all came home without a loss.

Meaning & Purpose

We lived to return home. We were patriotic, red-blooded American boys with families at home. We knew we were defeating evil. I gambled my life so that my sons would be safe from a similar fate. I felt that I was born on a certain day in 1921 so that I could be involved at that moment in history, 23 years later. If a target was important and would make a meaningful difference in saving lives and ending the war sooner, we'd go down and press the attack without regard for self. We became almost obsessed with the importance of saving other guys' lives. It sounds strange. You'd think your primary concern would be saving your own life, and often it was. But there were several times when we literally counted our lives expendable to hit that target. I came to peace with my own mortality. I accepted death but wanted to make sure it would count for something. We were committed to a cause, even if it involved suffering. I wrote the following to accompany a painting of me done by a New York artist, showing me standing in front of my airplane late in the war. The painting depicts not a hotshot, cocky fighter pilot, but rather one who has seen a lot of war: *"The burning spirit of patriotism he brought to the war is no longer visible, yet somewhere down within him the spark has not been extinguished. But now he fights not for any grand cause but rather for his buddies in the squadron and the poor suffering foot soldiers on the ground who count on him and his weapons to save them."*

Two years after the war, I remember spending several hours one afternoon walking around City Park in Baton Rouge, all alone, wondering what I should do with my life. Why was I a survivor? I had to sort it out. I concluded that I owed it to my buddies who were killed to make something of my life. I committed myself to creating, not destroying. My commitment to that has never wavered. Because of the impact of our film, Jackie and I feel we have almost become representatives of a generation. We want to live our lives with character, principle, and dignity, and feel we are doing that.

Too many who went off to war became impaired, because they had never been taught what to expect. This film has put a face on war, and has helped people have a better understanding of what a generation of young Americans went through during World War II.

Morality

As the war worsened, casualty rates increased and there was more battle fatigue. The flight surgeon told us when we were going on leave: You need to break the routine and change everything. Forget the war, you need to escape the pressure. But there were some things I couldn't do. I was stressed to the limits, but like most of the guys, I never broke.

Pride is a part of recovery and is needed to prevent depression. I was proud of being a fighter pilot, an American who did his duty in combat. I knew we were making a difference. While I knew I had killed enemy soldiers that day, I could go to bed knowing I had saved some American boys' lives by going a hundred yards further down the strafing run that day — and no one knew but me. Morality is part of that pride.

I grew up in a time where a man's word was his bond and shaking hands on an agreement was a contract, and its hard for me to move off that center line. And I won't. It is part of our generation.

Love

Our love and marriage was very healing. Jackie's sweet, beautiful voice and carefree ways tempered the pressure I had lived under while in combat.

There was a brotherhood among fighter pilots. The commitment level (something like the SEALS or Rangers, any of those special groups) raises the bar. Once we became fighter pilots, the bar was raised. No one wanted to let the squadron or a buddy down.

Optimism

Johnny and I would philosophize about life after the war. Our dreams kept us alive. My dream was to marry Jackie, and Johnny and I talked about going into business together. As long as you had something to look forward to beyond the next mission, there was an element of hope. I don't think I'd have been afraid to die, except that I had so much to live for. At the same time, I had a sense of realism, an acceptance that I could die anytime.

Humor

You had to have a few absolutely disarming moments, generally in the Officers Club after the mission. Prior to the mission there was not much kidding around. Humor is also the attitude that makes the best of things.

Jackie says he is not usually a cut up, unless he gets on a streak and then he can be the funniest thing around.

Long View of Suffering

The military service was a very positive experience that made me stronger and more disciplined. It made stronger men out of most of the guys, although it revealed weaknesses and left a sense of guilt in some. We had clearly defined goals. If you got through the worst in one piece and were equal to the standards, then you gained certain strengths that stayed with you throughout life: greater confidence, perspective, and the ability to judge people and their qualifications more quickly.

Maintaining Balanced Living

I take care of myself. I have never been a smoker; I've always been a very moderate drinker. During the war I drank very little. I didn't want to impair my flying or judgement while on missions..

I still exercise every morning. There is a regimen I go through. We watch our diet—three balanced meals a day. I'm not a huge eater. My weight hasn't fluctuated more than ten pounds for 50 years. I have always been a poor sleeper. It has been a handicap, but I have learned to live with it.

Jackie and I met on a dance floor and we danced together a lot in our social life. We were very socially inclined. If I go on a trip I'd prefer to visit historical areas and enjoy good restaurants and hotels. Jackie and I just returned from Louisiana. We visited New Orleans and enjoyed good restaurants. We also spent time in the boat and visited scenes from our youth.

I've always had an intellectual curiosity. I have a great interest in reading history—political, war, and inventions. I also like Tom Clancy's books. I don't watch television shows that lack substance, such as some of today's comedies.

Advice to Younger Generations

To the extent that you can, try to understand what you are facing. Then prepare in every way you can to deal with that situation, knowing that a situation will change on you. With a perfect plan, you still have to have a plan B.

Come to peace with the fact that you have a job to do that is worth risking your life for.

P-47 Thunderbolt pilot

Jackie, back home in Louisiana, during the war

Quentin and Jacqueline Aanenson of Bethesda, Maryland

Chapter 13

Kenneth John Sawyer
Gold Beach

Of a calm and strong temperament, Kenneth John Sawyer served in the British Army, landing at Normandy and fighting throughout Europe. He was the youngest Regimental Sergeant Major in the British Army. He is presently retired and lives in North Yorkshire, England. According to his wife Dorothy, who nursed the wounded soldiers from D-Day, "He is very reliable, constant, old-fashioned, and easy to live with; he gets on with most people."

I was born in 1922, in county Wiltshire, in southwest England. I had an older sister and a younger brother and sister. Dad was a WWI veteran and a farmer. When I was five, we moved to a suburb of Bristol on the west coast of England. We were a typical city family then. We made fun for ourselves, and played lots of games in the house, such as card games organized by my mother. Dad did various jobs, including dock foreman and driving a lorry *[truck]*.

I joined the Territorial Army, which is similar to the American Reserves, in 1939 when I was 17 years of age. I joined the Royal Engineers as a sapper *[like a private]*, specializing in mine clearing. My wife was in nursing when we met in 1942. We married during the war, in 1943, when I was 21 years of age.

I was in an assault division on D-Day at Gold Beach, next to Omaha, clearing the beach of mines and other barriers before the infantry landed. We had regiments with tanks that had flails in the front and rollers. I fired a machine gun from my tank. The tank in front of mine was hit right after hitting the beach. People were dropping all around me. The sea was red with blood. I saw 200 to 300 casualties. I pulled some of the wounded to safety behind the sea wall. If you saw the film "Saving Private Ryan," you'd know precisely what it was like. We suffered 25% casualties—75% had been anticipated—because of our armored support and because our artillery had suppressed the German defenses. My tank had a special gun that could demolish the concrete blockhouses. I was on the front lines for eight weeks until we broke out of Normandy at the end of July 1944.

All of us were frightened to death, but all were glad to get off the boat after two days on rough seas. I determined to do my job regardless of the mines and shells. My father had said, "If a shell or bullet has your name on it, there's nothing you can do to get out of the way. So if you're not being hit, don't worry about it." He was fearless. I wasn't. We felt exhilarated to have landed and still be alive ten minutes after landing. By the evening, when I could finally relax, I shivered. I couldn't stop shaking for an hour. Whenever I go back to France, I see the names of boys on the gravestones and thank God that I got away from that day.

After D-Day I was used in every major action, through France, Belgium, Holland, and Germany. Eventually I was in a brigade headquarters to organize the tanks for specific jobs. I was the youngest Regimental Sergeant Major in the army at age 21. I was wounded going over the Rhine, and received the Oak Leaf for valor.

Going through Germany in April 1945, we were the first troops to come across the Belzen concentration camp. We walked around rounding up the German guards. I had great difficulty stopping my troops from shooting the arrogant commandant, Mr. Kramer. We made civilians come to the camp to see it, and made them place the bodies in the mass graves for burial. That camp experience caused me more grief internally than anything else I've seen before or since. I had nightmares for many years.

After the war, I went back to the old job I'd begun in 1937 — a clerical job; I was studying to be an accountant. I then went to Yorkshire, where my wife was from. I worked in data processing, now called information technology. In 1950 I joined Sperry Gyroscope and worked there until I retired in 1987 as Director of Information Systems.

I remained in the reserves until 1977 and finished as a lieutenant colonel in the regiment. In 1951 I had my second stint in the army, when I was called up for Korea. I served as Regimental Sergeant Major. My service also included the Suez Campaign in 1956. I received the Member of the Order of the British Empire award for service at Buckingham Palace from the Queen in 1972.

Dorothy and I have two children, a daughter, Judy, and younger son, Robin.

PTSD Symptoms?

My wife says that the war did not effect me very much. I saw friends with PTSD, friends who were tougher than I, who had nervous breakdowns. One friend who turned to jelly will never talk about it. I didn't have it —I was very fortunate, except for nightmares about the concentration camp, which stopped 20 years ago. They stopped when I saw a film about Americans who entered camps with humor —a sergeant for instance who joked about the camps —and I realized that the war was over.

What Helped You Cope?

If you're in charge of a bunch of guys, as I was, you can't afford to show your feelings. In spite of fear, you must be an example. The British have the stiff upper lip. We didn't show fear, or show that we wouldn't carry on. This seemed to help me control the fear. You train yourself to say, "I wouldn't ask you to do it if I wouldn't do it."

I had a stable family life. My parents lived a frugal life and made the best of it. My wife was always there—during the war, she waited for me three years after we married to live together. In Normandy, she gave me great strength—she was one of the things that made me realize I had to come back.

My father was always a tower of strength, a real tough guy. When I was on leave in Bristol, there was an air raid. He would make cocoa at home and bring it to the elderly in bomb shelters. On the way there I ducked down when I heard the eerie whistling of an incoming bomb. He asked, "Why are you doing that? If it's got you name on it, it will get you. If it hasn't, it won't." Mother was also a great source of encouragement. She ensured that we did our homework. I always respected her.

Before the war, our environment was poor. Father was unemployed. We learned to make due with little. It strengthened character. We all helped out wherever we could.

The inner city had a greater sense of community than it does today. I joined the choir with most of my friends and attended services in the Church of England. I was active in Boy Scouts, which got kids together. There was a sense of order in life that carried on in the army even more so.

We were not only innocent, but hardened. Life was both harder and happier. We had very few pleasures, such as passive television. We were happier because expectations were fairly low. We made our own enjoyment. We played cricket, and football (soccer) with no equipment. We'd jolly along for a couple of hours and be as happy as Larry. We had no distractions. At school we played rugby.

During the Depression, three million men were unemployed, yet there was minimal crime due to the family structure and morals. My grandmother died at 96 years of age. Being deaf, she never realized how things had changed. Kids today are pampered.

CALM UNDER PRESSURE

It was drummed into our heads to do our job—and not look around and get distracted. So that's what we did when we landed at Normandy. We actually felt exhilarated when landing.

We captured a German captain and three of his troops at Normandy. He said, "The war's over, isn't it. " I replied, "It is for you." I had no gripes with the Germans, no real anger—they were perhaps the finest army in the world and the German prisoners were just like you and me—until I saw the concentration camp. I realized that there was a streak in some Germans that permitted them to obey such orders. After the war, I was sent to Italy to take over a POW camp of 500 German Engineers who had been prisoners for three years. I told them Germany was flattened. I got to like them very much. My interpreter had been the assistant organist at the Cologne cathedral. He would play the piano to entertain our troops. I could tolerate them any time. My friends who fought in the African desert said it was a most gentlemanly war. Our losers were treated well and respected by Rommel's troops. The wounded were helped. On D-Day, German doctors operated on British and German soldiers alike.

RATIONAL THOUGHT PROCESSES

Fear is normal. I was afraid many times. It's normal that we should all be frightened.

I didn't let mistakes, mine or others, prey on my mind. I'd let people know that I was aware of them, and do something about them if it was not trivial, but I wouldn't keep fussing over it.

SOCIAL SUPPORT

Letters from home were frequent and powerful. They meant a lot. They were my lifeline. A few soldiers had unfortunate marriages, which shook them up quite a bit and made quite a difference to them. I would try to muck in with them and help them get through it.

COMFORT WITH EMOTIONS

During the Battle of Britain in the early days of the war, there were nightly bombings. A bomb dropped in the underground barracks I was in. Several were killed. I was frightened. For one week after, I was afraid to go down to the barracks to go to bed. Thereafter, fear didn't bother me. Several others had the same feelings. It's normal to be frightened. My buddy dismissed my fear. He said, "What the hell's up with you?" And I said, "It could happen again." He said, "If it does, too bad." He believed lightening wouldn't strike twice in the same place. Ironically, he later cracked, became jelly.

On patrol in no-man's land, I could hear German voices in the fog 10 yards away. I was frightened. Everyone had fear. But, if you did what you were trained to do, you felt you had more of a chance. We were highly trained.

Dorothy adds: Ken was able to talk about the war. Things kept coming out in bits. Most men just want to talk about other things.

SELF-ESTEEM

I quite honestly believed in myself, more as the war went on. I was confident. I knew what I was doing. I was too young to know otherwise. Dad hadn't spoken much about his WWI experiences. I certainly felt that I had something to contribute. Doing well at school helped me feel reasonably well esteemed.

ACTIVE, CREATIVE COPING

You will cope if you are adaptable and know what you're doing. My generation was brought up to accept situations and believe we were capable of doing anything, if given the training we needed. We didn't question orders. We were disciplined—a word unknown today.

Dorothy: He is very determined in all he does. When his knee was replaced a few years ago, he was religious about physical therapy.

SPIRITUAL AND PHILOSOPHICAL STRENGTHS

God

Spirituality was always a strength. A wonderful padre in Normandy who held services said, "There are no atheists in slit trenches." Everyone prays in his or her own way. I always felt better in myself after services before combat; it led to a feeling that God was a Britisher, on my side. Church now is happy-clappy (guitars, waving hands), so I don't go. I like old-fashioned religion (hymns, prayer, sermons). I was a religious kid. I attended Church, and believed what I listened to. I wondered if God existed sometimes with what we saw. How can He let this happen? Perhaps for a reason that eludes me. I still believe He's there and keeps his eye on us. I think twice before I do things.

Mom was religious; she pushed me into choir. We always had to say our prayers before bed, which was standard for most kids. Just after the war, three buddies in camp knelt down to pray at night before bed and weren't chastised or laughed at. They'd done it all their lives.

Meaning & Purpose

My wife was the major reason to come back — to start again the life I'd stopped midstream in 1939. I was close to my brother and two sisters. We were close knit, and I wanted to see them too. Since the war, my wife and children have been my strength.

Morality

Any order you give must be moral. If you give an immoral order, you can expect an immoral reply. That's what was wrong with the Germans. I said to a German, "How could you believe you could do that (i.e., the camps), no matter who told you to do it?" He replied, "If I didn't, I'd get shot." I said, "I think that getting shot may be better than what you did."

I never robbed prisoners or looted them of watches or binoculars. I wouldn't want it done to me and I wouldn't do it to others. My family didn't have much, but we were taught not to expect things from others without working for it.

I was never licentious in the army. *(Dorothy adds: "We were both virgins when we married, and are still married for 57 years.")*

My parents were very strict, and were not far removed from the Victorian era. At age 17, I had to be in by 9:00 p.m. I wasn't alone. We respected our parents — that's the key. We stayed innocent far longer than kids today. The innocence was there until the '50s. Then it started to go wrong.

Love

I still see many comrades today, more than 50 years later. The British Army was very regimental. There was a family feeling about it that never leaves you. Especially in the engineers, everyone knew everyone. Buddies always helped each other. We knew our people intimately and looked out for each other.

I was amazed at how such a diverse group got on so well for so long, with so little aggravation or nastiness, because everyone had a job to do. It shook us a little that the American white soldiers didn't mix with the black soldiers. A lot of the black people were drivers on the massive trucks on the beachhead right up through Germany. I found them all very nice guys, always smiling, big cigars.

Optimism

I was very optimistic throughout the war, even in the darkest days of bombings. It never dawned on me that my nation wouldn't survive. I picked up a fallen German pilot in July 1940, who said, "We shall be in London soon." I said, "You will be, as a prisoner, but not the rest." I always felt I'd come home and it was quite as I'd expected, though I had to adjust to a less rigorous life. I always felt I was going places. I was never depressed. I've always felt that tomorrow will come and will be better, or not any worse. I'm still that way. I still look forward to returning to the U.S. in two years, to go cruising and having the grandchildren with us. We come every two years, and they come to England on alternate years.

Humor

I always enjoy a good story and try to be as humorous as I can. When we meet old army buddies, in a half-hour we can recount all the funny stories that happened. One drunken buddy was singing at the top of his lungs "Lead Kindly Light" as he was crawling in the gutter looking for the badge that fell off his hat. The vicar walking down the road says, " Well I'm certainly glad you remember the words."

In Holland, a black GI rode up on a motorcycle with a message. It had been pouring rain. The adjutant said, "You're a bit damp, Jackson" The messenger said, "Sir, I is wet right up to my asshole." Of course we never heard that in England before, so that always brought a laugh.

Long View of Suffering

It was difficult to see the seriously wounded. You realize how brave some wounded can be; with a gaping stomach, all they wanted was a cigarette. There was no griping. You expect them to be moaning and groaning at the point of death. You came to accept suffering. You got inured to it until you didn't shy away from suffering, danger, or trouble. It made you stronger.

Maintaining Balanced Living

I am a member of the Lions, and Probis clubs for service and sociality. We built schools on Cyprus. For recreation, we like to walk and eat out. I'm an avid reader.

I've kept fit through playing games. I play golf, and until recently played cricket and soccer. I always slept six to seven hours and awoke early. Eating well has been a priority. We've eaten balanced meals—meat, vegetables, and fruits.

I drink socially, but not to excess. I never felt the need to get drunk during the war. I only got drunk once, and got ill, so I never did again. I did start smoking during the war when cigarettes were plentiful, but stopped six years ago.

Advice to Younger Generations

Be prepared for what you choose. If you take a job, expect to meet the difficult situations that come with that job. Develop discipline. Be innocent, but hard. There is too much stress on counseling today. We turn too quickly to counseling. It is probably better to prepare before the situations are confronted.

I believe training should include realism and live ammunition to get used to the sounds. Troops should be advised: when you see your first dead body, here's what you'll feel. That's essential. Troops should be presented with hypothetical traumatic situations and asked: "What would you do if....?"

Kenneth John Sawyer

Kenneth John Sawyer

Wedding day, 1943

With Dorothy, returning to Normandy for fifty-year commemoration

Kenneth and Dorothy Sawyer at home in Yorkshire, England

Amos E. Small
With the Band of Brothers

Amos and Eleanor Small live in the peaceful rural setting of Raeford, North Carolina. Amos was an original member of the new, all-volunteer 506th Parachute Infantry Regiment, 101st Airborne Division, which landed at Normandy. He was in the same battalion as E Company, which inspired the Band of Brothers *book and movie, and often fought with them. According to historian Stephen Ambrose, the 101st earned the reputation from Normandy, Holland, and Bastogne as "the most famous and admired of all the eighty-nine divisions the United States Army put into the Second World War "(Band of Brothers, p. 219).*

Eleanor describes her husband as: "Easy going. Nothing bothers him, unless something will hurt his family. He is my friend and confidant. He is an absolutely wonderful father and family man. Even today, he goes to the kids right away when they need help. He is like a father to the men in the Knights of Columbus." He stands 6' tall and weights 173 pounds, which is about what he weighted during WWII.

I was raised in a place called Hells Kitchen, on the west side of New York City. There were three children. I was in the middle. My brother was three years younger. My older sister died at 10 years of age. She cut her ankle while roller skating and got blood poisoning. In the hospital she got double pneumonia and died. I was seven years old.

After school you did homework and played in the house. In the summertime, you got a baldy haircut, a pair of overalls, and sneakers. The fellas on the block left the house at 8:00 a.m. and played stickball all day long, maybe scooting home at lunchtime for a peanut butter and jelly sandwich.

During the Depression it was pretty rough. My father lost his job as a truck driver. Then he found work as a hospital orderly, working six days a week and making $30 a month. He walked at least two miles to work each day. At that time a nickel was a lot of money. You'd walk to save a nickel on the subway. You got a hotdog with sauerkraut and a lemonade for a nickel. That was a big treat then.

In high school I worked as an usher at the movies three nights a week. You had a flashlight and showed people to their seats because the movie was continuous—a newsreel, a comedy, and the main feature.

On Sundays father had his day off. We went to Coney Island or Rockaway after the 6:00 a.m. Mass to spend the day at the beach. Or we would drive with my aunt and uncle to the country for a picnic. Sometimes the men would get together and hire a bus to go to Lake Ronkonkoma on Long Island, where the cousins would spend a couple of weeks in the summer at my aunt's house.

My parents were both quiet, hard workers. We rarely heard them argue. Mother helped me with homework, because my father didn't get home until late at night. Many times I saw her down on her knees scrubbing the kitchen floor. My father was as tall as I and didn't have a grey hair on his head when he died.

In high school I took up stenography. I graduated high school in 1941, and worked for a loan company at $12.50 per week.

WORLD WAR II SURVIVORS - LESSONS IN RESILIENCE

War broke out and I had to fight for my country, so I enlisted at age 18. The Army Air Corps never notified me after I took a test, so I went to find out why. I saw a paratrooper looking all spiffy. He described fighting behind the enemy lines and talked us into joining. He took us to Governors Island to be sworn in. We shipped to Camp Toccoa, Georgia, to form the original 506th Parachute Infantry Regiment. I was assigned to Headquarters Company of the 2nd Battalion. My machine gun platoon supported rifle companies D, E, and F. I fought with E Company many a time. I fought four campaigns. I jumped into Normandy and Holland. I then fought in the Battle of the Bulge (and Bastogne) and took Hitler's Eagle's Nest. I got the Purple Heart, two Bronze Stars, two Presidential Citations, other awards, and sore feet.

The thing I remember about training in Georgia was running up and down Mount Currahee, three miles each way, every day. We ran obstacle courses, jumped from jump towers, and did all the basic parachute training. We learned to blow up bridges and communications, and handled every vehicle in the U.S. Army. We even had three days of riding horses. Anything you needed to know to fight behind enemy lines.

After joining the 101st Airborne Division, we shipped out to England on September of 1943. There we had lots of night training and night jumps. Little did we know we were jumping on a replica of Normandy.

We landed in Normandy, behind enemy lines, around midnight on the morning of June 6, 1945. Everything was pitch black and, in all the confusion and anti-aircraft fire, we landed about eight miles from our intended drop zone. We were also flying very low. Maybe six or eight seconds after I left the plane I hit the ground. I landed in a farm. If you kept low, you could see people moving. I headed toward Americans and away from German machine guns. I had walked an hour toward my objective. I heard someone say, "Ah, rats." I recognized the voice of a buddy who'd landed in the water in the flooded hedgerows. Soon there were 30 or 40 of us with an officer heading to our objective. We were to establish a roadblock about a kilometer from the beach to stop Germans moving to and from the Utah beach. I was a corporal, a squad leader at 19 years old, and I hoped to see twenty. All around were German machine guns and artillery. We stayed at the roadblock until the beach party came up to us about 10:00 or 11:00 that morning.

We pulled out and went to help take Carentan. This was a key to expanding the beachhead. On the way, we hit a few towns that we had to take and it was hell. The favorite saying was "Machine gun up front." That is, we were called up to support the rifle companies when units were pinned down, or mostly on the attack to lay down supporting fire, or to cover them when they withdrew. We sneaked past a whole division of German paratroopers one night and went into Carentan. Then we had a battle as the German division was pinned between our forces. After about a month, in July, we were pulled out and sent back to England.

We were all ready to jump into the forest outside Paris, where General Rommel's headquarters was, but Patton got there first. We were ready to jump into Belgium at an ammunition and equipment depot, but Patton beat us again. However, in September we jumped as part of a coordinated effort with the 82nd Airborne and the British to secure a road in northern Holland that would let us go to Berlin. The operation was called Market Garden. The American troops were successful but the British got slaughtered. I was in a patrol to bring a lot of the British and Canadian troops back. We were in Holland for 72 days. The Germans would break through and flood the area. Whenever they surrounded us, they lost. With our backs to the wall, we fought like hell. My squad of 12 men occupied six foxholes and covered an area one hundred yards wide. We'd take a town, give it to the English. They'd lose it and we had to take it back. When we took a town, the Dutch would take their flags out. When the Germans retook it, the German flags came out.

We were pulled back to rest in early December of 1944, and then were sent up to Bastogne, because the Germans had broken through the Ardennes Forest [*the Battle of the Bulge, Hitler's last offensive*]. We hardly had any ammunition. I had one box of ammo, two hand grenades, and four clips of ammo for a carbine. We slept in a farm house, and the next morning started moving to attack the town of Foy. Our scouts went into the town and ran back out saying that there were so many German tanks you couldn't count them. We were told to pull back and set up a defensive perimeter around

Bastogne and a roadblock and hold it at all costs. We stayed there until after Christmas. It was freezing—so cold we'd lie back to back in the foxholes and cover ourselves with pine straw. We wrapped burlap bags around our boots for warmth, and we put white flour sacks around us for camouflage when we went on patrol. The Germans shelled us mercilessly and knocked the tops of trees off. We put the limbs over us for warmth. They always seemed to know when we changed over companies on the line and shelled us. A lot of guys got trench foot. We heard that General McAuliffe had said "Nuts" to the Germans demand to surrender. We agreed. I thought we were winning. We lost a lot of guys, but we took five or six for every guy we lost. Yes, we were surrounded, but airborne units were always surrounded. In January, Patton's tanks broke through the encirclement and got to us. We thought we'd be relieved. Instead, we went on the attack again.

We then took trucks south to Alsace, the Black Forest between France and Germany. It was rumored that the Germans were breaking through there. In the town of Haguenau, we set up our machine guns in a hospital and fired across a narrow river at a row of houses where the Germans were. When we fired at them, they fired back, and vice versa. Mostly we left each other alone. Little by little they pulled back.

We entered Germany in the spring. We rode DUKWs [*boat-like trucks with big rubber tires*] along the autobahn in Germany. We saw about ten German jets on the ground. They had used the autobahn for runways. In Belgium I had seen one of them leave one of our P-47's in its blast, as though the P-47 were standing still. We entered a work camp of Buchloe, part of the Dachau complex. You could smell it a mile away. Corpses, starved slave workers—it was disgusting. We got to Hitler's Eagle's Nest in Berchtesgaden and took that without a fight. For a week we enjoyed the German sausage, pork, and fine liquor and wine that was stored there. We were there when the Germans surrendered.

We headed deep into Austria for occupation duty. We herded the many German prisoners into a big field. We were near Zell am Zee in a resort area of the Alps. We skied in the mountains and swam in the lakes. I was assigned to supervise the making of a baseball field for our troops, with the help of a detail of German volunteers. Before it was finished, there was a lottery for the 35 of us in the company who were left from the original 160 from Georgia. I won and was in a truck heading home with five others. The truck went off the road on a cliff. A buddy and I locked arms and grabbed the ribs of the truck and rode the truck into a river. The others were knocked off the truck. One drowned. After being hospitalized for a short time, we continued home. I made it back to the states. I was a section sergeant.

After the war I stayed in the reserves and became a first sergeant. I went to work driving a truck for various companies. I took tests to work for the city and was hired as a correction officer in 1953. Because of my stenography experience, I was the warden's secretary for 19 years. I met Eleanor in 1953. I bought a house that year under the GI bill and she lived next door. We were engaged in 1955 and married in 1956. We have five children, three girls and two boys. To help support the family, I worked part-time as a bookkeeper, after schooling in advanced accounting. I retired in 1974. On the way down to Florida to seek a retirement home, I stopped in North Carolina to see my nephew. We purchased four acres next to him and now live here. It was virgin land that I cleared by hand, mostly by myself.

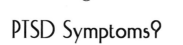

PTSD Symptoms?

For the first year or two I had occasional nightmares, usually on the weekend after drinking a few beers and relaxing. Otherwise, I was fine. I kept busy.

What Helped You Cope?

I had to worry about a squad of nine men — their food, safety, ammunition, getting them back from patrol. There was no time to fold. I kept on thinking of others, not myself.

My Catholic education helped very much — believing in God and knowing that he would watch over me. I carried pictures of Our Lady and carried a rosary with me at all times.

I had the idea of coming home. I always knew I'd make it home, even though on some days you had your doubts.

The weeks that I spent in summer camp, sponsored by the Boys Athletic League, made me familiar with the woods to the point that I wasn't afraid of the outdoors.

CALM UNDER PRESSURE

You concentrated on your mission, which was to cover the guys in front of you. You don't think of self, but the other guy, to get out there and do your job and bring everyone back with you.

Major Winters [*a universally respected and beloved officer and leader, one of the original members of the 506th*] never got excited. I remember seeing him sitting with his rifle across his legs, watching us come off the line. He said that we machine gunners had a bad reputation. We took that to mean that, if there was a firefight, those guys would fight like hell.

The German soldier was a good soldier and had to do his job, but I was a better soldier and I was doing my job. There was no animosity toward the Germans. My mother and grandparents in New York were Germans, although they were American true blue. I spoke German fluently. My father's side was Irish.

RATIONAL THOUGHT PROCESSES

You never see water stay on a duck's back. Things don't bother me. When we were getting pounded, we'd think, "Oh, they'll run out of ammo and stop soon." In other words, bad times will pass. You had to pass it off as a big joke, or you'd go crazy.

Mistakes are something we do as we are learning. But you learn and don't make costly mistakes in the future. If we screwed up in training, we had to dig a 6x6x6 [*foxhole*] by midnight. Screwing up was nothing unusual. We made a game of it. But you don't screw up in combat. Then it costs lives.

I wasn't perfect and made plenty of mistakes. I learned from our platoon sergeant. Many a time he'd come over to my bunk and say, "You know what you did wrong today?" as if in general conversation. And you'd remember that. Otherwise, if someone yells you turn a deaf ear.

To my troops who made mistakes, I'd talk man to man, but with authority. "You loused up, now we all have to take the brunt of it." In combat, screw ups were minimal. Everyone was trained and retrained. You correct with authority, but calmly and firmly, no demeaning. I'd talk to them off to the side, away from others so as not to embarrass.

As a parent, I'd talk in the beginning. They were usually sort of scared and didn't do much wrong. I talk calmly. Screaming leads to walls; talk calmly and they'll be calm.

SOCIAL SUPPORT

I got letters all the time from parents, aunts, cousins and my brother who was in the Navy. Letters gave news from home and let me know they were still thinking of me. It made me feel good. My mother sent cookies.

Everyone in the platoon knew everybody else. They were your buddies. We'd go out together. I was good at making friends.

We trained together to the point that you could look at the back of someone's head or hear someone talk behind you and you knew who it was. It was the greatest feeling, when a firefight started, to look over and see a buddy next to you shooting, too.

We had unit pride. Mention the 506th and your chest went out and buttons on your chest started to pop. We walked from Toccoa to Atlanta, 120 miles, in only 33½ hours walking time—not counting eating and sleeping. We didn't lose anybody. When we went to jump school, we didn't have one drop out.

Since the war, everything is the family. They're the ones that really count. Like the old saying, blood is thicker than water. When my daughter got married, her husband, an only child, couldn't believe all the people who come to our family gatherings from New York, Minnesota, and Texas. We usually have a reunion every two years and have 35 of us.

We still have reunions from the 506th and I still see some of the originals. We were all so glad to see each other years later, even though we've concentrated on our families. Now we can afford to go to reunions. We have a lot of fun. It means a lot to go to them.

COMFORTABLE WITH EMOTIONS

I was an 18-year-old kid, and only grew up after I went into combat. Hell, yes, I felt afraid, scared going in. All of a sudden, when the fighting starts, you become oblivious to the fear. Then, after it's over, you think, "Holy mackerel, I could have gotten killed." But at the time adrenaline is rushing so fast you don't realize you've run toward the enemy when maybe you should have been running away. With all that adrenaline, sometimes I had to be told to stop shooting.

A few times we'd talk among ourselves and laugh about the fears of others. The laughter helped break up the fear. For instance, once we were out in an open field when German artillery opened up on us. We were scared and running toward ditches. Two of our guys ran to an outhouse and jumped in, but there was no floor. Boy, oh boy, did they smell! But laughing about it helped break up the tension.

SELF-ESTEEM

I was very proud of what I did. I liked the person I was. I was well trained and I feel I did my job. My squad came back with the original eight guys when I left them to be promoted to section sergeant. I went in as a kid and came out as a man.

ACTIVE, CREATIVE COPING

If you wanted the job done right, you followed the plan. For example, if you were surrounded by Germans, you set up your machine guns to catch the enemy in a cross fire from any direction. You kept to that. Winters told us, if we got overrun, to pull back to make the last stand. We thought, "If we get overrun, come bury us, because we ain't leaving." That was the determination we had.

SPIRITUAL AND PHILOSOPHICAL STRENGTHS

God

He made us in his image and likeness and so loved people that He gave up His life for us. We go to Mass every Sunday and on holy days, and try to make first Friday novenas. During the war I had the belief that if I'm gonna die I'm going to go to heaven, and that's the most peaceful place there is. Faith kept me peaceful inside. Even today, if I can't sleep I say some prayers and go right to sleep. I carry the rosary in my pocket in a little pouch alongside my 506th medallion and a cross. If Eleanor and I are traveling in the car we say the rosary. It gives a sense of security. I said the rosary in the war.

Once, when a plane was hit at night, it started screaming and it appeared to be coming right at me and the hole I was in. I promised God if he got me out of that I'd change my ways. I said many a Hail Mary over there.

Meaning & Purpose

I was serving my country. President Roosevelt declared war and it was the duty of every American to protect our country. It was definitely clear to me that we were fighting for freedom. I saw the regimentation of the Germans. At first, the people in Normandy were scared of the Americans, after being under the Germans' thumbs. I wanted to get the job done, get the war over, and get back home to my family.

Morality

It was important to have principles, principles you were brought up with regarding caring for others. There's a difference between right and wrong. If you do what you're supposed to do, it's right. Shortcuts are wrong. You don't reach into someone's pocket and take a dime. That's stealing. I give back money to clerks who have given me too much change. In war, you didn't steal from your buddy. You only killed in self-defense, because you had to. I took five prisoners in Normandy. We could have shot them, but we didn't mistreat them. I'd expect the same treatment if I were captured. It's do unto others as you'd have them do to you. I wouldn't take rings or things like that from prisoners. When we took a town, we never had one incident of rape. That wouldn't be right.

It's very important to be honest with yourself and your men. That's how you get respect from them. They'll follow you by example.

You don't go out and commit adultery. I'm married 47 years this June and I can say I've been faithful. You have to have love and respect for each other, and being unfaithful isn't being respectful of anyone. Even in Hollywood, many of the older stars like Jimmy Stewart stayed married.

Love

You felt so comfortable knowing that the guys on both sides and to your rear were guys you knew and trusted. I can still name them all. You knew they wouldn't run on you. They'd stay and fight with you. No one called us a band of brothers then. It was a sense of camaraderie, of being buddies, though. Everything in our routine was to check on others—that they had water in their canteen, ammo, food. If someone was hit, you put sulfur powder on the wound and bandaged them up. You didn't leave him alone until a medic arrived to take over, or you carried him back to safety. Once a week, I talk or email old buddies from our original group.

Optimism

I think that tomorrow will come and I'll be here, I hope. If not, I'll be in heaven, definitely so.

I couldn't be in the war if I didn't think we'd win. No one in Bastogne told us we were surrounded. In every conflict we were in, we were surrounded, so why was this different? We thought we were winning. Those poor bastards had us surrounded. Only after Patton broke through were we told we were surrounded.

Humor

Humor helped you forget. Everything wasn't roses. It was blood today and blood tomorrow. The only way to live with it was with humorous incidents that happened, like the guys who jumped into the outhouse. Once, there was a German who would come and walk along the wood line every day, three hundred yards from our position. We watched him do this. I don't know why he did. Then we decided to have some fun. The next time he did this, we fired rounds in front of him. Then behind him. We had him running back and forth until he ran back into the woods. Everyone had a good time. Nobody hit him.

Long View of Suffering

The worst part of the war was seeing Buchloe, the concentration camp. You don't forget that one. The prisoners were treated so inhumanely. There were bodies all over.

I was 18 years old and still growing up when I enlisted. You had your ideals and character going in, but the Army strengthened my ideals. It taught me to be a leader and self sufficient—not just out of a book, but by doing it. Your worked hard and had to be conscientious. You learned to be sincere and honest. I learned that I respected leaders who gave sincere and honest orders. I tried to be that way. You learned to be caring for others, to look out for other guys' feelings. You didn't improve yourself by stepping on someone. There's enough freedom and opportunity in our country that people can get along.

Maintaining Balanced Living

My wife keeps me physically healthy. She makes sure I eat properly and get plenty of rest. We always have three good, balanced meals. We're in bed by 10:00 and sleep until 7:00 in the morning. Even when working I got almost that much sleep

I quit smoking in 1974. I picked up smoking in the Army. The doctor recommended I quit, so I threw them away and haven't had one since. I quit drinking in 1981, after I had a heart attack. I'd been a light social drinker, a couple of beers at a party every month or two.

I play cards with friends once a week. We alternate houses. During the 72 days in Holland, we played pinochle whenever we could to keep our sanity.

We both are active in church. I am very active in the church's Knights of Columbus. I was instrumental in forming the group here. It works doing charity, helping the community, the handicapped, visiting people in the hospital, and so forth. I volunteer at the airborne museum once a week. That keeps me active, too.

My wife and I go shopping in the mall, Eleanor's favorite pastime. We go out to eat on Friday nights. Most of the times we're both busy with the home. I keep busy with maintenance of this house. I paint and cut grass. I build things, mostly out of scrap would. I built an armoire, a desk, the extension on the home, and the gazebo.

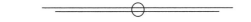

Advice to Younger Generations

Be honest with yourself. Don't cheat. Be honest with others and you'll be respected.
Slow down and appreciate things. Today's pace is too fast. We don't notice the beauty in nature.
Show respect for elders. They still do this around where we live.
Get more active in your church. You learn values, leadership, and morals.
Learn respect for yourself by working for what you get—you feel you've accomplished something.

Light machine gun squad after a training jump,
Camp MacKall, 1943

Amos and Eleanor Small visit a
monument to the 506th in
Toccoa, GA, 2001

At home in Raeford, NC

Chapter 15

Russell Dunham
Medal of Honor

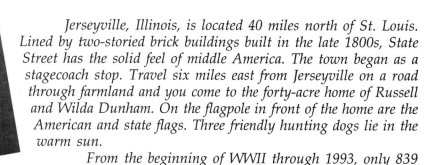

Jerseyville, Illinois, is located 40 miles north of St. Louis. Lined by two-storied brick buildings built in the late 1800s, State Street has the solid feel of middle America. The town began as a stagecoach stop. Travel six miles east from Jerseyville on a road through farmland and you come to the forty-acre home of Russell and Wilda Dunham. On the flagpole in front of the home are the American and state flags. Three friendly hunting dogs lie in the warm sun.

From the beginning of WWII through 1993, only 839 men have received the Medal of Honor, the nation's highest award for valor. Most of those men died earning the medal. Russell Dunham earned the Medal of Honor in Europe. He served in eight major campaigns in North Africa, Sicily, Italy, France, and Germany. During his 31 months of foreign service, he was credited with 407 days of combat. He was wounded in Italy and France. His brother Ralph, with whom he served, was wounded more than five times. Despite his outer toughness, Russell Dunham is an unusually thoughtful and sensitive man.

I was born February 23, 1920, in East Carondelet, Illinois, in a converted boxcar on the Mississippi River. Dad worked then for a barge line. I was the sixth of eight children—three girls and five boys. When I was three, we moved because of my mother's health.

We moved quite a bit. Mother was sick with tuberculosis most of my life. She died when I was seven. I don't remember her walking. At one point the family moved to Springfield, in southern Missouri, where my mother had a sister and the weather was warmer. We traveled the distance of 400 miles in a covered wagon.

The whole family had to work real hard, all the time. My dad was a gardener all his life and my first Christmas present was a hoe. As everyone said, my dad was a good boss. Dad rented farms. He moved around when the rent came due. I had an older sister who took pretty good care of us.

After my mother died in 1927, we had a number of housekeepers before Dad remarried. The older children left as soon as they were able. Dad remarried in 1932. My stepmother had three children of her own, and together they had three more.

During the Depression, we oftentimes didn't know where our next meal was coming from. Everybody was expected to do their part from the time they were able to do anything at all. Dad checked on us as we worked. He was busy selling produce, mainly butterbeans, to the produce market in St. Louis. Dad was strict, no doubt about it. Nowadays, welfare probably wouldn't have put up with the way he handled us kids. He was mean to us. My stepmother was worse than he was. I didn't go to high school. He needed us to work at home.

I left home at 16 or 17, when he broke my plate and said get out. It was my stepmother's idea that I leave home. I went to stay with my older brother in St. Louis, peddling hot tamales at night, and brooms and mops by day from carts. I also distributed advertising circulars for stores door to door at thirty-five cents an hour. Overtime was fifty cents an hour.

My dad coaxed me into going into the Civilian Conservation Corps in 1938. I always tried to help him. CCC paid $30 per month, $25 of which was to be sent home. He said he would give me back some of the money I sent home, but he never did. I worked on farms, setting out trees, building dams, placing tiles to drain farm fields, clearing out farm fields. After my six months were up, my buddy and I took a freight train to California to pick cotton. Business wasn't good, so I came back to St. Louis to sell hot tamales, brooms, and mops until spring.

My buddy and I decided to go back to California. We got to Tulsa, Oklahoma, and joined a carnival. I traveled over the country until the fall of 1939. Then it was back to selling tamales, brooms, and mops in St. Louis.

In August of 1940, my brother Ralph, a buddy, and I went to Peoria, Illinois, to look for a job. Finding none, we joined the Army. We knew that eventually war was on the way. I was so dumb I didn't know any better than to join the infantry *(chuckling)*.

We went to Fort Ord, California, to the old 7th Infantry Division under General Stillwell.

In March of 1941, they transferred all three-year men to the 3rd Infantry Division. I was in "I" Company, 3rd Battalion, 30th Infantry Regiment, and stayed with that unit throughout the war.

My brother was with me all the time. When we transferred to the 3rd, my brother stayed with the 7th Division because he was on the boxing team. Meanwhile, we went to Ft. Lewis, Washington, for maneuvers. When the war broke he joined us at Ft. Lewis.

In December of 1941 we traveled up and down the West coast on guard duty, watching bridges. We had a grand ol' time. Because we'd trained so much, we always said, "Let the Japs come, we're not afraid of them." We also trained in amphibious operations with the Marine Corps. Then we took the train to Camp Pickett, Virginia, a staging area to go overseas. We shipped out to North Africa in October 1942, getting there in November 8, 1942. We saw our first combat there under General Patton. We fought against the French three days before they surrendered. We were shelled when we landed; we scurried. This was the first time we were shot at. After things settled down, Patton paid us a visit. He learned that some of our guys were in the stockade for drinking. He said, "Whoever heard of locking up a GI for drinking? Release them." By 1943 the Germans had given up.

July 10, 1943 was our first fighting in Sicily. We walked across Sicily under Patton for 38 days. We lost a lot of men to the Germans. There were also lots of casualties from malaria and trench foot. Patton was a slave driver. That's where he slapped that boy and was relieved. We used to get mad at the Italians because they wouldn't fight.

We fought up the boot of Italy in General Clark's 5th Army. We were in the bloody battle for the monastery at Cassino. Only a few of us —32 of the 800 men in the battalion— walked away from Mount Rotundo. Ralph landed in the hospital with trench feet. Anzio was a real blood bath. We went in with 202 men and the next day we were only 22. By mid-March of 1944 the division had lost 6000 men, killed, wounded, or missing. I got hit on the 28th of January, 1944. I was in the hospital for 30 days from shrapnel wounds in the leg, mouth, and chin from white phosphorous. I rejoined the unit and the fighting was still going on hot and heavy.

In June, my company commander assigned me to lead a patrol of six into the town of Labico. We surprised a group of about fifty Germans preparing for a meeting in a building. Just as we'd disarmed them, a German tank approached. Leaving a man to guard the prisoners, the rest of us hid in the shadows of the building. When the tank came, two of my men jumped on the tank and surprised the crew. Now we'd captured a tank. Then an ambulance with a high-ranking German doctor came down the road and we captured that. We were the center of attention when my little patrol returned with a column of sixty Germans, a tank, and an ambulance.

We made the famous breakthrough to Rome. We were there only a few days, when the Normandy invasion took place. When people ask where I was during D-Day, I say we were over there waiting. We had already been there over 1½ years before they came over.

We landed in southern France on August 15, 1944, joining up with the D-Day invaders under Patton, who had been forgiven and now had the Third Army. Thousands of Germans were trapped, along with horses, vehicles, and giant railroad guns, in southern France.

In September we got into the Vosges Mountains, with rain and snow coming in, fighting determined Germans for each position. We finally broke out of there in November and went into Strasbourg.

From there we were attached to the French 1st Army. A key target in the "Colmar Pocket" (a bulge west of the Rhine River) was Kaysersberg. Near there I received the Medal of Honor for action on

January 8, 1945. After a quick prayer ("God, give me this day."), I led my platoon in the attack on Hill #616. We were pinned down by machine-gun fire in the snow on the hillside. Our own artillery was also landing near us. There were three enemy machine gun nests. I crawled in the snow, about seventy-five yards, toward the first one. I got close enough to heave a hand grenade, which killed two German soldiers. I reached into the nest and yanked the survivor out and threw him down the hill (our mission was to take prisoners for interrogation). As I moved toward the second nest, I felt a stinging sensation across my back as I was hit. I rolled down the hill. When I stopped rolling I went up the hill again toward the second nest. I tossed a grenade and killed the crew. I crawled uphill toward the third gun emplacement and cleared that out with a hand grenade. Back in town, someone asked what all the shooting was about. Someone said, "The Dunham brothers were on the loose again." Later, as I lay on a bunk at the battalion medics, I realized that my earlier prayer had been answered. *[The citation credits Dunham with killing nine Germans, wounding seven and capturing two. In addition to neutralizing the machine-gun emplacements, he also fired his carbine and a rifle (from a wounded GI) and threw grenades into supporting foxholes, dispatching and dispersing the enemy riflemen. Throughout this attack, Dunham was under intense enemy machine-gun, automatic rifle, and mortar fire. At one point he kicked aside a German egg grenade that landed at his feet. His white camouflage robe, turned red from the blood from a 10-inch gash in his back, made him a conspicuous target against the white background. In the episode Dunham expended 11 grenades and 175 rounds of carbine ammunition.]*

I was captured on January 22, 1945, in the fatal attack on the little town of Holtzwihr.

We didn't know the tanks weren't behind us. They caved in on the bridge behind us. German tanks came in and captured many from our company. I had flown through an open window and hid in a sauerkraut barrel by a barn all night. This was possible because my weight had dropped from the usual 150 to 117 pounds. When I got out and stopped to relieve myself, I was captured. They searched me and took my grenades, but missed my concealed shoulder pistol. They got into a fight over my candy bars and cigarettes. Two guards placed me in the back seat of a jeep headed to Germany. When we stopped, one guard went into a building. I shot the other. I traveled through the woods at night heading toward the sound of our guns. During the three days coming back I almost froze to death. I went back to the hospital. My feet froze up and I had a piece of shrapnel in my foot. It was operated on. I rejoined the company in Germany, but I never did go back to combat again.

After the war, I got out and felt lost. I went from job to job and couldn't find one I liked. Finally, President Truman said that all Medal of Honor recipients could work for the Veterans Administration. I took him up on his offer and did this from 1946 to 1975. As a VA representative, I advised veterans of their rights and benefits. I mostly lived near St. Louis, where the main office was, and also worked in Vietnam, Germany, and Korea.

I met Wilda in 1955. She was a city clerk in Alton, my home. We moved here to Jerseyville in 1985. We built a house on property we'd owned for several years. Our grandchildren still live in my place in Alton.

PTSD Symptoms?

In the service, I saw guys foam at the mouth and curl up. One sergeant at Anzio came to me and said he was not going to fight and ran away from the front. My ability to function was never impaired in the military or after. I got credit for 407 days in combat. After the war, I had an anxiety condition off and on, and always tried to hide it and fight it. I'm often anxious and in a hurry. But I find it sometimes relieves me to talk about it. You don't want to keep it cooped up in you. You have to let it out.

I never did have too many dreams. I have no trouble sleeping. I never shut down from people and wasn't bothered by memory problems. Watching the movie *Saving Private Ryan* didn't bother me. Maybe I'm short tempered at times, but I always was. I think I got that from my dad. I still have pain in the leg. I didn't use drugs. I saw my brother drink himself out. It killed him, so I shut drinking off altogether.

What Helped You Cope?

My childhood strengthened me. I always had it rough. The two-mile walks to school and handling the animals and the chores strengthened my body. Many a night we went to sleep without anything to eat. I learned to fend for myself and to defend myself against my older siblings. My sister, bless her heart, even said that it would be best if Ralph and I got killed. We had nothing left to come home to, so we might as well get killed and let some of the other guys live. It makes you stubborn and stronger in some ways. My dad, bless his heart, had four or five women and they all wanted to whip me 'cause I was little and ugly and mean. I didn't have a bath or a change of clothes. Every Thursday night we got a whipping whether we needed it or not. Other families had it as rough. My dad never accepted welfare. That was out. When I graduated from 8th grade, I had no shoes to wear to the graduation. My stepmother ordered them through welfare. Oh, boy, dad really ranted and raved. In St. Louis, you couldn't get a social security number until you were eighteen, and so it was hard to find jobs. But some people liked me and hired me anyway.

We used to walk night and day hunting. We were strong. If we got tired we just figured we had to put up with it. I knew what it meant to persist. In the Army, I didn't want to get court-martialed for goldbricking. I was downtrodden and had no help from Congressmen or relatives, so I knew I'd better perform. Our company commander said, "I didn't train you guys to get hit." He would court martial you or not promote you if you couldn't prove the wound was legitimate. But he liked me for some reason.

CALM UNDER PRESSURE

It was just pride that kept me functional. I didn't want anybody thinking that I couldn't do it, just like a pitcher in a ballgame. Then, too, if you have men under you that you are responsible for, if you have something to do for them, it helps. I didn't only have myself to worry about. I was in the same platoon all the way through, from the time I was transferred to the 3rd Division. I ran the whole platoon for a long time.

A lot of people think that heroic acts are done in a blind rage, where you forget what you are doing. During the incident on Hill #616, where I earned the Medal of Honor, that wasn't the case. I was very aware and thinking about what I had to do at each point. If you forget what you're doing, you're lost and can get killed in action.

I admired the Germans, really, because of their stamina and fighting ability. I felt no bitterness. The first thing we did was give them a cigarette. Most German front line troops in Africa and Europe treated us pretty well if captured. When I was captured in France, I was treated alright.

RATIONAL THOUGHT PROCESSES

There were a number of times when I thought I might break. But I summoned my reserve strength and pushed that thought aside, knowing I had to carry on as part of the team. After seeing so many friends wounded and killed, I couldn't dwell too long on this for my own sanity. I'd think of happier times and think that I had to press on for awhile.

When someone made a mistake, I was a good actor. I could make out like I was mad as hell, but at the same time I was laughing way down deep. I never actually got mad at them. I still hear from a couple of the guys who are still alive. I didn't promote one to PFC because of sand in his rifle. He still throws it at me. He says I'm the only sergeant who told him why he didn't get promoted. When you have eleven openings for twelve guys what are you going to do? Of course, a week or so later I promoted him. I bawled out another for dragging his rifle in the dirt. I would correct people but I wasn't mean.

My sister wrote and said I probably give people hell now that I'm a sergeant. I just thought, "You don't know the conditions that we're in here." As a leader, and in my own life, I always felt that no matter how low you go, you can usually come back. I always saw some good in any misfit. That's probably why I could relate to my men, and why later, working in the VA, I could talk to the soldiers.

Sometimes you really felt bad if you messed up, or sent someone in there when you knew you shouldn't have, and someone got wounded or killed. That hurt. In time it wears off, or you find out you were actually right, or that maybe someone else upstairs gave an order that made it bad. Now in this one attack, when Sergeant Palmer with 25 years of service was killed, the Germans had captured a recon car with two .50 caliber machine guns. The company commander wanted us to attack it point blank. I told the captain if he'd let me sneak around, rather than head on, I could take it. I lost 28 men in about 15 minutes. I never did get over that. There was nothing I could have done. The captain would have relieved me if I'd disobeyed. So I didn't feel guilt but sorrow for the guys lost.

SOCIAL SUPPORT

I never did hear from my dad. My sister wrote letters every two weeks. If I didn't respond, she wrote my company commander and, boy, did I catch it. A girl in California wrote all the time and sent me cookies. After you're on the line, letters became oh, so dear. In the bitter fighting in the mountains of Italy, I read and re-read one letter from home several times.

We really had a lot of good friends in the unit. I'd take guys to the tavern to get to know them. There was constant turnover. Ralph was the only one who went all the way through with me. My brother was braver than I was. I saw him do things I couldn't have done. He had a fist fight with a German in the combat when Sergeant Palmer got killed.

Some guys would die for me. One guy from North Dakota would come to me every time we were in a tight spot. We were together all the time.

Men call me today. It really does you good. It helps your morale a lot when friends say a lot of us wouldn't be alive today if it hadn't been for Dunham.

COMFORTABLE WITH EMOTIONS

The killing bothered me—especially when people were killed because of leaders' mistakes and when I lost friends. Tears ran down my cheeks when I had to identify the bodies of friends killed on Mount Rotundo and had to carry their bodies down the hillside. I didn't like the hardness that war caused.

I could acknowledge fears. You had to have a certain amount of fear to protect yourself or you wouldn't live to tell about it. As a private, we used to talk about how scared we were. I had some friends I could really open up with. I had one buddy, especially, that used to tell me about eating apple pie in Alabama. We went on a patrol with a lieutenant in Italy, 20 miles behind the German lines. I don't think he was afraid of anything. We sat there in an olive grove and watched him shave and sing and mark targets on his map. My buddy and I were really afraid. We said, "Don't let us get on a patrol again with this stupid dude," because he was too brave. He got killed not too long after that. Another I knew, that didn't seem to be afraid, got killed. Sometimes I wasn't afraid. Sometimes I *was*, but maybe not as much as the next guy. Back at the tavern, we'd talk about it.

Once you're in the thick of it, you lose all fears. You don't have time to be scared. But it gets you when you are waiting to move out. I didn't like it when we were sitting off the coast of Africa in a ship. Confidence and eagerness to get into battle were mixed with reluctance because of what might happen. Approaching the shore, shells were landing all around and you couldn't do anything about it. As experience and confidence grew, fear tended to subside somewhat. There was still strong fear, but it seemed that the more intense the fight, the more the survival instinct took over and the calmer I became.

When I was a sergeant, I kept fears under my hat because I had to. If the men asked me what I thought I'd say, "We'll be there alright. We'll be drinking wine in Rome in a couple more days." I took pride in not showing fear. They all thought that I was not afraid. When people asked me why I wasn't afraid, I was. I just said, "You gotta do what you gotta do."

I can understand people who need to talk about their fears, and even those who crack under the pressure.

SELF-ESTEEM

I thought I was a good leader most of the time. I was pretty confident because of the other men. They thought I was better than any officer, and they actually helped me believe it. When I asked for volunteers to go on a patrol with me, they'd be willing to go. Other guys had to appoint people.

I knew I was worthwhile. That was acquired. I knew it to be true because everybody depended on me. That makes you feel good. They'd go AWOL from their own outfit and want to be with me under the same circumstances.

ACTIVE, ADAPTIVE COPING

I didn't want to die, and fighting like mad was the only way to keep from dying. You had to go forward, otherwise our own artillery would get you, as we learned in Anzio. In rolling artillery barrages, the first barrage lands in front of you, and the next barrage advances. Then they'd fire behind you to protect you from flank attacks.

I wanted to pull my load. I didn't want to be a burden on someone if I got wounded. I figured, if they get me, let them get me good. There are worse things than dying. In fact, I didn't even want to be in the hospital. I got mad when an officer in the hospital interviewed me to see if I was goldbricking. I told him that I was put in for the Medal of Honor, I was there legitimately, and I didn't want to be there.

Sometimes I thought I wasn't going to get out of this world alive anyway, so take it as it comes, one day at a time. I always had hope it would end. Every time you broke through the lines you thought, "We gotta keep it going." When you had them on the run you had to keep them on the run. Having had so much training in the year before the war is the only thing that saved me.

When captured, I knew I was going to escape. All I was waiting for was the chance to do it. I wasn't going to stay captured. I would have died getting away. It was humiliating to be captured.

Even on the line, we'd talk about creative ways to go AWOL—never to avoid fighting when we were needed, but for brief respites and fun. There were some times between fights when I would drink to try to block out the memories. I found that this didn't really help much because the hangover only added to my other woes that hadn't changed. Now I find when I get anxious, it helps if I find something to do that tires me out in a comfortable way.

SPIRITUAL AND PHILOSOPHICAL STRENGTHS

God

You always had a prayer on your lips. That was natural. At times I could almost feel God's presence, as if He were sitting beside me. I was a believer in someone greater than us and felt that I knew God in my own way. Even today I believe, although on Anzio I thought that God went on a coffee break. When I was a child, we went to church and Sunday school, but not too much. We said the Lord's prayer every morning before school started. I always believed in God. It gives you comfort. When it's over, you thank God that you made it. The war actually strengthened my belief. I say my prayers still.

Meaning & Purpose

We knew we had to win. We knew enough about what was going on in Germany. The Jews were dead meat, and we knew that the colored were next. The Germans would then dispose of everybody if they could, even Hitler's own people that he didn't like. I went through some of the prison camps around Munich. You didn't have to be a Jew to be gassed. You saw thousands stacked in the boxcars. Some of them weren't even dead yet.

I wrote my autobiography in hopes that people will consider the mindless and wasteful suffering of war and perhaps eliminate wars in the future. Greatness is achieved over the conference table, not in war. I agree with the saying, "Only God and a GI know the misery of war."

Morality

We always felt sorry for people and didn't kill them needlessly—prisoners and civilians. It was important not to harm them. But, you couldn't even trust some people to take prisoners back. I got on several people for shooting Germans with their hands up. In Africa, I stopped a French guard from beating two Arabs.

As a platoon sergeant, I was always truthful with my men. I never did like a lie and never was much on that. I had to report a soldier next to me for a self-inflicted wound. But I told the company commander that I wouldn't lie by saying that he did it on purpose, because I hadn't seen him do it.

A thief in our company didn't live long if he were caught.

Ralph wasn't getting promoted in the heavy weapons platoon, because his platoon wasn't having the casualties like the other platoons. At Anzio, the company commander asked if I could be impartial if he came into my platoon. I told him that I figured everyone in the outfit was my brother. So I became his boss. When my brother was complaining, I realized that I had been picking on him so as not to appear to be favoring him. I was trying to be fair.

I worry about killing people. You know down deep that mistakes were made. A lieutenant was on the verge of a nervous breakdown. He was sending one man at a time into a clearing to make an attack. Three guys got killed before I got to him. I said, "You aren't going to send my men to get killed." I went back and told the company commander and I never did see that lieutenant again. Instead we flanked and attacked all together and lost no more men.

Love

You can't explain the bond that forms between comrades in arms. I had a lot of respect for my men. I cared for my men. As a private, I was inseparable from my friends. Returning to my unit after being wounded was like returning home—the only one I had at the time. I had tears in my eyes when I said goodbye to them at the end of the war. You needed your friends before, during, and after the battle. I'm sure the friends that I made in the hospital helped in my rehabilitation.

Optimism

I was optimistic to a certain extent. There were times I thought that we couldn't go further, but we knew we'd win eventually.

Humor

We had a lot of humor in our outfit. You had to think of something funny to say. We'd laugh at letters we'd get. One guy sent his girlfriend a Purple Heart. She wrote back and told him to get one for her mother. One guy's brother worked in the shipyards. He said he wished the war would last long enough for him to pay for an automobile. We had a Jewish lieutenant in our outfit, a good guy. We'd ask him who held the world speed record—a Jew going through Berlin on a bicycle.

Long View of Suffering

In my early years in the Army, I'd been a screw-up, a yardbird. I didn't want the responsibility of leadership. But in Italy, we had so many casualties that I had to take over. In fact, I was threatened with a court martial for shirking from duty if I didn't. I'm grateful for the opportunity that I had to become a leader. I determined to become a good one and gained an appreciation for good leadership. I knew I was a good soldier, and wanted to be a good man. I came to treasure my stripes and felt that I had earned them.

The fact is that combat helped we with my VA work, to realize what the soldiers were up against. I saw some of my best friends succumb to battle fatigue, and understood that it could happen to anybody. I could tell if a man was a goldbrick or genuinely stressed. I got in trouble for helping them. I don't think a man should stay on the line more than a year.

My Congressional medal also shaped my life. It gave me a sense acceptance and recognition for being the fighting man I had tried to be, and helped me to feel a greater sense of value inwardly.

Maintaining Balanced Living

For exercise, I like hunting, fishing, and gardening. On my 40 acres, you name it and I grow it. I walk and mow the lawn. I get seven or eight hours of sleep regularly, from 10:00 p.m. to 5:00 or 6:00 a.m. I eat regular meals. I don't believe in junk food. I never smoked. I gave up alcohol years ago.

For recreation, I enjoy lots of cards, parties, hunting in the winter, and fishing in a nearby lake. I lecture at schools. I used to go to Disabled Veterans meetings, but that has tapered off since my wife got sick.

Advice to Younger Generations

Take care of your body and lead a good clean life. Stay away from drugs and smoking. Don't overdo anything.

Don't hold yourself above others. Don't think you're better than people who had less opportunity. See yourselves as equals. I saw a number of leaders who didn't understand this, who created resentment.

No matter how low you get, you can usually come out of it.

Russell Dunham, wearing his Medal of Honor,
at Arlington Cemetery.

Chapter 16

Roy A. Freitag
Tank Commander

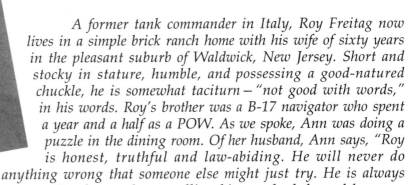

A former tank commander in Italy, Roy Freitag now lives in a simple brick ranch home with his wife of sixty years in the pleasant suburb of Waldwick, New Jersey. Short and stocky in stature, humble, and possessing a good-natured chuckle, he is somewhat taciturn—"not good with words," in his words. Roy's brother was a B-17 navigator who spent a year and a half as a POW. As we spoke, Ann was doing a puzzle in the dining room. Of her husband, Ann says, "Roy is honest, truthful and law-abiding. He will never do anything wrong that someone else might just try. He is always there to help someone. People are always calling him up for help and he never refuses. He'd do anything for you. He is very calm under pressure. Nothing seems to rattle him. He seems to accept problems and goes on."

I was born in Rumson, New Jersey, the older of two boys, in 1918. We moved to the Bronx soon after, where I lived through high school. I was a very active youth, doing something almost every night. Most of my family's activity was around the (Episcopal) church—Boy Scouts, Sea Scouts, choir, plays. Church leaders took us ice skating. The men's club of the church had a bowling league. I set pins for them. In return they let us bowl when they weren't busy. We played stickball in the streets and got chased by the cops because we weren't supposed to play there.

My family was warm and quiet. Mother kept house, and Father worked in the grocery business. He was never out of work. Every Saturday night he came home with a package of food from the store. So we never hurt for food during the Depression. Both were involved and active in the church. At that time you couldn't be grounded because kids didn't have cars. I never remember harsh restrictions.

After high school I came to Montclair, New Jersey, to help in my uncle's garage. I met Ann through my friends there in 1937. I played baseball every Sunday morning. Ann's brother, Bill Johnson, started a semi-pro league. Later he starred as a third baseman for the Yankees. I also played in a touch football league.

In October, 1940, I signed up for the draft in the Bronx, and went into the Army in November, training at Ft. Dix, New Jersey, with the 44th Infantry Division. I was returning from maneuvers when Pearl Harbor was hit. After going down to Louisiana, then to Ft. Lewis, Washington, for coastal security, I went to Ft. Knox, Kentucky, for Armor Officers Candidate School. Three of us from the division were sent there. I was actually trained as a maintenance officer because I had mechanical ability from working in my uncle's garage. I was commissioned July 4, 1942, and Ann and I married July 8, 1942. After training at Ft. Benning, Georgia, with the 10th Armored Division, we shipped overseas in 1943 as replacements to Africa a few days after the war there had ended. I was then assigned to the 752 Tank Battalion. The battalion was attached to different divisions as we worked our way up the western side of Italy, under Fifth Army control.

I was made commander of A Company as a 2nd lieutenant when the company commander and executive officer were injured or wounded. My battalion was with the first troops who rolled into Rome on June 4, 1944—two days before D-Day, which took all the headlines. I spent two months in a

133

hospital, after being wounded by artillery fire in Cecina, Italy (near Livorno). The Germans had blown up the bridge in front of us and I had gotten out of the tank to talk to an infantry officer. My mother got the card from me, saying that I was wounded. The next week she learned that my brother was a prisoner. My unit received a presidential citation for 315 consecutive days on the line without relief. We wound up just below the Brenner Pass, on the Italian side, when the treaty was signed in May of 1945. Ann and I had a late honeymoon after the war. We took the car and drove to Philadelphia, Washington, and Florida.

I retired from the Army in 1961, and then worked for the post office for 20 years. I have two boys and a girl. The boys both served during the Vietnam era. One was wounded three times and was awarded two Bronze Stars. My daughter is a talented artist *[her beautiful paintings hang in the living room]*.

PTSD Symptoms?

I did not have any PTSD symptoms that I can think of. The only thing that kept on my mind was the death of my lieutenant, which I'll explain later.

What Helped You Cope?

Boy Scout training helped me in my infantry training and living outdoors. Otherwise, there wasn't much about city life that especially prepared me for war.

CALM UNDER PRESSURE

I thought I stayed calm under pressure. I don't know how, I just did. I took things as they came. I probably learned that at home from my parents. Mother was an old Connecticut Yankee, who said, "It won't help any to get mad. Straighten out and move on." She would do everything she could for you, but wouldn't let us go too far. Dad was calm too. Practically every Sunday we took the subway to Central Park to watch parades or the miniature sailboats in the pond. It was very peaceful. Experiences like that helped me be calm. Maybe being an officer, we were trained to be calm, but mostly I was that way before the war.

My father's side was German. I had no animosity toward the Germans. I always felt that they were doing their job, as we did. It was the Nazi regime, not the Germans, that was causing the problems. I always felt that the people would probably have been shot if they didn't join the army.

RATIONAL THOUGHT PROCESSES

We didn't give much thought of what could happen then. Whatever came up came up. We didn't worry about it. If you worried about it, it would be worse for you. I think I just took it as it came along.

People make mistakes. One of our tanks was blown up by friendly rocket fire. When I was at battalion headquarters, a headquarters half-track was parked under a tree, contrary to our training. A shell burst hit the tree and killed two of the guys. I don't remember going off the handle when others made mistakes, but I'd try to minimize them. For example, I once commanded a lot of troops who were in a headquarters company because they couldn't do anything else. I threw the book at the first offender, as an example to let them know who was the boss. It worked. It seemed to me that word got out that you couldn't fool around without paying a penalty. I did not do it with meanness, just to straighten the others out. If I made mistakes, I'd get mad at myself. Then I'd drop it and start all over again, and try to get it right the next time.

Ann adds: "It didn't matter when the kids made mistakes. He is very forgiving. He was also very strict. When he said something, he meant it. Once, at the pool, one of our sons was banned for a day for running. When he made the mistake of telling us about it, Roy banned him for several weeks."

SOCIAL SUPPORT

My wife and I wrote once a week at least. I also got many letters from my mother, and my wife's aunt was always sending care packages. It was important to let us know they were still thinking about us.

In a unit of about 120 men, you have to get along with everybody. You're all in the same boat. I had two or three close friends that were important. When I was in the hospital, I ran into a good buddy from Ft. Benning. We were both wounded and helped each other pass the time. We kept up with each other for years. We have a whole book of people we keep up with from the service.

My wife and I don't argue. If we do, it's over quickly. Life is too short and over too soon.

COMFORTABLE WITH EMOTIONS

I think I was comfortable with emotions. I don't remember being extra afraid. I imagine I would have been more afraid if the circumstances had been more difficult. Unlike Vietnam, we generally knew where the enemy was.

SELF-ESTEEM

(Laughing), I never gave it a thought. I just did my job as best as I could. While serving at Ft Lewis on coastal security, I saw guys put their names in for Officer Candidate School. I figured I could do as well as they did, and did the same. I didn't doubt myself, even though having only a high school education limited my promotions.

ACTIVE, CREATIVE COPING

I was actually trained for the infantry and as a maintenance officer, with no field training with tanks. I just tried to be flexible and pick up knowledge as I went. With its narrow roads and mountains, Italy wasn't tank country. As Patton used to say, "Grab 'em by the nose and kick 'em in the ass." In other words, you'd normally go for a frontal attack and bring your tanks around the side. You couldn't always do that in Italy, but you learned to adapt. There were lots of opportunities to train as a leader. I thought I could perform as well as the next guy.

Wherever I've gone, I seem to get jobs of responsibility. If you're going to join, you might as well get involved—even though the Army says, "don't volunteer." If you get into something, like the VFW or American Legion, do something to make it go. Don't just sit there and do nothing. I wouldn't join an organization unless I could participate.

SPIRITUAL AND PHILOSOPHICAL STRENGTHS

God

As kids, we went to church every Sunday, sometimes twice. I was an acolyte, and later sang in the choir. In the war I carried a little Bible that my wife gave me and read it in the evenings. It made me feel more at ease. I believe He is there and will help. He's been loving so far. After all *(with a smile)*, we're still here at 83.

Meaning & Purpose

We were there to put a stop to the ravaging of the Germans and get things back to normal. We had a job to do and did it as best as we could. I also wanted to return to my wife and have a family and see my kids grow and be happy.

Morality

We learned as youth never to deliberately hurt anyone. In the war we never hurt civilians. To me, morality means being honest with people; don't do what you shouldn't do. The Scouts and Church helped teach me that. When we rolled into towns, there could have been lots of opportunities for infidelity. I had only been married six months when I went overseas. I kept myself clean.

Love

In the Army we were taught not to get too close to others, because something might happen to them. You show your love by helping people, doing what you can. I gave my monthly officer's liquor ration to my platoon sergeant to pass out to the men. In the States, I gave my passes to people who lived closer to their families than I.

Optimism

In Italy we wanted to keep going so as to get the war over with. I still have hope. I hope to wake up in the morning. If something is upsetting, I think: "Wait until tomorrow. It will probably straighten out by then."

Humor

(*Laughing*), Humor is good for the soul. We'd pull tricks on people to laugh. I like to laugh and hear a joke.

Ann opines: "He has a quiet humor, and says funny little things now and then, like his comment about hoping to wake up."

Long View of Suffering

After Rome, my lieutenant was killed by anti-tank fire in a narrow bend in the road when I sent his platoon forward. I thought if I had gone ahead instead of him he would have lived. But I reasoned that I had done the right thing, as doctrine directed, by staying in the middle of the column to maintain control of the company. I had deployed him correctly, as far as I thought. You accept that these things happen. Then I just tried to take my mind off it. The war made me appreciate living and what I had.

Maintaining Balanced Living

I was always very active. During the war, athletics helped us keep close as a unit. After the war, I played softball, bowled, and played golf. I coached little league and took the kids to Boys Scout camp. Ann and I have participated in cruises and time-share vacations in the summer. We go to a luncheon theatre. I actually organize it and sign people up. I am very involved in the VFW and American Legion. I am out all of the time.

Our eating is simple and nutritious, low fat, balanced, with lots of fruit and vegetables. Nothing fancy.

I had been a light smoker, but the doctor told me to cut back in 1991. I gave it up cold turkey. I drink moderately, perhaps two to three drinks a week.

Throughout my life, I've gotten seven or eight hours of sleep. I'd usually be in bed by 11:00 p.m.

Advice to Younger Generations

All should get military training. It would make people much better citizens, realizing what the country needs. A two-year draft wouldn't hurt and would give people much discipline.

If you have problems, remember the experiences you've had and know you can get through it.

Take care of your comrades.

Roy and Ann, July 8, 1942

Infantry training, Ft. Dix, NJ

At home in Waldwick, NJ

Chapter 17

Colonel Douglas Clark Dillard
Battle of the Bulge

COL Dillard greeted me at the front door of a beautiful, tree-shaded white house, trimmed with red brick and green shutters. He possesses a calm sense of quiet authority. At about 6', he is strong and fit in appearance. He speaks with a pleasant Southern drawl and has an easy laugh. He and his wife, Virginia, raised four daughters. There are swings on his lawn for his grandchildren. Dillard's parachute battalion played a key role in the Battle of the Bulge.

The Battle of the Bulge was the largest, bloodiest land battle for U.S. forces in WWII. The German offensive through the Ardennes began in December 1944. On January 3, 1945, the 551st Parachute Infantry Battalion (The Lost Battalion) spearheaded the 82nd Airborne Division's counterattack in the northern sector of the Bulge. The battalion's mission was to capture the bridge at the town of Rochelinval, the last avenue of escape for the Germans. Four-fifths of the more than 800 men of the battalion were wounded or died. Company A lost 40% of its men in the first two days of battle, which included a rare bayonet charge. On January 8, 1945, Hitler ordered the first pullback from the Bulge. The 551st had accounted for 700 Germans killed or captured and achieved its objectives against punishing artillery, mortar, and machine gun fire, unfavorable terrain, and a numerically superior enemy. On February 23, 2001, the battalion received the Presidential Unit Citation, the highest honor that can be given to an Army unit.

Among the dead was the battalion's inspirational commander, LTC Wood Guice Joerg, West Point, Class of 1937. He had moved through intense enemy fire to extricate his troops from an enemy trap and prevent other troops from moving into the trap. During this action, he was fatally wounded. In his pocket was found this prayer, signed by him:

"Oh God, Commander of all men, we stand before Thee asking Thy help in the execution of the many tasks which confront us. Give us strength, courage, daring, intelligence and devotion to duty, so that we may from day to day perfect ourselves as fighting men – so that some day, in some foreign land – we may, by our fighting ability, bring glory to ourselves, our country and to Thee.

And, Oh God, if the price we must pay for eternal freedom of man be great, give us strength so that we will not hesitate to sacrifice ourselves for a cause so sacred. All of this we ask in Thy name. Amen."

Because of its losses, the battalion was inactivated on January 27, 1945, and the survivors integrated into other units of the 82nd Airborne Division. Hence the term, Lost Battalion.

Following WWII, Dillard remained in the Army, and served with distinction in the Vietnam and Korean conflicts.

I was born in Atlanta Georgia on September 14, 1925. My parents separated when I was a little older than a toddler, at three or four years of age. I was raised in the home of my grandparents. The Depression times were very trying. My grandparents lost their land, a big farm, and had to move into town and start all over again. Grandmother was a very caring lady, who had three sons still living at home, along with my mother. Grandfather paid an awful lot of attention to me. He ran a tire store. More people, then, bought retreads than new tires. He gave me the run of the store, and turned me into a super salesman, which helped me develop a sense of initiative and independence.

In the middle of high school, mother had remarried, a sergeant in the 62nd Signal Battalion, the only signal battalion in the peacetime Army when the war broke out. It deployed to North Africa.

I was intrigued by the Army. At 16, I pressured my mother to let me enlist in the Army. In 1942, I went to basic training at Camp Wolters, Texas. By the time I was 17 I'd already had three months in the Army. While there, I saw posters of a soldier in a parachute descending, with Uncle Sam saying (sort of like "I want you"), "Pounce like a falcon onto the prey." Parachuting was very new on the American military scene. In the past, the cavalry had been the elite unit, and suddenly it was the paratroopers. Hundreds volunteered for parachute school. Rigorous screening and conditioning tested one's physical and mental agility and determination.

In 1943 I met Virginia, my future wife, at the annual carnival at Lakewood Park in Atlanta. I visited her on weekend passes from Camp Mackall, North Carolina, and corresponded with her for three years before marrying her in 1946.

I left for Europe in May of 1944, and jumped into southern France in August of 1944, with the 551st, liberating the city of Draguinan. We fought along the coast up to the Italian border. My unit was the only unit to capture a German general in his headquarters. I have his pistol. So we were in action for almost 100 days before the Bulge. We moved north, reaching the Bulge in late December and being attached to the 82nd Airborne Division. General Gavin had us infiltrate enemy lines on December 27 to disrupt the Germans, gather intelligence, and let the Germans know that we weren't just going to be defensive. That night we killed 100 Germans and destroyed a captured tank destroyer and a company command post.

On January 3, 1945, the whole division started a massive counteroffensive to push the Germans back across the Salm River. We started with about 800 men and lost more than 500 in three days, either killed, wounded, or disabled due to weather conditions, because the snow was waist deep and it was freezing cold. And the German artillery was just awful— constantly shelling us.

On January 3, we were going across an open field. I could see hundreds of Germans digging in and two tanks. When we were in the middle of the field, they opened up. We had a lot of casualties before we could get out of that area. That night Dick (Lt. Richard Durkee) got his platoon out on the right and flanked the German positions. This caused the Germans to pull back. Because of casualties, Dick, who was the senior surviving officer, reorganized the company into two platoons, and I joined his platoon. On January 4, Dick did not want to risk firing on the other platoon who were enveloping the Germans, so he ordered, "Fix bayonets and attack." We charged and surprised the German machine gun positions who were preoccupied with the envelopment, killing perhaps a dozen.

On January 7, we had about 300 effective troops left to attack Rochelinval, Belgium. By noon only 98 were combat effective. Durkee's platoon was annihilated in that attack on Rochelinval. But about 400 Germans surrendered to us. My feet were totally frozen. I was evacuated to a hospital for six weeks. After a few days, General Gavin and General Ridgeway came down and got the unit together and announced that the unit was deactivated and all of us were reassigned to other units in the 82nd. So that was the end of our battalion and I think that was tougher to take than being shot at.

In September, 1945, I signed an extension and was promoted to first sergeant in a rifle company on my 20th birthday, probably one of the youngest first sergeants during that period. I liked the Army and stayed on. Upon rejoining the 82nd in 1947 as first sergeant in the 504th Parachute Regiment, I received a direct appointment as warrant officer. I was reassigned to the 82nd Division Headquarters, serving with LTC William Westmoreland, who was Chief of Staff of the 82nd Airborne Division.

When the Korean War broke out in 1950, I received a direct appointment as a 2nd Lieutenant in the infantry reserves. I submitted a request to be called to active duty. In Korea, I joined a unit that was the forerunner of today's Special Forces. I lead a clandestine airdrop team that dropped one to three Chinese or Korean agents behind enemy lines to collect intelligence. I also led the Tactical Liaison Force of the 1st Marine Division, a team that passed through enemy lines on the ground to gather intelligence. In addition to myself, the team usually consisted of an American sergeant, and one to three Chinese or Koreans agents. These agents dressed either as civilians or as members of the North Korean or Chinese armies.

After the Korean War, I trained for intelligence and counter intelligence activities, which included the study of the Czech language. I arrived in Germany in 1957 as the Hungarian uprising was settling down, and monitored the Eastern Block for three years.

Following other assignments in intelligence, I returned to Ft. Bragg to help prepare intelligence units for Vietnam, and set up a program to train Special Forces intelligence personnel for duties there. I returned to Vietnam in 1968, working under the CIA in the Mekong Delta and serving as staff coordinator for over 1800 province reconnaissance unit personnel (Chinese we could trust or defecting Viet Cong). In 1969, I was assigned as Director of Security for the Joint Chiefs of Staff in the Pentagon. Subsequent assignments included Assistant Deputy Director for Human Intelligence Operations for the Defense Intelligence Agency, which meant I was the coordinator for intelligence operations worldwide with CIA and all the services.

Retiring from the service in 1977, I worked for 21 years in contract work and later real estate management. I presently serve on various military organizations, including the 551st Association, and other organizations dedicated to recognizing Korean and Chinese partisans who served the U.S. Today I am the keeper of the colors for the 551st [which stand in his living room].

PTSD Symptoms?

Things of that sort didn't affect me. I had no nightmares, no dreams, no depression, or anything of that sort. Neither did my close buddies. Before the bayonet attack, I only saw perhaps three or four people freeze psychologically or lose control and scream. Some things bothered me momentarily, and have left lasting impressions, however. For example, the company commander had directed me to move some of our dead who had been killed that night off the hill. I remember Yellow Robe, an American Indian in our unit, who was nearly cut in half by machine gun fire, and another person whose head was nearly blown off by a shell.

In Vietnam, what got under my skin the most was to see six-foot long body bags on the airstrip. It never gets any easier, but for some reason I think I may have developed some type of a mental defense that keeps it from getting to me. I made up my mind that I would do my dead level best to protect our troops by training the indigenous soldiers to defend their country well—not to fight their battles for them. It's a mistake to think our troops can do it all. If the indigenous soldiers won't defend their own country, we're wasting our time over there.

What Helped You Cope?

From the tough conditions of the Depression, you absorbed strength; it probably had a grounding effect. We were in a survival environment. My mother and grandfather worked really hard to provide. You had to hang on and make your own way as best you could. This might have had an effect on me, seeing my family not give up.

That physical rigor in my early years and in the Army has helped me over the years in having good health. As a youth I enjoyed and actively participated in the high jump, broad jump, long-distance running, and swimming. On weekends, we went on family outings to the Chattahoochee River, where we played games and swam. Before joining the Army, I was part of an ROTC drill company. We drilled every day—calisthenics and close order drill. You had to conform if you were going to be competitive, which lead early on to an acceptance of regimentation and listening to instructions in order to carry them out in the best manner possible.

CALM UNDER PRESSURE

When you are on the offensive, you are just trying to cause losses on the other side to facilitate your actions, whether you are patrolling or advancing. Then, in situations like the Bulge, you had times where there was a sense of rage because of what had happened to your buddies, and that emerged during the bayonet charge, to pay back for all the carnage. However, this was only an occasional feeling. From what I've seen from three wars, the American soldier does not have a proclivity to want to kill people. It's just not our way. When we made the charge across the fields, we captured several Germans, but had no thought of killing them once captured. Our objective was to capture the next objective. If you could do so without casualties, great; but we did not have a sense of constant revenge. Regarding the Germans who were killed, there was a natural hesitancy to admit killing. You certainly didn't want to brag about it.

We were imbued with the spirit that we could do anything. The pressure never seemed to bother me. I was okay after Korea and Vietnam as well.

By nature, I've always been able to pretty much control my emotions. This is not to say that at times I've not been infuriated, but I never lost control of my emotions or acted without considering ramifications. I never had the sense that I was on the edge of doing something wrong.

Watching people die, many veterans voiced the feeling that if you thought that you'd be next one to get killed, you'd be ineffective. So we thought, "It's not me, it's the other guy that's going to get hit, and I need to keep on moving forward and try to accomplish the mission. I simply have to do this regardless." If it's that gun that is causing casualties, you focus on getting it, come hell or high water. I think for every Medal of Honor winner, there are probably a dozen in the wings that just were never recognized.

Even today, you might have fears of litigation, but you make a balanced judgement and consider the ramifications of whatever decision you make. In combat, there's the probability that you are going to be wounded or killed or separated from your unit. But you focus on the task and go ahead. For me it was kind of a natural thing to do. I was given responsibility. I accepted it and was willing to carry it out.

We had a respect for the German soldiers' experience and professionalism. We regarded them as very good soldiers. They had superb training and good equipment. The SS was a different story. You really wanted to go after them. Our propaganda had highlighted their atrocities in Russia, and we had heard about some of the activities against some of our units who had fought them.

RATIONAL THOUGHT PROCESSES

I found it personally very upsetting when I fell short. I'd think that I didn't try hard enough, or prepare myself well enough. Maybe I made the wrong decision that contributed to less than success or failure to accomplish something. But I would then try my best and not dwell on what might have been.

If another's mistake had something to do with character or integrity—one should never lie or steal in the military— I had no patience for that. If the individual just absolutely made a mistake from lack of training or professional knowledge or just made a dumb decision, then I had a bit of compassion for him. As president of a special court martial board in the Vietnam Delta, I had the authority to sentence people to up to six months confinement, reduce them in grade, and fine them. A sergeant was brought in from one of these districts, where we had five-man teams out in the rural areas in the Delta, essentially fighting the war by themselves for months. He had gotten drunk on New Years day and fired his rifle recklessly in a village. The soldier had a good combat record. He admitted his mistake and said he had too much to drink and just lost control of his senses and recklessly fired that weapon. We found him guilty but I had compassion. I considered the environment and conditions and tried to put myself in his position. We found him guilty, reprimanded him sternly and reminded him that he was fortunate that no one was injured, and only fined him a month's pay. I have never been one who is hung up on blaming, punishing, or being mean, if one takes responsibility.

SOCIAL SUPPORT

In your unit, it was important to be a cohesive unit and have a common mission. We had the feeling that our unit could do it better than yours. I felt very close to the people in my unit. Today it's even closer. It was sort of like a family. I was the youngest one in the battalion. A lot of people wanted to protect me and see that I was okay. We developed very strong friendships. You felt you could rely on any one to help you with anything and they could rely on you. Our young 29-year-old battalion commander, LTC Wood Joerg, was a charismatic figure. He was briefly replaced by an older commander that treated us as if we were recruits—even though we were the oldest and best trained parachutists. The day LTC Joerg came back and took over the battalion, you could feel the morale surge. It was the old unit again. He created the espirit. You felt you were special with him. We each felt we were part of his family and he of ours. He did what you did. As a separate battalion, we were scroungers who didn't belong to anybody. But our commander was in our hip pocket—you could see him every day. He was on the march with us, played athletics with us, and went on jumps with us. He encouraged us to straighten up and be proud.

My family has always been supportive and a priority. During WWII, my step-father was already in Africa. He'd write periodically. I was proud he was overseas. When being considered for promotion to general, I was told that if I were to make certain moves to become better known, I'd have a better chance of promotion. I had just settled my family and the idea of packing them up and moving again just for my possible promotion would not do. I said, "My record stands for itself." So I'm at peace with that decision. I have no sour grapes and don't dwell on what could have been. Ironically, when I was later chief of the Military Intelligence Branch, I helped my contemporary expunge his record of an apparently unfair report that would have damaged his chances for promotion. As it happened, the next year our two files were the only two that went to the general officer board. He received the promotion that I might otherwise have received. Again, if one dwells on what could have been, he'll have a miserable life.

During the Vietnam War, my family was 1000% supportive, as contrasted to the media and certain elements of society. When I came home, we bought this house. My daughter was in grammar school. She came home one day and said, "My teacher told me that all the GIs in Vietnam were murderers." I said, "Well, do you think I'm a murderer, I just came back from Vietnam?" She said, "Well, no, Daddy." "Well why don't you tell your teacher that?" She feared she'd get in trouble. That's the only time that that kind of thing bothered me, but it wasn't coming from family. It was the general attitude of the populace that was being portrayed in the media.

COMFORTABLE WITH EMOTIONS

I think I'm comfortable with my emotions. Afraid sometimes? Oh sure. We'd express it in GI ways, like saying, "Man, we're going to get clobbered going out in this field." (You could see the Germans digging in with tanks). It was like saying, "Some of us are not going to make it," but you didn't talk about it in those terms. Or we'd say, "I'd rather get shot than step on a German mine." That was our way of letting out the apprehension.

When LTC Joerg was killed, we really felt we'd lost our best friend. It upset me. We'd been together three years. We talked about it, and that helped us grieve. We also talked about Yellow Robe's body. Maybe we could have saved him. The medics assured us that we couldn't. Even today, when the unit gets together, we still get choked up over the loss of them.

SELF-ESTEEM

We all felt that every man in our unit felt totally competent to carry out the unit's mission. The unit developed a character of its own— a bunch of renegades in a separate, elite unit. LTC Joerg imbued individual initiative. Every Thursday, we broke down into small training units and you could learn anything you were interested in: flying small aircraft, handling a small Higgins landing craft, operating locomotives, communications. We had people in our unit who could do practically anything you could think of. This is the concept of the Special Forces today. I think this is what helped build my self-esteem and confidence.

ACTIVE, CREATIVE COPING

As I developed confidence in my ability to absorb training, that overcame my hesitancy to be proactive. I've always wanted to be innovative in whatever I do. If there are any injustices that exist, then I want to clear that up. In my development, I patterned my conduct after LTC. Joerg. I tried to visualize what he would do, because he made a lasting impression on me. I tried to turn bad things around by seizing the initiative.

I could accept what I couldn't control. When a young corporal, I led a detail to clean up the service club. A fellow who was older by 10 to 12 years wouldn't obey me. I just said, "You're dismissed, report to the first sergeant. " I stayed calm knowing he'd get his comeuppance eventually if he did that again. It was no big deal. I tried to control it by getting that irritant out of the group.

SPIRITUAL AND PHILOSOPHICAL STRENGTHS

God

My wife and I were extremely active in the church in the States (I was raised to be a churchgoer and went to summer camp on a farm every year), and overseas we frequented the military chapels. I am a strong believer. I perceive God as kind and loving. Sometimes when struggling with why God would permit physical suffering, I thought that the explanation is that God is interested in your soul. What people do to your body isn't controlled, but your spirit is of great concern to God. There is a spiritual importance to each person that is bigger than the trials we go through here. We believe in the kindness of the Lord. Over three different wars, faith surfaced. As I grew older, it grew stronger. As a youth going into the Army, I was on a learning curve that tested my character. In the 35 years that I was on active duty I've been tempted and seen a lot of my buddies go down the tubes by succumbing to those temptations.

Meaning & Purpose

We had the big picture before WWII. It was a just cause. The newsreels at theaters showed us what was happening in the war effort. Scenes of battles made us angry — threats to England and our country. The Japanese had attacked Pearl Harbor. We had news of the Bataan death march. At that point in time, I think we were more angry at the Japanese than the Germans. However, once deployed, our focus was on the immediate picture — the next hill, the next village, survival, and the survival of our buddies.

Afterward, (May 1945) when we moved into Frankfurt I saw the prisoners of the concentration camp for the first time. That's when what we had accomplished came to the forefront. General Gavin had the mayor turn out every citizen of the local town of Wöbbelin to dig graves and bury the prisoners from Ludwigslust concentration camp.

Morality

The military really shaped my outlook. I detest lying and stealing. Any other moral traits become questionable if one is untrustworthy. Eventually, people who are morally corrupt have a premature ending of their career. It eventually catches up to them. I have *never* wanted to do anything that would embarrass my family or the service that I spent the better part of my life in. If people were corrupt, I would try to move them out of my command.

In WWII, all in all, our group was fairly clean morally. After we formed our association, we got to know the wives and it reinforced my respect for the individual, because during the time that I knew him I didn't see anything that would reflect poorly on his character. On the other hand, there were others who were going to do what they wanted to do, and didn't worry about the ramifications, as long as they weren't caught. I tended to gravitate to groups with good character. You formed your affinities early. You kept yourself separate from activities you didn't approve of.

Optimism

In the Depression era, you had to be an optimist. Every day was a struggle. You had to have hope of improvement or you began to get into bad things. You might think, "Nothing is going to get better, so what the hell."

Humor

This was extremely important. I developed a feeling for it over the years. I always try to inject it, to weave it into talks to establish rapport. I appreciated GI humor, and found it funny that one guy was putting cans of beer into his pack when getting ready to make a jump into France. I thought that was typical GI to prepare for the immediate future with a libation after he got on the ground.

We ribbed each other often. Once, we were resting in a French village. I was sitting in a barber chair with the hair on one side of my head cut short when I saw my unit marching by the window. So I dashed out of the chair and joined my unit, and got ribbed for a week about my haircut until I could get another. Something always came up. I lost half a trouser leg of my jump suit in climbing one of the hills, and as we walked along through the French villages, people pointed at my leg and laughed about it, and we had to put camouflaged paint on it. We must have looked like a bunch of clowns to the villagers. And, of course, all my buddies were ribbing me. I could hardly wait to buy another pair of pants to put on. Little humorous things took the edge off. As we walked through the French towns, people had bottles of wine. One guy would uncork a bottle and hand it to you. There would be an interval of two or three GIs before he had the next bottle uncorked. So, as soon as guys saw this, they'd try to pace themselves so that they'd arrive by the time he'd uncorked a bottle.

Long View of Suffering

Between the 3rd and 7th of January, 1945, the elements were at their worst and there were mounting casualties in front of our eyes, people you'd been with for three years. The good that came out of this was the comraderie and elan of the unit to keep going, the individual acts of courage and heroism. They met the test and plunged forward. The fraternity that developed among the survivors was as close as one can be without being blood relatives. I also matured fast in that situation. I learned to accept responsibility and do whatever I could do to avoid the loss of the men in my unit. An ingrained sense of responsibility came out of this situation, and remained with me throughout my career. As I mentioned before, adversity helped me develop character and faith.

Maintaining Balanced Living

Physical activity with the unit was extremely important. Besides the exercise that was a part of the daily routine in the airborne infantry, we also had organized sports—companies competing in softball, baseball, or volleyball. We didn't have cars so we naturally made our own recreation on the post when we were off duty. Stateside and overseas, horseshoes would appear to occupy our time or someone would find a baseball and bat.

Except when I was in the field, my wife was very good about insuring that we had balanced meals. I attribute the physical activity in the Army and the wholesome meals over a lifetime to my good health. I've tried to be moderate in my consumption. I'm basically a meat and potato guy. In the summer, there was a much greater amount of fresh vegetables. Or we had canned vegetables when they were not available.

Over the course of my adult life, I have been a regular swimmer, and still swim today regularly. I've walked a mile or two a day. I still walk up stairs whenever I can. Last year I made the 18-mile march through the Ardennes with the 325th Glider Infantry Regiment. The year before, I completed a 13-mile march with the 504th Parachute Regiment and my battalion, the 551st. I've been a regular sleeper. We developed a habit of retiring at 11:30 p.m. and arising at 6:00 a.m. almost religiously over the years.

I've never been a regular smoker or drinker, only drinking occasionally socially. I've seen some really bad cases of my military friends who have gone down the tubes from drinking. I had a young captain from a prominent family in Boston who was loaded on duty. For his good, I reported it, but nothing was done regarding his condition after he was removed from my unit. He ended up in the hospital with cirrhosis of the liver. He was on IV tubes, ripped them out, and bled to death. I was infuriated that his superior did not follow up on my report and make sure that his problem was known and treated.

For recreation, my wife and I *really* like to travel. I paid for her to travel with me on business. We often went together to Europe, Korea, and stateside locations for military commemorative events. I am an avid reader and like to keep up on politics—my graduate degree is in international affairs. I am writing a book on clandestine airborne special military operations in Korea. In researching the book, I found a Ranger who deserved an award, but never received it, and I'm working to gain that posthumously. I like a good movie on television or in the theatres. My wife and I have enjoyed cultural events. But she's in pain now with her back and I don't want to subject her to discomfort if she doesn't enjoy it. She would encourage me to go, but she doesn't need to go just for me.

Advice to Younger Generations

One must decide early on to accept the regimentation that goes along with certain chosen professions. If you're getting poor leadership that borders on immorality or illegality, have the courage to decide between staying in the activity or taking a stand to clear it up, because people's lives are endangered, particularly in professions such as the military. Have strong enough character to stand up. Don't succumb to the illegality or immorality you observe. Once you begin to accept corrupt behavior, the more likely you'll become a part of it. Taking a stand may even risk your career. So you really have to have strong convictions.

Doug and Virginia, 1946

Doug and Virginia Dillard

Chapter 18

Robert R. Vanover
Infantryman on the Western Front

A fit 5'7", Robert Vanover fought in three major campaigns on the western front. He lives in an immaculate home with a well-groomed garden in the town of Manassas, Virginia, with his wife Joeclyn, to whom he has been married since 1948. He has a most pleasant smiling face and a twinkle in his eye as he speaks. Joeclyn says, "He's never met a stranger—he can talk to anyone and always clicks with people. If someone in a crowd isn't popular, he'll pick them out and make them feel good. He is very honest. He can talk to people about problems and give direct advice, but no one ever gets mad at him. He's never hurt anyone's feelings."

I was born in 1926 in the West Virginia mining town of Lorado, and was raised in a religious family of eleven children. Two girls died in infancy, and one of the nine boys died as a child. I played football in high school and managed the movie theatre from age sixteen to the time I enlisted.

I enlisted in January of 1944 and was called up in July. In November of 1944, I went overseas to the western front in Europe as an infantryman in the second phase of the Battle of the Bulge. I was with the 70th Division of the 7th Army. During the time I was in combat, I served under Generals Patton and Devers in three of the seventeen major campaigns on the western front. In those three campaigns 84,000 GIs were killed of the total of about 178,000 killed in the European Theater of Operations. Those campaigns were Rhineland, Ardennes-Alsace, and Central Europe. Once I was in a company of 200 men, of which only 34 survived. I re-enlisted in 1945 and was discharged in 1947. I worked as a coal miner in West Virginia until I broke my back in 1954. I then worked for the Department of Motor Vehicles as a safety inspector in Washington, DC.

I met Joeclyn when I returned from the service. Her family had moved two doors down from mine a few months before I enlisted, but we didn't meet then, even though we could see each other's yard. She was five years younger than I. When I returned from the war, she was a senior in high school. We met on a snow day, when school was cancelled. She was sleigh riding. Apparently the girls had a bet on who would be the first to date me. I asked her to the movies. Within a year we were engaged. We married in February 1, 1948. We have a daughter and a son.

PTSD Symptoms?

I had no PTSD symptoms at all.

What Helped You Cope?

My youth gave me great strength. There was never much food on the table, but we were raised healthy, and had no trauma in the family. I was strong. There wasn't anything I couldn't do with my hands. I helped Dad do things outside of the home and enjoyed working with him. We lived in the part of town known as Little Italy. Because there were so many boys, our home was the center. Everyone seemed to gather there. No one was ever turned away hungry, even though there was not much food. We had uncles and aunts all over the place, who often stayed over. Grandparents lived with us. I enjoyed sports and girls. I was happy. I hated for the dark to come. I whistled in bed until I fell asleep.

CALM UNDER PRESSURE

An infantryman presses straight ahead. I could look at dead bodies, but then focus on the job—straight ahead. I once took needed rations off a dead soldier. It was just a matter of thinking, "Thanks brother, this is the Lord's gift."

I got mad when my lieutenant was shot, but I didn't do anything stupid. Later I shed a tear over him. I never lost my cool. I ran at times in fear, as did the others, but I never lost my head.

I had to fire to kill, but never fired my rifle in anger. I liked the Germans. They seemed like nice people. Several were just kids. They had a job to do, just was we did. It was just like playing soccer. We had to knock him out of the game, but not to hurt him if possible. How could I kill someone I don't know, who could turn out to be a buddy? Yet Patton told us: "Kill or be killed." So killing was an obligation and duty. When you meet a person on the front you shoot him as an enemy. Then you near weep. I always felt bad for my sergeant, who shot a prisoner of war in anger. He told him to get out of here, then shot him as he was running away.

Once I was being a bit smart, as I was marching POWs to a holding point. A German kid looked me right in the eye and spit at my feet. I was almost proud of the little sucker for being so brave. Somehow or other, I liked the German soldier. Not Hitler, though. Today, I might get mad at you during the day, but by night I hold no grudges.

RATIONAL THOUGHT PROCESSES

When I made a mistake, I didn't get angry—I just straightened it out. I never get mad when people more experienced or qualified corrected me. It never hurt me to make a mistake in front of others.

(Smiling) Next to my wife, I am my worst critic. I never made a bunch of mistakes because I try to do what I'm told. If I do something that needs to be corrected, I work on correcting it.

I'd paddle my kids, but I wasn't hard on them and didn't get angry. I tried to teach them to do better.

SOCIAL SUPPORT

I felt a deep bond with my buddies. Once on patrol, a flare went up and eleven of my squad retreated, while the sergeant and lieutenant were pinned down. I stayed with them to protect them. I gave a wounded comrade my own first aid pack although we'd been told never to do that. I made friends with everyone I could. I was once told, "Not everyone is as friendly as you"—meaning you can't trust everyone. But I'm very friendly. I like people. I never met anyone I couldn't eventually get along with, if they acted half decent. I knew my family would stick by me, as well.

COMFORTABLE WITH EMOTIONS

How could I fuss with others getting scared, when I was scared myself. But I was never so scared that I couldn't do my job. In other words, I acknowledged my fear, but didn't let it get the best of me.

I was not afraid of getting killed. From being raised in a religious family, I just knew that if I did what I was supposed to do, God would protect me.

I didn't talk to others about emotions, except to try to encourage them. I am sure there were many with the absolute right to be traumatized. Where I drew the strength not to be traumatized, I don't know.

SELF-ESTEEM

I don't have too many problems with myself. I felt that I had worth because I felt close to the Lord. I thought He was pleased with me for the efforts that I put into His children's behalf.

ACTIVE, CREATIVE COPING

That attitude is encompassed by the infantry concept of moving straight ahead. You didn't sit around.

SPIRITUAL AND PHILOSOPHICAL STRENGTHS

God

I knew God was kind, absolutely. He loved me and would help me any way He could, if I let Him. I would pray hard. I was serious in believing you could pray for anything that was expedient.

Meaning & Purpose

I had a reason for going into the service. I and six of my brothers were in the service, including four brothers in combat. Two older brothers were on the same front. I was pleased to go to combat to do my part and to be with and protect my other brothers. Otherwise, infantrymen had no big picture. We just focused on moving straight ahead and following orders. I was satisfied to do that.

My family was my main purpose to return home. I wanted to have my own family. I just tried to get the job done. My main purpose over the course of my life has been to be in a position to help people.

Morality

When I did something wrong, I'd repent. God is quick to forgive. I always knew right from wrong and tried to do right.

Love

I was always scared, but I always volunteered to be with foxhole buddies, because I wanted to help keep them alive. For example, when my squad leader told me that I had to recruit volunteers to go on a patrol, I volunteered, knowing my buddies would be in the patrol. I did that every time I was asked. We got together and talked. You shared your love with your foxhole buddy.

I enjoy people and doing things for them. I'd give away all my furniture, if not for my wife. I want to do things not for my own pleasure, but so that others will say I'm a nice guy and know that I'm there if they need my help.

Optimism

Whatever I had to do, I knew that if I could make it through the night, things would be better the next day. Get a good night's sleep and the mind has a chance to square it away.

Long View of Suffering

The Army gave me three pretty good meals and a roof over my head. I learned many things about life, not just to like people but to be involved and to help them overcome stress and strains, calm fears, and know that tomorrow will be better.

Humor

I'd try to have fun in the foxholes. For instance, as people were socializing around a foxhole during a lull in the action, I pulled a prank. I'd made a dummy grenade by emptying it of explosive powder. A buddy started playing with it. He pulled the pin and "accidentally" dropped it. I yelled, "Grenade!"

and eleven people jumped into the foxhole. We were always saying or doing something to break the monotony, so guys wouldn't go berserk.

My humor is a kind humor. I can't say anything harmful about others. I can't hurt someone's feelings. Making a fool of myself was my way to entertain people. People draw strength from me because I'm always smiling.

Maintaining Balanced Living

Although moonshine was prevalent when I was growing up, I only drank socially during the war, but I don't drink or smoke now. I smoked as a teenager, but my children saw a film about what that does to your lungs and came home and fussed at me until I quit. That was in 1955. My health was always important. I've always exercised, and I'm still using the rowing machine and do isometrics and go for walks with my wife. We hiked the parks of Washington, D.C. I liked to help her with the flower garden. I usually slept from 10:00 p.m to 5:00 a.m.

I'm a grazer. I like to snack along with three meals. I eat cereal for breakfast, lunch at work, and for dinner Joeclyn would try a couple of new recipes each week. So there was big variety. We'd eat lots of vegetables, not a lot of meat—mostly chicken, some beef.

I enjoyed lots of reading, including sports and western books. I love crossword puzzles. I enjoyed doing repair work and woodwork around the house, and being active in my church community.

Advice to Younger Generations

Sleep on it and give it a night's rest and it will look better tomorrow. Be good and be kind to each other, including your buddies. Never fail to know that you are a child of God and that God has as much respect and love for the other person as he does for you.

Robert Vanover during WWII

Robert and Joeclyn Vanover in West Virginia, circa 1948

Robert Vanover

Chapter 19

Seymour D. Selzer
Standing Against Hitler

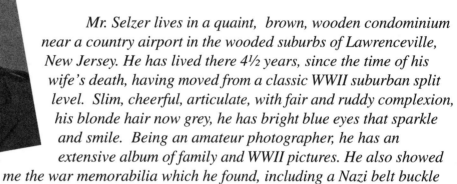

Mr. Selzer lives in a quaint, brown, wooden condominium near a country airport in the wooded suburbs of Lawrenceville, New Jersey. He has lived there 4½ years, since the time of his wife's death, having moved from a classic WWII suburban split level. Slim, cheerful, articulate, with fair and ruddy complexion, his blonde hair now grey, he has bright blue eyes that sparkle and smile. Being an amateur photographer, he has an extensive album of family and WWII pictures. He also showed me the war memorabilia which he found, including a Nazi belt buckle that said, "God is with us," a tanker's winter cap, a bayonet, and a photograph of an angelic-looking German boy dressed in a Nazi uniform.

I was born into a large and very loving family in Jersey City, by far the youngest of five children, perhaps an afterthought. My oldest sister was thirteen years older, my brother nine years older, and twin sisters seven years older. I might have gotten a little special treatment and mothering because I was the youngest. I guess we were standard middle class.

My father was an insurance salesman. In fact, his nature was so outgoing that one year he sold more insurance than anyone else in the whole country. Then he owned an old-fashioned diner during the Depression years. In 1900, at age nineteen, Dad emigrated from Austria-Hungary. He was a linguist. German was his native tongue—but he also spoke fluent Hebrew and Polish, which helped him later at the diner, since there were many Polish people living nearby. Dad came to America because he was enterprising. Many of my cousins stayed in Europe and were murdered in the Holocaust. He came knowing little English and boarded at the home of my mother's parents.

Mother was American born. Her parents came to America from Lithuania in 1870, with a large group of Jews who settled on free land in Michigan. The strange thing is they didn't like it there and went back to Lithuania. Fortunately, my grandmother was either ill or pregnant, and so in New York City my grandparents left the group and stayed. The rest of the group returned to Lithuania and their descendants were later murdered in the Holocaust. So you can see what fortuitous circumstances I'm the tail end of. Mother was blonde—I guess that's the Russian element of blood. There are a lot of blondes on my side of the family. Prior to marrying, my mother was a classic working girl and worked on a sewing machine in a factory. When she did sewing at home she was unbelievably good at it. She used a machine that you pumped with your feet.

My parents married in 1910. I was born in 1923. That year Grandmother died, and Grandfather moved in with us. I remember he had a Tolstoy beard. Since mother was a very busy woman, he took care of me until he died when I was seven or eight.

Father was very loving, and he worked long hours. We'd see him in the evenings. He was somewhat of a discipline figure. Never harsh, but his word was law. He started to buy real estate in the 1920s. He had over thirty parcels of rental units. In the late twenties he finally bought us a one family house, and extended it. Then, in the Depression, we lost our beautiful home and essentially all of the land. Dad was heartbroken over the Depression, but didn't collapse. Those were tough years, but we never really experienced poverty. We became tenants in another house for one to two years. Father was very enterprising and was pulling us out. He borrowed money and bought a two-family home. In the depths of the Depression, he bought a complete diner for $200 to $300. They were tearing down buildings, preparatory to building the Triborough Bridge, and the diner was under one of the buildings. He moved the diner to North Bergen, and, lo and behold, we were in the restaurant business. Most of the family worked in the diner. I started part-time while still in high school.

Mother was a great reader and very philosophical, telling us things like, "God couldn't be everywhere, so He made mothers." From her, I learned my love of books. While she was the mothering type, it didn't phase her to have a strong husband. She stood right up to my father verbally. She was very religiously involved in the synagogue or temple. She was a huge fundraiser, good at twisting the arms of the diner's suppliers to support synagogue programs. She was not the retiring European-style wife.

We had a very active family. There was no real jealousy among the children. The children played board games and ping-pong on the huge dining room table. My nine-years-older brother took me places and took me fishing in the summers.

I graduated from high school at 16, but didn't go to college because of the looming war. In 1942, I saw an announcement in a paper for pre-induction test for the Army Specialized Training Program. I took the test and I passed. After I was drafted in 1943, I went to basic training at Fort Benning, Georgia, and learned to use all of the infantry weapons. Then I was sent to Cornell University, where I trained in communications for a semester, and discovered I had academic ability.

By then the war was progressing and I was assigned to the 75th Division in Louisiana, and sent to England in December 1944. We were in the first counterattack at the Battle of the Bulge in Belgium, and it was murderous. One platoon was mowed down in an ill-advised charge. More than half of my company was killed or wounded in Belgium.

Christmas Eve was a major attack. Christmas day was crystal clear, and our planes were finally able to operate. I still remember being in the foxhole, watching thousands of our bombers coming over. We later saw the American bomb craters every 20 to 30 feet. I received the Combat badge, the Bronze Star, and frostbite in a finger.

The best part of my life was my wife Rosamond. I had such good fortune, but none of it exceeded that. My mother was away one summer, renting a room in the country because her medical condition would not permit her to stand the heat. My father was trying to run his business, absent both his sons, and had a heart attack. Their good friends, Daisy and Jack Garfunkel, drove to get my mother and bring her home. I came home on emergency furlough from Camp Breckinridge, Kentucky, where the 75th was training. My mother told me to go down to visit her friend Daisy, who was working in her father's store. While I was there to say thanks to Daisy for picking up my mother, I saw a beautiful girl working behind the counter. My future mother-in-law said, "Can I see you outside?" She said, "Promise me you'll write." Guess who answered the letter. I guess Rosamond's arm was twisted because she was only a teenager then. We corresponded, which is good, because you learn more about a person writing than you do just looking, especially if it's a beautiful girl. She sent me a picture of herself while I was in France and I reciprocated. By the time I came out of the service, my mind was essentially made up.

When I returned from the war, I became an engineer, completing my bachelors and masters degrees in civil engineering. After working eight years in Manhattan, I specialized, becoming a water resources engineer, working on New Jersey reservoir projects. At my retirement, I was head of the planning branch at the Delaware River Basin Commission. I lost my wife in 1997, when she was 69.

My three children are another blessing. All are very loving, capable individuals. The oldest son, Gary, is a computer scientist, the middle girl, Wilma, graduated from Purdue and works in consumer services, and the youngest, Hal, is an accountant and rock musician.

PTSD Symptoms?

I never felt that I was on the edge. I don't have nightmares about the war or anything like that. Never did. I saw suffering all around me, but it didn't affect me personally. Perhaps I might have cracked if I were in bloodier circumstances, but I don't think so. Very few in my company did, even under tough conditions. It just wasn't the thing to do. I'm inclined to think that those who did had a lack, a deficiency.

What Helped You Cope?

I don't claim any special strengths. I had this stabilizing influence, family. I knew I had to get back and see my mother and father, and even more, I had a girl about whom I had serious intentions. I never even had another girlfriend. My life seemed to be lining up. I had a goal to be an engineer. I expected and intended to go through this thing without cracking up, which never even crossed my mind. My frame of mind was: I'm in this thing with my buddies. We were sort of happy-go-lucky in some ways. I was twenty when I went in the Army, so I wasn't a child. I'd been through the Depression and I had seen my father be resourceful.

CALM UNDER PRESSURE

It was all the guys and me—we supported each other. They were your buddies. Being a Jew, it was kill or be killed. I kept my dog tags in my duffle bag, because we knew of Jewish GIs who were killed in atrocious ways. But after that, I remember going into Germany. I saw a picture on a wall, showing a German soldier sleeping. It was entitled "Soldier's Dream." Knowing Yiddish, I understood that it said the soldier was dreaming about parents, Sunday dinner at home, his girlfriend, and a good meal. These guys were no different than we were. I don't believe that most were indoctrinated. Other GIs kicked German prisoners, but I couldn't see that. *[At this time he showed me two photographs. A beautiful little boy with an innocent face and the swastika on his uniform. Another was a young German soldier in a Nazi uniform. He said, "They're just like us."]*

I did hate the Nazis that represented Hitler, the SS, but in spite of that, it seems to me, most of the Germans weren't really died in the wool Nazis. I understand Germany's resentment over the treatment after WWI. Germany had some of the greatest musicians, composers, and philosophers. I can separate the German culture from Nazism. We even thought that German Jews felt superior because of their culture. I don't criticize the whole German Army. This one SS unit machine-gunned the arm of an officer off, and bayonetted a Jewish GI in a most cruel way. I was so angry hearing this. But I would not have killed German POWs as some did.

RATIONAL THOUGHT PROCESSES

I thought that I was born with three balls, not two strikes. I rarely complained and wasn't compulsive or driven to excel or be perfect, although I was always a good student. In college, I wasn't invited to join the honor fraternity, although I was equal to those who made it, but it never bothered me. I worked hard but never expected to be top man. I did expect to be in the first rank.

SOCIAL SUPPORT

I had a lot of support. For example, my brother served in North Africa. He wrote me long letters explaining what would happen and what to do, which I still have.

My wife was very loving, better than I deserved. Her letters were very innocent. One of her last letters, when the Armistice was signed, described service men kissing all the gals they saw. That was the first time she signed it love and kisses. She saved all my correspondence, tied with a ribbon.

We were all in the war together and my buddies and I helped each other. We had a highly varied mix of people. In my basic training, I was probably in the first integrated unit in the Army, with a squad of black soldiers, all, like us, slated for college. Nobody had anti-war feelings, unlike Vietnam. A conscientious objector, then, was something quite shameful. We all knew it was a just war. I didn't have a single best buddy, but knew people generally.

At various times, Jews segregated in communities in Europe couldn't own land, and were excluded from learned professions and many businesses, but we live in the greatest country in the world. In this country now I know of practically no discrimination. To give you an idea, though, my first job in New Jersey, six months out of school in 1951, was at the Hackensack Water Company. After I was hired, people said to me, "Are you sure? They don't hire Jews." I might have been the first hired, but subsequently that policy collapsed.

I grew up in a predominantly Italian neighborhood, and encountered no vicious prejudice. We all lived together. The war cured much prejudice. Even in the Army, I saw anti-semitism, but half was good natured. I felt that I wasn't a subservient ghetto Jew and that I belonged in this country. My generation saw the transition from the last residue of anti-semitism.

COMFORTABLE WITH EMOTIONS

Maybe it's my generation, but I didn't really think about feelings. It was matter of fact. In the foxholes, understandably I feared for my life. Of course I was afraid and I know the others were afraid. We accepted that. I was afraid I wouldn't have the opportunity to come home and lead a normal life.

SELF-ESTEEM

I never thought of it. I thought I was good academically. In the Army, I discovered I could do a lot of things I hadn't known before. I wasn't competitive athletically. I didn't exert myself in high school, because I didn't want to appear too smart or strange, but I was generally confident and in the upper levels of the class.

ACTIVE, CREATIVE COPING

We were well trained and we felt that we knew what we were doing. I qualified on the machine gun and all other infantry weapons. I'm a pretty good shot. We felt we had superior weapons, and a huge supply system. I believed in the individual soldiers.

My father's resourcefulness set the example of problem solving. In 1948, I was in my second year of college and in love with Rosamond. I was afraid she wouldn't wait to get married, or would choose someone else. When my father died, he had three houses left. One was a house that my mother lived in. One was a store and two cute three-room apartments above that he had remodeled. Rather than sell off the third house to pay off Mom's mortgage, I came up with this solution. I paid off her mortgage with my savings, and explained that we could rent out the store and live in an apartment above the store, essentially rent free. Rosamond's salary could pay the other bills until I graduated. After some discussion I gradually got the families convinced. My mother-in-law, Daisy, in fact, supported the plan. I think she had her eye on me the first time she saw me. So we got married and things fell into place. I was glad we didn't wait until I graduated, because we had those extra two years together.

SPIRITUAL AND PHILOSOPHICAL STRENGTHS

God

My family was not extremely religious. We weren't orthodox. My mother led the trend away. Most of our lives we belonged to Reformed congregations.

I still believe in God. I came as close to being an atheist in the foxhole as I ever did. Why should a just God permit these things? On the other hand, the human race has everything we need to make a paradise, but we screw it up. Finally, I came to the conclusion that I don't think we understand God. We don't know God's purpose. I think there is a purpose and we gradually reach understanding.

I feel my life has been blessed in many, many ways by God—a beautiful wife, beautiful children and grandchildren, and being steered to the right doctors. I think, "Thanks for everything I've had and get." I can't say I'm bitter or unhappy. Every week I read a portion of the Torah and go to the temple.

Meaning & Purpose

As a Jew, particularly, the war was meaningful. I felt this country accomplished something enormous. We did it. Hitler would have conquered England. Then we'd have had a really bloody conflict.

When I saw all the destruction in Europe, everything that was blown up, I decided I wanted to be a builder. So I became a civil engineer. I wanted to do something concrete. You can be constructive in whatever profession you're in. I feel good that the Delaware River is a lot cleaner now than it was forty years ago.

And of course I was corresponding with my beloved, a reason to return.

Morality

It was important to be ethical. I think I got that from my mother—not to steal, lie, or take advantage of others, and to serve. The Ten Commandments are a serious thing. There are 613 commandments in the Bible. More than half are prohibitions. During the war, the rules of behavior for our army were laid out in no uncertain terms. We did not abuse the civilian population. No way.

We learned to help each other. If you grow up that way, it's ingrained. For example, I saw my father buy ties from peddlers during the Depression when they were less expensive in the store. In our diner, people came in wearing rags. My dad always motioned them over and gave them a bowl of soup and bread.

Love

I love my family and they return it. There's love all around and it is reciprocated.

The reformed movement is socially inclined—clothe the naked, feed the hungry. We participate in the Trenton area soup kitchen. I think this is good training for the children. We should help all people, not just Jews.

Optimism

I had a feeling there was a life ahead of me, and I wanted to get on with life. It was not just me. Our generation had a tremendous optimism. We started building cars, housing for veterans, etc. It was a very optimistic age. There was a phrase, "we're fighting for motherhood and apple pie." We were fighting for what we had and were going to have—a car, a wife and children, a very ordinary, good American life.

Humor

We had all kinds of humor and jokes. Plenty of laughter. Some was maudlin or ironic. Before the war, Burns and Allen, Eddie Cantor, and others taught us to laugh. I enjoy humor, although I'm not a jokester. There's a humorous streak in many of the books I read.

Long View of Suffering

We weren't really the greatest generation. Every generation has strengths and ways of coping with adversity. I don't consider what I endured suffering. My parents suffered with two sons in the war. I missed the freedom of being my own master in the war, but we took it with good humor. The war was a maturing process, not all negative. Certain things happened that changed my life positively, such as my selection for the Army training program, which eventually led to my going to college. My decision to be a rebuilder turned me in the direction of civil engineering, which was a career I really enjoyed.

It seemed very random who got killed. I can't explain suffering or why some seem to have worse luck than others. At my age, I have health conditions people never even heard of. And yet ,somehow, I have been steered to the right doctors so I've been able to cope without much hardship.

Man is mortal. We're here for a period of time and must value our time. I wouldn't change my life in major ways, but I'd be nicer, more helpful. I suppose I'm saying that we get through suffering if we keep it in perspective, and if we focus on what we have, on what's still possible, and on loving. Good deeds help people endure suffering.

Maintaining Balanced Living

I ascribe some of my longevity to a low-fat, balanced diet, with fresh produce at least twice daily. I walk on the treadmill 30 minutes a day, six days a week. I've kept regular sleep hours, usually getting six to seven hours of sleep.

I picked up smoking in the Army, like many did, but stopped at the first Surgeon General's warning, I think about 1950. I didn't go out drinking in the service. Occasionally, I only have a glass of wine at dinner.

I have been quite a reader. I started with Socrates and Plato and then moved to the Jewish philosophers such as Heschel and Maimonides. I have read much of Jewish medieval history. Although some of it is unhappy, much of it is happy. I was active as a Scout Leader. My wife and I had separate interests, but also did everything together. We kept busy with family activities. We have relatives all over the world. We traveled to South America twice, to Israel three times, and around the U.S. three times.

Advice to Younger Generations

At the age of high school, start thinking of selecting a profession that enables you to give something to society. Doing something productive brings huge satisfaction. Be productive and moral.

The most important thing is to select the right spouse. That helps you a lot in your perspective.

To stay intact and still be functional and want to go on living you have to have certain attitudes. These include gratitude. I don't pray for things. I say a prayer of thanks. Feel fortunate for a good life. Love is the key. If you start out with three balls, help someone who started out with two strikes. There is something absent in what we teach in schools.

As I was leaving, he said, "I appreciate the opportunity to unload, to have a summing up." Then, smiling, "Of course, there is nothing to uncover," as if to say, "Don't live in a way that causes regrets."

At home in Lawrenceville, NJ

Chapter 20

Brigadier General Don Rue Hickman
Rifle Company Commander

General Hickman and I met in a sleepy town in the rolling hills of western Maryland, which was surrounded by horse farms and woods. With his wife of 60 years, LoRee, he had driven from Utah to visit his daughter and her family. Tall (6'2"), a trim 220 pounds, and distinguished, his warmth and humor put me at ease immediately. LoRee graciously served us orange juice and apples during the interview. The house was on a wooded hill. We sat in a comfortable, wood paneled room that was full of books.

Following WWII, General Hickman remained in the Army, serving in Korea and Vietnam. He counts raising with his wife "four beautiful daughters, who all married honest God-fearing men," as his greatest accomplishment. His grandson John R. Giles, III, wrote the following poem in honor of General Hickman. It was patterned after General Douglas MacArthur's poem, "Build Me a Son."

Give Me a Man
Give me a man—
A man who is true to righteous principles.
Who treasures the life given to him,
But is willing to lay it down in defense of another.
Give me a man who is motivated by honor and duty,
But tempered with love and compassion.
Who has been through the refiner's fire
And withstood the heat, and come out stronger for it.
Give me a man who knows the importance of truth.
To whom honesty and integrity are more important than gold.
To whom virtue is more valuable than vice.
Who sets his values and sticks to his conscience.
Who is willing to listen—when he has a burning story of his own to tell.
Who values friendship, but is willing to stand alone when others are too cowardly to stand with him.
Give me a man with character.
Give me a man of strength, a man of patience.
Give me a man who is willing to forgive,
    Whether for transgression or omission.
Give me a man of God.
Give me a man who knows whereof he speaks, but is willing to listen to the words of others.
Give me this man, and I will follow him wherever his footsteps may lead.
Give me this man, and I will fight every battle with faith to overcome.
Give me this man, and I will honor his name.
Give me this man, and I will revere him and call him—*Grandfather*

[Fittingly General Hickman's autobiography is entitled No Regrets.*]*

I was born in Torrey, Utah, a small town in southern Utah, in 1918. Brigham Young sent our people down there to settle. My father had three girls from his first wife, who died. At 28 years of age, he married my mother, who was then 18. She bore me, another boy who died at birth, and then another girl and boy. We were raised as one happy family, with no talk of half-siblings or stepmother. It was just sister, brother, Mother.

Dad could do anything and I knew it. He was affable; people liked him. I felt very close to him. He was responsible for state roads in the county. He'd take me with him to build a road, which were some of my happiest days. He liked horses and would bet on anything. He was a fun guy. He also never missed one of my ball games. He taught me character: He always looked at me and said, "Never take a rusty nail if it doesn't belong to you. Be completely honest, and do what you're supposed to do." He taught me to do more than my employer asked, and to be on time as a way to show that my word counted. Dad wasn't religious. His father, a bishop, probably pressed his kids too much. But we had prayers at meals together. He led by example.

Mother was an educator. Possessing an eighth grade education when she married, she earned her three-year normal degree after she married, then started to teach grammar school in small schools in the "boonies" when I was five. She enrolled me in first grade, but she had taught me so well that I ended up skipping that and going to second grade. I was a smart aleck who corrected the teacher. I knew I was the smartest kid in the school and told everyone.

My mother also taught me character, with a little willow switch sometimes. For instance, I took candy from a store when I was five or six years old, then lied to her about finding the money to buy it. She took away my privileges for six weeks—no ball playing, cowboy movies (which were then shown at the school), no nothing. I couldn't leave the house. I learned a great lesson about honesty. I wasn't afraid of her, but she was a strict disciplinarian and I respected her. Mother stressed education, constantly telling me, "I don't want you to grow up to be a great big nothing." It never occurred to me that I wouldn't graduate from college. She also taught me to work hard, that things don't come easy in life.

I was aware of quite a bit of dissension between Mom and some of Dad's sisters— probably because it was a small town, and they compared her to Dad's first wife. Yet Dad was supportive of Mom's schooling, and there were many happy times. My family fished together, and were all involved in the July 4 celebrations. Dad always won the fat man's race and Mom entered sewing contests.

I worked hard raising sugar beets and hay for little pay, especially during the Depression. One summer I pitched hay for $1.25 per day, from sunrise to dinnertime. Then I'd sneak off to fish. At age 17, I graduated from high school.

Two men in the community had an influence for good on me and caused me to think seriously about the importance of religion in my life—through discussions while hunting, or mini-sermons while I was doing odd jobs. Our bishop asked my parents if they'd support my going on a church mission. They said yes and for two years sent me $21 to $35 a month. I served a great mission, believing the harder I worked, the more good I could do. I was a district president at 18.

At nineteen, I attended Snow College, played basketball, and worked on the National Youth Administration recovery projects at thirty-five cents an hour. At Snow College, I spotted my future wife. I thought she was the cutest thing I'd ever seen and wanted to meet her. She was playing the trombone in the marching band, so I walked up and tapped her on the shoulder and said, "You can't fool me—you're not swallowing that thing." She thought that was clever. After two years, our little school defeated Northern Arizona. Their coach invited me to play for them. So I thumbed my way to Flagstaff, where I played two years of varsity basketball and earned a degree with majors in elementary and secondary education. I had a contract to teach when I received my draft notice on July 5, 1941. I was drafted from Arizona along with six Navajo Indians, a Ph.D., and two others. With my schooling and mission experience, I thought they'd never make me a rifleman, but that is what I became, and I resolved to serve my country proudly. Because of my education, hard work, and military competence I was invited to Officer Candidate School at Ft. Benning, Georgia. Assigned to Ft. Meade Maryland, we had a policy that no one could get leave. I asked the colonel, however, if I could get leave to get married. He said I'd have to talk directly to the general. Not being shy, I told the general that some of us deserve leave in order to get married and I'm one of them. So I was the first among 25,000 soldiers to get leave, and I married in 1942, as a 24-year-old Army lieutenant. Thereafter, the policy was changed to allow a few soldiers at a time to take leave to get married.

I was a rifle company commander in the 76th Infantry Division during the Battle of the Bulge and as we attacked eastward into Germany. I saw dead people from both sides all around. I saw soldiers lie down and cry. Some ran or wandered off. Others froze and refused to move. My best platoon sergeant, a hard worker and a good guy in the states, fell apart in combat from the stress that he just couldn't handle. Perhaps 8% had such problems. Then I became the operations officer and later the executive officer for the battalion. In March 1945, the American Army was moving rapidly toward the heart of Germany. I was sent ahead with a small party to reconnoiter for a new battalion command post. We were well ahead of the other U.S. forces. Returning at night, we discovered that we were in the middle of a German platoon. We fired on three approaching Germans and took one as prisoner as we sped away in our jeeps. During the next phase, we liberated thousand of Allied POWs. I was at the Buchenwald concentration camp as it was liberated. This was my most terrible experience of the war. I saw bodies piled up like cardboard and remains in the furnace. As the Germans from the nearby town were marched through the prison camp, many cried and said, "We didn't know." Most didn't want to know. There *was* a Holocaust! I saw the remains.

My wife and I have four daughters. All my sons-in-law are successful. The girls were all are musical, thanks to my wife's influence. I retired in 1972 from the Army.

PTSD Symptoms?

I was just happy to be home, and was not troubled by such symptoms. Once in awhile I had nightmares, but nothing major.

What Helped You Cope?

My mission. Prior to that I thought I knew everything and could do anything. You see, that was one of my problems. I had to calm down a little bit and say, "Hey, you're not that great." I realized there were others who knew more. I learned to deal with people, lead with kindness, and consider others. I did not lose my confidence, however. This combination of qualities helped me go from private to general in the Army.

My early training with weapons, as an enlisted man, lead to confidence in battle. I wasn't afraid to walk up to a machine gun group and tell them that something was wrong. Same with the mortars. I was at Fort Benning for a year, where we played out problems and prepared.

My parents' character training. My mother also taught me poems about sharing the sunshine and laughter that you feel with others.

Athletics helped a lot, to learn competition. Leads in plays and operas in school also taught me to perform before the public and *(chuckling)* enjoy their praise.

I was inclined to be a good soldier, being athletic, smart enough to be an officer, not afraid to talk (I could handle the chaplains)—all that background helped.

CALM UNDER PRESSURE

Knowing what was going on helped—to see the big picture and understand the situation. I knew the geography. I knew where I was and what was happening on our left and right, knew that our planes would be called in to help, and knew how they were being called in. The worst thing is for soldiers not to know what's going on. So it's important to keep them briefed! Being briefed, possessing character, and having the training background help people maintain focus under pressure.

I never felt hatred for the Germans, and I don't think they hated us. They were clean, industrious, and decent, but duped or misguided by Hitler. I felt compassion for them, but also knew we had to protect ourselves properly. After the war, they seemed tired of Hitler's oppression, happy to change for the better.

RATIONAL THOUGHT PROCESSES

I never felt like I didn't have control of what was going on. That's innate to a great degree.

When there's a problem, I spring into action and solve it. There's always a way to do it. In combat we learned, "He who fights and runs away lives to fight another day." That is, get yourself in the best possible posture for tomorrow. You can't just keep running. I felt sorry for people who kept running because of lack of training, character, or knowledge. Maybe some of that was our fault. With proper training, people can learn to take a proper stand; knowledge is power.

When others messed up, I felt compassion, but they'd be responsible for irresponsible acts. For example, my platoon sergeant was the best in peacetime, and the first to run in combat. Later, I helped him to get a job he could handle. If I had had him in my home when he was five or six years of age, I believe I could have taught him how to stand firm, by teaching character and work ethic. Also, in the military, I feel it is important to teach military history; teach about people who stood up for their country; indoctrinate properly concerning the importance of a war and what the country is trying to do. But it seems to me there's some point where a person becomes a great or weak character.

SOCIAL SUPPORT

Friends were very important. The first thing the Army taught was the buddy system, to have friends to look out for each other, to help each other. It gives you strength.

I had regular letters from Mom and Dad. My wife's letters were a great asset. I still have those letters bound. I almost cried for some soldiers who got no letters when mail call came. My wife was a great and supportive Army wife. Wives ruin more officers' careers than whiskey.

COMFORTABLE WITH EMOTIONS

I was afraid—only a fool or one who didn't value his life or his family's welfare wouldn't be. But I accepted the risk and overcame my fear. In our first combat, we were hit and I was shaking. I told myself, "What in the world is the matter? Are you going to be a coward and fall apart, or stand up and be a man and do what you're supposed to do?" I calmed down, and never again had that problem. I made up my mind there would be no more of that.

In combat, I kept a journal, which helped me write my autobiography. I kept it in foxholes, and sometimes it got rained on. Writing helped me remember; it's probably a release.

I always had some confidant. My first sergeant was one with whom I could always discuss the business of the company. He said, "If the captain doesn't mind, I'd like to make a suggestion." I appreciated that. He was never offensive.

SELF-ESTEEM

Self-esteem was no problem. People thought I had too much. I'd kid, "I'm humble. I don't think I'm half as good as I really am."

ACTIVE, CREATIVE COPING

I can't see how anyone could be passive under pressure. Something needs to be done, to be solved, and you'd better solve it or else you go away talking to yourself. I was lucky to have parents who modeled that pattern.

On one occasion, while I was doing reconnaissance, my company executive officer moved my company into a bad place to defend. The troops had dug foxholes and made a comfortable home of it. When I returned, I took one look and knew the enemy would attack. We wouldn't see them and would get knocked out. So I ordered them to move up to a better position and dig in. When the attack came, they were in a good position. My troops watched what happened to the company in the foxholes below. Their commander was popular and didn't want to inconvenience them. They got clobbered. Thereafter, my men never questioned me.

SPIRITUAL AND PHILOSOPHICAL STRENGTHS

God

I believe in God and Christ. I think of God as supportive, or else I wouldn't have prayed. In combat, I prayed whenever I needed a prayer, including and mostly in foxholes. At headquarters, I supported the chaplains in their duty to pray. I appreciated them. They were a big help, particularly in calming down frightened soldiers or comforting the homesick. However, once a chaplain was the first one on the chow line. I always taught the officers to feed the men first. I finally had to take a bite out of him and explain that he'd go through the line with me—after the men were all fed.

I taught Sunday school wherever I went, and served a mission with my wife in 1992.

Meaning & Purpose

It is most important to know why you are there and why you're fighting. Otherwise you are dead in the water. I had that understanding. We were taught not to question an order. Often there isn't time to explain. I accepted that. But if you can explain things to the troops, you should.

Morality

I always felt good because of my religion and background. I never had a problem with immorality or fraternizing with the German girls.

Love

I had a great love for all my men, particularly those that were right close to me. I just did. I knew them. I had brought every man in my company and sat them down, just like we are talking, and asked them: "Where you from? What do you do? What's your dad and mother do? What do they think about your being here? Are you married? Have you got a girlfriend? Do you write her regularly?" So I knew every man in my company and knew them well. I thought that was very important. I had to censor all their mail as well, which helped me know them.

Optimism

I was always optimistic. I always saw the glass as half full instead of half empty. My hope was for peace and to return to my family. I dreamed of coming back to my family in one piece and teaching.

Humor

My wife used to joke that I loved football and basketball better than her. I said, "Yes, but I like you better than baseball." I enjoy joking, but humor is more than joking. Humor was always been important to me. It helps you to look at situations and not get too serious. People who crashed often had tunnel vision, couldn't see the light at the end of the tunnel. They only saw worries. I felt that life was good all around, which permitted me to have a light heart. Some see the thorns on roses instead of roses on thorns. I've always felt that things are pretty good. If you want to mess them up, though, you can with pessimism and worry. Keep your eye on the ball and don't veer off the happy course. It seems like the gospel is a pretty good guide, provides excellent boundaries for life. You know why you're here, where you're going, and where you came from. That helps.

Long View of Suffering

I saw a lot of it *[long pause]*. A lot of guys, after seeing their buddies killed, were shook up for life. I took it with a grain of salt. I expected some to be killed and some to live. You had to move on. You couldn't stay stuck in suffering. If you know them, you suffer. You don't want to see any of them dead. They were somebody's son. It was easier to see the enemy suffer than our guys. If I hadn't won, I'd have been dead like him.

My great friend and aid, PFC Jack McKenna, was a kid from the state of Washington. Smartest kid I'd ever seen. He had one or two years at Harvard. He knew what to do in a hurry. He was not afraid to talk to me. He could have become anything. The hardest thing for me in the whole war was when he was killed. He had volunteered to help take German POWs to the battalion and was killed by a German machine gun ten minutes later. He could have stayed in safety at my headquarters. After the war I drove clear to the state of Washington to see his family. They lived on an island near Seattle in a great big mansion. The parents were so thankful that he could make the sacrifice that he made for his country. I told them what a great man he was and how much I appreciated having him by my side. They felt like they'd made a contribution to the country. I went away knowing why Jack was such a great young man. Though you suffer when you lose such a person, it helps to understand the big picture—the meaning of what the country was trying to accomplish. That's why it was difficult in Korea and more difficult in Viet Nam, when you didn't know what you were fighting for. You'd see people killed and you'd say, "Why?" You didn't understand the big picture, and so you had to have confidence in those guys back in Washington, confidence that President Johnson didn't have you there just for nothing.

Maintaining Balanced Living

I was always an athlete. After the war, I joined a basketball team in the town industrial league and played for four years. Every place I went, I joined a spa, where I swam three to four times a week. I still swim most weekdays. It's not good to weigh too much. My wife helps me watch my diet and has always made balanced meals. During my career I got seven to eight hours of sleep. Now I retire at 11:00 p.m and arise at about 7:00 a.m. I was not a smoker or drinker.

We liked to go to shows, be it in London or New York. I always took a vacation. I felt I owed it to LoRee and our children and parents. We tried to always take my 30 days each year, in 15-day increments, to get our girls acquainted with their grandparents. Each time we moved, every two to three years, we tried to make it a vacation for the kids. We talked it up and made it fun so they wouldn't resent moving.

Advice to Younger Generations

Keep yourself physically fit. Especially for the military, continue to read, particularly military history, the history of your country, and lessons learned from all wars. Develop a thorough understanding of tactics, strategy (which is different), and the weapons you have to use, whether you're preparing to fight in battle or a fire.

It's very important to keep knowledgeable about what's going on every day. I can't wait to read the paper each day and often read two.

For people in general, it's very important to have a basic knowledge and understanding of your religion, which is the basis of everything. Have faith, which might have to be developed. The true faith of a nation is measured by the morality of its citizens.

Don Rue and LoRee Hickman, Camp McCoy, WI, 1943

General Don Rue Hickman

Chapter 21

Michael DeMarco
Footsoldier

The son of immigrants, mild-mannered Michael DeMarco lives with his wife June in a house that he built with his own skilled hands. He served with the 106th Infantry Division in the Battle of the Bulge and fought into Germany. He still works to this day. Says June, his wife, "He's a faithful husband who always keeps me happy, a hard worker who takes pride in his house, and one who helps others."

I was born August 22, 1925, in Brooklyn, New York. We didn't have too many material things, but we had a big "playground" on the waterfront—the railroad terminal. We'd jump on the railroad trains when they were moving or when they were being loaded at the factories. And of course we'd go down with my father and brother with a wagon my father made and we'd put railroad ties on the wagon. We'd saw the wood in our dirt cellar and it would go into our wood burning stove, in a cold water flat—a four-story high apartment.

There were two boys and two girls. The girls were the oldest (one was born in Italy) and I was number three. My mother wanted to be a nun in Italy, but the family pushed her into marriage. She seemed like a good mother to me. My parents stood together, but they were always at a distance from what I could see.

Things were tough. I used to pull on my mother's apron when I was hungry. My father owned a lot of property in Italy, chestnut farms passed down through the generations, but he was poor because of the Depression. He was a blacksmith in Italy, and was respected because of his trade. He built gates and made locks, and people called him master. He migrated to Brazil and couldn't make out, so he came to America as a concrete worker and sent for my mother. He also worked for the WPA. He was too proud to go on welfare.

Although I had no money, I had a ball playing in the freight yards and swimming down at the docks. I snuck on the subway and went to the 1939 Worlds Fair, where we'd wait in lines for free morsels of food. A kind shop owner kept the bad potatoes on the end so the kids could steal them and bake them on the streets. Plus, a bread man delivered bread every day even when we couldn't pay for it, and never charged.

Dad used to take me mushroom hunting on Staten Island, where a lot of people who were so hungry went. He was a genius when it came to distinguishing the good ones from the poison ones. A lot of people died from eating poisonous mushrooms. We'd take the nickel ferry. He also made his own excellent wine. My father was short and very cunning. There was nothing he couldn't do. He had tools down in the cellar and taught me how to work with wood and forge iron. Whenever he did something, I had to watch him do it. I'm still handy with my hands. He was tough, fast to pull his strap out. Being the oldest boy, I'd get it and my younger brother got away with murder. We always had a radio. He liked to listen to all the Italian music. The kids listened to Bobby Benson, the Witch's Tale, and The Shadow. My parents didn't understand English well enough to listen.

My mother was very religious. She went to church every Sunday and during the week, and brought whatever pennies she had. We went to church every Sunday because we had to. She wasn't affectionate, but she always cooked. My father left fifty cents under the sugar bowl each day and that was her allotment to produce the day's meals. We ate supper together, but my father got up early to go to work, so we didn't eat breakfast together.

I made my own shoe shine box and shined shoes at a train station for two years and then sold bananas for a penny apiece. I worked on a truck that sold produce on Saturdays. I also went junking—picking up papers, rags, and metal from the street for the junk yard, anything that could sell. I gave my mother the money I earned from the jobs.

I didn't graduate from high school because I wanted money, over my school's objections because I was a pretty good student. My first job was with a baking company filling out orders for the truckers. Then I took a job in a printing company, setting up a big printing press.

I went into the Army on November 3, 1943, at 18 years of age plus two months. I could have stayed out of the Army because I was the only one working in my family, but I didn't. I took basic training in Mississippi as an infantryman. Then I went to Camp Atterbury in Indiana, the headquarters for the 106th Division, which was ready to go overseas. I got to England in the summer of 1944 for advanced training, learning the ins and outs of hedgerows. We landed in France and were trucked to the front lines, a 27-mile front. We replaced the 82nd Airborne Division. They complained because we took over their foxholes. It was so quiet at that time, but not for long. My 424th regiment was in the center of the 106th division sector. I was in company L. This was about two weeks before the Battle of the Bulge. It was freezing cold.

I was in a foxhole on December 16, 1944. All of a sudden I saw a German heavy equipment truck approach. They slid out machine guns. They didn't know we were there. My company commander, Captain Benjamin Bartel, told us to let them have it. The truck went on fire. That started the war for us, and the Battle of the Bulge. Then the Germans shot screaming rockets at us from trucks. It was frightening. The Germans got behind us with donkeys loaded with ammunition and were coming at us from all sides. When we went down the hill to our mess hall, I started seeing guys lying there dead. At one point, a piece of shrapnel hit me in the helmet. I went to grab it and it burned my hand.

We got prisoners and put them in our bunkers. My captain said we were surrounded, every man for himself. We paired off and were given a westward azimuth to follow to get out. As my buddy and I were crossing a field one night, they fired parachute flares and then opened up with mortars and rockets that came very close. We couldn't believe that they would expend so much firepower for two GIs. As soon as the flares went out, we got up from hiding and took off running. It took a couple of weeks traveling at night to regroup. We regrouped and started forward, now in white camouflage uniforms, with tanks. We were taking a lot of prisoners.

I was behind a tank one day. There were two snipers in a wooded area. I pleaded with my buddy to get behind the tank. My buddy tried to be a hero. He got shot, and the medic who attended him also got shot and killed because of my buddy's foolhardy behavior. The tank fired at the snipers, who gave up. When they saw the medic, the snipers laughed. Two of our men shot the snipers in the back, but I wouldn't do it. I destroyed their rifles in anger, because they'd killed the medic, but I wouldn't hurt them.

I was outside most of the time for the next five months, until the war ended. You become like an animal. You become so desensitized that GIs sat on German bodies to eat lunch. After living outdoors, we couldn't breathe in a house. We had to break the windows to let air in. There were a lot of snipers. Once, I was standing behind a barn, eating from my mess kit, when wood splinters from a sniper's bullet came down on my food. I just sat down and kept on eating.

When we occupied Germany, I was made acting first sergeant. I was discharged on April 2, 1946. I got GI Bill training to be a tool and die maker and have been a tool and die maker ever since. I'm still working today. I met my wife June in the summer of 1946 in Brooklyn. She lived only a couple of blocks from me. She was in the neighborhood walking around. We married December 16, 1947. We had a girl and a boy.

I built this house that we live in. I was my own contractor when I was 28 years old. We moved into it in 1953. My wife's family was Scandinavian, all carpenters. I learned a lot by observing them. If I saw someone do it, I thought, "He's not better than me—I can do it."

PTSD Symptoms?

If I was walking down the street and someone ran behind me, I turned on them with fists up. This lasted less than a year, although I still don't like people behind me when I'm walking in the park at night. Sometimes I'd have dreams and would lash out, for just a few months. I can't hear from nerve damage from the rockets.

What Helped You Cope?

Growing up, it was miserable to try to eat a decent meal. We didn't have much food on the table. I was always hungry—that was normal. I said to myself that I wouldn't be one who was starving anymore. I made up my mind that I'd have a house and food in the refrigerator, to better my life and get out of the slums. After the war, my wife was a good influence. Her family owned houses and I got more determined to do that.

CALM UNDER PRESSURE

I saw guys cry out of fear when we were advancing. I saw our medic, Mike Mueller, put his arm around many of the soldiers. Nobody was laughing about it. Some of these guys came out of safe homes and now they were seeing guys getting killed. I don't even know why I didn't crack. It wasn't my makeup, I guess. I was never spoiled and I never had it easy. When guys started falling asleep on the front I used to stop them because they'd freeze to death. I stayed focused. A guy would go into a barn and try to jump a German girl, when he could be shot any second. You're not going to stay alive if you let your mind wander. Same thing with my being behind the tank.

I looked at combat as I had to be there and I made the best of it. I didn't try to be a hero. Who am I trying to impress? I wasn't looking for a medal of honor. I wasn't foolhardy. I watched where I walked. I was very careful of booby traps.

I saw a German get on his hands and knees in the snow. He took out pictures of his wife and children and begged to live. This GI standing over him was a nice kid with a good heart, and he told him he wouldn't kill him. I approved of that. I didn't hate the Germans. I had a German girlfriend before the war ended. What did anger me was that the German officers wouldn't work alongside their men when they were prisoners. I wasn't averse to firing in self-defense, but I felt no animosity.

RATIONAL THOUGHT PROCESSES

Why complain or feel sorry for yourself? What will that get you? Make the best of it. A lot of times I'd take my shoes off and couldn't get them back on because my feet would swell. We were tired and our feet were wet. Everybody had lice. We hadn't had a bath in three months.

When I made mistakes I felt bad, but I allowed that I was human. Everybody makes mistakes, so what? In Germany after the war, I was guarding an American who was in the stockade for being AWOL because he was in love with a German girl. He'd cracked up and was crying; they were both crazy about each other. I told him I was going to get a drink of water. I told him to disappear out the open window. I have a soft heart. That's my weakness. The captain in charge discovered his escape. He pointed his captured German Lugar at me. I wrestled it out of his hand and threatened him with bloody murder. I almost broke his arm. I gave him the gun back without the bullets and warned him never to try that again. He never mentioned the incident again.

SOCIAL SUPPORT

I got letters from my sister and I wrote back. My Mother wrote perfect Italian letters to her brothers, but that didn't help me. After the war, my family visited Tibby Ladda, a Hungarian, and his family in

Michigan. He was my squad leader. My wife and kids were close to him and his wife. They were nice people. We'd trade visits for many years. We're still in contact with the wife, his childhood sweetheart. Once, we were on patrol and I had a sinus cough. He said, "DeMarco, if you cough once more I'm going to shoot you." I told him to get lost. Paul Mitchell, the platoon sergeant, watched me like he was my father. He told me to keep my butt down so I wouldn't get shot. He cared about me. I appreciated that. He visited me after the war with his wife until his wife died.

One guy in my barracks in Mississippi and I pal'd around. He set me up with the sister of his girlfriend because I didn't smoke or drink. The father had a watermelon farm. I still have pictures.

COMFORTABLE WITH EMOTIONS

I was comfortable with my emotions. I was scared in combat, but isn't that what keeps you alive? But you can't get carried away with the fear to the point that you don't know what you're doing. When my buddy got shot by another GI accidentally, that really hurt me. It was devastating. You just kept it inside. It happened so fast. After the war Tibby, Mitchell, and I talked about everything. Sometimes we'd laugh and joke or talk about the serious losses, too. Things didn't eat me up inside, though, because I don't feel I did anything wrong.

SELF-ESTEEM

I didn't realize how stupid I was. I wasn't educated, but I was confident. I felt like a person of worth, who wanted to come out of the war alive. I had a strong will to survive. I thought I was strong and tough. Maybe some of the confidence came from the skills I'd acquired with my hands. I felt I could do anything I wanted to do. I wasn't afraid to do anything. I loved the firing of all the different weapons.

ACTIVE, CREATIVE COPING

I set up booby traps around my foxhole with blasting caps and TNT so I could sleep. I learned that from another GI. Once, my company passed through a village. When resting there for the night in a house, I took old radio batteries that were being thrown away, stacked them up in parallel, and made a light. The company commander was impressed. He confiscated it to read his maps. It made me mad, but it kept me alive making things. I enjoyed that. In school I had loved making scientific projects. I even made an electric chair as a prank.

When I was going up to the front in Belgium, we passed an old house. I thought this would be beautiful for a good night's sleep. So a buddy and I ducked in. We got a nice sleep upstairs in the nice, dry room, and rejoined the company the next day.

I had a "can do" attitude when it came to building my house.

SPIRITUAL AND PHILOSOPHICAL STRENGTHS

God

I did believe in God during the war. Some of the guys carried statues of saints and put them in their foxhole. They'd chisel out a spot with their bayonets. I never heard of any atheists in the foxholes. I went to church with my buddy and the two girls we were dating in Mississippi. My wife and I are regular church attenders now.

Meaning & Purpose

If we hadn't won the war, the Germans would have had complete control of our country. We were fighting for freedom of thought. I cherished freedom more than anything else, that I could do what I want. I wanted to defend my country; it was the honorable thing to do. You have to realize that the Germans were smart and powerful.

I knew the war wasn't going to be a forever thing. I wanted to return to my country to be free and I knew I wanted to get married and have a family, a house and property, and a car. That was my

American dream. I was tired of doing without, as we had during the war. I wanted to see my brother and sisters, get home to my family. I was happy as a lark when I came home.

Morality

I just couldn't kill soldiers who had surrendered. When we were moving forward in the Battle of the Bulge, we were taking prisoners. At one point, a sergeant and I captured a machine gun team in a house. They were nine German Air Corps kids, maybe not a day over 15 years old. They were waving a white flag. This sergeant said that we'd kill the Germans. I pointed my rifle at the sergeant and said, "You aren't going to kill these guys because they could have killed us." He knew I meant business. When I was behind a tank, a sergeant told me to kill a defenseless German who was running toward us. I refused.

I shared in the Army. I wasn't the greedy type. I never stole from my buddies. I sold my cigarettes to the French restaurants and sent the money home to my mother. We got $20 a carton if we sold it to an expensive restaurant.

I wouldn't harm a girl when dating. I believe that when a married person is tempted, if they really pray about it, it will go away. You'll feel better. It doesn't pay. The anguish that would follow would be overwhelming. There's no percentage in being unfaithful. It's not worth it. The anguish outweighs the rewards that you think you'll get. When I was young, I'd rather get married than mess around. I preferred the family and home life to fooling around.

I searched prisoners from day to night, confiscating maps, drugs, weapons. Sometimes, I bought watches from prisoners and loaned them to my buddies and never got them back. I admit that sometimes I took watches from prisoners if they were nasty. I'm not proud of it, but it was probably growing up in poverty. I traded them for pancakes; you always wanted a little extra food. I wouldn't do that today. I was a tough dead end kid. The Army and marriage straightened me out, put the finishing touches on me.

Love

I am kind of good-hearted. In basic training, I gave away my socks to people who needed them. There was a very poor person from the South, who was making more than he ever had, $30.00 a month, and was sending the money to his wife. He was wetting the bed and I knew it. He asked me not to tell anybody. I told him not to worry and kept my mouth shut. Somebody squealed and he got a medical discharge. Before he left, he gave me his socks. I felt a bond with a number of my buddies and we maintained our friendship after the war.

I loved my family. That was part of what motivated me to come out alive. My brother and sisters and I have been inseparable since I got out of the Army. I'm glued to my family. After the war, I'd see one every weekend at least. My whole life, from the minute I came home from service, was family. We survived the Depression together.

Optimism

I always look on the good side of things. Except for the time we were surrounded, I felt that we were going to win the war. In general, I think things will turn out well.

Humor

Everybody uses humor to ease tension. It's not a military secret. Tibby was always a joker. We had a play before we went overseas about a famous hotel in Indiana. One guy put a mop on his head like he was a girl. When we were in an R&R area in Belgium, we made a dummy grenade. It would pop but not explode. We rolled the grenade along the floor and it went pop and the guys went running. It was funny. I enjoy a good laugh. Now, all I do is laugh when I get together with my family.

Long View of Suffering

I have to say, I think the Army did me a lot of good. It taught me a lot about life, death, and adversity. It makes you grow up. Going into the service was the best thing that happened to me, even though it was miserable at times. The good outweighed the bad. It taught me survival, discipline (you had to do what you were told), patience, and respect for others. Being in the war has made me more determined. I look at my life and I can't really see any failures. I supported my family.

Maintaining Balanced Living

I'm not much of an exerciser, but I do a lot of walking. I'm always doing something. I don't sit down on the couch; I'm very active doing work around the house or entertaining family. I always worked 50 to 55 hours a week. Now I work 32 hours a week on my job and then go to my son or daughter's house to help, or else I work on our house. Now I walk an hour a day. My feet froze in the Army. Walking helps the circulation to my feet.

I sleep with a clear conscience. I average at least eight hours a night, getting to bed by 10:00 p.m. usually. Sometimes I get up early to water the garden.

I eat very healthy, at least five or six pieces of fruit per day. No salt or junk food; I rarely eat candy or chocolate. I rarely go to restaurants. We eat very little meat, mostly chicken; a lot of vegetables, especially broccoli. I can attack broccoli. I don't eat butter or margarine and won't touch caffeine. I have a ginger ale once a week or month. I drink bottled water. The doctor says I have the blood pressure of a young kid.

I wasn't a drinker in the barracks. Right after the war, I'd have wine with dinner, but I haven't drank since the sixties. I never smoked during, before, or after the war. I never used drugs.

My wife and I traveled a lot—Italy, Canada, Mexico, various states. I used to hunt, but I can't kill that innocent deer. I fish once in awhile. My hobby is to make furniture and cabinets around the house.

Advice to Younger Generations

Get as much education as you can get, but also be active and try to create things. Make things with your hands, because it gives you great satisfaction and esteem—even though you think it's not much. Don't always buy things. In the process of trying to make something, you learn about electricity or plumbing, and you broaden your mind in ways beyond school work. Don't be afraid to try to make something and fail.

Be respectful to the opposite sex. Get married young. When you are biologically ready to get married, get married. Otherwise you create bad habits. The most important thing that any youth should do is get married young. Find the right one and fall in love. It will keep you secure and safe.

Be compassionate. Have empathy for people. Some people can't walk or cross the street. Help them.

Keep your morals. Don't degrade yourself and you can readjust more easily.

Michael and June DeMarco of Valley Stream, NY.

Chapter 22

Glenn Howard Hamm
193rd Glider Infantry Regiment

Glenn and Loy Hamm live in Wall, South Dakota, in a white ranch house with the American flag out front. Horses graze in the expansive pasture in front. A walnut grandfather's clock and other woodwork that he has built adorn the house.

His wife Loy says that family is very important to him. "He always listened to the kids and backed me." He has a dry, self-deprecating humor and an easy laugh. His granddaughter said, "He always listened to us and made things simple." He replied, "Coming from me, it would have to be simple."

Hamm served with the 193rd Glider Infantry Regiment, 17th Airborne Division, in Europe, earning the Bronze Star and Purple Heart.

I said hello to the world on February 3, 1923 in Quinn, South Dakota, six miles east of Wall, in my grandparents' home. I grew up on a wheat and cattle farm and went to a rural grade school.

When I was older, I worked in the summer for different farmers. I helped them cut hay, cultivate corn, and do general farm work for a dollar a day. Everything was done the hard way. Most places were farmed with horses. Nothing was hydraulic or easy. It seemed like it was always hot. There was no air conditioning or electricity for refrigeration. Light came from gas and kerosene lamps. We had a radio run by battery. My dad listened to the news and we listened to baseball games.

I'm the oldest of four children. My younger brother was in the Korean War. I also had another sister and brother. We came along about every two years.

In high school, I played football and basketball, and on a loosely organized baseball team in the summer. We lost my first high school football game 73-0, playing in bib overalls or borrowed uniforms. In the wintertime, we had skating parties on frozen ponds, and country or high school dances every two weeks.

My dad was a farmer—real easy to get along with, didn't push too hard. He had homesteaded here, coming from Missouri in 1909. He was quiet, a baseball fiend. We worked together milking ten or twelve cows morning and night, planting wheat and corn, cultivating, and harvesting. Most of the time there was no harvest because it was always dry.

Mom was small and real quiet—about the sweetest person in the whole world, everybody's dream mother-in-law, my wife says. She didn't care for discord, and kept peace at all costs. She was not bossy. Mom and her mother went to the country church every Sunday. Dad preferred fishing. On Sunday we often visited relatives.

I didn't get many spankings. One time, Mom had a swing, about like a kid's car seat with four straps that were tied to a spring and hung in the doorway. The little kids could sit there and bounce. I wound my sister up and spun her around. All I could see was her mouth open and she was screaming. I outran my mother for awhile but she finally caught me. I got in trouble once with Dad when I shot a bird outside the window with my BB gun. I also got in trouble for breaking a window with a slingshot and wading in the pond without asking.

When we weren't working, we had baseball games on Sunday (my dad had a team, too), played cards, listened to the radio, and went to bed early to get up at 6:00 a.m. to do chores. We'd swim with the neighbor kids in a country pond. On the Fourth of July we always had a country celebration with ice cream and firecrackers.

I graduated from Interior High School in 1941. After graduation, I was carrying mail on a rural mail route until I received my draft notice. I was sworn in at Fort Crook, Omaha, Nebraska, March 18, 1943. I came home on a 14-day furlough, and then reported to Fort Leavenworth, Kansas, for shots and clothes. I was assigned to D Company, 193rd Glider Infantry Regiment, 17th Airborne Division, at Camp Mackall, North Carolina, near Fort Bragg. I was there for basic and advanced training from April of 1943 to February 3, 1944. I went to Tennessee for maneuvers for seven weeks, training on the machine gun in the snowy mountains. One day, a native brought us a tray of biscuits and ham. I've never forgotten their kindness.

After maneuvers, we went to Camp Forrest, Tennessee, until August of 1944. We deployed from Camp Miles Standish, Massachusetts, to Europe in August of 1944. We landed in Liverpool, England, staying until Christmas Eve of 1944, when we flew to Reims, France, after the Bulge started. We set up machine guns on a bridge over the Meuse River, near the town of Soissons (where Loy's ancestors had come from, 300 years earlier). On January 6, we went up to the Bulge. On the 7th we were near Bastogne, helping to get the 101st out of that city.

There was a bad blizzard. E Company was supposed to come up beside us, but instead came up behind us. They thought we were Germans and shot many of our guys over the next hour, before they found out their mistake. My best friend, Bill Brown, *(tears)* beside me behind the machine gun, was shot in the back and died. I don't know why they missed me. We had known each other since our induction at Camp Mackall two years before. *[Says son William, "It's no coincidence that I am named Bill."]*

That evening the Germans counterattacked. We were told there were just a few Germans in front of us, but there were more than four thousand in an SS Panzer division. We really got our butts kicked. We were retreating. I came back alone to the same foxhole that I'd been in that morning. The snow was over knee deep. Tracer bullets went between my legs and made a hole in my pants legs, and burned my leg. Out of 235 men in my company, only 65 were left that night. Half of the losses were from friendly fire. We stayed two to three days to regroup. So many were killed in the 193rd that they did away with it and absorbed us into the 194th.

We attacked again. This time we followed the outstanding and dedicated 761st Tank Battalion—all black people—from about January 10th through 14th. One black tank commander shot at a church steeple (where German snipers were hiding) five or six times and missed. Finally, another black fellow in another Sherman tank hit it the first time. The first stood up and said, "You black n___r, that was my steeple." They laughed. The black troops were kind of by themselves until after the war, when General Gavin assigned the 555th Parachute Infantry Regiment to the 82nd Airborne.

We were outside the whole winter until April. I had never been that cold in my whole life. They claimed it was the coldest winter in Europe. Sometimes we got to sleep in barns or burned out buildings.

Neither did we receive mail or pay until April.

I got to meet General Patton once. He really dressed me and another guy down for not having rubber overshoes on. But we didn't have any; they weren't issued. That didn't fly with him. He finally cooled off and got in his jeep and left. When we came back from the Bulge in February, I went to the hospital in Paris for three weeks with frozen feet and trench foot. When I got out, I had to hitch my way back to the unit.

We trained in Chalons, France, getting ready to cross the Rhine River on March 24, 1945. On that day, the formation was nine planes wide and 500 miles long—C-47 transports with gliders and paratroopers. I was in a glider with 15 men. My glider landed in Belgium because the tail came loose. We landed going 85 miles per hour into the ground, but no one was killed. We were supposed to land in Wesel, Germany, so we started to walk there. My squad leader asked an M.P. how we could find the front. He was directed to a headquarters building, where he knocked on the door and saluted. There were Generals Bradley, Montgomery, and he thought Eisenhower, and some more generals. He came out and joked, "I don't know what they told me. I think they said, 'There's the door.'" So we walked several days through Belgium and Holland until we caught our unit in Germany on the east side of the

Rhine in the Ruhr pocket. We were there until the war was over. We captured Franz von Papen, one of Hitler's cabinet members. On the outskirts of Warstein, Germany, Harry, my partner, and I had set up the machine gun. About 30 feet in front in the road ditch lay a "dead" German boy about 15 years old. The riflemen moved out across the field as we covered them. One of our men nudged the German boy, who jumped up and surrendered. He had been lying over a machine pistol, apparently waiting for the right time to kill me and Harry as we passed by. Later Harry and I were set up at an outpost next to a barn in a drizzling rain, when Harry remarked, "Wouldn't it be something if this barn were full of Germans?" So he opened the door and hollered, "All right, you so and so's, get out of here." Seven of them threw up their hands and walked out. Incidents like these made your hair pull.

After the war, if you had 85 points, you could start going home. I had 67, so I joined the 82nd Airborne and went to Berlin with the American Honor Guard. I got home January 7, 1946, a year to the day when Bill and so many got killed. Coming home, there was a bad storm in the Atlantic and our ship tipped 44 degrees. I didn't know if we'd make it.

At home, my saddle horse was dead and so was my pick up. I worked three years for Standard Oil Company, delivering gas to farmers and filling stations. I worked for my future father-in-law for 11 years. He had a 1400-acre cattle and wheat farm. Wages were a percentage of the crop. I met my wife Loy working there in 1948. I had my eye on her earlier in Interior where she was attending high school. We married May 20, 1950. After we married, we had a little ranch house on her father's farm.

In 1960 we went to Spearfish, South Dakota. I attended Black Hills State College. We were there for five years. I majored in biology to be a forest ranger. We ran out of money, so I quit. Loy graduated with a teacher's degree.

I worked for the National Park Service for 11 years, starting in 1954 in the summers. I worked in maintenance, and the last year, 1964, as a ranger. I drove around the park to contact visitors and answer questions and help out.

Loy was teaching school at Ellsworth Air Force base, near Rapid City, and I was custodian three years there until 1968, when we moved to Iowa for ten years. She taught art and I built campers. Then I worked in a furniture factory until 1977. We moved back to Wall. In 1978 I went to work for the Post office. I worked there for 14 years. I became postmaster at Quinn, six miles east of Wall. In 1992, I retired at age of 69, and haven't done much since *(laughing)*.

PTSD Symptoms?

Once in awhile I get a dream. Otherwise, I transitioned smoothly.

What Helped You Cope?

I didn't talk about it much until years later, going to reunions. I was just glad to be home. I'd had a stable home life. My parents didn't fight or threaten divorce. I always had something to eat and a place to sleep, which was more than some had.

I always said that WWII was won by high school graduates. Being raised in the Depression, we didn't know we were poor, because everyone was. We didn't have anything except hard work, and maybe that's why we could take the conditions. In the Army, we were getting paid and had something to eat. We got $30.00 a month. They took $6.50 for insurance and $6.50 for laundry. Airborne troops got $50 a month more for hazardous duty. That was a lot of money.

CALM UNDER PRESSURE

I stayed calm despite the fear. I always thought I was going to come home. Bill Brown, my buddy, always said he wasn't coming home. On the ship from Boston, he said, "I won't see Boston again, and you probably won't either." In 1995, I visited his grave in Kansas with his brother and four sisters. His sister said he always said he wasn't coming back. So it was probably positive thinking—I assumed I was going to make it.

I had no real hatred or blood thirst for the Germans. Most of us came from Europe. Going into the German city of Munster, a German soldier came up and asked us not to shoot. He showed us some others who were wounded—one was really butchered and had a leg gone. He wanted to know if there was a doctor. We could have shot him, I guess, and maybe could have gotten into trouble for letting them go, but we just pointed him to the aid station.

RATIONAL THOUGHT PROCESSES

When times were tough, I thought that it could be worse. I think today, and have taught my kids this: You're not sleeping out in the cold and nobody's shooting at you. It could be worse.

I guess we all make mistakes. You try to learn from them. I wasn't aware of others' faults too much. I always said I had the best platoon sergeant in the Army and the best company commander.

SOCIAL SUPPORT

Our company commander, Captain Sturhman, was a Missouri farm kid. At 30, he was younger than my platoon sergeant, who was 33. Neither was a pushover, but they were nice to all of us and they'd talk to us. They'd explain things to us, and we could talk to them about our problems. On the last day of basic training in August, we took a 25-mile hike. It was hot and I was exhausted. My squad leader put smelling salts under my nose. The company commander came back and said, "Can y'all take one more step? If you don't y'all will have to take it again next week, so keep trying." He led in a nice way.

We were always one in the unit. We all knew each other just like you do in a small community. If one got hurt, the rest were there to help and take care of each other. It was like going through high school with the same kids. We'd talk about what we were going to do when we got home. We played football and baseball in the states. I was friendly—always anxious to talk to someone and always visiting with people. There was no use in being crabby. I kept up with the South Dakota soldiers. I preferred the quieter, kinder people to the blustery. Even now, they have reunions in August. This year will be the 49th and I've been to six. Most of the time I didn't have enough money to go.

Training together and being in the same company without being transferred helped to increase our confidence. We all knew each other and what our buddies could do. It was just like a football team.

I got a letter once a week from my parents and grandparents, except during that four-month period. They were real important. I wrote someone almost every night.

COMFORTABLE WITH EMOTIONS

We were all scared to death. We were only 18 and 19 years old. It was okay to admit we were scared. Sometimes it came out in other ways, like griping about the chow. The captain always said, "The ones that do the bitching and griping, I know they're going to make it. The ones that scare me are the quiet ones." So we'd gripe a lot about the K-rations.

SELF-ESTEEM

I felt that I was as good as the next guy. You have to have confidence in yourself. I guess I thought that I had just as much chance as anyone else. My dad always said that every boy could be President if he had a million dollars. I saw a lot of people start out with nothing, learn to talk just as I did, and become successful. General Eisenhower was just some kid from Kansas.

ACTIVE, CREATIVE COPING

When passive, you think of bad things instead of driving on. Maybe you feel sorry for yourself. Being raised on the farm and doing chores you learned to keep busy. I think it helped me adjust to combat. If I was told to do something, I did it.

SPIRITUAL AND PHILOSOPHICAL STRENGTHS

God

My beliefs gave me strength and comfort. We always went to service every time we could in Europe and the States. The platoon sergeant and I always went together. I believed in God and thought of him as fatherly, even though I today wonder why he lets some things happen.

Meaning & Purpose

We were fighting for freedom. That was the big goal. If we hadn't won we wouldn't be sitting here today. I can't imagine the world today if Hitler had won. I also wanted to come back to farming, my first love.

Morality

I tried to get along the best I could and treated others nicely. I never saw it as an advantage to be bad or sarcastic. My dad always taught me to leave things that I liked alone if they didn't belong to me. I never did steal anything from GIs or Germans. I always tried to be honest and taught our children to be. I have never been unfaithful to my wife. One of the worst things I saw was the starving children after the war. We tried to sneak them food. On guard in Germany after the war, a German man asked for a good square meal. I helped him get a job for food working in the U.S. kitchen. He had lived in the United States longer than I had.

Loy: "He always looks out for the underdog. I've only seen him in two fights in his life. He stepped in when a man was going to whip a 17-year-old drunk who was too drunk to handle himself. Another time, an Indian man's boss was dressing down the wife like she was a dog for trying to get her husband's pay check so she could buy groceries. Some of his best strengths are his honesty and kindness.

Love

Outside of family, the bonding in the military is the tightest one. Being together so long in training and battle formed very strong bonds. You helped each other even in the chaos of battle. I even recall seeing one buddy help a wounded person with whom he hadn't gotten along. He dragged him, crawling for a half mile, to safety.

Loy explained: "At Army reunions, the bond is different completely from the one he has with his family, in a way that none of the family can touch. It was forged under different circumstances. There's a closeness you can't describe."

Captain Stuhrman was the only company commander we'd ever had. We had an airborne reunion in 1990. Six of us enlisted men were discussing where we'd hold the next reunion. After a half-hour, we agreed to vote for Cedar Rapids, Iowa, because one of the men had a farm there that was convenient and we could stay there for free. Well, the master of ceremonies announced it was time to vote. The first city mentioned was St. Louis, Missouri. Silently, Captain Sturhman—still distinguished at 77—stood up to vote, because that was his home state. In unison, all six of us stood with him to vote for St. Louis. His ability to lead hadn't diminished one iota. That bond had never been broken. He had led us through all our training and the war and had earned our respect, and it never went away. It really hit me when he passed away. He was tops in my book.

Fifty years after the death of my best friend, Bill, I tried to find where he was buried, to say a final goodbye. On May 6, 1995, I visited his grave in Kansas, along with Loy and my son, Bill, and four of my buddy's siblings. One advantage he has over us is that he'll be forever 20.

Optimism

I am and was an optimist. I always thought I was coming home and that we'd win. I looked on the bright side of things and never did quit anything. I think that anything that happens could be worse. In cabinet making, I always think they will turn out well. When waking up my wife, I always said, "The sun is shining, coffee's perking, birds are singing, and it looks like it's going to be a lovely day."

Humor

Humor was so important. I never got too serious about anything. There's always something nice and funny. In the Army, we'd kid people for doing something wrong and getting caught, like throwing an orange peel on the ground and having to dig a four-foot hole to bury it. We'd tease the guy who got sick in his helmet in the glider and made the rest us all get sick. Tragedy is always funny afterward. In a foxhole, my buddy said that he didn't think anybody was out there. He raised his shovel and before he could pull it down there were five holes in it.

I took a German girl to a party in Berlin. There were sandwiches and she was interested in eating. I asked her if it was hard to learn to speak English. "She said, "I don't know what you mean by *hard*. Do you mean *difficult*?" She spoke English better than I did. I should have paid better attention in school.

I have a dry sense of humor. I wasn't mean to the kids. I might get old someday and have to go live with them. Once Loy was having trouble with my daughter and said I'd have to give her a spanking when I got home. I was sad, because I rarely spanked, but I put her over my knee. She sobbed, "Daddy, why did you spank me?" I said, "Well, it didn't hurt, did it?" It didn't, but she could hear it.

I always liked Will Roger's humor. He said that our government was an open book— checkbook, that is.

Long View of Suffering

If there was something good, it was the friendships, which I wouldn't have had otherwise. I also learned to hunker down and take difficult things and not give up. I walked 33 miles once on maneuvers carrying a machine gun 19 of those miles. I made it when a lot of others dropped out. Training was tough but it paid off later. I had open-heart surgery in 1987. Remembering helped me have the strength and determination to persist in the recovery program.

Maintaining Balanced Living

I usually get six to seven hours of sleep, from eleven until 5:00 or 6:00 in the morning. I nap after lunch. I am a cheerful early riser. I walk a half-mile nightly. I used to walk more, before my knees got arthritis.

I ate meat and potatoes until the '80s. I pushed away from the table. If the table moved and I didn't, I knew there was a problem. Then I got diabetes. Now I eat heart healthy, lots of vegetables.

In 1987, with open-heart surgery, I quit smoking. I never smoked more than a pack a day. I drank moderately, not every day. Now I don't drink at all.

For recreation, I read and do crossword puzzles to keep my mind exercised. That's as important as keeping the body exercised. In 1975, I started reading books and read all the time now—history books, Lewis and Clark, war books, Southwest history. I love to work in the shop, building things like cabinets, cedar chests, decks, and lamps. Friends always bring me something to fix or build. I enjoy country western concerts and music, music in general. In the hospital in Paris, I watched and listened to Glenn Miller's band, and still like his music. (He died around the time that we flew over to France). My wife and I travel and visit the three children. I like to fish but I don't have much time to. I think I'll go back to work so I can take some time off.

Advice to Younger Generations

Be optimistic. Have confidence in yourself, knowing you can do it. Give your best. Know you are going to make it, and don't look down. Be decent and honest.

There's a sign in my shop that says, "Wear it out, use it up, and eat it all." Like Grandma's nightgown, I guess that about covers everything.

With Honor Guard in Berlin, 1945

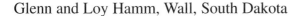

Glenn and Loy Hamm, Wall, South Dakota

Chapter 23

Lin H. Johnson
Scout Corporal

Tall (6'), slender, and fit from a lifetime of outdoor work, Lin Johnson is a most amiable and gentle man, and a keen observer of human nature who writes for his local newspaper.

I was born in Idaho's upper Snake River Valley, the third oldest of twelve children. I lived on a farm, in a hardworking, happy family. We were disadvantaged as far as material things, but we had an abundance of love and lots of fun. My parents were salt of the earth. Dad was college educated, very talented, and not afraid of hard, dirty work. He was understanding and not severe. He didn't countenance wrongdoing, but was not harsh about it. He gave us gentle correction if we were out of line. He seldom spanked us, and then only if we really deserved it. Mom was patient and gentle, and loved her kids, who were foremost in her life. She made every one of us feel worthwhile and important and like we wanted to achieve the potential in us. She never wanted anything for herself, but family was first priority. There was not a selfish bone in her body.

We were a musical family. Dad was a gifted musician. After we boys got the cows milked and evening chores done and the girls did the dishes — usually it was dark by then — the family sang around the battered piano. We learned to harmonize. All my life, we sang in duets and quartets and choirs. We were poor but didn't know it, because all the people around us were poor. There was no radio or other distractions. Education was important. When we were little, Mom would read stories from her rocking chair — no junk books, but good caliber literature or scriptures. My parents saw to it that we did our homework, and they would help us with it. All the kids went to college, the family producing a doctor, dentist, and a Ph.D.

My family was very self-sufficient. Almost all of our food came from the farm: vegetables and fruits — sometimes canned — and butchered meat. We went to the store only for a few essentials. Mother sewed clothes for the family. We attended church regularly and had family prayers night and morning on our knees, every day.

During the Depression, Dad lost the farm and we moved to several farms.

I was drafted in 1942, into the 95th Infantry Division. I was sent to England and came across the English Channel in landing craft soon after Normandy's D-Day, to temporary dock at Omaha Beach. Exploring one day, I found a cemetery with white crosses for American soldiers killed at D-Day and ensuing battles. An elderly French couple stopped at each grave, said, "Merci, merci beaucoup," and would then lay a flower on each grave. My Division entered action in the fall of 1944 in Patton's 3rd Army. I was a scout corporal (forward observer for the artillery). We started to hammer the Germans. We shifted to the southern flank of the Bulge, and inflicted heavy damage on the Germans. In May 1945, we pushed into Germany as far as Hamburg. I had a number of brushes with death. For example, a colonel kicked me out of a building and turned it into his headquarters. The next day I carried six to eight bodies out of that building — they'd been killed by German artillery. In the Ardennes we were so tired, cold and numb. Once, I led a unit into a location at night. We traveled over a frozen road containing a land mine. The next day the road thawed, and a messenger was blown up as he traveled over that same road. My division overran one of the smaller extermination camps. I saw the rotting corpses and the barely living. We rousted the locals out of their homes to see it and know that it wasn't a "convalescent hospital." Many vomited and fainted. A Nazi SS POW asked me why we didn't mind our own business and permit the Germans to cleanse the earth of Jews. I thought of all the women and children they had slaughtered and thought of my own grandmother, mother, and sisters, and knew why it was my business.

Most GIs were very considerate to the civilians, and except in a few isolated instances, were kind. This was very distinctive for an army. During the occupancy, I tried to befriend and help the Germans. Has history ever recorded a victorious army trying to feed the conquered? We shared our rations with civilians. Some adopted little homeless kids like big brothers. Civilians had been led by Hitler to fear us, but, to our credit, we helped them. We fought the war for the right purposes and, when we won, we did what we should. One woman, mayor of a Belgium town, had been active in the resistance movement. She was amazed that we were so kind and helpful.

After the war in 1945, I received a medical discharge for injuries. I finished college and married a young wonderful woman who was much like Mother. We started farming, buying Dad's farm and the one next to it, and I continued irrigated agriculture until the age of 77. We have six children, including one daughter and five sons. My first wife died 17 years ago, at age 59. I was remarried to a widow 14 years ago. We live on the outskirts of Idaho Falls

PTSD Symptoms?

After the war, I had some momentary fits and jerks, but nothing serious. The passing of time allows me to view the war with a somewhat mellow detachment. This was perhaps the cruelest war in history. But when I got home, even though we were trained to be killers, we were so grateful to be home and free of all that, that I didn't notice anyone of my personal acquaintance who was changed from what he was before into someone who was cruel and unfeeling. We were glad to slip back into civilian life and be done with the war and have it in the past.

What Helped You Cope?

We were so busy with raising families and positive things, that we didn't dwell on the negative. If we hadn't been so occupied, we might have tended toward PTSD.

CALM UNDER PRESSURE

Initially, I hated the Germans, though this changed. The SS divisions were raised from boyhood to believe Nazis were superior, to hate, and to kill. They became brutal, efficient killing machines. Later in the war, Hitler had to draft others, many of whom were older men. We found them decent guys, like our fathers. So I modified my opinion. Then, when we saw how devastated the country was, I felt compassion. Lots of Germans were victims of their system, but I learned they weren't all that way. I never lusted to kill. I had more contempt for members of our own Graves Registration Units who removed watches, rings, and other personal effects from our dead boys and sold them on the black market, items that would have meant so much to their grieving survivors. This, of course, was a very rare occurrence.

RATIONAL THOUGHT PROCESSES

When you're young, you tend to see things as life and death. As you mature, you learn that everyone blunders, and many things in life are not so critical. In the war, we made lots of tactical blunders, but still won the war. I concluded that the Germans made blunders too, but more than we did, and that's why we won.

We all had combat fatigue to a certain extent. At one point, I didn't think I would come home, and wrote letters to my parents, telling them that and instructing them about how they should use my insurance money for the family. But I told my dad that I never broke my moral code or did anything to be ashamed of. I felt that as long as I was true to my principles, I could die without regret.

SOCIAL SUPPORT

Friends were vital. Most everyone had a special buddy in the unit, and a nickname. I was Johnny. We had Rabbi, Hog Meat, Pappy and others. In combat, you realize that you depend on others. Personal dislikes must be put into perspective. I'd never have associated with some of my buddies unless the fortunes of war had thrown us together. I found out that, deep down beneath the surface, we're mostly similar. Without a sense of kinship, you don't make it. War is the crucible that strips away phoniness and pretense. Despite differences, we're mostly alike.

I had a girlfriend back in the U.S., a choice girl I hoped to marry. And letters from back home were so important. Oh, my, they were my lifeblood. I got letters pretty regular but some of those poor guys were hungry for a letter and they'd go to mail call day after day and started wondering, "What do I amount to—is my life worth anything? Does it matter?" One nice kid was so starved for a letter, he said, "Johnny, I hate to ask you, but I haven't had a letter for so long. Would you let me read that letter from your mother." I said, "Sure." He read it and he had to wipe a tear from his eye, and said, "Oh I wish someone would write to me like that and say those nice things and tell me about the good things that are going on back there. I can hardly remember." And I felt so bad for him and after that I'd share my letters with him, because the poor guy— I don't know when he ever got a letter. One of the best keys to survival was the constant flow of letters, so we knew we mattered and somebody cared. Otherwise it seemed hopeless.

COMFORTABLE WITH EMOTIONS

We were scared kids, a long way from home, never without fear; we just accepted the low-level fear. Sometimes fear became quite intense.

At one point, we had moved into a German house. My sisters had sent me a miniature Christmas tree, which we decorated and set on the mantle. A Polish slave girl emerged from hiding in the straw in the barn. When she saw the tree that child cried, and so did all the soldiers, unashamed. It was okay to cry then. Crying is a great tension reliever, as is laughter.

SELF-ESTEEM

We were confident from our training and experience. Of course, after the Bulge, we had to relearn some lessons. We were raised with a free spirit, to think no one had a right to tell us what to do.

ACTIVE, CREATIVE COPING

To keep warm, I showed the guys how to build dugouts — underground log and dirt shelters— that were just like the potato cellars we built in Idaho with timbers.

Because of the culture we were raised in — the American system gives more choices than anywhere else—we were not repressed. So we could adapt, improvise, make do. The SS was efficient until things broke down. We could function better without rules. When Americans couldn't get out of the hedgerows in Normandy, some American took a tank and built a brush cutter on the front of the tank. He didn't wait for someone to design one. In winter combat in the Ardennes, the Yanks built snowplows, also on the front of tanks. The Europeans were used to being told what to do. We chafed under regimentation; underneath was a free spirit.

War calls for creativity. Regimentation and textbook fighting don't work, because you don't run into textbook situations. We had to discard what we learned at artillery school, in favor of Yankee ingenuity. The Germans went by the book.

SPIRITUAL AND PHILOSOPHICAL STRENGTHS

God

I had made promises to God before shipping overseas. I felt obligated to obey them and this was a great source of strength. I felt that He was mindful of me. I took lots of ribbing for not drinking or fooling around with women, but I became more and more appreciated over time. I gave away my cigarette rations (we were issued seven packs a week in combat) to friends. After the war, worship gave perspective, focus, stability and balance.

Meaning & Purpose

This was a war to preserve civilization. I felt that God would help us come out on top. Had we lost, it would have meant the end of civilization as we know it. The Nazis would have controlled the world. Yet my long view let me realize that mortality and war are temporary. It has an end. I knew we'd win. Someday I hoped to be home or buried with honor. Once home, I focused on raising a family and living a good life.

Morality

On R&R in a Belgian town with two buddies, we struck up an acquaintance with three young women at a café. As we were leaving, the young women invited us home to spend the night. One said to me, "I'll make you so happy." I said, "I'm so happy now, I can hardly stand it." I was ribbed for that. One buddy said, "You have to be dumb. Is it because of your religion?" I said, "Yes." He said, "You sure passed up a deal. Who would ever know?" I said, "The Lord and I." I remembered promises I'd made to God. Whenever the severest trials came, I felt that strength. I came close to the breaking point a lot of times and a lot of guys did. We were pushed to the limit in such sustained, unrelenting, unrelieved combat conditions. We all had combat fatigue. The body starts to break. You have to dig down somewhere and find some strength or you can't go on. It would have haunted me if I'd given in.

[When I asked him, "Why did you do that?" he said, with tears] I knew my parents and younger brothers and sisters wanted me to be an example. I knew every morning and night our family knelt in prayer. My mother told me in a letter how they prayed for my safety and well-being. And I knew instinctively every morning and night my family was on their knees petitioning the Lord for my safety, and that thought never left me. My Dad wrote me and said, "In prayer, Mother asked the Lord to protect you and your brother. She couldn't finish. I had to finish the prayer for her." I never forgot the impact to know that, thousands of miles away, they felt they could ask the Lord to protect me, and they had the faith to believe that would take place. In saying goodbye to me as I was leaving Europe, my buddy told me that my buddies had bet that I would break down and abandon my moral standards, but I never did.

Optimism

I know my family was praying for me. I'd kept my promises and if He wanted to take me I wouldn't have a lot of excuses to make. That's basically the way I felt. I prayed for strength to do what I knew I should do. I felt a fatalistic resignation to die at one point, I was feeling so low. But I felt that if I lived the way I should, I would be peaceful.

Humor

When fear got intense, such as when the Germans were bombing us or shelling us with artillery, offbeat humor and horseplay relieved the pressure. We'd say, "If the Germans are aiming at us, we don't have to worry."

At one point Patton's army was laid low with diarrhea from drinking bad water—oftimes rivers were polluted by decaying bodies. Our captain said he'd court marital anyone who got sick from not drinking out of the lister bags. The captain was the next guy to get sick. One guy with really bad diarrhea was running to the latrine. A guard said, "Halt or I'll shoot." The guy said, "Go ahead, you'd do me a favor." In one German town, a GI farm boy found a workhorse and rode it down the street. His buddies ribbed him, saying, "All you have is one horsepower," and he rejoined, "That's all I need—I'd just like to be back home and have this horse hooked up to something and be out of this cockeyed mess."

I think humor gave GIs an edge. They were not so suppressed that they couldn't think and improvise.

Long View of Suffering

Overall, we were just kids out of high school, pitted against the more experienced Germans. We were overmatched at first, but persisted with ingenuity. I guess we didn't realize that deep down inside we were growing in perseverance and maturity and gratitude. We appreciated that we lived through it and that we returned to a country where our farms, schools, and cities were safe and secure, just as we'd left them. So many European homes were blown apart and they were left homeless. We were grateful to come home to the same circumstances.

Maintaining Balanced Living

I farmed until age 77, up to 16 hours a day of hard work, and that kept me exercised. Since then I've kept active tending the yard. I eat well. I go to sleep early and rise early, getting six to eight hours. I've never been a drinker or smoker.

I've enjoyed writing a weekly column for the local newspaper—light-hearted observations about farming. I once wrote an article about battle fatigue and cattle fatigue. I've stayed involved in my church.

Advice to Younger Generations

I don't know if I'm qualified to give advice. I'd say, have a right sense of values and stay involved with church. Without a concept of religion or God, it is only what can I get materially, what goodies, what play things, rather than the concept of eternal, meaningful things.

Appreciate the sanctity and enduring value of a good marriage. I learned in census work that there are fewer traditional families today. Marriage is ordained of God, a sacred covenant, whether by minister or judge.

Little kids are growing up not knowing what a good stable family is. In my home, the girls worked in the home—making bread, doing laundry, cooking meals, etc, while the boys worked with Dad in the fields. Regardless of one's religious affiliation, society can't be stable without stable homes, and that starts with united parents.

Learn how to enjoy meaningful things, and not be set on material abundance, worrying about how others have more. Appreciate what you have and make do. Don't waste or throw away.

Lin Johnson, circa 1942

Lin and Madge Johnson,
September, 1945

Lin Johnson, Idaho Falls, ID

Chapter 94

Jackson Brownell Vail
Infantry Squad Leader

There is one traffic light in the town of Cumberland, Maine, the home of Jack and Helen Vail. The road through town passes between a church and the cemetery. They live in a Cape Cod house with cedar shingles. The American flag hangs on the front of the house.

Jack is the oldest of the four Vail brothers, all of whom served during WWII. He fought through France, winning the Silver Star for gallantry and the Purple Heart.

Jack and Helen raised two daughters and a son. Their relationship is a love story. Helen has Alzheimer's disease. He takes care of her with loving tenderness and patience — cooking, baking biscuits, cleaning, doing laundry, taking her for walks and to church, and occasionally taking her camping. He is a trim 5'11."

I was born just across the Vermont border in Monroe, Massachusetts, in 1917, the oldest of four boys. Our home was a warm one and I feel nothing but thanksgiving for it. Dad was away selling a lot. In some aspects, my mother was the strength of the family. She put up with us fellows.

Dad's college baseball pictures were on the walls. He was one step out of the major leagues pitching. I wanted to be like him, a great ball player. I played third base. He loved to hunt and fish and we had a good time going with him. We didn't know much about girls, being four boys. We had a collie dog that used to get between us every time we had a scrap and quell that fight.

Dad didn't bring home a lot, but we got by. In summers each one of us worked. I did manual work—mowing lawns, and working for the town, shoveling gravel into a truck and spreading it onto the roads. I couldn't afford college after high school. I went to Maine Central Institute, an inexpensive prep school, so I could play ball. They had good teachers. Then I got in a year of business classes in a junior college in Portland. During the fall of 1937, during the Depression, an aunt invited me to come stay with her and look for work in the Newark, New Jersey, area. After driving a delivery truck for an auto parts store, I answered an ad and became a salesman for Fuller Brush Company, selling door to door. I thrived on the challenge of earning commission on sales of a good product. Late in the summer, I returned to Portland. I continued selling Fuller Brushes and led the state in sales.

In June 1941, I was drafted and got to travel and sightsee quite a bit. I completed basic training in Camp Croft, South Carolina. The training was strenuous. There was good espirit de corps. There was a West Pointer who had a troublemaker under his command, a heavy set private who rebelled against authority. They settled it out between the barracks with boxing gloves—a real show. That was the kind of lieutenant he was. He would have the respect of his company. I don't regret my time there. We spent a cold winter training in Pine Camp (later Fort Drum), New York. The day after Pearl Harbor, the disciplined sergeants had us out in the snow doing bayonet drills. I had signed up for more training at Fort Knox, Kentucky, but I told the first sergeant that I wasn't going to go. I wanted to stay with my outfit. He insisted that I go. I had one meal at Fort Knox and returned to my outfit. I had a mind of my own and it wasn't very good. I hitchhiked back, and didn't get a very warm welcome, but I was allowed to stay with my outfit. We then did maneuvers and training in Tennessee, the Mojave Desert, and Camp Bowie, Texas. During our six months in the desert, I wore the knees out of three pairs of fatigues, from running and hitting the ground. We had to just sew up the holes and make do with what we had, because the first priority was to supply the troops in the Pacific.

We shipped out to England in December 1943, for more demanding training in the cold weather. We went into Normandy July 12, 1944, about a month after D-Day, to relieve part of the battered 29th Infantry, twelve miles inland. I was a squad leader in the 10th Armored Infantry Battalion of the 4th Armored Division as we fought through France. I can tell you, I wouldn't be here if the shots had been a little to the right or left. In our first engagement, our company commander went down, mortally wounded. We were in an open pasture with tall grass. I put my platoon's machine gun into operation against a heavily fortified German position. Within minutes, we were drawing heavy mortar fire, because the Germans had the positions zeroed in. We had to dodge them by rolling side to side.

I was impressed at the way our engineers welded blades to tanks so that they could plow holes through the dense hedgerows. I was wounded in late September. My squad was located in defile. About a mile below us, our tanks were engaging the German tanks. Our tanks were no match for the enemy's bigger guns. The one thing that made a difference was our P-47 and P-51 fighters, which came in low and dropped bombs. I noticed three Germans moving along the slope above us. I got up to discourage others that might be there. I had to swing my legs over a barbed wire fence. As I reached the height of the hill, I heard the "phift, phift" of sniper bullets passing by me. By now, the Germans were out of range, so I returned to my slit trench. I was lying in the slit trench and, as I raised my head after a few minutes, a sniper's bullet entered my neck, passed under my spine, and traveled diagonally across my body to the kidney area. While recovering in a hospital, I missed my outfit and the camaraderie. I rejoined the unit at the end of November. By then, there was only one man left from my squad.

One of the hardest places was close to the German border, where one of our Sherman tanks was hit in a duel with a German tank. The lieutenant's burned body was thrown from the vehicle. In the Battle of the Bulge, my unit and other forces of Patton's Army fought through the German ring surrounding Bastogne to free the 101st Airborne Division. The last month or two, we were in the snow, wearing long overcoats. Some mornings it got down to below zero in the slit trenches. There was a long stretch of cold, until a thaw came mid-March. Somehow you managed to get accustomed to the cold and we survived that.

I was discharged in May of 1945. Following the war, I worked three years. I went back to selling Fuller Brushes. Then, between 1948 and 1952, I went to Springfield College to study physical education on the GI bill. I met Helen there, and we married in my last year at Springfield College. After teaching for five years, I worked at the state institution for the mentally and physically disabled as a recreation teacher. I ran sports programs and field trips, sometimes taking "my boys" on camping trips *[According to his brothers, he worked wonders at the place]*. I saw some of the boys get out. I worked there for 23 years. I then worked in a brick yard until it closed—the old way of making bricks. I remember writing to my son about all the things I learned, how they mixed sand, clay, and water. I also worked in a convalescent home as a handyman and as a substitute teacher for three or four years. Sometimes that was pretty rough. I retired in 1984.

PTSD Symptoms?

I had no PTSD symptoms. I did have an energy that wasn't harnessed yet—a quietness that I needed—but I got to work and put the war behind me.

What Helped You Cope?

During the war, I felt a loyalty to my unit. Right after the war I joined the telephone company, working with a line crew that was something like the Army. This helped me to transition and settle in. I also joined the American Legion, working to get a ball field for the town.

CALM UNDER PRESSURE

The training I had helped very much. I knew the simple things. I knew how to follow orders. As soon as I heard firing, I gave the command to put the machine gun into action. We drew a lot of fire, but I did what I was supposed to do. We trained probably longer than we needed. We were together as a unit.

I didn't have any negative feelings toward the Germans. We didn't get a lot of indoctrination against them. It was probably just as well. We were taught the rudiments of combat. I was dumb enough not to think about where I was and what I was doing. My primary thought was to push the Germans back.

RATIONAL THOUGHT PROCESSES

We could always say that someone above us goofed up. In a convoy at night, we stopped and were told to dig in into the hard, frozen clay. About the time we got blisters from digging fast, we were told to mount up and move out. I look back and laugh at the GI hurry up and wait. We just tried to do what we could.

SOCIAL SUPPORT

I really missed my outfit when I wasn't with them and after I came home. We did things as a squad. If someone was sick or had a problem we knew about it; we cared for each other. I was close to several. We fulfilled our obligations as best we could. I felt loyalty to my company commander, Captain Leighton, and the lieutenants, but mostly we thought of the squad. After the war, I had contact with two buddies from my unit who came to visit.

Letters were important to me. Mother wrote fairly often. The war shook my father up a lot, with his boys in the service at the same time. He started to go to church with my mother.

While in England, I met my brother in London. He was in a B-17 that would go down later on the border of Switzerland, where he was interned. We spent a few days together. That was good. We toured the beautiful countryside and towns on bicycles. A constable in a little town loaned me his bike. It had bad hand brakes, though, and going down a hill I almost killed myself.

COMFORTABLE WITH EMOTIONS

Of course I was scared. I guess it was the unknown. Once, while on patrol along the woods, I came upon a German machine gun nest. Two of the enemy jumped up and ran instead of shooting at us. They could have killed us. But you did what you could, despite those feelings. I didn't keep it inside.

SELF-ESTEEM

I was confident, and attributed it all to the lengthy training. We didn't have to figure things out or think about it under pressure. I think our company trained harder than most.

ACTIVE, CREATIVE COPING

I was one who aspired to be a somebody and have some part in the company. That was my ambition. I became a sergeant and did my job. I was also a leader when we played softball.

SPIRITUAL AND PHILOSOPHICAL STRENGTHS

God

I called out to God and prayed during the war, although I didn't have a great affinity initially. I felt the encouragement of others' prayers following me. I felt it was God that allowed me to survive the war.

I commit each day in prayer. Oftimes, I feel inadequate, but I know He doesn't look at me that way. I know He forgives and is merciful and longsuffering toward us. These things are written in my mind.

Just before being discharged, I was in Washington to begin a tour of war plants to compliment and encourage the workers. I was standing in front of the USO, when a young fellow said, "Do you know where you are going?" He led me to Christ, which was stabilizing. My faith was established and that gave me something to go on for a long time.

After the war, I'd fellowship with friends for Bible study at Springfield College. That's how I met Helen. These friends were important, although most of these friends have passed away.

Meaning & Purpose

We belonged to the United States as citizens and we had a job to do. I knew where I was supposed to be and what I was supposed to do. I didn't cuss God or my fate, but went along stoically.

Morality

There were times when unarmed or wounded Germans were walking toward us. I never hurt them.

I remember a married man weeping for what he had done during the war. God has his commandments. It isn't so much about judging my neighbor. That's none of my business. But my integrity is important. To me morality means doing what I know is right, being an example to others if I can, and protecting principles. I ask myself, "Am I really loyal to God?" For example, a co-worker wrote an article for a newspaper that was rather base and suggestive. I wrote to the editor, saying that it was offensive to readers. I also wrote to editors for offensive advertisements. I knew when I got off the track and it wasn't very good. I try to put my mistakes behind and fill out my days as best I can.

Love

Once, in training, we crossed a river in Tennessee and slept on our raincoats in a barnyard. In the morning, eight of us were sitting along the road waiting for our platoon leader to lead us on another hike. A woman and her mother were so good. They invited us to come to their kitchen, which was nearby, and gave us beans and hot biscuits. What a feeling that was! That was quite a bit of hospitality. Those kinds of things strengthen you.

As I was taking the train back to England to recover, a woman walked down the aisle with little homegrown tomatoes. She said to all the wounded, "Now just open your mouth and I'll pop it in." I'll never forget that kindness.

My wife and I had some hard times. I acknowledged that I was wrong. Ever since then, our relationship has been 100%. We have a good loving relationship, and look forward to things we can do together. We enjoy going out shopping. We went camping last August for three days. People were so kind to us. They helped us set up our tent and brought us supper. Helen and I sat by the water and watched the ducks swim by. My, what a time we had.

Optimism

Sure. I'm an optimist. I could leave this world tomorrow. I love life and know it won't last many more years, but I'm an optimist. A lot of people don't measure up, yet are called friends of God. God deals with us kindly Why shouldn't I be an optimist? I'm not successful every day, but God is over all.

Humor

There was always something to laugh at. Someone would be the life of the party wherever we were. Sometimes you would gripe or laugh at how bad the food was, but of course you never said anything to the mess sergeant. At least I didn't, but I wondered if the mess sergeant made a career of cooking.

Long View of Suffering

I'm glad the war is over. As I look back, the Army was good. The training was tedious, but we had good espirit de corps. Hardship and discipline pay off if you are committed. You learn something about character. You learn how education makes people better leaders and instills purpose. You gain from observing both the leaders and the goof-offs.

During the three years that I taught school after the war, the best thing was to learn that I wasn't really a teacher, just because my brothers were. It taught me some things about myself.

Maintaining Balanced Living

I usually exercise in the morning, walking, sit-ups, a lot of stretching. I garden and mow the lawn. I've usually eaten well. I'm not a heavy eater. I don't need to go to a full course restaurant. Helen is a good cook. We always had a salad and balanced meals with vegetables with the meat. I've usually gotten seven hours of sleep, generally arising at 6 a.m.

I tried smoking for a short time, but it never became a habit. I've never been a regular drinker. I don't have any need for it.

I've enjoyed fishing. For each of the past ten to twelve years, I've gotten together with my brothers to camp for two or three days. We play tennis together, too, but that's a laugh.

Helen and I like to go sight seeing. My wife loves to paint places we've been to, like the ocean. All of the paintings on the wall were done by my wife.

For five or six years, before Helen's illness, I teamed up with another man to visit prisoners at the county jail, a Bible teaching ministry on Monday nights, bringing encouragement to quite a few

Advice to Younger Generations

Be friendly. Have a hobby. Take hold of something, whether it's boating or a simple craft. Develop some skills.

Don't neglect the wisdom of older folks. Latch on to someone you can listen too, like grandparents, and have a listening ear. In your formative years, stay under the care of your parents as long as they are concerned about you. Don't neglect your responsibility to your parents. Keep a good relationship. Be considerate. Obey curfews. Tell your parents when you're coming home. Be conscientious and obedient. It's not good to get loose.

WORLD WAR II SURVIVORS - LESSONS IN RESILIENCE

The Vail brothers: Jackson, Ted, Robert, and Tom, circa 1943

Ted, Jackson, Tom, Robert, 2000

Jackson and Helen Vail

Chapter 25

Joseph Robert Curcio
Surrounded and Wounded

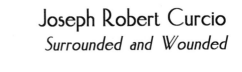

Joseph Curcio lives in a beautiful ranch house with crab orchard stonework (like sandstone), atop a wooded hill in Huntington, Long Island, New York. He built the house and the cabinets in it. Although he walked with a noticeable limp from his war wounds, his stocky, granite 5'7" frame reminded me of photographs I've seen of Vince Lombardi and the "Seven Blocks of Granite." His expression was open and friendly. He began the interview with "Anything I can say that might help," and was gracious, patient, and enthusiastic throughout.

My birthplace was Brooklyn, New York, near the Brooklyn Navy yard. My family was large, very close knit— a traditional Italian family. Both parents were from Italy. I was the youngest of seven— four sisters and two brothers. I had the best childhood in the world, with no real worries. I attended Alexander Hamilton High School.

Growing up, if we had an argument, it was over and gone the next day. We never held grudges. As the youngest, my siblings catered to me, and gave me a lot of attention, especially my oldest sister, who would hide candy in her coat and I would search around for it. My mother spoke very little English. We'd speak to her in English and she spoke back in Italian. My father had his own laundry business. He was a hard worker, and easy to get along with. I couldn't get away with things, but I wasn't spanked. My mother loved to cook and catered to all of us. We never had dinner unless everyone was there. This often meant waiting until my brother got home from work late. Like all Italian families, our regular Sunday meal was a four-hour dinner. Mother did all the cooking. First, there was soup (minestrone or chicken), then antipasto (cheese, salami and cold cuts, sausage, mushrooms). Then macaroni and meat (sometimes breast of veal, a roast, chicken, or sausage, peppers, potatoes). Then fruit; then coffee with dessert. Then we'd start picking all over again.

I didn't feel any lack from the Depression. In those days, the neighborhoods were very close. They were mixed —Jews, Germans, Italians, all nationalities. We all seemed to get along very well. In my honest opinion, there was no such thing as discrimination. I was very friendly in school with a black boy and never even thought about it. For some reason, it got worse in later years. If you did anything wrong, the neighbors threatened to tell your parents. You couldn't really get away with anything without the neighbors knowing about it.

As a teenager, I worked on Saturdays, delivering orders for a grocery store. I also worked with my father in the laundry business after school and on Saturdays. We used to joke around a lot.

I was drafted in 1943, completed basic training in Camp Blanding, Florida, then tested for the Air Corps. I passed the test and went to Texas, but was called back to serve in the infantry, because soldiers were needed overseas. When I was nineteen, I went overseas as part of a weapons platoon. I shipped out to Liverpool, England, in the late spring of 1944, with the 1st Battalion, 117th Infantry, 30th Infantry Division. We landed on Normandy about a week after D-Day, and advanced inland. In July we engaged in fierce fighting —the battle of Mortain, near St. Barthelmy, France. First, we came in and took over the town. Then, the Germans counterattacked with infantry and tanks. Then we took it over again. My battalion bore the brunt of the assault. The town was a shambles. There was not a building left standing. We fought from one hedgerow to another. After taking over Mortain, I was out as an advanced scout with ten to fifteen others, when we were encircled by German tanks. Machine gun rounds ripped into our foxholes from the hedgerows above us at night, and we were eventually captured.

After being captured, it was frightening, because we didn't know if we'd be shot. The German officers interrogated us. We wouldn't answer their questions, although they already knew everything we knew. My interrogator said he'd gone to Yale or Harvard, and spoke English fluently. We were used to carry the German wounded—some of whom were pretty badly wounded. At one point, as I was doing this, I was hit by shrapnel from American artillery and knocked over.

We were then trucked toward Paris. As we were traveling, a British Spitfire came over the treetops and strafed the convoy. I was in the first truck, which took the bulk of the strafing. Quite a few in my truck were killed. A bullet hit a metal-covered prayer book that my mother had given me and which I carried over my heart. *[He pulled out the book, which had an indentation from the bullet.]* My mother said, "Carry this with you always, Joe, and the Lord will protect you." However, I was hit twice in the side, three times in my left arm, and three times in my left leg, where a bullet still is lodged.

They dropped me off at a field medical unit, where I lay for many hours; then I was driven by ambulance to a Paris hospital. I was treated there by the Germans. One German doctor saved my infected leg by punching a drainage hole through the entire leg. I was there for a week or two. Then the French underground liberated the hospital as Patton was approaching and the Germans were retreating. But the hospital was then bombed by German planes.

The Americans flew me back to England. The infection was so bad as to prevent operating. Then I went back to Walter Reed Army Hospital for surgery and rehabilitation for eighteen months as the war was winding down. I was discharged in 1946. My leg today is partially paralyzed.

After further rehabilitation, I trained as a linotype printing operator and mechanic, and worked for the *New York Times* for awhile. Mostly I worked in downtown New York City.

I met my wife at a July 4 dance in Kings Park. My sister introduced us. We courted for about two years. In 1950, I married and began building this home in Huntington. It took three years and some chutzpah to complete it, since I learned how to build it by reading as I went. My wife and I lived with my parents while I was building this house. My wife took full advantage of the opportunity to watch my mother cook and became a very fine cook herself.

I commuted to work for 25 years, and then started a partnership in a printing business, buying a printing shop in East Northport, which I operated until I retired in 1992. My wife and I raised four lovely girls, all of whom graduated from college and are doing well. One is an oncologist.

PTSD Symptoms?

I can honestly say I had no PTSD symptoms.

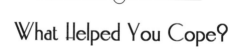

What Helped You Cope?

CALM UNDER PRESSURE

In combat, it was frightening, but we were so involved we sort of forgot about the fears. I focused on what I had to do. Everybody was afraid to a certain extent, but we were all in the same boat.

Nobody panicked. You had to do your job, work together, and stay alive. After we were captured, I thought of making a break for it, but we decided we could get killed.

The Germans weren't that bad. They didn't give us great medical attention or food. They used crepe paper for bandages and aspirin for pain, but only because they didn't have these things for themselves. I didn't hate them. I just felt they had to fight because they were German, just as we had to fight because we were American. They didn't treat us badly.

I have no grudges. The British Spitfires—that was their job. I'm sure that the pilot didn't realize he was firing on allies or he wouldn't have fired.

I never even had a thought of dying, just didn't think of it.

RATIONAL THOUGHT PROCESSES

I never even thought about mistakes.

SOCIAL SUPPORT

I wrote my family every day and they wrote me every day. Because my mother didn't read or write, my sisters read my mother my old letters so she wouldn't know I was captured.

People around us were very supportive during my rehabilitation —nurses in the hospital, USO girls, and volunteers gave us crafts and things to work with to keep our minds occupied. Being around friends really helped, especially during the rehabilitation.

When I got home, being with family helped a lot. We were very close and loving, and joked around a lot. We were always together for Sunday meals and holidays. Sometimes, my cousins and uncles joined us.

I had very good friends in my childhood. Even now, five to seven of us meet each month in a Hicksville diner—fellows I played baseball with in Brooklyn. *[He showed me pictures of the old team, the St. Lucy Colonels, with whom he continued to play after the war. His injuries restricted him to playing first base, but he still starred as a potent hitter, as the newspaper clippings attest]*. I was friends with a lot of people in the service; I didn't have one special buddy, rather a circle of friends. I think that having many friends helped me to cope. I always tried to be helpful. If anyone asked, I'd help with money or with talking. I'm still that way. For example, I help widows in the neighborhood with their homes.

COMFORT WITH FEELINGS

I would have spoken about the war if asked, but until recently never spoke about it. I guess I never felt the need. Also, my life after the war was very good.

SELF-ESTEEM

I always felt very confident. I thought there was nothing I couldn't do, if I really wanted to. I'm that way today. I can't pinpoint why that is. My brother was mechanically inclined. I worked with him, as a helper in a gas station, and learned about automobile repair. I still do all my brake jobs, minor repairs, and, until recently, tune-ups. I can watch and pick things up pretty easily. It was the same with building this house. I got a set of plans, and picked it up right away. I learned to do the stonework by watching a relative, who had been a sculptor in Europe. He hand carved all the stones on the outside of the house and I helped him. Then I did a whole section myself.

We had chores growing up. We weren't idle. There were always things to do. We didn't have steam heat. We had a coal stove, then an oil stove, which I had to maintain and clean each spring. I chopped wood for our stove, on which Mother cooked and which we used for heat.

ACTIVE, CREATIVE COPING

I do everything around here. I'm very handy. I do all the garden work —weeding, trimming, mowing the lawn —house repairs, car repairs. I just did the driveway and the sidewalks over.

SPIRITUAL AND PHILOSOPHICAL STRENGTHS

God

I never lost hope for anything. In the war, my faith was important. I was always religious and went to church every Sunday. I still do. Of course, in combat you couldn't go to church, but in the hospital I always went to Mass, and I think that had a lot to do with keeping my morale up. My whole family went to church every Sunday and on religious holidays. I prayed every night before bed in the service.

God is the only reason we're here. God is very kind, really, even though a lot of things happen to you that you feel shouldn't. That's the way life is. We were brought up to believe that we're only here temporarily. I have no fear of dying. I believe and hope we'll be with loved ones after this life.

Meaning & Purpose

I was only nineteen when I went to war. At the time, I thought it was great that I got to fight for my country. I think most of the kids did then. I didn't have a girlfriend. My family was number one — getting back and seeing them.

I always wanted to be a star baseball player until I was injured. I'd wanted to try out for the pros (I was a Dodger fan), but the war came. After the injury, I had to figure out where I was going in life. I had my family. I loved being in the printing business. I loved to go to work — the people, the work. I had very good relations with others. I get along with all people. They can be whatever they want. I don't care if the person is a millionaire or a bum. I still treat them the same. I never was one to name drop. Celebrities don't phase me. I like and respect people.

Morality

I didn't think about morality much, but I don't think I'd have done anything wrong, or tried to hurt anyone. I didn't believe in fighting. That doesn't solve anything. My religious principles were definitely important. In fifty years of marriage, I never cheated on my wife. Honesty is important. Why would you want to lie? Lying wasn't part of my upbringing. My brothers and sisters were always honest, and always tried to help people, as my parents did. My mother didn't have a bad bone in her body.

Love

My wife died a year ago. It is hard, because we had a very, very good relationship, and were very close. We played golf together, went on trips, and liked to entertain.

Optimism

I had hope. I never got down when I was in the hospital. I always thought things would get better every day. My injury would heal and I would keep going.

Humor

I like to laugh. In the service we joked and took things as they came. We certainly had a lot of laughs in training. Basic training to me was very good. I think all kids today should spend six to twelve months in the service. It's the best thing in the world. It teaches discipline, the lack of which is the biggest problem today. Years back, there wasn't violence; people didn't fly off the handle for little things.

Long View of Suffering

I have no bitterness. I think of all the things that happened in my life — I met my wife, I had my children, we built this house — that were good. We can honestly say that we didn't have any misfortune over the years. I never got bitter about my limp. Don't get me wrong. I wish the injury had never happened. On the other hand, I survived while many others didn't. So I have something to be thankful for. My injury prevented me from playing sports, and limited my golf game and bowling. I like to excel in those things. But I made the best of it, and today I play as well as I can. I think the war made me more mature and gave me a greater sense of responsibility.

Maintaining Balanced Living

I am very active, keeping busy with golf, the house, and the car. When my wife was alive, we had parties. We liked people. We enjoyed traveling and recreating together.

Eating? *(With a laugh)* That's a problem. I try to watch my weight. I have good nutritious meals. My wife was a nutrition nut. We ate the right foods. I never required much sleep. I get four to five hours of sound sleep a night, and go all day. I don't take a nap in the afternoon. I never used drugs. I never drank excessively. Perhaps a glass of wine at meals. I stopped smoking twenty-five years ago.

Advice to Younger Generations

The first thing is that you must have respect for other people, regardless of race, creed, or religion. Once you have that, I think that clarifies everything.

Have good morals. If you have that, you won't harm anyone, and the whole world will get along better.

Joseph Curcio of Huntington, NY

Flanked by his daughters

Chapter 26

Robert B. Jacobs
Supporting the 9th Army

Warm, friendly, humble, gentle, and tall (6'2"), Robert B. Jacobs resides in a lovely apartment with a stunning view of northern Virginia from the balcony. Pictures of him with Congressmen adorn his bedroom, reminiscent of his years working for the House of Representatives. The apartment contains a beautiful Pennsylvania Dutch cabinet from the 1930s and a table, which he stained and finished. He was widowed four months ago, after nearly sixty years of marriage.

I was born in 1920 in Hazleton, in the northeastern coal mining country of Pennsylvania, into a rather typical coal-mining family. I was the baby. I had three brothers and a sister. Father was a civil engineer and surveyor in the mines. His family was Dutch, from upstate New York. Mom's family were what I would call "Molly Maguires," Irish immigrants who worked in the coal mines and lived in company houses and could only redeem their salary in company stores.

Hazleton was a third class city, made up of many ethnic backgrounds—Irish, Polish, Lithuanian, Slovak — and surrounded by smaller towns of immigrants, who were brought over to work in the mines. It was a good place to grow up. We had a good family structure for awhile.

My parents separated when I was about seven years old. I guess I was too young to understand the friction between them, which arose in part because of their different backgrounds. You just took life the way it was.

After my mother died, I ended up living with my brother, who was more than twenty years older than I, and his wife. My sister-in-law was more like my mother. She was a very strict, level-headed person. She came from a Slovak family, and was a very good woman. Their children were like my own brother and sister. I worked part time delivering milk from a horse and wagon on weekends during high school. The Depression never bothered me that much. My brother had a job, so we ate. Every now and then the train came in and announced you could get free prunes and Mother's oats. Everyone in town raced down to the stations with wagons and got a supply. No one was ashamed to do that. My brother moved out of town in my senior year, and I stayed on with a close friend and his family to finish my senior year. We used dynamite to de-stump their country property.

After high school, I took a job in a furniture factory in Beacon, New York, where I had a sister. Then I returned to Hazleton. My brother got me a job at Christmas time working for F.W. Woolworth. A New Yorker in the store evidently liked my work and asked if I'd like to join Woolworth as a lifetime profession, since there was a store in Washington, D.C. So I came to Washington to be trained as a manager. This was a top-flight job during the Depression. But, as things would have it, they hired this beautiful young lady to be in charge of the candy counter. She caught my eye and I caught hers. Well, Woolworth had an ironclad rule that you didn't date employees in the store. That was death. Well, you know—love takes over all of us. We started dating, and got reported. The manager told me, "Either you give her up or you give up Woolworth. So I gave up Woolworth in 1941, and she and I got married.

WORLD WAR II SURVIVORS - LESSONS IN RESILIENCE

I worked for the Baltimore Transfer Company, a trucking company in D.C., checking freight from the railroad cars to the trucks, for about a year, until I was drafted in 1942. I went into an Ordinance Medium Automotive Maintenance Unit and was shipped to Pamona, California, for basic training. Our job was to travel with front line units to take care of vehicles that got hit or broke down without having to take them 500 miles back. In that way, I got to see a lot of action. We trained for Africa in the Mojave Desert in the 2nd Armored Division. I was the company clerk. My wife moved to Palm Springs to live. We then went to Texas to train for a short period.

Since the African campaign had ended, we shipped overseas to England, then took a British destroyer to Omaha Beach, Normandy, September 1944 — a few months after D-day. We stayed there until the end of October.

A new 9th Army was formed under General Simpson. We were called the Will o' the Wisp Army, because nobody knew where we were or who we were. We convoyed through Belgium and Holland. On November 19, we crossed the Siegfried Line and started the invasion of Germany. We were among the first troops in Germany. I'll never forget the sight of 5000 war planes flying overhead, in the biggest air attack of the war.

During the Battle of the Bulge, we were in a little town near Aachen being surrounded by Germans. We could see German tanks skirting us to get to Antwerp, Belgium, a fuel depot, and shells were firing overhead. Here a funny incident happened. We were having trouble with Germans dressed as GIs infiltrating our lines. So guards at the roadblock had to ask new faces questions that only Americans would know, such as how many players are on a baseball team. I was on guard with a big Jewish guy stopping vehicles, while three others were in a shell hole with a 50-caliber machine gun and some bazookas. We stopped a truck with a lieutenant and a black driver. One of us said, "I hate to stop you, but we have to ask you some questions." The lieutenant said, "I have no time to fool with you guys," which we were told would be the typical reaction of a German. We insisted. He told the driver to drive, but the driver refused. The lieutenant then unclipped his 45. We said, "If you un-holster that weapon, two bazookas and a 50-caliber machine gun will take the top of your truck right off." The driver said, "Man, you know I ain't no Nazi." The lieutenant apologized, but said he was in a hurry. We said, "Lieutenant, we're surrounded. There's nowhere to go."

My commander was from the Citadel, but most of the troops in my unit were from the North. Two quartermaster trucks brought in supplies, but then couldn't get back out, because we were surrounded by Germans. The drivers were from the South, and my commander told me to take them out on the roadblock with me. Hearing German gliders overhead in zero degree weather and pitch dark, one stands up in the shell hole and starts shooting in the air. "I'm not going through the war without shooting my gun one time." His buddy said, "Malcolm, when was the last time you fired that gun?" "In Louisiana," the first answered. "I thought so," said the second. "When you shot, I saw frogs and snakes and everything else flying out of your rifle." You talk about GI humor right in the middle of the war. Soon afterward, as company clerk, I wrote certificates certifying that they were brave under fire. They said, "Wait until the folks at home see this. Nobody will believe it." They were real happy about that.

Before we got to Aachen, our mess unit was preparing turkey for Christmas to replace our C-rations. However, a German plane came over and strafed our mess truck and blew it up. We never got the turkey. After the Bulge subsided, we finally got into Aachen, where we set up a field repair. We took captured troops and ordinance to 9th Army Headquarters in Holland. While we were in Aachen, the Germans started shooting V-1 rockets overhead into Belgium. We could see them. They sounded like a truck without a muffler. We were told not to worry about them unless they stopped making noise. That meant they were out of fuel and would land. Well, one V-1 stopped making noise and hit across the street from us and blew a huge hole in the ground. My helmet blew straight up in the air from the concussion. Around this time a Canadian RAF plane crashed into the building I was staying in, killing the pilot.

We were supposed to cross the Rur River, between Aachen and Jülich. We sent welders to do the bridge. Combat engineers were trying to put together Bailey Bridges. They were tangled in German barbed wire, sunk in the river, and the Germans fired on them with machine guns from the other side. So our general gave orders for all who could shoot to fire across the river into the German town—air power and artillery. Next morning, we entered Jülich. It was eerie. The town was dead. They say it was the most devastated town in the war. I saw many dead people and animals all over the place, including a woman still holding onto a baby carriage. This was without a doubt the worst site I saw.

Then we headed for Berlin. Trying to cross the Rhine was the next big step. I went with my lieutenant in a truck with a machine gun to recon the river. All of a sudden, shells fired from the other side of the river start falling all around us. The German townspeople on the banks of the other side of the river were watching this, as though watching a soccer game, and clapping each time the Germans fired. I was scared to death as I felt the concussion of the shells. Yet I really wasn't worried in another sense, feeling I wouldn't get it — it would be the other guy.

One or two days later, we were about to cross the Rhine. On that day, the engineers were putting pontoons across. I had about twelve guys in the back of my truck. As I was driving down to the pontoon bridge, we heard the darndest noise we'd ever heard. We looked up and saw German jets flying right through our planes, which were protecting us, as if they weren't there. Our planes tried to chase them, and ten minutes later the jets were coming back the same way. They didn't seem to be intent on doing harm; more like they were playing with our cocky pilots and showing them what they had. I'm told that this was the first appearance of German jets recorded by the Army. Had the Germans had more of these jets, we'd have had a hard time.

We stopped at Helmstedt, near Berlin. In Helmstedt, a German civilian named Richard Held owned a big estate and cheese factory there. His Dutch laborers had a rope around his neck and were ready to lynch him when we arrived. My buddy and I went over and put a stop to it, saving his life. Herr Held said that after the war he was going to make chewing gum since all the German kids preferred the GI gum to the cheese he made. He offered my buddy and I jobs if we would cut him down. Little bits of humor always floated into everything.

Near Helmstedt was Bergen-Belsen, where Anne Frank was incarcerated. As company clerk I took reports from the troops who had been there and saw their photographs. You had to wonder how anybody could do that. In Helmstedt, the GIs took turns being mayor for a day. The department store remained open for business. We had orders to confiscate the blankets and warm clothes for the slave laborers. The owner kept saying, "Nein, Nein," until a GI next to me fired a machine gun into the ceiling. The slave laborers were very grateful for the clothes and blankets.

Ending up so close to Berlin, we were PO'd that the Russians were allowed to take Berlin.

After the war I went back with the Baltimore Transfer Company and decided to take the civil service exam. I worked in Virginia for the VA for a year, until a reduction in force occurred.

A neighbor's father had a new automotive paint business called Mattos. So I went to work with them to learn not only about paints, but also chemicals, lacquers, and synthetics— which I was interested in. I found out that I could go to school at the National Paint and Varnish Institute at night. I went there for two years. So I learned pretty well the basis of the automotive and industrial paint business, which was something new at the time. After working there for a while, I changed to another paint company, which was more diversified. They specialized in house paint and furniture lacquers, which was again something new, but something I was schooled in. They decided to branch out, and I became the manager of a store in Arlington, Virginia.

In 1969, a friend working on Capitol Hill for the House of Representatives told me, "You know, they're looking for someone that knows furniture lacquers and paint." I applied and was hired to work for the office that managed the office furnishings for all of the House. Under me was the furniture finishing shop, draperies, carpets, etc. I stayed there and eventually became assistant chief of the office. It was a nice paying job. I made a lot of friends before retiring in 1991.

PTSD Symptoms?

Once I got out and came back home, I didn't give the war much thought. My thought was, "OK, lets start over. You've got to make your living; you're married and want to have children."

What Helped You Cope?

Emma, my sister-in-law, made sure we attended church each Sunday. You couldn't find a better woman. She came from a good Slovak family of coal miners. There was no pretense from those people. Everything was basic. She demanded respect as a mother. In no way were you disrespectful. That was the unwritten law of the house. Her habits were aboveboard. No swearing or dirty talk. Consequently, that's what I learned from her. Family discipline and respect in the family were the basis of life. You didn't talk back. You were expected to behave.

From my background, I learned individual strength, independence, and trust that God would provide, despite the ups and downs of moving to other families and sometimes feeling like I was an outsider. I learned to accept the cards I was dealt. The Army was tough on guys who'd never been away from home, but that never bothered me as much as others. Although I never liked being in the Army, I was able to confront it better than those who were too sheltered.

CALM UNDER PRESSURE

The troops in my company were a sharp group. I can't recall anyone really cracking up and that helped me. We just accepted that these things happen in war. My mother taught me to face whatever came up and not hide or turn my back from a fight.

We had a lot of respect for the German military. Germans were similar to Americans in the way that they were and lived. Many would say that being in Germany was just like being in Philadelphia. I had no ill will after the war. They thought they were doing right. That's life. After the war, we had German neighbors we were friendly with, and I hired their boy to work for me.

RATIONAL THOUGHT PROCESSES

Nothing too much bothers me, coming from a broken home, and that's still true to this day. I've been through so much. I realized I could survive almost anything, so I tended not to panic.

We're all human and we all make mistakes. I tried to understand others peoples' sides. I was raised that way. The one big thing that I learned form my Sunday school teacher was to think how I would feel in the same situation and not judge. Coming from a broken home, I observed that Dad, a civil engineer, couldn't stand ignorance. Yet my mother's people were simple Irish coal miners. All they knew was hard work and raising a family. My mother's brothers would never come to our house if my dad were home because he had a way of looking down on them. Mom instilled in us the idea that everyone is capable of rising. So I looked at both ways and decided how I would go. I decided I wouldn't be my dad's way. As a company clerk, you were kind of a psychiatrist, listening to people's problems. I would try to listen as best I could when someone needed a day off, a pass, a trip ticket to use a jeep, or something like that. People said that I had a way of listening to people. My wife, a farm gal from Virginia, invited me to her home when we were first married. When I came down the stairs, there was gravy out for breakfast. I apologized for sleeping so late. I assumed it must be dinnertime, because people up North only have gravy with dinner. I had to learn how people are so different and how little we understand of each others' culture.

I probably made my million mistakes, like other young men. In going to live with my brother, I learned to accept my mistakes. My sister-in-law had a way of raising me with a level head. She made me feel accepted and treated me well. If I made a mistake, that was just part of growing up.

SOCIAL SUPPORT

Letters were very important. Mail call was the crux of the day. I got V-mail *[letters condensed by the government]* from my wife weekly.

I was friendly with everyone, but five or six guys stuck together—birds of a feather. I had one special friend. We were in the foxholes together, bunked together, went on leave together. Everyone had a buddy. It was the natural thing to keep the spirits up. It would be hard to be a loner. You always had to rely on one another for something. I always had respect for others. I also pal'd around with a Jewish lieutenant, a real nice guy, and didn't let rank separate us.

Back then, people looked out for each other. My wife arrived unannounced in Palm Springs, California. She left her home and a good job to follow her GI husband. Palm Springs was the movie stars' playground. We were walking down the main street looking for a place, when we passed a store with a 'for rent' sign. The owner was surprised that my wife had no place to stay and said she'd rent her store for little or nothing. It only had a single bed, but we didn't mind. We stayed there for a day or two. In the meantime, some of my buddies in the orderly room had met the wife of the dietitian in the hospital, who had one more little kitchenette to rent, and she rented it to us for next to nothing. She only rented to enlisted men, because her husband was enlisted when they married. Our neighbor across the street was Eddie Cantor. I don't know where this woman is, but I bless her every time I think of her. As company clerk, sometimes I got couples a tent and a cot, so that they could be together until we found a better place. We once had a reunion of GI brides and their husbands who'd lived together all over, wherever our camp was, and had looked out for each other. My wife said it didn't matter where we lived or ate or slept as long as the family was together, as long as she was with her man. This support was one of the most important parts of my life. I'll never forget it. These women who followed their husbands, you can't underestimate the strength of the American women and how much they helped us. There's more to war than what happens on the battlefield.

COMFORTABLE WITH EMOTIONS

You had to be comfortable with your fears or else you'd break. I wasn't very scared. I always felt I was in God's hands.

SELF-ESTEEM

I think we were strong-minded individuals, with good feelings about ourselves. My self-esteem has always been high. I was raised to always look proper, talk proper, and be proper, keep my head high and never let myself go low—always have respect for others. Most of the guys in my company were that way. They always had a good outlook.

ACTIVE, CREATIVE COPING

The crazy American "can do attitude" got us through. If you have that attitude, you're going to win. Even the Germans said that being over-disciplined could be a hindrance. If the German leader was killed, the troops said, "What do I do now?" and surrendered. In the U.S. Army, there was always some GI to take over leadership. The GIs could adapt.

SPIRITUAL AND PHILOSOPHICAL STRENGTHS

God

My sister-in-law was a church woman and a Christian. My early Christian training followed me through—as it did most of the fellas in my company. I had a belief. I felt I had an unseen protection, a spirit that seemed to live within me, that everything would be OK. If you didn't have that, you'd end up in a mental hospital. Most of my buddies had that. Whenever we'd get to a town with a church, we'd attend worship service whenever we could. It didn't matter what religion the church was. I was Protestant, but I'd go with my friends, most of whom were Catholic. A religious belief is the strongest protection from worry. I don't think too many men feared dying, because we understood it might happen. The idea was that "if I do go, I'm going to a better place anyway." Even now, my wife and I were married sixty years when she passed on, and I still feel that we'll be together again. To me death does not end a person.

I think God is a loving God, and He has high expectations of you. To this day, I go to church every Sunday. It's what kept me going, even during this period. Most GIs griped, but never damned the Army. Most had a religious background, mostly either Protestant and Catholic. Three Jews in our unit took a lot of kidding. Yet somehow the Army molded a company of men from many walks of life. Most guys pulled together and had a good moral background.

Meaning & Purpose

The government had excellent films called "Why We Fight." It showed that the treatment of the Jews in Europe could happen to us. Had Germany won, they could easily have come to the U.S. They already had the V-2 rockets that could cross the ocean. Freedom is dear to any American. You learned from grade school that we are a free country.

Morality

When I went into town, I remembered that I had a beautiful wife and I didn't want to ever hurt or disappoint her. Most of the single guys were pretty high morally. We didn't talk dirty or fantasize. I went back to one rest area in Holland — a little town. Five of us went to a monastery for R&R. We were invited to the home of a Dutch family by some girls we met on a trolley. It was nice to see how they lived, but there was no inappropriate activity.

We heard stories of Russians raping routinely. Apparently it was considered the spoils of war. But our Army forbade that kind of thing.

I've always tried to be truthful.

Love

The feeling of friendship that I felt toward some buddies, some of whom I knew from the States, helped very much. We did favors for each other. It made life more bearable.

In Helmstedt, there was a young Dutch woman who'd married a German soldier and had a baby. I smuggled cans of evaporated milk or Spam to them. That was illegal, but who cared when you saw a baby. I couldn't pass a child who was hungry. We felt sorry for the civilians. We had so much more food; we'd try to share it with them and asked nothing in return.

My wife and I were very close. Coming from a broken family, when I met my wife's close family, it was a different world, seeing them together. My wife was so pure in mind, she wouldn't do anything wrong. A letter from her was the greatest thing in the world. Knowing she was waiting for me, that's what kept me going.

Optimism

I always had a good outlook. I was never depressed and never thought of death. I never heard a GI say, "We're gonna lose." Every GI had confidence in his Army. We were well trained and there was no doubt we wouldn't win. I never heard a defeatist attitude.

I had a beautiful wife and a job waiting. It was just the idea to get going, get a car and your own place — the American way of life.

Humor

The American GI, as opposed to the German and French, could find humor in anything, something to laugh about. I don't care what it was. We'd do anything for a laugh. I did get one package overseas in Aachen around Christmas. A Jewish guy from Philadelphia was sent a food package from his parents' deli like you wouldn't believe. But my brother worked for JC Penney's, and his wife sent me a box with a big powder puff. We hadn't had a bath in months. My buddies passed it around, putting it under their arms through their uniforms. They were all laughing and saying, "Hey, this is great."

In Aachen, I heard an airplane. A Canadian RAF plane crashed into my building and was stuck half in and half out. One of my buddies said, "Who in the hell invited him?"

In England, as we were returning home, German POWs were serving us eggs. A buddy said, "What's your home town and street?" Whatever the German said, my buddy said, "Oh yeah, I've been there. The houses there are perfect." Then he'd get more eggs from the POW.

In Helmstedt, we heard that German SS officers were in a house in the woods. The company commander sent me on a patrol with five or six others to capture them. He told us to take our sharpshootber, a tall hillbilly from Tennessee. We went through the woods and saw the command car outside, with the SS officers in the house. We wanted to capture them and thought this would really be a feather in our cap. We heard a shot and hit the dirt. Here comes this sharpshooter with a deer over his shoulder. The German officers took off.

In the states, our first sergeant from the South hated Northerners. On maneuvers, he put everyone out at night digging foxholes. Then he'd sneak around trying to catch guys sleeping. So we strung thin strands of wires with bottles and cans around the foxholes. Then we took our rifles, loaded with blanks, and jammed the end of the barrel into soap. When he came and made noise, we fired the soap at him. He went on sick call the next day, shot up with soap. The referee got the company together and said that we could not only get courtmartialed, but also get charged a dollar for the bullet. Everyone reached in their wallets and waved their dollars. The referee realized that his guy wouldn't last. Sure enough, we got a new first sergeant, an Italian fellow, a real gentlemen.

I noticed that my buddy Bill Mauldin died recently. We enjoyed his humor. It kept our morale up. One I remember best is Patton overlooking a cliff at a beautiful sight, and saying, "That's a beautiful view. Is there one for the enlisted men?" Eisenhower liked Mauldin, but Patton didn't.

Long View of Suffering

You saw so much suffering. After the first impact, suffering became commonplace. You just adjusted. Humans can endure a lot more than we think, if we're put to the test. Man's endurance is beyond understanding. The survival instinct will come out as long as you're mentally even. It has to effect you to see people endure adversity and realize you could too. I watched people, released from the concentration camps, walking the muddy roads. Although they looked stunned and lost, they also had the look of "something must be better down the road."

In the Army, I learned to deal with different kinds of people. For example, one of my buddies was a very intelligent Jewish fellow, whose family started a large grocery food chain. Most of the guys in my company were of a high caliber, which made it easier to get past superficial differences.

Maintaining Balanced Living

I used to walk a mile each day until arthritis set in recently. Now I do at least twenty minutes on the health rider daily. I am a very regular sleeper. I sleep 8 hours a night and nap every day. My wife was a fine southern cook—three meals a day, lots of farm foods and lots of fruits and vegetables with the meats. I still eat well.

I was a heavy smoker until twenty years ago. My wife was, too. Then my wife came out of a smoke-enders meeting and said, "You know, the instructor said it would be a lot easier to quit if my mate didn't smoke." So I threw my cigarette away and I haven't had one since. I basically wasn't a drinker.

My wife and I were very compatible and inseparable. We liked the same things. Everything we did, we did together. We didn't do anything separately — entertainment, shopping, we just had a closeness. I was fortunate to get a good woman with a good family background. She was a farm girl from Culpepper, Virginia. I went to Sears the other day by myself and just felt lost. What am I doing here? We were in love.

I like non-fiction and read voraciously about WWII and paint chemistry.

Advice to Younger Generations

Be yourself. Don't try to impress anyone with what you're not. A fake can be picked out in no time at all. Know your limitations and when to quit. Don't try to impress people beyond your capacity.

As a father, grandfather, and great grandfather, I think of everything I do and always remind myself, "Family respect— never do anything that would embarrass your family." I always consider whether or not they would respect me for what I do. So I've kept a straight and narrow path in life.

One's relationship to God is foremost whether one is Jewish, Catholic, or Protestant. All good hinges on that.

Self-respect is very important—when you can walk through your community and hold your head up and feel you have nothing to feel ashamed of.

Be tolerant of another person. One of the biggest problems in society today is that we're not tolerant of neighbors because of different religions, physical appearance, beliefs, etc. Two of my closest friends are a Jewish couple. They commented that they appreciate how I feel toward them, because not everybody feels that way. I show it by my friendship and willingness. For example, the husband had a heart attack and couldn't drive, so I've offered to drive them places—mostly just kindness and respect for their beliefs. I have not an ounce of hate. I just take people for what they are. In the House, 99% of the labor force was black, maybe two hundred employees. So many said they appreciated the way I'd go over and talk with them. Even today when I visit they say, "I miss you." I always treated them with a level of respect. Growing up, I never heard anything racial or religious.

The heart of everything is the family. It needs to be close. Be honest and have mutual respect. With my wife, I don't recall a spat in 60 years of marriage. We had that mutual feeling. My daughter often said, "It's so nice at our house to have no bickering like other families." I would never do anything to embarrass my family. That would kill me.

Robert, second from right, with a captured German staff car.

Robert and Fran Jacobs, 1942

At home in Alexandria, VA

Chapter 27

George S. Everly
Signal Corps

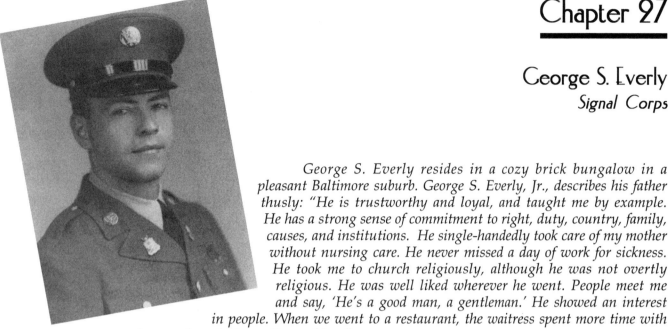

George S. Everly resides in a cozy brick bungalow in a pleasant Baltimore suburb. George S. Everly, Jr., describes his father thusly: "He is trustworthy and loyal, and taught me by example. He has a strong sense of commitment to right, duty, country, family, causes, and institutions. He single-handedly took care of my mother without nursing care. He never missed a day of work for sickness. He took me to church religiously, although he was not overtly religious. He was well liked wherever he went. People meet me and say, 'He's a good man, a gentleman.' He showed an interest in people. When we went to a restaurant, the waitress spent more time with us because he asked questions of her."

I was born in 1916, an only child. So that makes me 86. My family lived on a small farm in Ilchester, Maryland, west of Baltimore. It was a small agricultural truck farm. We grew tomatoes and corn. I had no neighbors to play with. It was very lonely. My main friend was my dog. When I was seven we moved to Ellicott City, a small town nearer to Baltimore. My family was quite normal. There was no screaming. My father was pleasant, gentle, and well liked. Mother was a nice disciplinarian, a frugal German.

Going through the Depression, we had little money, and jobs were hard to get. Dad was always employed, though, with the Baltimore Transit Company.

Ellicott City was small town life. Everyone knew everyone. All stores had charge accounts for steady customers. There was no television, so you found your own entertainment. I was active in Boys Club, athletics, and music. I was a good musician. I started playing music at 11 years old. I frequently performed publicly. I joined a band and played firemen's carnivals and parades for $2. Clubs had dances and I would play. I made lots of friends and knew everyone in town.

I enjoyed athletics. In high school, I made varsity in soccer, basketball, track, and softball. I was offered three scholarships for basketball. At six feet tall, I played center and forward. I also interviewed visiting celebrities for the high school paper.

I graduated high school in 1934, took business courses, and worked for a corporation. My parents couldn't afford to send me to Peabody, so I studied for five years with a Peabody professor, early in the morning before he went to teach in Baltimore. I decided to go to Baltimore College of Commerce, now University of Baltimore. I finished two years of accounting before I was drafted. I also covered the local music scene in Baltimore and its suburbs for the *Down Beat* magazine. I'd take a tuxedo to work and school, and worked as a musician at night. We played big band music—Benny Goodman, Guy Lombardo, Glenn Miller, Count Basie— '30s jazz. I played the saxophone, clarinet, and flute.

I was drafted just before Pearl Harbor was bombed, and served 4½ years in the Army Signal Corps, from 1941 to 1945. I went to South Carolina for three months of basic training. I went for infantry training to Fort Benning, Georgia, and spent another three months there learning to be a high-speed radio operator. Then I went back to Fort Jackson, South Carolina, for combat training.

I met my wife, Kathleen, in the latter part of 1941 at the Georgia Warm Springs Foundation, which was 45 miles from Fort Benning. She worked there as a secretary. USO set up dances there. FDR visited the springs for his polio. He died there. He was good at remembering names. He remembered Kathleen and her sister's name. Kathleen said he gave the guards fits. One time, they found him sitting on the porch of a farm, visiting with a local farmer. I went up there about every weekend before going overseas.

Our first assignment was Iceland in 1943. Our job was to keep the German submarines from hiding in the fiords as they were patrolling the North Atlantic. Then we went to England for training and to prepare for the invasion.

We landed in Scotland, then trained to Southampton. It was rainy and cold there. We slept in tents on cots. I was freezing. We endured nightly bombings for several weeks prior to the invasion, and would have to leave our tents and run to fox holes. We landed on Normandy two weeks after the invasion. My unit, the 29th Infantry Regiment, got behind General Patton's 3rd Army. He moved very fast. Going through France, a lot of times there was no time to pitch tents. In Belgium, during the Battle of the Bulge, Europe was experiencing one of the coldest winters in years. There was snow all around; we slept sometimes under porches. There was much bombing from German buzz bombs. They sounded like cheap lawnmowers. When we heard the motor shut off, we'd run for cover. I was in a building when one buzz bomb came. I ducked under a bed. The bomb sheared off part of a room and a radio I was working on. I saw many dead bodies, including those of members of the French underground who had been executed. I rose to the rank of staff sergeant.

After the war, I served for four months in the occupation force. The Army established a huge sports program to keep the troops occupied. I became the sports editor of the newspaper. And I spent time rehearsing with some of the Army bands and having jam sessions. The occupation was lots of fun. The Germans got friendly with us and invited us to dinner. We went to parks with oom-pah bands; there were men in lederhosen. Three of us took over an ornate home. We were eating breakfast one morning when we heard a knock on the door. A German officer in uniform, just released from prison camp, said it was his home, and asked if he could come in to get some clothes.

In civilian life I kept busy finishing my education. I became an accountant (after finishing two more years of accounting) and a musician, and married. Kathleen joined my band after we married and I used her as a vocalist. Several years after we married, my wife developed bipolar depressive disorder, and caring for her was in many ways more difficult than the war.

PTSD Symptoms?

I experienced no PTSD symptoms

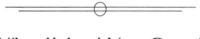

What Helped You Cope?

CALM UNDER PRESSURE

I stayed calm by keeping busy doing my job. I always had something to get back to after the bombings, such as cleaning up. For example, once, I stepped over soldiers who had been killed in a bombing, but focused on helping others. I was so busy, I glanced at them, but didn't focus on their injuries. I had the ability to turn things off like a spigot and replace them with other things that I had to do, such as my next assignment. I didn't dwell on negatives.

The Germans were told to fight. I didn't hate them or take personally what they were doing. After the Battle of the Bulge, many Germans gave up. I remember remarking to a friend that they were supposed to be supermen; but they were youthful, not supermen, just men. I made friends in Germany, and couldn't obey the non-fraternization rule. I was invited to many friendly homes.

RATIONAL THOUGHT PROCESSES

In basic training, our instructors were good about imperfections. They taught you rather than criticize you. I once spoke up about getting demerits for utensils that were not shined. The sergeant acknowledged a mistake. If I did something wrong, though, I'd accept that and let it go. I don't remember making too many serious mistakes. However, in Iceland, I was on the radio detail one night. It was very boring, so I sent a practice message. I thought I'd jazz things up. I said that an enemy sub was sighted in the harbor. Everyone around the island emptied their huts and went to their foxholes, cold and wet, on alert. The colonel called me in the next morning and laughed. He said, "George, at least you've proved that our system works. In the future please preface practice messages with 'practice repeat practice'."

When I was young, I was very well trained as a musician. I was sometimes bothered by other musician's mistakes. But I got over it, and learned to accept that some people have little talent.

I wasn't too strict with my son; I'd just explain what had to be done and let mistakes go.

SOCIAL SUPPORT

I've always been good at making friends. I like people. Once I made a friend, I kept him. Music helped me in many ways to connect with people. I had good civilian friends from my musical experiences. During the occupation, I was invited to join Army musicians to rehearse. I also made friends covering sports for the Army paper.

When you sleep and eat every day with the same guys, you become close. Early on, we had a lot of career men who resented the draftees. But the longer we lived together, the closer we got. By the time we reached Europe, everyone was treated the same.

I was close to my family at home. I received frequent letters from parents, friends, and girlfriend.

COMFORT WITH EMOTIONS

During the war, I didn't feel it necessary to talk about traumatic events. Today, I don't mind talking about the war at all. Crying doesn't bother me, but I don't do that.

SELF-ESTEEM

I think I had self-esteem, although I didn't think much about it. I wasn't overconfident or arrogant.

My musical training and public performing gave me confidence and a sense of worth, as did my participation in athletics. My Peabody teacher gave me confidence also. He was a big tough German, very strict. I didn't want him yelling at me so I practiced hard. It paid off.

In high school I was the president of the public speaking club. That also built confidence.

ACTIVE, FLEXIBLE COPING

I had the habit of jumping in. I was always an officer in my high school classes. I was class president for three years, president of the student council, and I led my own orchestra. As a staff sergeant, I took over the company for drills, calisthenics, and marches. The top sergeant complimented me for my close order drill.

I could also go with the flow when I couldn't control things, such as my wife's mental illness. Music was wonderful therapy. After the war I played reed instruments. You have to concentrate when you play. There is no room for thinking about anything else. Golfers say the same thing.

SPIRITUAL AND PHILOSOPHICAL STRENGTHS

God

My faith helped me get through the war. I had a quiet faith and tried to live it. I came from a religious family. My mother was an active Presbyterian and a Sunday school teacher. I believed in prayer. I tried to live by the basics. I lived a quiet moderate religious life. I pretty much attended church each week, and was active in youth groups. I played in the church orchestra. I tried to find a church wherever I was in the service, and listened to the chaplains overseas about being morally correct.

The future is a mystery regarding the afterlife. I'm curious. I try to dig into other religions to find out what they think. I attended Japanese Shinto temples on a recent trip with my son. My Jewish friends invite me to synagogues. I try to find out as much as I can.

Meaning & Purpose

I looked forward to marrying my wife. We married on December 7, 1945, four years after meeting at Ft. Benning, Georgia. I wanted to finish college and be active in the music business. Music was my one love, a burning desire. I wanted to play with a big band. I wrote to managers of Glenn Miller and all the other big bands. My main goal was to become a musician, until I worried about supporting my family. I eventually went into accounting.

Morality

The theme of my life was leading a good life. One classmate said, "I used to think of you as staying on the sidelines and smiling and watching the world go by," since I didn't do drinking or partying.

When we visited the Riviera on leave, my friend Carmine from New York asked if he could come with me. He said, "I know, if I go with you, I won't get into trouble."

I was quite conservative in my dating. I tried to treat women with respect. I don't believe in cheating or stealing, and never did that. I didn't run around. I was faithful to my wife. I never used bad language or told dirty jokes. I never took things from the dead soldiers I saw.

Love

I felt a strong bond with my comrades, and have kept in touch all these years. After the war, the members of the regular Army who came to Fort Meade, Maryland, to train came up to see me. I made a lot of friends, from first sergeant down to the privates.

I still send Christmas cards and receive them. Sometimes the widows write to let me know of a buddy's passing.

Optimistic

I feel everything will turn out. I look forward to the next day and try to make life as pleasant as possible. I've looked forward to goals. I think that there is always something better in the future. Something will happen to make it OK. Optimism would get me through the tough times. Why waste time being upset?

Humor

We picked out humor whenever we could. I appreciated how many boys in the outfit cut up and joked.

One officer liked my rifle manual, so he gave me the opportunity to conduct the inspection. I grabbed the officer's rifle and told him he had a dirty bore. I found it funny that people lined the roads and cheered the GIs in France and threw fruit and flowers. The minute we crossed the border into Germany, everyone was grim faced, as if to say "we don't want you guys here." Our 250-pound mess sergeant flung mashed potatoes into the messiest thing on the POWs' plates to splash them.

There was also black humor. There was not a building left standing in Aachen, Germany. The artillery had leveled the town. A work crew was shoveling debris off the road to permit trucks to pass. Two workers found a dead German soldier. One put his shovel under the legs, another under the trunk, and hefted him into the truck like the other debris. To the troops it somehow seemed funny.

Long View of Suffering

I saw parts of the war as not so bad, and even enjoyed some parts. For example, the Army sent us on leave, so we went to the Riviera or to Belgium, and saw beautiful cathedrals there. When things were quiet, I enjoyed morning walks in small French towns and talking with the shopkeepers, but I couldn't lose the local kids when I needed to dig a latrine in the woods.

In spite of the war, I met fine people—a diverse population. After being in combat together I was able to make friends even with tough southern soldiers who had problems, such as having illegitimate children. I learned to tolerate new habits and customs, such as how to live with brash New Yorkers or southern rednecks. I had been taught to be a segregationist in Ellicott City. But I learned to be ashamed of myself for looking down on people. I learned to appreciate black and oriental people. In the Battle of the Bulge, a black unit, that was lost, came to our camp and our commander told the mess sergeant to feed them. The mess sergeant wouldn't do it until he was finally threatened with a court martial. I also saw what people in the South did to blacks and the way they talked to them. I felt empathy. I started to think better of them and treat them better.

Mental illness in a loved one is the hardest thing for anybody. There were times I thought I would lose my mind. Occasionally I had to get out to take a break. I kept playing music. You can't worry about anything when you're playing. That kept me sane. A psychiatrist friend at Johns Hopkins plays in a band called the "Mood Swings." Otherwise, he'd lose his mind. My wife died over ten years ago. A lot of people ask me if it is difficult being alone. Being alone doesn't bother me, because as a child I was alone. We each have strengths and find ways that help us through adversity.

Maintaining Balanced Living

I avoided smoking and drugs, and always tried to stay in shape. Even now, I walk and run on the treadmill, or use the stationary bike. I lift weights every day and follow a regular regimen that I learned in the Army. I used to take my son to the health club when he was a boy. I've generally retired at 11:30 p.m. and awakened at 5:45 a.m. I don't need much sleep. I try to eat healthy—green vegetables, little meat, and pasta. I love fruit—I can make a meal of it, and make sure I have lots of fruit around. My doctor says that the secret to living to 86 is exercise, eat well, don't smoke, and have good genes and good luck. I never drank much. In the war I had an occasional beer or wine to celebrate with the French, but not to drown my sorrows or escape my troubles.

Music was always my hobby. I surround myself with music as much as I can. I've attended many concerts, dinner theatres, bands, and symphonies. I have friends that I take with me. I like to read Civil War books. My wife and I traveled to vacation together. I regularly attend church now.

Advice to Younger Generations

Your relationship with the people you work with is important. People who get promoted are those who get along with their co-workers. It is important to respect the people you work with and to try to work with them.

Don't hold grudges. You never know when another might have to help you. Don't judge people the first time you meet them. Try to see their perspective.

Get a good education. Then, it is most important to do something you like and are interested in. Find a job you like. When I was promoted to secretary/treasurer of the Baltimore Transit Company, I enjoyed meeting people, discussing finances, and visiting different cities to audit contractors. I loved to go to work and couldn't wait to get there in the morning.

George Everly

George and Kathleen in Georgia, circa 1942.

Being recognized for service by Maryland Governor, Harry Hughes.

Chapter 98

John David Blumgart
Captured at Inden

John David Blumgart resides in a contemporary house in the woods of suburban Maryland. In his home are pictures of his family and grandchildren. Tall, with a cheerful disposition and cordial smile, he worked for the Agency for International Development for most of his post-war years. His son Dan observes, "He was a role model for me as a military and police officer, responsible and uncomplaining." Mr. Blumgart was wounded in an attempt to escape a German counterattack, and spent six months as a prisoner of war.

I was born in Manhattan, an only child, and went to high school in Riverdale, New York, in the Bronx. I played tennis and enjoyed that very much. I entered Oberlin College in Ohio in 1942, and attended one year before entering the service.

I was blessed with a very supportive family. You're advantaged when you have a loving family. My parents were good to me and encouraged me to lead a full life and develop my capabilities.

My father, a physician, trained under Freud in Vienna. He was one of the pioneers of psychoanalysis and had a thriving practice in Manhattan. He was a first class person, loving, very tender, very wise. I was very close to him. My mother was more in the social science field. She worked for Friends of Democracy, a voluntary organization, opposing right wing and racist groups in the U.S. She was also very tender, loving, and supportive. We went to the theater and movies as a family. We often had guests at the house and had a good time with them.

I have vivid memories of the milk trucks, clopping along the pavement in the wee hours of the morning. As a family, we were not affected by the Depression, but I remember seeing people out of work on the street and suffering from hunger.

After training briefly to be an engineer officer, I was sent to Europe as an infantry replacement in the autumn of 1944. I was in England for two weeks, then landed at Normandy about three months after the invasion. We trained in Belgium, then were parceled out to the 104th Infantry Division. I became a company radio operator and runner, because of my one year in college. My unit drove from Aachen, the first German city occupied by the allies, to attack toward Cologne. I saw casualties along the way and felt fear and horror, which I often remember, but we pressed ahead.

We attacked the town of Inden early in the morning of November 29 and entered the town with covering fire from our artillery. We occupied parts of the town during the day. In the afternoon, the Germans sent in reinforcements and tanks. We discovered we were cut off from the rear. Tanks pummeled us with tank artillery for an hour and a half. I saw an engineer have his leg blown off, which was terrifying. We were short of anti-tank weapons, and had no tanks of our own. We were surrounded in the basement of a cement plant. They attacked and stormed our position, then ordered us to surrender. I tried to sneak away and hide, but was wounded by a grenade in the back of my leg.

We were taken in troop carriers to a receiving area. I woke up in a hospital train and saw a picture of Hitler looking down at me. We were sent to a hospital and subsequently joined others near Frankfurt am Main, Germany. We stayed there for two weeks. Then, we were transported by train to central Germany, which was my low point. It was one of the coldest winters on record. We were in freight cars for three or four days with very little food and no sanitary facilities. We were scared to death that we'd be strafed by U.S. planes. I spent two months in a prison camp hospital at Stalag 12A, near Limburg, Germany.

I was transported near the Elbe River near the town of Torgau, where the Russians and Americans would meet months later. I was assigned to the prison camp Stalag 4B, billeted there with the British. We had meager rations—ersatz coffee and bread for breakfast, turnip soup for lunch (to this day I can't stand turnips), and soup at dinner. Thanks to the Red Cross, we received portions of parcels from time to time, to supplement our diet. We were treated much better than the Russians; we were not treated cruelly and had better housing. They blew a whistle each morning to line up for head count. We were enlisted for work parties to build anti-tank obstacles. Some actually volunteered because the chances of escape were better. I didn't, because we knew from our clandestine radios that the war was coming to an end, and I figured the war would come to me. We were supplied with reading material, a good selection of American literature. We were allowed to walk in the recreation areas of the camp to pass the time. I was liberated in May of 1945, six months after being captured. I had dropped 40 pounds, from 180 to 140 pounds.

At the end of the war, the Army sent me on rehabilitation furlough to Lake Placid, New York. There I met my future wife Mary Margaret (May) at a USO dance. After the war, I went back to Oberlin. I spent a summer working in the mines and forests of Czechoslovakia— a Unitarian church-organized work camp, to help the country get back on its feet. I married May on graduation day in 1948. I then went to Columbia University. I did research overseas on a Fulbright Fellowship.

Between 1952 and 1958 I worked for the American Committee on United Europe, which supported Western European unification, and was headed by Benelux, France, West Germany, and Italy. I accepted an offer from the Ford Foundation to work in Indonesia for two years. I worked for the Agency for International Development, part of the State Department, until my retirement as an economist and program officer.

PTSD Symptoms?

I had no PTSD symptoms.

What Helped You Cope?

We got lonesome, homesick, and bored in the prison camps. We read Red Cross books, talked, and shared experiences about our lives, including the details of our capture.

CALM UNDER PRESSURE

During the war, I just tried to keep my sights on what I had to do. I felt neutral toward the Germans. They didn't bother us. It was just a duty to fight them. A German surgeon operated on my injured leg, saving it from possible infection and amputation.

RATIONAL THOUGHT PROCESSES

After I was captured, a British medical officer cleaned me up and dressed my wound. I told him how ashamed I was about being captured. He reassured and comforted me. He was older than I. He recognized the causes of my reaction and explained that sometimes being captured can't be helped. That thought was very steadying.

In the boxcar, I just thought I had to carry on from moment to moment; there wasn't a great deal of choice. We were all miserable, but we didn't make it worse by dwelling on it.

I almost made a mistake that could have been horrible. In the early hours of the morning, when we took the town, going up the stairs of a building, I remember looking across at an adjacent building and seeing a soldier. I thought he was a German and drew a bead on him, and suddenly I shouted to him thinking he would surrender. He spoke to me in English. I look back on it often, with gratitude that I didn't kill him. I probably would have told myself that these things happen in war despite your best efforts, but I'm glad I didn't have to apply that lesson.

SOCIAL SUPPORT

I made friends with fellow POWs. I grew acquainted with one who lived near Oberlin. It was very important to have that friend to bare my breast and talk about anything I wanted to, including fears and worries. Mostly, of course, we talked about our past experiences and the future. I looked him up after the war. We meticulously and fairly shared Red Cross parcels with buddies whenever they arrived.

I had a lot of contact with my company commander and I felt close and comfortable with him and admired him.

COMFORTABLE WITH EMOTIONS

We were terribly afraid of strafing in the boxcars. So uncomfortable and frozen, we just existed.

I learned a good lesson from the British medical officer: that it is good to get something off your chest and resolve it. In the prison camp, I talked a lot with fellow prisoners. After the war, the war wasn't discussed much, although I'd talk in response to questions. I was happy to oblige. It wasn't a burden sharing.

SELF-ESTEEM

I feel like I had reasonable self-esteem, and the prison camp experience increased it. My interactions with others made me feel more self-confident. I found I could handle problems and cope with situations. I think that just enduring the camp made me realize I could handle other problems.

ACTIVE, CREATIVE COPING

As a prisoner, we had limited options. I managed through talking, reading, playing games, and exercising. I got out of the barracks to exercise and did a lot of walking, which was a release and a diversion. One guy in the prison camp never left his bunk. He gave up on life. He withdrew, stared at ceiling, and didn't take nourishment. I had a will to cope with my situation—to make the most of it, and not to be overwhelmed by it.

Even in prison camp, you couldn't just sit around. Being next to a V-2 rocket launching site, my prison camp was bombed by the British. I crawled under my bed. When I got up, I found that a piece of shrapnel was embedded in my bed just where my head had been.

SPIRITUAL AND PHILOSOPHICAL STRENGTHS

God

I developed my belief in God later in life, going to church to fill the gap from the absence of my wife, who died in 1997. I belong to a dynamic and interesting congregation, which helps a great deal. I still go every Sunday.

Meaning & Purpose

I knew we were fighting for a good cause. I was a political science major. I was clear on why we were fighting. After I was captured, I got into an argument with a German soldier in an armored troop carrier. I said we were fighting for democracy and he was fighting for fascism. A friend advised me not to argue politics, and I realized I'd be wise to be quiet.

Morality

I felt a sense of morality as a result of my home life and education. My school emphasized principles and morality in relationships. To me, morality means to know right from wrong, being kind and honest, looking after others, being helpful, and not criticizing people. In the camp, I knew I could trust my buddy and he trusted me. We shared equally and wouldn't take what wasn't ours.

Love

I'm sure my family's love helped me get through the war.

Optimism

We listened to BBC and the Voice of America on smuggled radios. The promise of returning to college, seeing my parents, enjoying the good food I was missing, and my interest in international affairs kept my hopes up.

Humor

Humor gave me a certain buoyancy that helped me with POW problems.

I was amused that one group of prisoners started a drama club. They performed Claire Booth Luce's "The Women," depicting the interaction of women in a dormitory. That was comical with an all-male cast of grimy soldiers.

Shortly before the Russians overran our camp, the Germans tried to recruit volunteers to join a special Anglo-American unit, fighting the Russians on the eastern front. No one of us thought too highly of that idea.

Long View of Suffering

The overall war experience was good. It increased my confidence and self-esteem, and toughened me psychologically. Getting through with little psychological damage made a difference. The war also matured me in terms of working hard and making the most of what came my way. It helped me achieve at Oberlin, which was demanding.

Maintaining Balanced Living

Since the war, I have gone for a brisk walk each evening and watched my diet—not much junk food. I drank mostly beer and wine, not a great deal, but stopped in recent years. In the prison camp, everything was priced in cigarettes. I smoked a pack a day, but stopped several years later when I learned that they were linked to cancer. I got eight hours of sleep at night, usually from 11:00 p.m. to 7:00 a.m.

I enjoy culture. I love to read. I enjoy going to plays and movies, traveling, and spending time with my family. My wife and I enjoyed each other's company and did many of these things together. I also enjoyed tennis and sailing,

Advice to Younger Generations

Make the most of the current situation. If a problem is unpleasant, take the long view—"This too shall pass."

Exercise moderation in your habits, such as eating and drinking. The consequences of excess ruin the pleasure of what you are doing. Never volunteer *(laughing)*.

John, center, at a work camp in Czechoslovakia, where he returned after the war to aid the rehabilitation effort.

John and May Blumgart in New York.

May and John Blumgart

Chapter 29

Colonel Robert "Butch" Carroll Kendrick
Paratrooper

COL Robert "Butch" Kendrick resides in a brick, single level home in Fayetteville, North Carolina. At 5'9," this eighty-five-year-old man is still lean, muscled, spry, and athletic looking. His hearty, ready laugh and enthusiasm are the trademarks by which he is known.

He and his wife raised a daughter and two sons — one served in the Air Force and the other was a carrier pilot who retired from the Navy. He is a charter member of the Old Soldiers social group, and is especially appreciated for his crooning of old tunes to his comrades and their wives at their quarterly dinners.

A career Army officer, he fought in Europe and also served in the Korean and Vietnam wars. He earned the Silver Star, five awards of the Bronze Star, the Legion of Merit, and the Purple Heart. COL Kendrick is the leader of the soldiers depicted in the Korean Memorial in Washington, D. C. He is number seven from the front.

I was born in 1917, in Shreveport, Louisiana, the second of two boys. We moved to San Antonio, Texas, for a year when I was a little tyke because we had family there, but we returned to Homer, Louisiana, for the rest of my boyhood, until I went to college.

My life was wonderful, a very happy childhood. I thought Homer was heaven. It was a typical little country town of about 4900, a blip in the road, a fine little town. To get through the town you had to go around the beautiful court square. I guess the town got started because, at one time, there was a cotton gin there. Cotton was the big crop in those days. They also raised a little tobacco, some peanuts, and field peas.

Dad was in the automobile business. He ran a Ford maintenance shop and his friend ran the sales. He sold out his interest and went into the Chevrolet business, again running the maintenance department as a part owner. Then he bought a filling station and had a service department in his own garage and did most of the work himself. He was one of the most respected men in town. He was tall, honest, clean, and didn't drink or smoke. If he told you something, you could believe him. He was one of the most honest men I've ever known. He was also a volunteer fire chief and a Mason. My brother was just like him, one of the finest men I've ever known — highly respected in our town.

I had a wonderful mother, too. Mother was a little, wiry ball of fire, the disciplinarian in the family — with a switch. If you had any faults, she brought them to your attention very strongly. She was very religious. I'm still religious. If it's good enough for Mom, it's good enough for me.

We were very close as a family. We ate and worshipped together. We went on picnics. Every year or so we'd go visit my grandparents in San Antonio. A grandpa, three aunts, and two uncles lived on a farm nearby and we'd visit once or twice a month. I had chores at home. On weekends I ran my dad's filling station. We lived by the Golden Rule.

My brother was the student, the smart one. I was always involved in sports. I knew everybody in town and was kin to probably a third of them. It was a happy existence. We had admiration for each other and we all got along fine together. The kids had a good social life. We had a good high school, with good teachers who I knew most all my life.

We weren't rich, but we had plenty to eat and were well clothed, had a nice home and a car. The thing that depressed me about the Depression was to hear about people. Like, one day I was out at my uncle's farm. He came back crying. He'd been to a little farm near a lumber mill. The people were cracking hickory nuts from the ground for lunch. That's all they had. So my uncle went out to the smokehouse, got ham, eggs, and flour and took them to the people to eat. People stood by each other. Dad and Mom insured that the nieces and nephews went to Sears to buy clothes and shoes every year for school.

In high school, I played football (halfback), baseball, basketball, and track (100-yard dash and the 220-yard race). My family came to all the football games I played in. I graduated high school in 1936.

I went to Louisiana State University. I played fullback on a football scholarship, and was red-shirted my sophomore year. I took basic ROTC for the first two years. My trainer had been in the Navy in WWI and steered me into advanced ROTC. I decided to be a coach and teacher, so I majored in PE and minored in English. I graduated in June of 1941, commissioned as a 2nd Lieutenant. I married a fine young lady in the same month.

I had met my wife in 1937, my sophomore year. A big ol' tackle asked me if I'd like to go with him to his girlfriend's. She was living in her mom's boarding home. Her mother ran it in the heart of Baton Rouge. While there, I saw my future wife, Agnes. Her sister—the tackle's girlfriend— was having a birthday on Sunday. I got her to invite me. I saw Agnes at the party and I latched onto her like a cat's squirrel. I thought she was the prettiest thing I'd ever lay my eyes on. She was one fine lady, a wonderful companion, a great mother. I courted her for 4½ years. She was a secretary for an optometrist. Every summer I worked on the campus to take additional courses so I could court her. Almost every night I visited her at the boarding house. I knew I was going to marry her. I borrowed $20 from her mother to get married. That was the best $20 I spent in my life. She was crying about losing her daughter, but I moved into her boarding house the next morning. I went and got my other shirt before I moved in. We were married 56 years.

After graduating, I worked for Westinghouse, then Dupont. I was operating a blending tower that made ethylene gas in Baton Rouge, on the banks of the Mississippi. Shortly after December 7, 1941, I got orders. In January of 1942, I reported to Ft. McClellan, Alabama, living in an ol' pup tent at this branch immaterial training center, training replacements in basic training. I stayed there several months. My oldest boy was born there. I had the fastest time on the obstacle course, so my battalion commander, COL Albert Dickerson, promoted me to 1st Lieutenant and sent me to Ft. Benning, Georgia, for the Infantry Officers Basic Course. He was going to join the paratroopers and wanted me to join too.

While I was at Ft. Benning, I was impressed by the paratroopers in those brown boots, leather jackets, and airborne wings. I told my wife I was thinking about joining. She said, "You join that suicide outfit and I'll divorce you." After I got my first jump pay she didn't mention it.

I went back to Alabama and volunteered for the Airborne. Shortly thereafter, I got orders to the 506th Parachute Infantry Regiment, which was being organized in the mountains of Georgia. I was assigned to H Company. To be accepted, you had to be in the top sixteen qualifying in various events, such as the obstacle course, pull ups, pushups, situps, jumping from a thirty foot tower, rope climb, and running up and down Currahee mountain. When you got picked, you made five jumps and qualified. I was the proudest human being when I got my wings, boots, and leather jacket. I slept in the boots. When I went home on vacation, I hated to take them off at night. Most paratroopers were the same way. I made my last jump in 1972.

COL Dickerson was organizing the 513th Infantry Regiment. He invited me back to Alabama to command a company of the 513th as a captain. Two weeks later, I got orders to the 513th in Alabama. I took over C Company, organized it, and took it overseas. I left it when I was wounded on January 4, 1945 in Belgium in the Battle of the Bulge. I spent about five months in a hospital in England. I rejoined my company in Germany. When I came back, I brought my company home with only twelve of the original members—due to casualties, transfers, or assignments to occupation forces. Maybe thirty or forty, at most, survived uninjured or weren't captured. All the officers were wounded, captured, or killed.

Colonel Robert "Butch" Carroll Kendrick

From Alabama, we moved to Ft. Bragg, North Carolina, then to Camp Mackall, North Carolina, to train for a year. After maneuvers in Tennessee, we went to Europe in the fall of 1944. We landed in Andover, England, to train. We went to Reims, France, in December, 1944. Christmas Eve night, we moved up to the Our River to set up defensive positions for a week or so. Then we loaded on trucks for Belgium and the Battle of the Bulge. I caught the flu about then. It was cold. We were part of Patton's 3rd Army. We traveled all night, and were strafed. My truck was hit. We left the trucks like bats out of hell. No one was killed, but one fellow got a hole in his canteen.

The next day we moved up to a little town, to relieve the 11th Armored Division that had caught hell. The situation must have been desperate for a lightly armored outfit like ours to replace it. The snow was three to four feet deep. There were a lot of dead frozen people, including a lot of Belgium civilians and some Germans, and knocked out tanks—mostly American. People were flattened by tanks, like a squirrel. We were getting sniper fire from the woods. The Germans knew we were there; we had no idea where they were. We cleaned out the woods.

We were trying to dig into the frozen ground at 8:30 p.m., when my battalion commander told me I'd be lead company to follow a trail that went between a patch of fir trees. B Company would follow my company. We got half way there, and the moon came out. The company executive officer said that nobody was behind us. I stopped for fifteen minutes. Everywhere I looked there were dead civilians. I waited awhile and we went through the woods. German vehicles were parked there, but I figured they'd been knocked out. We got to the other edge of the woods and swung around to the right and set up a perimeter. I heard digging over to my right flank. I thought maybe it was B Company, lost. I sent out a patrol to check it out, but the digging stopped and they didn't see a soul. B company showed up and moved to the left. A Company brought up the rear.

About one o'clock, we were told we'd attack first thing in the morning. I would take C Company and take the little town below us. B Company would take another town on the left, with A Company in reserve. We were told the artillery would reduce the town to rubble. An hour before daylight, I made my way back to the battalion commander and told him I hadn't seen the artillery forward observers. He said, "Don't worry about it. If they show up, I'll send them down." They never showed up.

Just at daylight, we went across the snow-covered field in battle formation. After 500 to 600 yards, I heard a commotion. We'd spent the night in the woods with the Germans. They put the biggest artillery barrage you'd ever seen in your life right on us. While I was on the radio, they killed my radio operator. I got hit by a shell fragment through my right leg. The binoculars on my chest were torn up. Snow was flying in all directions. Two platoon leaders ran to town to escape the barrage. We didn't get one round of artillery support and got no air support because of the bad weather. My operation sergeant lay over me to keep me from getting killed. He then got me to the aid station. Talking to what was left, my platoons got into the town and took it, but the Germans came in with infantry and tanks and killed and captured what was in there.

We just went in without any preparation and got the hell kicked out of us. Maybe only 65 or 70 men in my company of about 120 were left. We made every error we possibly could have and it cost us. We were too eager to get into battle. We underestimated the enemy. They were one of the best led, trained, disciplined, and equipped armies in the world. They knew where we were, but we really didn't know where they were. We attacked without any recon or fire support. Although we had no forward observer an hour before we jumped off, the battalion commander told me not to worry. He didn't send the reserves into the town. He was relieved shortly after. I learned a lot. We lost many fine young men. They loved America.

I was evacuated to Luxembourg. They operated on me. I went to Paris, and was then loaded on a cattle car to Le Havre. The train was full of people with frozen limbs. From Le Havre, we went to South Hampton. They operated on me again there. I was in the hospital there in England for five or six months. When I got out of the hospital, I was limping. I was given five officers and 240 troops. I was to escort them to Le Havre. From Le Havre, we were put on box cars to Nuremberg. I was told that the men I was escorting would fight with Patton into Czechoslovakia. I tried to get back to the 17th Airborne Division and my regiment. Finally, I saw a truck driver who told me where they were. I got my stuff and the next morning got on the road, hitching to rejoin my regiment in Oberhausen, Germany. The war ended just before I rejoined my company. They had been across the Rhine and come back, what was left of them. I took over my company. We went to France to ship home.

At Camp Shelby, Mississippi, they operated again on my leg, did a beautiful job fixing it and I haven't had any trouble since. I got out of the Army and worked with the Ethyl (for high-test gasoline) Corporation in Baton Rouge, Louisiana. My old paratrooper friends said I should come back into the Army and get a regular commission. I talked it over with my wife. The Army had been good to us. My boss told me I could have a year's leave of absence and my job would be right there if I didn't stay in the Army. I got a direct commission at Ft. Benning and ended up on the staff at Ft. Benning, in the Infantry School's physical training committee.

In 1947, I got orders to Japan, joining the 11th Airborne Division as a company commander. 1950-51, I went with the advance party to southern Japan and then to Korea. I took part in the Inchon landing and our battalion helped the Marines take Seoul. We later made a beach landing in North Korea and fought all the way to the Yalu River on the Chinese border. For six to eight months, it seemed we were fighting every day.

I served in Vietnam as the special operations officer for Mac V (Military Assistance Command, Vietnam), which helped establish the U.S. Army special forces effort there. The special forces and helicopter pilots were among the real heroes in Vietnam

I later took over the 2nd Brigade of the 82nd Airborne Division and was promoted to colonel. I took that brigade to the Dominican Republic for six to eight months in 1964, when the division was sent to clean up the civil uprising mess.

Sometime after I retired at Ft. Bragg in 1972, I was at a cocktail party at the home of Brigadier General Oscar Davis [See Chapter 41], who is a great friend of mine. He was one of the finest generals. He has saved so many young officers. If you did something wrong, he'd call you in there. He'd nibble about a foot or two out of your behind. And you wouldn't resent it at all, because you knew you needed it, and he'd never hold it against you. He and I had the two top scores on the PT test when we were instructors in the airborne department of the Infantry School at Ft. Benning in 1953. The city executive was organizing a bank and he invited me to be a banker, because I knew a lot of people, even though I told him that I couldn't write a check. I have managed four branches. I now take care of outside teller machines. I'm my own boss and that's great.

In 1996, I lost my wife. Life will never be the same without her.

PTSD Symptoms?

PTSD really never bothered me. We weren't smart enough to have some syndrome. After the Korean War, my wife told me that sometimes I'd be over at the window talking in my sleep looking for the enemy.

What Helped You Cope?

My childhood helped to strengthen me. Being an athlete and playing sports helped. In high school I was a heavyweight champion, even though I wasn't a member of the boxing team. I beat a much bigger man in my first and only fight. They thought the other team didn't have a heavyweight, so they asked me to just go and win by forfeit. Well, they were wrong and the coach told me to fight him. He hit me and my mouthpiece flew out of my mouth. I just started hitting him, and the other guy's coach threw in the towel.

CALM UNDER PRESSURE

It's an old cliché, but you do like you're trained. You have faith in the man on your right and your left. When you attack and you know there are bullets or shells aimed at you, you go because you know people are depending on you. Combat was a job we were sent to do to save our country and way of life. I had great admiration for our two enemies. I knew the Germans were trained to kill me and I was the same, but I had no animosity toward them. I had great respect for the German soldier. When I lived in Japan, I admired those people, too. Our servants were completely honest, even though they were very poor. I admired their code of conduct. They worked hard. I respected our Korean and Vietnam adversaries as well. You don't have to have blood thirst or hatred to be an effective soldier.

RATIONAL THOUGHT PROCESSES

Some things you can't control, there's nothing you can do about it, like when I asked why my forward observer didn't show up.

Everyone makes mistakes; you learn from them. Going into battle, I was so proud of my company that I thought we could whip the world. When we were going into the first woods, I saw a man I played football with at LSU. He was in a jeep, trying to retrieve some of the tanks. When I told him where I was going, he said, "Boy, it's hell over that hill." I said, "These are paratroopers following me." There was no doubt in my mind. Since then I've learned there's a right way and a wrong way. Of course, some things are beyond your control, but you must rightly estimate the enemy, be sure to the best of your ability that the job you give people is within their capability. Take time to have a fire plan and secure communications and tie in with the units on your flanks. I was pretty bitter that we were thrown to the wolves, but maybe my leaders had orders to go. I don't know; Monday morning quarterbacking is easy. But I know the right way. The right way doesn't take that long. I was told that two tanks tried to help our troops, but the German tanks knocked them out.

I've always been patient with my troops' mistakes. I'm honest and will tell someone if he does something wrong—I don't hold it against him, but he'd better not repeat it. When I fail, I feel bad and resolve to correct my course.

If I see a problem, I try to solve it. You don't let problems keep happening. I can't understand people who do nothing. That's what leaders are for. The leaders I had in the service were great. If you got into trouble, they'd be there to help you, with one or two exceptions. I did feel we were let down in the Battle of the Bulge, but maybe the situation was so desperate that we had to do what we did.

SOCIAL SUPPORT

If someone gets near me, he's going to get talked to. I make friends. I was close to my buddies. After the war, they wrote and told me to come back. That was what influenced me to come back. Our unit was a family. We all got along real fine. I felt pride and mutual respect.

I got letters from my mother and brother during the war (my father had died by then), and, of course, my wife. Those letters meant everything to me.

I loved LSU. I was vice president of the student body. It was a beautiful campus and had great people. My professors wrote me when they found out I was in England in the hospital.

I loved my troops and looked out for them. I got them everything I could that they needed. I made sure they weren't overloaded like pack mules. There is no doubt in my mind that they thought a lot of me. I hear from a lot of them still, including quite a few enlisted men.

This is the home of the airborne here, so there are many, many people retired here that I've known for decades. Every Saturday morning we all go, six or eight of us, for breakfast. On Wednesday, another group of WWII veterans go to a different restaurant. I'm a charter member of the Old Soldiers club. We have a dinner party once a quarter. And the retired officers association goes out to eat. Almost daily, I see someone in the bank that I know.

Since my wife is buried here, I'm not going anywhere.

COMFORTABLE WITH EMOTIONS

At times in my career I was scared to death, to put it mildly. On Wednesday I'd say, "I'll be glad when Friday comes to see if I'm still alive." You see a dead man and you think it won't happen to you—but you worry about it. But usually I had so much faith in our leaders. I knew they'd take care of everything, and they did.

I wrote my wife every chance I got, almost daily. When I came back, I talked to all my friends and neighbors. I never held it in. I never tried to make myself out a hero, but I was comfortable talking about the war.

SELF-ESTEEM

I thought I was something hot. I had faith in myself, because I had faith in others too. Paratroopers think they're hot. I was proud to be an airborne soldier. After we were well trained, I had a lot of confidence. I thought we could do anything. I loved and missed Army life.

ACTIVE, CREATIVE COPING

I had a soldier return from London a day late, for reasons that I understood. My battalion commander told me to crucify him, one of the best men I had. I told my battalion commander to relieve me or let me discipline as I thought best. After that, he let me run my own company.

I was active during the Bulge, in that I advised my battalion commander that we had no forward observers. But I had to follow orders. I've questioned orders, but never disobeyed one. Thereafter, I was always sure I led better and gave my troops better support, or at least asked for it. My leaders in Korea supported their troops in an exemplary way. I learned so much from my battalion commander in Korea, Denzil Baker. He asked for armor, air, and artillery support to augment our fire plan.

I learned there was a right and wrong way to do things. You do everything to protect your troops. You have to tie in with units on your flanks. You have to make sure you have a fire plan to cover all areas. You don't just make a fire plan. You have to test out the plan every day and every night when you stop. There can be no complacency. You must constantly check and test.

In Korea, you would attack a ridge. You knew you would take it, but you wondered how many men you would loose. You feel that everyone sees you and you're the one they're shooting at, but you keep going. In one battle, we were about out of ammunition. I was sent to get an ammunition truck. I had the driver drive us right up into the middle of the battle.

I stay active. I didn't want to retire; I was retired when I reached mandatory retirement age and thirty years of service. People think I'm a nut for working. I need to work, not for money, but I'm around wonderful people all day long. I always loved people and always got along well with people. After I had my bypass operation, I exercised right away. It makes me feel good.

SPIRITUAL AND PHILOSOPHICAL STRENGTHS

God

I believe in God and I pray a lot. I believe in heaven and that's a good feeling, because I want to rejoin my wife. I think I'll go to heaven. I think heaven is a nice place to be. I'm not a religious fanatic by any means, because sometimes I get upset and am prone to swear. I think God is kind, although I don't understand why some things happen. I still go to church every Sunday.

Meaning & Purpose

My meaning and purpose was my wonderful wife and family, and I didn't want to let my soldiers down. I knew they wouldn't let me down.

The purpose of the war was clear in my mind. The Japanese hit us and we couldn't stand for that. The war was a fight to preserve our freedom. There was no doubt in my mind that we were fighting for the USA. The war was justified. We had to do something.

I knew I had a good job waiting in Baton Rouge and wanted to return to my wife and family and a good life. My goals were to take care of my family, and make them happy. I did.

Morality

My, yes, morality is so important. To be moral is to have a fair life and treat others well. I tried to be firm and fair and see the other person's viewpoints.

When we ate, the men ate first, the NCOs second, and the officers third. If there wasn't enough food, the officers didn't get any.

You have to be honest. If you tell someone something you keep your word. I can't stand a fake or a phony. In the Army I was in, if you told a man something and you found out it wasn't true, you made a beeline to him and told him the truth. If you did it, you admit it, and face the music. In my units, if someone told you a lie, he'd be in serious trouble. Just to lie to favor yourself is a disgrace. The truth never hurts in the long run. You come out better and feel better. Your self-respect increases when you are truthful. When I got out of the Army, I was shocked that people in business would look you in the eye and be untruthful. I'm honest, although if some fellow is ugly as hell, I won't say, "You're an ugly SOB." I'll tell him his clothes look good.

Any man that hits or slaps a woman to me is a worthless SOB. All you have to do is walk off. I think it's a disgrace to abuse a woman. I open doors for women, and I still give up my seat for a woman. I did that this morning.

Troops would take a dim view of one who cheats on his wife. I do too. If you can't respect a leader, it makes you feel uncomfortable. The troops want you to be moral. I know my wife respected me because I loved her to death.

Love

I've always loved life. Just like now. I've managed four different banking branches and I love the people I work with in the bank. I get along with people. I'm honest and outspoken. In the service I had wonderful friends. Mutual respect and admiration are why I loved the Army so. I didn't care what color people were. I was raised with black people and thought the world of them, even though I've known sorry people of all races. My soldiers thought a lot of me, and I let them know I thought a lot of them.

The regimental intelligence officer in Korea was a good friend. His wife would send him a can of sardines or a few cookies and maybe a can of beer. He'd find me and we'd share those sardines or cookies. Now that's a great friend.

I loved my wife and kids. I couldn't wait to get home to see them. In WWII, I had two little boys; one was born while I was away. We had a new baby girl in Japan, just before I went to Korea. Every time I got home, I was so happy.

Optimism

I am an optimist. That means I can get things done. I'm a doer. If I think something is wrong, I tell my bosses.

I never thought about losing the war. There was no doubt in my mind that we wouldn't win. To be honest, I really never thought I'd be killed, either. When I was wounded, I was still optimistic; I thought I'd be back in a week or two.

Before I retired, I didn't really have a plan. My wife joked that I'd retire and we'd drive off the post and say, "Should we turn right, or should we turn left?" But I knew we'd find a place to live and enjoy ourselves. Maybe we'd start out on the Gulf Coast and enjoy the beach and good seafood, or maybe find a place somewhere else. I love life and don't plan to go anytime soon, either.

Humor

You just can't get too serious. Life is too short. In high school I was the class clown. I talked to my troops as often as I could. When I was brigade commander I'd talk to my battalions at least once a month. I'd kid them and remind them that the dumpsters were to put trash in. I'd tell the first sergeants I could barely see the antlers of deer out there in the grass. Next thing you know, the grass was cut. We knew we thought a lot of each other.

Sometimes I couldn't help but laugh about certain combat situations. Once, in Korea, we were eating C rations behind a ridge line, when some mortars started coming in twenty yards in front of us. I immediately ran for a crevice. I looked back and there was an officer hiding under a poncho, thinking it would save him from a mortar round. The next day we were moving across a creek, when a mortar round landed thirty yards behind us. The battalion signal officer ran over to the hole, thinking he could look at it and tell where the round came from, when another round landed nearby and he got a bunch of fragments in his behind. So he undid his britches and reached back and came flying back with his britches down. You couldn't help but laugh. Another time, I was in a foxhole with my battalion commander. I wore size ten boots and he wore size seven or eight. One of the few times I took my boots off to dry and to rub my feet, the enemy penetrated our perimeter. He kept saying, "You know, I think I forgot to put my inserts in." My feet were cramping. He'd put on my boots, and I'd put on his. I also had his field jacket on and he had mine on.

Long View of Suffering

Most people I knew felt like they were better men for being in the service. I loved the service. If I were a young man, I'd do it again. If it were up to me, all able young men would do at least two years of service. My experience in the Army to me was the greatest thing. The mutual admiration and respect made the suffering worthwhile. When I retired, I felt I was leaving the greatest love of my life. I hated to leave my unit after the Bulge. I felt things might have gone better for my company if I had been there.

Maintaining Balanced Living

You'll never see me with a potbelly. I exercise. I ran every morning with my brigade. I walk my dog twice a day. I used to jog, but my puppies couldn't keep up. I lift weights daily. I do light weights in the morning, along with thirty pushups and other calisthenics. At night I do heavier weights. If I ever had a headache, I don't remember.

I eat a lot of fruit and vegetables, vitamins, milk, orange juice, and cereal. I don't eat a lot of fried food. I watch my weight—about 155 pounds. When I played football I was only 190 pounds.

During WWII, I didn't even drink coffee. I didn't drink alcohol during the week. In 1965 I quit smoking, and I took my last drink in 1968.

I've slept eight or nine hours usually—nine or ten o'clock until 6:00 a.m. Now I also take a nap after lunch for fifteen or twenty minutes. It really helps me, if nothing else, psychologically.

For recreation, I was a rabid handball player. I tried to be a golfer, but my wife took a dim view of the long weekend hours. I've been an avid hunter and camper. Now I mow the lawn and keep my yard up. My wife and I liked to go out to eat and go to parties. I love to read, but sometimes I don't have time. I like to read military books and the paper to keep up with what's going on. I watch the news. I look forward to attending the Old Soldiers social gatherings quarterly. *[I was fortunate enough to hear him lead the singing of "On Top of Ol' Smokey"].*

Advice to Younger Generations

Warts and all, this is the greatest country that's ever been. Learn about other countries to appreciate what we have. Study history, especially American history. Young people think the rest of the world thinks just like we do. They don't.

Get as much education as you can. These days you'd better learn computers. Get a degree. It gives you confidence and pride. It gives your family pride in you. It makes you a better man and soldier. Education is your potential.

Learn your job. It never hurts to listen to other viewpoints. You'll be surprised what you learn.

Take pride in your appearance. It helps you be admired by others. If you see a jeep with rust on it, you know it's worse inside.

It's to one's advantage to go into the military, at least for a couple of years. The military teaches pride in self, respect for others, honesty, integrity, character, discipline, and how to get along with different people. If you're a parent, teach your kids those values and don't expect others to raise them. Teach them to be independent. Some kids expect their parents to take care of them their whole life. I don't understand that. Let them gain self-respect and pride from hard work.

As fullback at Louisiana State University

With C Company, 513th Parachute Regiment, Alabama. Captain Kendrick is holding the dog, front row center.

Home in Fayetteville, NC

Colonel "Butch" Kendrick, Brigade Commander

Part III
Pacific Theater of Operations

Chapter 30

Troy Dempsey Sillivan
USS St. Louis

Troy and Elizabeth (Libby) Sullivan live in a bright coral-colored home in Ft. Pierce, Florida, surrounded on three sides by water — bay, ocean, and river. They have two children, four grandchildren, and six great grandchildren. Troy is a trim and fit 5'6". His USS St. Louis *earned eleven battle stars for major engagements in the Pacific. Says Libby: "He's got a good sense of humor. He takes things very easily and is not easily upset. He is a good man. His faith brought him through."*

I was born in 1918 and lived on a farm in Goldsboro, North Carolina, for my first six years. We moved to a larger farm in nearby Turkey, North Carolina, the strawberry capitol of the state. We ran around with no shoes on. Those were the good old days. We planted ten acres of strawberries. In the springtime and every other time the weatherman said it would frost, we had to get up at 2:00 a.m. and cover them with pine straw.

In 1932, Daddy bought a big farm in Washington, North Carolina, where we raised tobacco, cotton, corn, peanuts, and chickens. Although the Depression had begun, we had no problems. We gave a lot of vegetables to people who had no food. We had plenty. We'd give away chickens and fifty dozen eggs a week. Everyone knew us and would walk out to the farm to see what we were giving away. People in the cities could have planted gardens, but they didn't. You never hear about farmers complaining during the Depression. We raised our cows for milk. I had to milk them before school and help clean out chicken barns. There were always chores to do, 24 hours a day. You'd work until you took fishing poles and left the farm. That was the only way to get away from the farm.

We were eight kids. I was third from the top. Mother made three meals a day. She had me help her cook. I preferred that to slopping hogs and milking cows. We all ate what mother put on the table. There was always so much—sweet corn, squash, beans, watermelons, cantaloupes.

Daddy was big hearted. We'd go fishing and catch a lot and then he'd give it to people in town. Everyone liked him. People were better natured and friendlier back then. Dad liked sports, which were free then. He played baseball. We put fields on the farm, and cities played against each other. Dad was six feet tall and 180 pounds. Nothing got in his way. He was a number one dad. I can't remember him ever hollering in anger. He'd tell you what needed doing, and you'd do it, no complaints. Then he'd hand you a dime. He was strict. We'd obey him, or, as he said, we'd get together. He made his own fish nets. He'd take all the kids into the mountains in a truck. We'd roam and climb cliffs and rocks without ropes. He never spanked, but he'd give us a good talking to. The sooner we got through our chores, the sooner we'd go fishing. Everyone would go head over heels to get their work done. Sometimes, in the afternoon after we finished chores, the neighborhood kids came over and we'd play ball in our ball field.

Mom was A1, the best cook in the world. She had a persuader, a four foot long by one inch in diameter tobacco stick. If I didn't move quickly, she'd head to the door where she kept it. I don't remember her using it. When we were young, my brothers and I would hide when company came. All our aunts wanted to do was hug us and make a fuss over us. Although things were tough, we were happy.

I finished high school in 1938. Daddy had plenty of help on the farm, so I left the farm at age nineteen to start in the doughnut business. In 1939 I opened up my own doughnut business in Carolina Beach, North Carolina. The doughnut shop is still there, making the same doughnut.

The name of the doughnut shop was Krispy Cream. However, someone patented that name and we were required to change ours. My shop was a spring and summer affair, and changing the name hurt our business, so my friend and I decided to check out the Navy to see the world. We hitchhiked to Raleigh and, on August 26th, 1940, signed up for six years. Two weeks later we reported to Norfolk, Virginia, for sixteen weeks of training. It was hard work, harder than making doughnuts. I was assigned to the cruiser USS *St. Louis*. A cruiser blasts out anything in its way, mostly on coastlines. We'd go two or three weeks ahead of the troops to bombard beach installations, usually at night. From 20 miles out, we could blast oil supplies, military installations, or troop transports. We usually operated with a task force of ten or more ships, maybe two or three cruisers, four or five destroyers, and maybe an aircraft carrier. I was in gunnery, either range finding or firing the guns.

My first cruise was to Guantanamo Bay, Cuba. Then we went through the Panama Canal to California. It seemed that everyone got seasick but me. I'd been used to water and fishing. After loading up with ammo and supplies, we cruised to Pearl Harbor. After two months of training, we went to China, in the spring of 1941. I think we were trying to gain permission for the Pacific fleet to maneuver in the China Sea and use airfields for the bombing of Japan. After a week we went to Manila to refuel and resupply. We went to Guam and Wake Island, and then back to Pearl Harbor in September, 1941.

On December 7, 1941, I was on the quarterdeck getting ready to leave the ship. We were going into town. On Sundays we'd usually listen to military bands, see military shows like boxing or singing contests, or play sports. I watched the enemy planes come in over my ship, dropping torpedoes on the battleships. Within five minutes smoke came up and everything was on fire. We were told to man our battle stations. Thirty minutes later we had enough steam that we could move the ship out of the harbor. As we were leaving the harbor, two torpedoes were fired at us from submarines. We had no room for evasive action, so we went full steam ahead to avoid them. We saw a submarine on the starboard side, which we fired on. We think we sunk it. There were two other destroyers with us. They threw depth charges in the area.

The first wave of torpedoes was followed by high-flying bombers and then strafers. I saw battleships on fire, dark smoke, and burning oil on the water. Battleships rolled and everyone slid off into the water. As we were leaving the harbor, you could see boats trying to pick up survivors.

We circled the island to see where the enemy was. Their nearest ship was 300 miles west of us in a big task force of four aircraft carriers, four battleships, and many smaller ships.

Two months later, we assembled a task force of seven ships, cruisers and destroyers, and went to the Marshall and Gilbert Islands, 800 miles west. At night, we successfully bombarded the naval installations from which was launched the raid on Pearl Harbor.

From May through about September of 1942, the *St. Louis* and about six other ships patrolled the Aleutians and bombarded two of the islands 400 miles west of Alaska, because the Japanese were setting up communications, prior to invading Alaska. This was actually a diversion for the Japanese attack on Midway.

Meanwhile, we heard that a big Japanese task force was moving east toward Midway. Two of our carrier task forces went to meet them. One went to the northern approach to Midway. Another went to the southern approach. We sank four of the carriers and a heavy cruiser, and disabled another heavy cruiser. Several hundred Japanese planes were destroyed. That stopped them. That was the turning point of the war, because Japan didn't have much left after that.

We went back to Pearl Harbor and then to the Coral Sea and the Solomon Islands to bombard and break up the "Tokyo Express." The Japanese were preparing to invade Australia. We were on standby when the five Sullivan brothers went down with the USS *Juneau*. There were air raids by high-flying bombers nearly every day through the Solomon Islands.

We lost our sister ship, USS *Helena*, in July of 1943, in the Battle of Kula Gulf. A few days later, we were torpedoed by a submarine. That was on Friday, July 13, 1943. The bottom of the bow was knocked off. It shook the ship and lowered it in the water. We were ordered topside to abandon ship, but we were still seaworthy. A destroyer escorted us back to Guadalcanal. We went back to Pearl Harbor for repair, and then to California for a better repair. We were there two months. Then we went back to the South Pacific. We went back to the Solomon Islands to bombard other islands in the group in November and December of 1943. We were dispatched back to Pearl Harbor in January, 1944

We went to the Philippines in the beginning of 1944, and on to Leyte Bay for supplies. One of the happiest moments was when a telegram told me to report to Washington, D.C., for 16 weeks of advanced fire control training in everything pertaining to the guns' electrical components. On May 27, 1944, while at this school, I married Mary Elizabeth (Libby) Savage. We'll be married 59 years in May of 2003.

I met Libby when she was still in school, when I was in the doughnut shop. She looked at me while on her bicycle and hit the curb. I helped her up, and off she went. Then she and her friends showed up at the shop. I had to tell them to only use one napkin each. She was in seventh grade. The second time I met her she was nineteen. When I came back to a Navy school in Washington, D.C., I went home and found that she was still there, working as a nurse in a hospital. I went to visit her at her home after she had her tonsils out. I sat on the bed without giving it a thought, but her mother asked me to move away.

I went back to San Francisco and a new ship, the troop transport USS *Missoula*. We carried two thousand Marines to Iwo Jima. I was a repairman for any gun that was out of order. The first flag to fly on Mt. Suribachi came from this ship. We were supposed to take the Marines out after three days, but the ship left with no Marines aboard. They were either still dug in or were casualties. One Marine that came on this ship asked me to send photos to his wife, and I did. I never heard from him. We were within two miles of the coast. Twenty Marines were lowered into each of the landing crafts. You could see them get hit before they got ashore.

The Japanese fired at us from artillery pieces on a train in a tunnel in the mountain. They'd fire and move back. They never hit us, but came within one to two hundred feet. You could hear the shells coming. It sounded like bacon frying. Everyone would duck and you'd see an explosion 200 feet off the bow.

We went back to the Philippines. The orders were to load Marines for the invasion of Japan. Soon after that the war ended. If we hadn't dropped the bombs, we would have lost about a million troops and they'd have lost many more. We were so happy when the war ended. Everyone was hugging each other and shaking hands.

I was discharged on December 18, 1945 from Mare Island Hospital in California. I had a lung condition, like emphysema, from the cold weather near Alaska, breaking the ice from the ship every morning. I enjoyed being in the Navy, but I was very glad to return home to my family.

I was fortunate. I escaped death two or three times by being lucky. At Pearl Harbor, the ship next to mine was bombed and then strafed. Our wooden deck also had a trench made by the Japanese bullets, but no one was hit. When the *St. Louis* was torpedoed, if we'd been hit two feet further back, we'd have flooded. Then, after I was reassigned to the second ship, the *St. Louis* was hit by a bomb and later by two kamikazes. The bomb hit topside and killed or wounded about forty sailors, right where I would have been. The person who took my place was killed.

After the Navy, I stayed in the doughnut business for thirty-seven more years. I went to Hopewell, Virginia, twenty miles east of Richmond, where my sister lived. Libby and I opened a doughnut shop. We rented a store for $15 per month. We couldn't make doughnuts fast enough to sell. We opened the first drive-in restaurant in the area in the same building. Later, Libby started a catering business there as well. So now we had three great-paying businesses. I retired in 1982 and moved to Florida. We really enjoyed our business and hesitated about retiring, but I think now that it's a good idea to retire in your sixties to have a good life.

PTSD Symptoms?

I still have nightmares. Other than that, I'm in good health. You can't help but think about guys in the water on fire at Pearl Harbor. We couldn't do anything to help them. They were yelling and screaming for help. Then at Iwo Jima, a launch was full of wounded Marines being brought back to sickbay for treatment. There were bodies with no legs. Legs were in the net, but we didn't know which legs went with whom.

What Helped You Cope?

After the war, I didn't dwell on memories, but tried to do something positive. My parents instilled in the children the work ethic, to work for something you want and not expect it to be given to you. We got into our business and didn't have time to be troubled. We were busy twenty-four hours a day. Wherever you saw me, you saw my wife right there helping. We were self-employed and working together. Sometimes we'd put the 'gone fishing' sign in the window and go off together. Working hard and making sufficient income let us take off and enjoy life. Our loving family and active church involvement also helped very much.

CALM UNDER PRESSURE

From previous training from my parents, I learned that when someone told me to do something, I should do my job. That's why I advanced so fast in the Navy. When you saw guys burning in the water you were trained ahead of time to know you had to keep your eye on what you had to do, to stand up under pressure.

I didn't hate the Japanese. I put myself in their place and felt sorry for them. They were obeying orders just as we were, even the admirals. The war wasn't their idea. Today, when I go to the Veterans Administration, I never use disparaging words for the Japanese. I just say *the enemy*.

RATIONAL THOUGHT PROCESSES

We were told all during our training what could happen and what we should do when emergencies happened. Because we were so well trained, we didn't give a thought to how bad things could be. I never knew anyone aboard my ship to not take care of his job well under stress or to think negatively. As far as mistakes, in four years we had no prosecutions or reprimands. It was a motivated group, that reached a fairly high level of precision. That's why we were called a fighting ship. In civilian life, with my children, I was easier on them because I knew what I went through growing up. I was strict and had rules, but I wasn't too tough. I took privileges away, but didn't holler. I'd set a punishment, but if they were good, I could back track and ease up.

SOCIAL SUPPORT

Libby still has my letters and I still have hers. We wrote several times a week. My parents also wrote each month. You were glad to hear from people back home, especially loved ones. After the war, my wife quit her job in the hospital to be with me and help me in the business. Family members will work three times harder than employees.

I knew what I had gone through, so I tried to give the younger sailors all the training I could. I taught them in practical terms, from my experience, in one hour what would take a month to learn in a class. I showed them that being cocky gets you into trouble. I gave guidance if they were willing to listen. Later, they'd slap me on the back and thank me.

COMFORTABLE WITH EMOTIONS

During typhoons in the Pacific, sometimes there were swells forty feet high. You could hear metal crack with every wave. It gave us the creeps, but we'd go check for leaks. You were afraid when you expected to engage the enemy. You'd start to bounce your feet. Or you'd kid with others. "I hope, if we go into another battle, I'm not with you." If they were reading their Bible, we'd kid that they were going to need more luck than that. You'd stay busy in a mock battle, setting up your equipment and drilling. You'd make practice runs with the fire control room. I've talked often about the war, but lately I try not to dwell on it.

SELF-ESTEEM

I had good self-esteem. I knew I could learn or do anything, if anyone else could. I felt I'd have been a lieutenant commander if I'd stayed in the Navy. I didn't know of anyone I wanted to change places with. I feel that way now.

ACTIVE, CREATIVE COPING

I went from the bottom to top in five years—from Seaman 1st Class to Petty Officer 1st Class—and was given the papers to sign for Chief. If you had a job to do, you accepted it. The chief in charge of my division told us to keep ourselves clean, study, do as we were told to without back talk, and say "aye, aye, sir," or "right away, sir." If someone outranked me, they controlled me. I accepted that. If you didn't agree with someone, you did what you were supposed to, and you'd later, as soon as you could, get permission to speak to the chief. Every nine months I got advanced. Then I had control. I never lost shore leave because I talked back or didn't do my job. I didn't mumble.

SPIRITUAL AND PHILOSOPHICAL STRENGTHS

God

I believed in God. I think that this belief strengthened me, because I did things that I thought God intended me to do. If you do the right things consistently, you have an open path and God will look out for you and respect you. But you can't be inconsistent. If you do what God expects, that's what's necessary. If you respect Him, He'll respect you. It is the same in life. The ship's captain had four bars. He was in charge and you abided his rules or took the consequences. I don't worry about the past or the future, because I know the road is open in front of me. Libby and I are quite involved in our church, and go about every Sunday.

Meaning & Purpose

I went into the Navy to see the world. After two years in the Pacific, I thought I'd be leaving. My marriage made me want to get out more than ever. I looked forward to advancing and to getting out. I looked forward to having a family. I was looking for the gold pot at the end of the rainbow. My gold pot then was to work until I retired and then move to Florida.

We were fighting because we were attacked, to defend our country and our lives. Later, I learned that if they'd defeated us in the Pacific, they had invasion plans for Alaska and Seattle. We learned this from information recovered from sunken ships.

Morality

Morality means you treat people equally and fairly. You don't blow smoke and brag. When I was promoted, I didn't wear my stripes to show superiority. You don't show superiority unless it is required by a work demand. I enjoyed training new men to help them advance. The guys I was working with hated to see me leave. When I treat people good and fair, I feel better myself. If someone is arrogant, then something is wrong with him. If you feel good about yourself, you'll treat others right.

It also means being honest. Last week I took a wheelbarrow from a yard sale that I thought had been placed out for the trash. I returned it when I noticed a $10 dollar price tag on it.

When you are married, your vows are to be faithful to that person for life. You're not interested in anything else. That's why we're married so long. We both feel the same way. This is very important.

Love

We had no enemies anywhere, no one that we couldn't talk to. You have to love nature, and if you do, you love everybody with it. There was no place that we went, that we didn't feel liked. Your own personality helps you get through life. If you show a good personality, others will show a good one back to you. I made friends with everyone, even guys on other ships. On patrol in San Francisco, I couldn't use my nightstick to butt other personnel. You had a love that you'd protect your own in the Navy. I felt especially close to guys on my gun station. You had to trust the men next to you and work as a team. Once a month, I still get together with our chapter of the Pearl Harbor Association. There are about thirty of us left.

Optimism

I figured that what was coming was what I deserved. If you did the right things you got favors, and things usually turned out well. Only goof-offs got mess duty. I didn't get any. I felt that if I were friendly with others, others would be friendly with me.

I felt we'd win the war after we took Guadalcanal, but not without cost. After the war, I thought things would turn out. The harder you work, the more you make.

Humor

This helped me 100% to get through. I had no enemies anywhere. Everyone wanted to go ashore with me. I could get along with anyone. If you have a good sense of humor and are pleasant, you feel good about everything.

One of my gun teammates was of German extraction. We kidded him and called him a Nazi. Sometimes, before a battle, someone would make a crack and break the tension: "Hey, you know what this means, don't you? You'd better kiss your tail goodbye because this is it."

I still try to keep things light. We thought my wife was going to need an operation, so we went to the store and bought her pajamas. When the doctor told us that the MRI showed that it wouldn't be necessary. I said, "Good, now I can go and get my money back." *(They both laughed heartily).*

Long View of Suffering

After seeing the bottom side of life at Pearl Harbor and such, you realize what could happen to you at any time. After seeing the worst, you appreciate anything that's left. Anything is better than that. The war also taught me to treat my fellow man right and don't expect favors from anyone, unless I work for those favors. If you want something good, you have to work for it.

Maintaining Balanced Living

I stay busy. I do a lot of walking—three miles a day; it used to be five. After our walks, we'd often go fishing. Fishing is a lot of exercise if you catch a big one. I take care of my own property. We don't hire people to do our maintenance. We do all the painting, every two years on the outside and every five years inside. We grow our vegetables. I eat three meals a day, little meat, lots of fruits and vegetables, and much lighter than our friends eat. We eat a lot of vegetables from our garden. I sleep eight hours, from 11:00 p.m. to 7:00 a.m.

I started smoking in the Navy, but quit in 1960. I've never been a drinker. I'd rather have a soda.

We travel and camp in our van. Over the summer, we take off. We've been to California twice. We are also in a group that plays dominos and cards once or twice a month and has dinner at each others' homes.

Advice to Younger Generations

Listen and you'll learn—much more by listening than by talking. Let other people talk and don't talk so much.

Keep your sanity by doing your job. Don't do it half way and depend on someone else to finish it. Don't expect favors or benefits without working for them.

My motto is "Be happy, go lucky." Be happy and you'll go lucky. Sometimes people think about that and find that it works—frowning doesn't. If my customers weren't happy when they came in, they would be when they left. I used to tell them, "If you are going to wear that frown, I'm not going to charge you." Look around. There's always someone in worse shape than you. Put yourself in their place and you realize how lucky you are. We volunteered and served 300 homeless people recently at Thanksgiving and Christmas. It was a good feeling to realize how lucky we are, to realize how many people will show up for a meal. One man had no legs. They all felt grateful. We felt good to give them a lift. You have to have a positive outlook. We could have felt gloomy because our family wasn't with us.

Troy Sullivan, 1941

Troy and Libby Sullivan, Ft. Pierce, FL

Chapter 31

Emil Paul Kauffmann
Platoon Sergeant

Eighty-three-year-old Paul Kauffmann was outside raking when I drove up to his split level home in Port Jefferson Station, New York. There is a basketball hoop outside for his grandson, who has cystic fibrosis. He and his wife Elaine have chosen to stay near him, rather than join the rest of his family in Florida. They are the parents of four children and have nine grandchildren. Paul is good natured and quick to smile.

I was born July 8, 1919, in the Bronx, New York, at home with a midwife. All of us were born at home. I was the second oldest of eight children. Only one was a girl. She and a brother died at young ages.

I had a good family, but my mother died very young from pneumonia, when I was 15 years old. I was raised by my father and aunt. All the children ate meals at my aunt's house. She did the laundry for us, too.

My first 15 years were excellent. When I think about it, it was a nice life. We didn't go without anything. My father had an electrical contracting business. We rented a five-bedroom apartment behind the store. My uncle owned the store and rented to my father. We had bikes and wagons; most kids didn't have those then. Aunts, uncles, and cousins all lived nearby, within a five-block area. Back then, families helped each other. We also moved nearby as we could find nicer places. Outside one residence we raised rabbits and chickens, and ate the eggs. I did my homework at night by the light of the kitchen's belly stove, which burned wood or coal. In another place, we took baths in tubs filled with water that was heated by a gas coil. Once a week we got a supply of ice for our icebox. We wrapped the ice in paper and it kept for a week. We had a close family. The boys fought like cats and dogs sometimes, but if someone from the outside stepped in to hurt one of us, there would be trouble. We did a lot together as a family. We'd drive almost every weekend of summers to Bridgeport, Connecticut, to roller skate.

My mother was a very good person, very pleasant, a pussycat, the best friend you ever had when you're boys. Boys are difficult until they settle down. She worked in the house. My father was very strict and very fair. He wanted us to do certain things, such as sift the coal so we could use it again, take care of the garden, make our beds, and take out the garbage. Everyone had a little job. He had rules: Do your work first thing after changing clothes. When you finished the chores, then homework, then you could play. If you didn't, you couldn't play. We all went with him on weekends to do electrical jobs, like winding motors for factories. If it wasn't right, he'd pull it down and we had to make it right. He was proud of his jobs.

Sunday, we went to church in the morning. My mother packed a lunch, and in the afternoon Dad and the boys would fish off the docks. Or we'd go crabbing. We didn't lack for much during the Depression, because he made good money.

At home we made marble games with a wood cheese box. My mother often played games with us, as did Dad on the weekends. After school, we'd ride ponies bareback in the Bronx Park, where they were being bred. We'd hop the fence surrounding the field and use a bridle we fashioned out of rope, and never were caught. We were lucky.

I left school in the eighth grade to earn money and be independent, working in a restaurant as a dishwasher, shining shoes, and working in a gas station.

I was drafted in 1942. I first trained in 40 mm artillery at Camp Stewart, Georgia, and then volunteered for the 677 Antiaircraft, Artillery, Automatic Weapons Battalion, a glider battalion heavily armed with many machine guns, whose mission it was to protect the fighter strips in the advanced combat areas. I trained at different camps in the states. Our battalion commander was a rebel, and every place we went, we had to be the best. In 1943, we went overseas to Australia for more training. Our first mission was to defend the airstrips in New Guinea from the Japanese—who were mostly using guerrilla tactics. After five or six months, we went to the Philippines and we were there when the atomic bomb went off. Thus, we didn't have to go to Japan, which saved a lot of lives. As platoon sergeant, I taught the guys how to take apart and reassemble the machine guns in the dark, by feel. There was a lot of shooting, but you didn't want to talk about the deaths you saw. You wanted to forget those things.

I met my wife before the war, when I was working in a gas station in the Bronx. She lived in the house next door. We were engaged when I was drafted. I sent her my allotment every month. When I got back, she handed me the bank book. Every nickel was there. I thought that was a good sign and I was going to marry her, and I was never wrong. She is a good woman. We married in April of 1946, so we've been married 56 years. In 1949 I went to work for the city and spent 32 years as a troubleshooter for welding equipment. I picked up the skills as I went along.

PTSD Symptoms?

I had malaria when I got out—sweats and chills, but no psychological problems.

What Helped You Cope?

My family was a good influence. Growing up, my father and mother were home all the time. You figured that you had to toe the line, because someone was around, which was good. The same with my extended family. They lived all around a two mile radius. They'd see you do something and tell your father, and he'd believe it. My brothers helped each other in everything, especially my oldest brother. He had a job and would buy us things; he was very generous with his earnings. He was a special person. He'd also separate us boys when we were fighting sometimes.

CALM UNDER PRESSURE

Sometimes guys came back from pass and shot up the tents to release built-up tension. Fortunately, no one got hurt. I was always calm. I wasn't too afraid. Same with heights—that never phased me.

I felt the Japanese were sneaky, but they had to do their job, just like I had to. I felt no hatred.

RATIONAL THOUGHT PROCESSES

Sometimes I made mistakes. Everybody makes mistakes. There's no one perfect in the world. Even Einstein, who was brilliant, made mistakes. Most of the guys in my unit were civilians, volunteers from New York and New Jersey. It was hard for them to learn their chores. You didn't want to be rough on them. You had to be patient as they learned their duties. When I had malaria and dengue fever (a mosquito-borne disease), I was in the hospital twice. You got a shot every three hours in the behind. Some nurses were good and some were bad. Some struck a bone.

SOCIAL SUPPORT

Support from home during the war was important. My future wife always wrote. Her letters helped to keep me alert all the time. I knew I had to go back; that was the most important thing. My oldest brother, who was in the European Theater, wrote me regularly, as did my aunt and uncle.

The guys in our unit pal'd around on their time off. I used to pal around with a couple of guys. I liked all the guys in my outfit. I was friendly with them. Most men abided by what I told them and with only a few did I have to keep at a leader's distance. Certain ones worked on you. With them, I had to draw the line. It's been the same with being a boss. On our time off, we played stick ball with a broom handle, like we did back in New York.

COMFORTABLE WITH EMOTIONS

It was awful to lose someone you knew. You'd go to pieces. Also, everybody is afraid sometimes. You just think of what is home, what you are returning to. That was always on your mind. You were serving your country. I don't believe anyone should back away from serving their country. If things got too intense, I'd talk to my buddy and get it over with. To keep things in you is no good. Things build up, just like hatred that builds up poisons you. Anything you have on your mind, it's better to talk about it. Don't keep it in you.

SELF-ESTEEM

I was very proud that I was in the war. I thought I was doing the right thing. I always thought I was a worthwhile person. I always had confidence. When I tackle something, I do it to completion. I get mad at myself sometimes, if I know how to do it and can't. And, eventually I'll do it. I was confident because I tried everything. If you don't try, you don't know what you can do.

ACTIVE, CREATIVE COPING

I volunteered for advanced training and figured I made better use of my time. I would tackle jobs when I wasn't a mechanic, even in the service. When I'd get stuck, I'd sit down and eat and go back and it would fall back together. Off duty on the islands, I volunteered to build kitchens and sleeping areas out of concrete forms to improve our living conditions.

SPIRITUAL AND PHILOSOPHICAL STRENGTHS

God

I went to church. It didn't matter which one, but I went every Sunday morning. God was very important. There is a God. God sees everything you do. If you do things wrong, you'll pay for it some way, and if you do things right, you'll go to heaven. I hope my spirit will live on in heaven. For comfort during the war, I'd say a prayer now and then and hope He'd listen to it.

Meaning & Purpose

I knew I had to go back to the life I had, which was good. You had your memory of what you'd come back to. That was very important. When I lost my stripes at the end of the war (I struck a drunken lieutenant who was mistreating a woman), I didn't care, because I knew I was going home.

I thought I did my job in the war. The war was just. You were fighting for your freedom. I thought everybody should do that. Since the war, I have a nice family and house—it's mine and my wife's. It's a fair world.

Morality

During the war this was very important. Morality means you have to be fair, honest, and respectful with people. You have to put yourself in the place of the other person. You have to be reasonable about what you're asking. If you won't do it, they won't do it. I want to be treated as I treat you.

I was always true to my wife. I wouldn't have what I have today, if it wasn't for her. Immoral behavior would risk that relationship.

Love

Love is very important. My wife is a good woman, a marvelous woman. If you can stay with one woman for fifty-six years, it's a treasure.

In the war, I had good men. The guys stuck together like a family. They were a terror sometimes, but they were good fighting men. You could depend on them. I liked all the men in my platoon, although I had to watch some of them.

Optimism

I'm an optimist, because anything could happen. I thought the war had to come to an end some way, and I expected it to end well. I always thought we'd win out. I expected to have a good life with my family.

Humor

I'd like a joke. Sometimes it would break the tension, but I don't remember jokes.

Long View of Suffering

After the war, I was more grown up in a lot of ways. I knew what I wanted to do in terms of work and family. I used to live in a middle income project in the city, but I realized I wanted to get a house. So, I hocked everything I had, and I bought one. The first year, they doubled the taxes and I thought I was going to lose it. My wife said we wouldn't lose it. The Army taught me that you fight for what you want, for what's important to you and your family.

Maintaining Balanced Livinig

I exercise—gardening, cutting the lawn, washing the car. After the war I weighed 176 pounds. Now I weigh 177. I fluctuate a pound or so. I'm always busy doing something. I've had pretty good eating habits— three meals a day. Breakfast is very important. You can go all day on a good one. I usually have cereal, juice, grapefruit, coffee, and toast. Lunch is usually a sandwich. For dinner, I like all fish and have it twice a week, with lots of greens and all kinds of fruit. We eat home most of the time, rather than eating out. My wife prefers that. I usually slept eight hours, from 10:00 p.m. to 6:00 a.m. I still do, and sometimes nap, now that I'm retired.

I quit smoking cigars 20 years ago. I realized smoking is no good for you. When the doctors quit, I quit too. I didn't inhale. I used to drink a beer or two a day, but haven't drunk in six years.

I fish whenever I can; it's the most relaxing sport there is. I like to watch sports— football, baseball, and hockey— and tinker with machines.

My eight-year-old grandson, with cystic fibrosis, is our recreation. We watch him. We'd like to move to Florida, where the rest of the family is, but my daughter has good health insurance with her job.

Advice to Younger Generations

Families are very important. You always go to family for help. Stay close to yours. Too many people are moving away from family.

You can do it. Anybody can do it. Americans are the smartest people around, if they use their minds. Education is very important. If you have an education, you can do anything. All my grandchildren have good, well-paying jobs. You can be smarter, if you keep studying.

Realize you have a lot to learn. You'll learn a lot, if you listen to the old-timers. When I was young, I wouldn't listen either.

Paul and Elaine, April 1, 1946

Paul and Elaine with their grandchildren

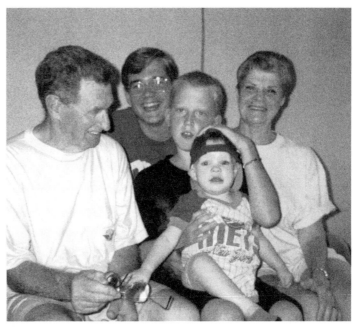

Chapter 32

Milo Louis Ballinger
USS Rocky Mount

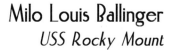

Eighty-eight-year-old Milo Ballinger was Chief Gunners Mate on the amphibious assault command ship USS Rocky Mount, *the command center that orchestrated invasions in Pacific combat areas. The phrase "Ask the Chief" reflects the respect with which these seasoned, wise leaders were held. The* Rocky Mount *earned six battle stars and the Navy Unit Commendation.*

Mr. Ballinger is a slender six-footer with a gentle smile. He drives a golf cart with two American flags on it around his Arizona retirement community. His wife Margaret (Meg) describes him as "a wonderful husband, father, and family man. The girls adore him. He listened to them. His strengths are his honesty, fairness, and patience. He never goes overboard; if he does get angry, it is with good cause." A Bible rests on his coffee table.

I was born on August 9, 1914, and grew up on a ranch near the little town of Mead, 30 miles north of Denver, Colorado. I had an older brother and sister. My family was a strong family. Mother's parents were immigrants from Germany and France. Dad's family has been here forever. My grandmother on his side was Cherokee Indian. My parents were good, honest, hard-working, people. I can remember that my dad, if he didn't think he could pay that year for a newspaper, phone, or other billings, would discontinue them in advance. My mother was a wonderful mother. I could always go to her with my troubles. She was very quiet and kind and would help anyone that needed help. If the neighbors were sick, she was always willing to take food in or care for the children, even when her health wasn't good.

We worked awfully hard. In those days, there was no modern equipment. Everything was done by hand. Nothing was lifted by tractors. All feed for the cattle was handled by hand. It was an extremely hard life.

Once or twice a year, my parents would take us to Denver to a park for a picnic lunch and rides. It was rare because it cost money. We had three or four family gatherings a year with various relatives, and always the whole family got together once a year—aunts, uncles, and cousins.

I went to high school at Mead. I had to be home for chores after school, as did most of the others. Because it was small, my school couldn't field a football team, so I started boxing during school hours and later went on to Golden Gloves. That was *good* experience. I won in my area, before going into the Navy. It taught me that you'd better take care of yourself and keep in good physical condition, or you'll get punched around in the world. I followed that all through my life. I boxed light heavyweight in the Navy at 175 pounds.

Because life on the ranch and farm was tough and we had no money, in 1933, at 18, I decided to join the Navy. I remember what prompted me to join. It was a dry year and the crops were bad. I was cultivating corn and my dad came over to see how things were going. I'd been thinking about it all morning and said to him, "There has to be a better way to live my life." He thought about it a minute and said, "If there is, son, and you can find it, take it." Joining was the best decision I ever made. He wanted us to do better for ourselves. He'd always provided us with a living, but died at 59 years of age from hard, hard work.

I did four years in the Navy, serving on the USS *Pensacola*, a heavy cruiser, in gunnery. At the end of my enlistment, I came home and went to work for the Weld County Highway Department for three years. I was a heavy equipment operator, which helped me out later in life. The service helped me meet my wife. In 1938, Margaret (Meg) was working in town. She was a young manager of a telephone exchange. My mom wanted me to go up and meet her. I thought to myself that she probably wouldn't want to know an ex-sailor, but I went anyway. I watched her work the old telephone board. I asked her if she'd like me to help her out, since, in the service I had been a switchboard operator at the main gate. She said, "You can't do that." I said, "Just move over," and she did and I took over and did fine. She was really upset that a man could do what was then a woman's job, and that someone might think she wasn't doing her job properly. In a way she was impressed. We went together and planned on getting married. And then the war started.

When Pearl Harbor was attacked, I re-enlisted the next day. I was assigned to the Armed Guard, the units that manned the guns on merchant ships. I picked up a crew and took it aboard the SS *John Erickson*, a troop transport out of San Francisco. On our first trip, we took about 5000 troops to New Zealand in preparation for the August 1942 invasion of Guadalcanal. We unloaded at Auckland and returned to New York. There, I got leave to marry my wife. Since I was proficient in small arms and automatic weapons, I was assigned as an automatic weapons instructor at Treasure Island, California, to train armed guards for the merchant ships.

In the first part of 1943, I made Chief Gunners Mate, and was assigned to Admiral Kelly Turner's flagship, USS *Rocky Mount* AGC-3. An AGC (amphibious group command) ship was specially designed as a command center for amphibious invasions of the islands of the Pacific. It was manned by all the specialists in the world at that time—all the intelligence and all the brains from different services and nations that it takes to invade—and had the most modern communications. Admiral Turner was the supreme commander over all forces in the group. As chief gunners mate of the ship, I was responsible for the use of all guns and the training of all personnel in the use of those guns.

Our first trip back was to the Marshall Islands in January and February of 1944. That whole operation was directed from our command ship, until the troops were on the ground. *[The main islands were Kwajalein and Eniwetok].* At that point, the ground services (Marines or Army) took over. Admiral Turner was Fifth Amphibious Group Commander.

Then in the summer of 1944, we went to the Marianas Islands *[Saipan, Guam, and Tinian in the Central Pacific, which would provide Allied bomber bases. The Japanese disastrous ambush of the American fleet during the invasion of Saipan was to become known as the Marianas Turkey Shoot, because so many Japanese aircraft were shot down.].*

Next was the Leyte and Lingayen Operations in the Philippines at the end of the year and into January of 1945. The brains running the war knew that the Philippines were critically important. There were some real battles there. The Japanese knew this was their last naval stand and they put everything into it. *[General MacArthur chose to land at Leyte because it could be used for an air base. The Battle of Leyte Gulf was the largest naval battle of the war and inflicted critical losses on the Japanese Navy. This marked the first appearance of the dangerous kamikaze aircraft.]* At the end of the operation, we were getting opposition from a little island called Zamboango. There was a sugar mill there. We wiped it out. Then we put Australian troops on the shore of Borneo in April, May, and June of 1945.

I'm proud to say that my service was an honest representation of the Navy. I was always proud to have served on good ships with good people. And Admiral Turner was one of the best. Admiral Turner was a two-star admiral—tall, red headed, mostly grey now, with a very, very strict set of rules, which we all operated by. On the operations, my battle station was on the bridge, where I could talk to all gun batteries, as was his, of course. As we were coming into the Marianas, we had bogeys on the screen all day, which meant we had enemy airplanes in the air all day around us someplace. It was just getting to be dusk. We were at general quarters and knew they were going to hit. Everybody was watching in every direction. Then I heard Admiral Turner say, "There the SOBs come." He was the first to see the enemy. I looked up and they were coming in just like black birds. I thought, "I don't mind serving with this man. I believe he's gonna fight." He had a very distinguished record before this time. I was proud to serve with him on that prestigious flagship. Now, of course, according to Navy tactics, the destroyers were a screen. Then we had the heavier ships, cruisers and battle wagons. But we were right in the center because the people we carried needed more protection. That night we used our guns, too.

On the Marianas, we really had trouble getting the guys ashore. There was very heavy opposition. The Air Force and our ships had been in and hit them, and after several days we got them on the beach. I can remember, we had so many dead on the beach. Ours were lying there stinking. The Japanese were burning theirs. You'll never forget that smell of burning flesh. One of the things I remember about Saipan was that we took people aboard that had lost their ships or for whatever reason. We got a group aboard of probably fifteen to twenty. I saw this one fellow who seemed familiar. It turned out to be a friend of mine from Colorado, whom I hadn't seen in years. He was a mechanic in an assault boat that had gotten hit. He had lain on the beach for a couple of days. We had excellent hospital facilities aboard, although ours was not a hospital ship. They brought a lot of the wounded aboard for treatment. In a passageway to the dispensary area, there was a gurney. On it was a young boy of about seventeen—red headed, big freckles, near death. Blood was running down. The thought ran through my mind, "I wonder if that kid's mother knows what's happening to him this morning."

I was sent back to Washington, D. C., to attend electro-hydraulic and officers training schools. That's where I was when the war ended.

The first few years was a difficult time. We came home expecting everything to be the way it was. I went to work for the Colorado State Department of Highways. But wherever you went to work, you were supervised by people who'd managed to stay out of the war one way or the other. That was difficult for some of us. I started at the bottom, doing menial work, inventorying a warehouse. This was quite a comedown from being Chief of Gunnery for a ship, as high as an enlisted man could go. But over the course of 18 years, I worked my way up the ladder—to the shop, and to field construction, heavy equipment operator, area supervisor, and division superintendent. My wife stood by me and encouraged me to stay at it, having to start all over. My wife and I have been together 60 years. We had two girls after the war.

Under the Marshall Plan, so much was done to help war-torn nations. Later, it was expanded to impoverished nations, including Afghanistan. In 1968, the state of Colorado was asked to provide a team of technicians to go over there to implement a highway department similar to its own. A team was chosen. I was asked to head the project. My family was there two years. It was difficult in an impoverished nation, yet we accomplished our mission, by setting up toll stations to accrue revenue. When we left, the ambassador wrote to my boss saying that the aid program would be a success if all projects had been as successful as the Colorado project. It's not that we were so smart, but that we were able to get down to the level of the people we were working with. Although we are a superpower, we don't know everything. The people of Afghanistan accomplish remarkable things with the crudest of tools. For example, this beautiful five-legged table [*in his living room*] was carved from one piece of wood. They are a good people, although years of war have ravaged their country.

I retired in 1975. We had 160 acres north of Denver. We raised horses. We both were raised on ranches and we never got horses out of us. In 1989, we came down to Arizona permanently.

PTSD Symptoms?

I'd wake up at night slugging it out. I don't believe you ever get over nightmares. Memories returned at night if I didn't go to sleep. Nightmares still come, although less frequently. I'd developed stomach troubles from the stress during those 3½ years of hell. You don't get over it overnight.

What Helped You Cope?

In order to move ahead you have to be able to know and work with people. It was difficult to talk with others at first. I made up my mind to move ahead and so I did the things I had to. I think I did it pretty well. I made myself do the things I needed to do to progress. Giving presentations was difficult at first, but I persisted. By Afghanistan, I really enjoyed it.

Determination was a factor, but I think a month or two of vacation would have been helpful before returning to work. After a year, when I was feeling unproductive, I talked to my supervisor. He told me to take off a month and a half with pay. I came back to work and was able to do a much better job. That was a turning point. I saw a good doctor to treat my stomach, and took a nice trip with Meg. I didn't take to drink or drugs to dull the pain.

Pride wouldn't let me quit or buckle. I had never quit before in a fight. In the old Navy, you were taught to do a job and do it right. And you were given the opportunity to be more responsible. I wanted to do what I was doing. My first four years of training prior to the war were the best thing for my life in the war. It was almost crucial; it gave me a stronger background.

I love baseball and boxing. My first trainer told me, "Anytime you go in the ring and you're not in condition, you'll get hurt." He taught me to be conditioned, and to keep myself strong physically. I think it is a crime almost to abuse your body by drinking and running around, because you need all your strength.

CALM UNDER PRESSURE

Anyone who says they weren't scared to death is lying, but after war starts everyone can adjust— some better than others. For instance, on the three-man 20mm gun crew, you had to insert the magazine in just the right way or you'd jam the gun. If flustered you'd screw up. But, if people were well trained, for the most part, they were able to do it. When kamikazes dived, you would be destroyed if you didn't focus. The properly trained crew will stand there and fight. You have to know what you're doing, then concentrate on your job. In war, more than ever, you need to focus on the one thing and bear down.

We had so many men who were so hastily trained. They looked to me to know what to do. I focused on doing my job, because they expected me to. If I didn't do my job, they wouldn't be able to do theirs.

I didn't really feel hatred for the Japanese. He was doing exactly what his country was asking of him. I just knew him as the enemy and I'd better kill him first, before he killed me. When I first got home, I stopped to buy vegetables from a Japanese farmer. I felt some anger, but got over it. I think it was just a transition. This Japanese man was probably a good person. I knew Japanese people and worked with them and never had any trouble. It was just that one time.

RATIONAL THOUGHT PROCESSES

I worked, I mean I really worked, at being a positive person. I never felt that being negative gained you a thing. I think that being positive got me through a lot of trouble. People are prone to be critical or make light of others, but I never ever thought this was right. I've worked hard on that and feel it deeply. I think that you should be positive about your approach. When going through the transition to peacetime, it was competitive. I always liked to be #1, but often I wasn't. So I'd look back at myself to see where I had dropped the ball, or where I had to be better prepared. I never felt sorry for myself. I'd be disappointed of course, but I didn't let it get me down on myself. I'm not perfect, but usually felt that if I didn't get the position, it was because I wasn't prepared.

As a technician, I was known as a perfectionist. As a heavy equipment operator, I took a lot of pride in being known as an "Old Master." When I became area supervisor, my expectations were too high and the men couldn't deliver. After a year, I learned that everyone is not perfect. But I learned to accept an acceptable job in their own way. When you learn to accept the acceptable, then you can calmly talk to people and look to make adjustments that really count. You can say, "OK, John, let's try it this way."

I don't believe that I catastrophized in the war, or at any time thought that I couldn't stand something anymore. When things got tough, you went to the chief's quarters to talk about your challenges with someone who understood. Some chiefs went off their rocker—one thought he was being chased by a black cat. When we were bombarding the beach and the noise was horrific, I had the flu and a terrible headache and I wondered what else could happen. But I just tried to do my job. I never felt self-pity.

After the war, I tried to remember the good things more than the bad, because focusing on the negative causes them to multiply. Finally, you just let them go.

SOCIAL SUPPORT

On board, you know you're not alone, and everyone feels the same way. The whole ship's company was all working together. Sailors are a pretty good group of people. They support each other whether they know it or not, even if they're ribbing you. You become closer than anyone in the world because you do everything together. There's not much room on the ship. We had a chief boatswain mate/master of arms. After an engagement, casualties were brought down to sick bay. Following the proper examinations, the dead were wrapped in canvas and a weight was attached to their feet so that they would sink. His job was to have the canvas down there and his men would sew them up. My job was to have the 5" shells down there to be lashed to their legs for weight. One night, he said, "Tomorrow night I'll probably be doing this to you, Ball." I suppose I could have taken offense or been afraid, but it tickled and amused me to have that much humor on our job. In that way, you were able to communicate with and support each other, despite this serious business. He meant nothing by it, and I knew that. It kind of broke things up. I'll never forget him.

A ship is large. I reached out to every chief so that we could support each other. We were friends. That's very important. All our jobs were linked. You had to know the other chiefs. You couldn't be a loner. It was somewhat different with those under me. I wanted discipline, so we weren't friends, but we respected and liked each other.

The guys in Vietnam were not sent to win the war; it was a politician's war. In WWII *everybody* worked together to win. I hear people say that there was a different breed of people in the Vietnam war, but the lack of support probably hurt them more than anybody will ever know.

Support from home was very important. Meg wrote a letter almost every day. We'd get them all at one time. My mother wrote often. Even high school girls were given the names of service people to write to. That really helped, even though we never met. It gave you a lift. You looked forward to it. The guys who got Dear John letters were the ones who really cracked up. You're holding on tight, and then you lose that little handgrip and they lose it all. It was probably the cruelest thing a person could do to another in those times. Probably no one would do that, if they really knew how hard it was on the guy on the receiving end.

My wife was a good person to come home to. I also had my mother and father. My wife's encouragement kept me going in my menial job. She said I'd someday be a superintendent. And I had two great little girls. My boss helped me, too. It was really the beginning to have someone have real feeling for the transition I was going through. All of us need help sometimes even if we, or the people we're with, don't realize it.

COMFORTABLE WITH EMOTIONS

I was comfortable with my emotions, able to talk about them for the most part. I could acknowledge that I was afraid. Oh, Lord, yes. I remember the first time I saw the enemy at sea. My knees might have buckled if I hadn't had a gun mount to hold me up. I'm sure some of the kids cried, but it was not acceptable for chiefs. Now, we're probably more open. I've become more open in expressing my feelings. I've not told my wife everything. We go to ship reunions. It is nice to go. Often the things you don't tell your family come out. I'll never forget our first in San Diego in the '70s. I saw fresh faced kids who are now bald with a tummy. It was great being with them again and talking.

All of us chiefs had one or two we were closer too. My best friend was a chief signalman. We could get together and we could talk about almost anything that bothered us. I thought I had a confidant. Although I enjoy being alone, I realize you must communicate with others. Everyone needs time by himself, but you must be careful not to overdo it.

Our letters home were severely censored. We'd write about the activities of the day, not feelings, except that I told Meg I loved her.

Sometimes at night, after an exceptionally bad day, in the hot quarters, you'd lie there and sweat, unable to sleep. I could get peace and relief and sleep by putting myself on a mountain top, with thick green grass. I could lie in that grass and put my feet in that grass and go to sleep. Honest to goodness, it worked. I would rest and go to sleep.

SELF-ESTEEM

I was proud to be a chief gunners mate. I knew my job and knew it very well. The self-esteem from that helped me do what I had to do. I was looked up to by our young seamen. We certainly didn't know everything, but we tried to. That confidence generalized. On the *Rocky Mount*, I replaced a very inefficient chief and was able to straighten things out. Thereafter, everyone knew that I knew my job and could help them do theirs. I wasn't God, but I did know my job.

ACTIVE, CREATIVE COPING

I never want to be classified as passive. That's the worst thing you can do. Sit around and you get lazy and careless. In the example I just mentioned, the guns were really in bad shape when I came aboard, but I didn't let things stay the way they were. The men thought we had to send them out to maintenance. Instead I showed them how to fix them. As soon as you do things like that, the guys take interest. Every day all along the line, I always gave the job the best I had, in the war and after. In Greeley (north of Denver), they transferred me one time to an area that had had little or no supervision for quite a while. The guys were older than I, but I had the supervisor's job. Things weren't right. They'd been passive. After two weeks, I called a meeting and laid it out. I told them that I'd been sent to do a certain job and I needed their support and expected to get it. One guy said, "If you do all that, you'll have no friends." I said, "Well, Joe, I wasn't sent to make love to anybody." In a few days that got back to the main office. But I changed things and everyone was far happier.

SPIRITUAL AND PHILOSOPHICAL STRENGTHS

God

I was a believer during the war. I'd been to church as a kid but wasn't a religious person and I never went to church in the service. Shortly after the war started, I had so much responsibility heaped on my shoulders. Those men knew nothing except what I'd taught them. They looked at me as if I were God and knew everything. Of course, I didn't. There you need some help. I mean spiritual help. The night before the first operation, I went into a ready room and I sat down and laid my cards out and asked for help. Before I left that ready room, I had the best feeling. All the problems were still there, but I absolutely knew I'd do the best I could do. I'd make the best decision on the knowledge that I had. That would be good enough. That load had been lessened. I think spiritual help is vital. I know you can't live a full life without Him. You have to have that support. Without it you have nothing. There has got to be something greater than we are.

I had an issued canvas back Bible. I read it at nights. I would say my prayers daily, but I stopped asking for favors. I didn't want to put God in a position to make choices as to who he would protect. During the armed guard days on the merchant boats, a ship was torpedoed and most of the crew was picked up. I said to my buddy, "Did you have a chance to shoot at 'em?" He'd been having a prayer meeting and not taking care of the business at hand. I believed in doing my share. I know you have to have help, but you have to do your job, too. God won't clean guns for you. I think what you are really asking Him is that if it's your time to go that you are prepared to meet your maker. In other words,

God expects you to do your share to the best of your ability, and live so that you are prepared when you meet Him. I'm not afraid to meet Him.

Today we go to a community church every week. When I was chairman of the council we had sixteen denominations. We were very actively involved, but in the last few years we have cut back to a more acceptable level.

Meaning & Purpose

My goal was to do the very best job I could do, and get home so I could get on with my life. On the way up, I had goals of advancement, and being a chief was as high as I could go. I looked forward to living in freedom and safety, being at home with my wife, and hopefully going out and generating a new life. My wife and her mother were good people. So it was just good to be back home.

Morality

You can't legislate morality. I think it comes from each individual. The worst thing you can do is cheat. Whether on your wife or your job, whatever you cheat on is wrong. I'm not pretending to be perfect, but I don't think anyone is happy unless they have something to be proud of. You're not afraid of what's going to happen, if you've done what is morally right. When you look at the business world today and the scandals, there is certainly no morality there. There is no way for those people to ever expect any happiness from what they've done. You need to live your life in a manner consistent with what you know is right. I'm no preacher, but "If you love me, you'll obey my laws," as the Book of John says. That's hard to do. But if we've done the best that we can do and ask forgiveness for mistakes, it's as the first verse of the 23rd Psalm says: The Lord is our shepherd and we shall not want. I think that this is true.

My wife and I discussed being true shortly after marriage. In essence, we said if you are not happy with me, just come to me and tell me and don't go out and mess around. I absolutely lived up to that. It just won't work out otherwise. Cheating just wouldn't have been worth it. I had it better at home.

Love

I felt love for my wife. Next to that, I'd call what I felt for my shipmates great respect as people. You need to know someone to respect him. You knew if someone was honest and true, did his job, tried to live a decent life, and treated people well, and you respected these men. If a man had good character, you could depend on him. You didn't have to wonder if he'd be there to be counted on. This is true for anyone—man, woman, or child. You can respect different things in different people. I find that you can find some good, something to respect, in everyone. Sometimes you have to look for it. I learned, early in life, that if you had a good employee and something went wrong, instead of chewing them out, you should have a talk to see what's going on in their lives. Lots of times you can do some good.

At my most difficult times when I didn't quit, there were things that kept me going—my wife and little girls— and I couldn't bear to think of them not loving and respecting me. I wanted this more than I wanted to quit. The will to do right was stronger than the will to do wrong. When I retired, there was a roast for me. I had over three hundred people working under me. People said they didn't always agree with me, but I was always fair. To me, they couldn't have given me a higher compliment.

Optimism

I believe I'm an optimist. Optimism is really a good word. You need it. I always tried to take the positive approach to any work that needed to be done. I resolved that if I was going to do something, I'd do my best. I always thought I could learn something every day.

Humor

It is extremely important to see humor in almost every situation, especially the bad. A little laugh goes a long way. In the chief's quarters, at night, the storytellers who gave you a little laugh went a long ways to make the night better.

The most humorous things involved a slight injury and how it happened. In construction in the wintertime, we'd come in to overhaul equipment. We'd sit down to eat our sack lunches. One guy was very particular where he sat down to eat his lunch. We were sitting there watching him. He was moving steel around from place to place, getting ready to sit down. After all his preparation, he finally had everything just right, except that he brushed a final piece of iron off the table. It landed right on his toe. His expression of pain was so funny. You shouldn't laugh at someone's expense, but we went crazy laughing. After all his careful preparation, it was just so funny. I've thought of it so many times and laughed.

After I became superintendent, every morning the supervisors would gather in my office and we'd go over the details of the day. One of those guys had a new story every time he came in. I really looked forward to those meetings. It just made my day and put everyone in a good mood.

Long View of Suffering

War *is* hell, but I wouldn't take anything in the world for my eight years of service. It has served me so well. It taught me discipline. You need that. If the war did anything for me, it taught me humility, and to respect people for what they could do. It taught all of us that we can't live alone. You have to learn to live with others. War teaches you strengths (and weaknesses) and you draw from that as you live your life afterwards. And in the very end, it made me know that there is a reason for almost everything. I'm grateful to have been able to get through it and get home to live the life I did.

The most difficult part was being away from loved ones, and the uncertainty of life and what would happen tomorrow, if there was one. You have no control. You coped by simply doing your job to the best of your ability, and perhaps putting uncertainty in the back of your mind.

Maintaining Balanced Living

I kept my weight to within five pounds of what it was when I entered the Navy. I now weigh 168 pounds. I was 164 when I went in the Navy. I've walked a lot. I do stretching exercises. Years ago, when I was a supervisor, I had back trouble and intense pain. I was driving a pick-up a lot. An older man referred me to an osteopath, who gave me a set of exercises, but no medicine. He said that if I didn't do them, he wouldn't see me again. I did them religiously, and that cured the back trouble. I eat lots of fruit, and mostly fish and chicken. We try to eat a balanced diet, three nourishing meals a day. Lately, we eat a smaller dinner. I never have trouble sleeping. I'm thankful to our good Lord that I can sleep at night. Now I get eight to nine hours, from 9:00 p.m. until 5:00 a.m. or so. That's about how it was when I was working, too.

I smoked a little bit when I was young, but gave it up in 1946. I knew it wasn't doing me any good, so I quit and I'm thankful I did. Everyone was sending us cigarettes. They were five cents a pack on the ship. The Red Cross gave us cigarettes. I knew they were doing harm. I quit during the hardest time of my life. I was so proud of myself and wouldn't have broken my hard work and gone back to smoking for anything in the world. I don't drink, but a shot of B&B occasionally is nice.

For recreation, we loved to dance: square dances, round dances, regular ballroom dances. We went weekly all of our adult lives. In the Navy, if you couldn't dance, you had trouble getting dates. We were with an exhibition square dance team in our forties. We liked to travel all over, to Europe and different places. Now we like to read—political histories, cowboy stories, the Middle East. I especially like Leon Uris. I chaired almost all the boards in town and worked in church, and I've also gone to about half of our Navy reunions.

Advice to Younger Generations

I think we have a lot of good kids, and only hear about the problems. I really believe that parental guidance, in most cases, has become a thing of the past. People expect teachers to raise the kids. Both parents too busy working to give kids the care, love, and support they need. A lot of our trouble starts at home. If you're going to have a family, be a parent. If you don't think you can stand up to that, then don't have children. My wife was home when our children went to school and when they returned. They had parental supervision all the time. They grew up to be good people. Parental guidance is the most important thing for the kids. We're a rich nation, accustomed to all the good things. But in order to support all those things, it seems both parents must work. And if they both work, they just cannot give enough time to their kids. Children are far more important than the wealth. If kids haven't built up a good sense of right and wrong at home, there will be trouble.

Choose the career that is right for you. You don't have to go to college just because daddy says so. Some are better suited for technical college. If you make a wrong choice, you can always overcome it. I had to go back to school a number of times. At one point, I took a course in human relations and it was the most wonderful course I ever took. It helped me correct my mistakes. That's where education comes in. Life is a learning experience. Keep your eyes open for life's lessons, whether in school or somewhere else. If you let yourself, you can learn something every day. Some of your best lessons come from people in the lowest rung. Life is hard; it isn't easy for anyone, so keep your eyes open.

If you are a war veteran and you leave the service, don't just jump into a job, but give yourself time to adjust to a new world. You need time to adjust before you return to real life.

Milo and Meg Ballinger

Meg Ballinger

Milo and Meg Ballinger

At home in Pearce Sunsites, AZ

Chapter 33

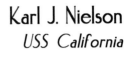

Karl J. Nielson
USS California

Youthful looking and active, Karl Nielson served on the battleship USS California *from age 15 to 18. After being hit and sunk at Pearl Harbor, the* California *saw extensive service in the Pacific Theater of Operations. The battleship played a vital role in the critical Battle of Surigao Strait, history's last fight between opposing battleships. It was struck by a shell from a shore battery, by a kamikaze, and by her own sister ship. After the war, Mr. Nielson played fastpitch softball for 36 years, and was inducted into the International Softball Congress Hall of Fame.*

I was born January 4, 1928, in Mesa, Arizona. Growing up was a super experience. Mesa was a little town where you knew every dog that ran down the street, everybody that lived in the town, who had problems, and who didn't. Nobody had any money, so houses were left open, and you didn't have stealing. When you haven't had anything, you don't miss it.

I am the baby of six children. I have two half-brothers, a half-sister, one full brother, and a full sister. My father's first wife died in the flu epidemic around 1918, and left him with three children. Dad met my mother and raised his three and they had three more children.

My mother graduated from Tempe Normal School (*today, Arizona State University*), a two-year teacher college. She finished college at Berkeley and then taught school in Arizona until she met my father. Her first husband died in the flu epidemic nine months after they married.

I felt you got your inner strength from what you did yourself. My parents were so busy making a living, that it was up to me to do the right thing. Kids basically raised themselves.

There weren't the temptations of today. We had no money to travel or to spend on drugs. Today, if you get picked up for drinking too much, you go to jail. In our little town, if you got out of line, police officers took you home.

My dad had a two-bedroom house. One room was for my parents, the second for my sister, and the boys slept on a screened porch, which was fine as far as we were concerned.

We were a pretty close family. My father had three loves: his family, his religion, and his profession. Our lives were organized. We went to school. Each summer, he went to school in Los Angeles for two weeks, and we went to the beach and had a nice relationship with each other.

If you wanted money, you had to work for it. Dad didn't have money. As a chiropractor in the Depression, he never turned anyone away because they didn't have the money, and was paid a lot of the time with chickens and oranges. He was dedicated. He'd go to people's homes if they were sick. People still remember him to this day. When I was 13, I washed dishes in a hash house. At fourteen, I went to the nearby air field, where they trained British pilots. I worked the line of aircraft from after school until after midnight, cranking them up and cleaning them up. I remember the accents of the British pilots, going through their checklists: "Switch is off, petrol on, throttle closed, crank up and start, ol' boy." The "ol' boy" made me feel good.

When I was a sophomore, I quit high school to join the Navy. My mother signed because I was a bit ornery and wasn't getting good grades. I was on the battleship USS *California*, which was sunk at

Pearl Harbor. It was refurbished at Bremerton, Washington. I caught her in 1943 at Bremerton and stayed on her in the Pacific until 1946.

Service was the best thing that ever happened to me. I kept bugging my mother to join until she relented when my dad was on a trip. In the Navy, I was taken on a grinder, or obstacle course, in the summer time. I was sick and throwing up, lying on my bunk. A boatswain's mate told me to get out of the bunk and eat. I wouldn't, so he ran me through the grinder again. I wrote and asked my mother to let me come home and I'd be a good boy. The Navy was no place for a young boy. There was swearing and smoking and drinking. My wife has this letter to this day. An admiral called me down to his office. He asked me how old I was and why I had joined the Navy. I told him I was 15, and I joined to fight for my country. He asked if I'd written a letter to my mother. And then I got the best lesson of my life. He said, "You volunteered. You quit this, and every time life gets hard, you'll be a quitter." I decided to stay. I began to grow up into a responsible person. Since that time, I've always finished what I started. The Admiral said he'd follow my career. They put me in the gunnery because that's what I was qualified to do.

The *California* was 624 feet long. I was assigned as a shell man to the number one turret, which fired the big 14" shells. We used bombardment and steel penetrating shells. With us were the battleships *Tennessee, Pennsylvania, New Mexico* and *Colorado*. I also worked in supply and ran the ship's store, which sold all of the things you buy in the grocery and department stores.

The first battles were in the Marianas in June and July of 1944 — bombarding Saipan, Guam, and Tinian. At Saipan, we were so close in that enemy shore fire hit us, and killed one or two men and wounded quite a few. The Japanese gun was mounted on a railroad track. It would fire at the ships and then dart back into a cave, so we couldn't hit it.

We were going down to Australia for R&R, zig-zagging to avoid submarines, when we got hit by our sister ship, the *Tennessee*. It took thirty feet of our bow off. We went to New Hebredes for repairs. A floating dry dock pulled us out of the water and made the repairs in two weeks — quite a feat for a ship that was longer than two football fields.

Then we came to Ulithi, in the Marshalls, where hundreds of ships were getting ready to invade the Phillipines. In October and November, we took part in the Leyte Campaign, bombarding for the invasion, and then taking part in the October 25th Battle of Surigao Strait with the Japanese fleet. We destroyed the Japanese fleet, sinking two battleships, a cruiser, and several destroyers. No U.S. ships were hit. That was the greatest sea battle in history. We broke their back. That was the last time the Japanese battled us at sea. The *California* was credited for sinking a battleship. Overall, we'd get credit for downing several other ships, and seven aircraft. My brother's ship, the USS *Haggard*, was with us much of the time, but was not there in the Battle of Leyte. His ship, along with two others, was in a different battle, in which each was hit by kamikazes, and one was sunk.

Then we went to the Lingayan Gulf and the invasion of Luzon in January of 1945. We caught a kamikaze and had nearly 200 casualties, but continued our mission for more than two weeks. You talk about traumatic experiences: One fellow was on a destroyer that was hit by a kamikaze and his ship sunk. He was rescued from the water and put on another ship. He hadn't been on it an hour before it was hit by a kamikaze and sunk. Then he came on the *California* and was so exhausted that he lay down on the floor of the barber shop, not knowing that the barber shop is used as a morgue when there are casualties. So, when we were hit, the bodies were put beside him. He woke up lying there among all these bodies. When he told us this at our reunion, he was still having nightmares about waking up and going through this ordeal.

One of our men left his post to go to the head. While he was gone, the kamikaze hit and killed everyone in sky-aft [*the lookout station*].

In June and July of 1945, after repair in the U.S., we bombed Okinawa. We were back to the Philippines when the atomic bomb was dropped. Everyone loved Truman for saving a multitude of lives. Japan had been told we'd rape and plunder and would fight to the end. From September to October of 1945, we covered the occupation of Japan.

When I came out of the service, I knew how important education was, so, at eighteen, I went back to finish high school and graduated in 1949.

In 1949, at age nineteen, I started an autobody shop business in Phoenix with a lifelong friend. In high school I had worked in a body shop to make spending money. I stayed in that business for 35 years. During that time I also had several other shops—other body shops, frame and motor service, autoglass sales, and auto wrecking yards. I'm still working. I have had seven bar-restaurants in the past, and now am working in two.

I met my wife Georgia playing fast pitch softball. I pitched for 35 years for a car dealer's team. The owner of the dealership asked his daughter and Georgia, her neighbor, if they'd like to come watch his team. I looked over in the stands, saw these two beautiful girls, and went up to meet them. About two days later Georgia called me. She was a senior in high school, and I was 21. After we'd dated awhile, I got cross and went my way. After two weeks, I really missed her and called her and said, "You want to get married, or not?" We drove to the courthouse and got a license. That was in 1949. I had $12 to my name. We had our fist three babies right away in a three-year period. We had to grow up real quick. If I hadn't married a girl with intestinal fortitude, I'd be in sad shape. I say that we had a planned family. The minute she said she was pregnant is when we planned our family. She went to college and graduated, while raising five children. We eventually had seven children, living in the absolute greatest country in the world.

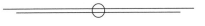

PTSD Symptoms?

I didn't have any of those symptoms, although a lot of people did. I was never wounded on the ship. Some who were didn't want to talk about it.

What Helped You Cope?

We were young. Wars are meant for young people because they don't know about death. After we experienced it, we were completely different persons. Most young people don't appreciate what the veterans did to preserve our democracy.

I was grateful to have been raised in the U.S. So much of the way we were raised rubbed off on us. Children see the examples of their parents, good and bad. I had very fine parents. I can't put a finger on the many ways my parents influenced me. My father campaigned against tobacco in the county. I never heard my mother ever say a bad word about anybody. They were supportive. She cried when she signed my papers and a neighbor had to comfort her, but she knew it was good for me in the long run. Their influences gave me a security and strength. I appreciated being raised in a small town. When you live in a little town, you relate to everyone around you. You knew when the people did things bad and good and could see the consequences.

CALM UNDER PRESSURE

At my battle station as the shell man in the number one turret, I was at the top of the turret and was responsible for the shells being injected into the gun. In a turret, there was a series of things that had to be done. You had to be careful around powder, carefully move the shell to be loaded, shove the projectile in, ram four-hundred pounds of powder in, and so forth. It took eighteen seconds to load the guns and have them ready to fire. You had a job to do, and it was a challenge, but you didn't think about the fears. It was easy to be upset at the enemy for what they did. But, you didn't even think about it. You had a job to do and you did it.

RATIONAL THOUGHT PROCESSES

I never had negative thoughts. Most young people think positively. We never thought we were going to lose or die. We didn't think about adversity or that we could get sunk. We were trained in what to do for crises, but we didn't dwell on negatives.

We all make all kinds of mistakes. I have compassion for people who make mistakes, because I make them. It took me awhile to find what I was good at in the Navy. Everyone has a comfort zone. Sometimes it takes time to find it.

SOCIAL SUPPORT

On ship, you feel a feeling toward your associates, like a town. We got very close with people in our own division, because we ate, slept, and worked together. We went on liberties together. We all became dreamers, sitting in our leisure time making plans. We often talked about what we were going to do after the war. My friends were very important. We were united for a purpose. In October, I'm going to my reunion in Alabama to see old buddies from the ship. Running into old friends is great.

Everybody looked forward to mail day. Family was where it was really all at. You can have a friend one day but never see him again. Family structure is the most important thing. Mail became a very important part of our life because it came usually came from family.

COMFORTABLE WITH EMOTIONS

After sitting with the Admiral, I really felt I'd made the right decision and knew it was important to finish all I started. I was pleased I'd made the decision, and knew I'd finish what I started. Had I gone home, I might never have known if I could do something. I was always positive from that point on. I got acclimated and actually started to enjoy the Navy.

Honestly, I didn't feel afraid. I felt protected and never thought I'd get killed. I only looked at the positive, what I'd do when I got out.

I lost a couple of good friends to kamikazes. I couldn't believe that they were killed. Nothing was sadder than to stand at a service and to see these men draped with a flag, hear "Taps" being played, and see their bodies slide into the ocean. I was just grateful to survive. It reminded me to make sure my life was balanced, because you never know when you'll go. You don't go to bed at night mad. You try to resolve such feelings.

Some of my friends came home, went on a continuous party, and died young, in their 40s. They wasted good lives. So I think that drinking wasn't a good way to cope with problems.

At reunions, people start talking and that's good. In talking they get memories that have been pent up for years off their chest. Sometimes we'll laugh together because some parts were funny. The process is therapeutic.

SELF-ESTEEM

I thought, and still think, that anyone could do what I did to help win the war. A lot of people did a lot of things, and nobody alone is important enough to win a war. It took a combination of great teamwork to get it done. In no way did I ever think I was heroic. I just did the job I was asked to. I always did it. So I felt I was a worthwhile contributor. I tried for excellence. I felt like I did my duty well. That gave me confidence and satisfaction.

When I was a kid, even after I came home, you didn't do drugs because you knew it wasn't good for you. If you think you're worth something, you won't expose yourself to certain things. That's part of being mature.

ACTIVE, CREATIVE COPING

We all felt pressure, but when something needed to be done, you got in and got it finished. Some people don't solve problems and then another comes along. Pretty soon your whole life is a problem. Everyone has stress and problems. You have to get rid of them and go on to the next one. I wouldn't let problems accumulate. I'd go after them.

Sports helped me to learn that you can't control everything. In playing fast pitch softball, I pitched eighty to one hundred games a year. You don't like losing, but you learn to be a gracious loser, as well as a gracious winner. You can't win 'em al. So you accept certain things and go on. I've gone to 18 national tournaments and won in 1979 in Fresno, a culmination of successes. But you realize that you can't be a winner 100% of the time, so you learn to accept failures along with successes. When I came back I played high school football with Wilford "Wizzer" White, one of the finest running backs. His son is the quarterback, Danny White. I made all-state end. The next year, I was to be a running back, but the coaches' association changed the age limit from 19 to 18 and this took me out of football. This was a blow I had to accept. Instead, I went into softball, which is how I met my wife. Sometimes ill winds blow us good fortune.

Yesterday is history; you can't do anything about it. Tomorrow is the future; you don't know what's in store. Today is the present. That's why it's called a gift. So I'm living for the present. I don't look back on things and worry about changing yesterday. The most important time is right now. I can only do something about it now. I make mistakes. There are things I must accept. I'm 74 and can't do what I used to. I used to shoot golf in the low 70s, and pitch softball. You must be gracious and enjoy what you can do, and not lament what you can't do.

SPIRITUAL AND PHILOSOPHICAL STRENGTHS

God

Each ship had a chaplain and services. Ours was a super guy. I went to services and talked to the chaplain when something personal came up.

I certainly believed in God. I went to church regularly growing up, and was taught from the time I was a little boy to believe in God. I prayed that we'd win and be kept safe from harm. I've felt blessed and thankful for being alive and having advantages in life. I have seven children and love every one of them. It bothers me that some children are born deformed or are born to drug addicts. It's upsetting. I've wondered why life isn't fair.

Meaning & Purpose

I wanted to fight for my country and be one of the defenders. My brother and next door neighbor had gone and I didn't want to be left out. We had a purpose to keep the country from being taken over and to preserve our way of life. We'd be in a terrible shape if Hitler had succeeded. There was never a time when we were so unified. Rosie the Riveter came out of the home and went to work. It was a superb era for unification of our people. I think our crime rates went down. We became a whole different people. We have a close kinship with England and Australia, which would have been taken over by Germany and Japan, if not for the Americans.

I had dreams. I wanted to see the U.S., go back to high school, and save my GI bill to go to osteopath school—although later I decided to go into the autobody business.

Morality

On shore leave, I didn't go to jump in bed with women. That didn't happen. Today, it's very important to me to be moral. It's like a bottle of green olives packed tight. Once you get the first one out the rest come easy. So you don't want to take the first immoral step. I've got a very moral wife and she wouldn't put up with me doing anything immoral and I respect that. But if she died tonight, I'd still be moral. Cheating betrays a trust. When we had a baby sitter, I'd never take her home alone, so as to avoid accusations. Each of us has to determine for ourselves what is right and wrong.

Love

I still feel very strong feelings for my buddies. Most are dead now. At our yearly reunion memorial services, we remember that a lot of good people of all faiths died. We that survived were the lucky ones.

Optimism

We never thought of defeat. I had an absolute positive feeling that this thing was going to be over. I've always been an optimist. I always think I'm going to win or come out on top at whatever I do. If you wait for something to happen you're always in a quandary, so it's best to go ahead and get in there and attack your problems.

Humor

We all cut up when we weren't on battle stations. I love jokes. I continually laugh at things that are humorous. I'd kid people about how tough it was in the Navy. Sometimes we had to go two days without butter.

Long View of Suffering

We didn't want a war to come. Certainly I didn't. The greatest thing, though, was when I wrote that letter to my mother and the Admiral told me that if I quit I'd be a quitter all my life. Saying "Yes, I'll stay" was the turning point in my life. I started my own business at age 19. When it was failing, Dad advised me to quit and go back to school. I wouldn't. And here's the lesson from the Admiral: I borrowed some money and told creditors I'd pay every cent back and wouldn't go into bankruptcy. I worked 16 hours a day. I paid everybody back. I got my business going and life went on. You don't start without finishing it. I've learned that the most important person in life is you. You have to have peace about your life—who you are and what you've done—and everything else comes later. You have to think well of yourself or you can't think well of anybody else.

Maintaining Balanced Living

I was always very physically active, although not with a structured exercise program. I played softball three times a week for 35 years. I played golf, hunted a lot, and did a lot of bicycling. I was a commissioner of the International Softball Congress for fifteen years and served as Western vice president for three years and president for three years. While I was president, I got to do color commentary on the public broadcasting network.

I need at least eight hours a day of sleep. I would usually, and still do, sleep from 8:00 or 9:00 p.m. to 4:00 or 5:00 a.m.

I've usually eaten two meals, no breakfast. I don't eat much meat, mostly vegetables and beans. My wife cooks healthy and I basically eat healthy, but I like junk food, too.

As a kid, I didn't smoke or drink. After the war I celebrated a bit, but I haven't smoked or drank since 1950. During the war, samples of cigarettes were given to all the boys on ship. On shore there was always free beer. A lot of bad habits, created during the war, were allowed by the government, so a lot of people took up smoking and it did a lot of harm. When I go back to my reunions, we don't drink.

Now, socializing is with my family. I see most of the children fairly regularly. We go to San Diego in August for ten days to a place on the beach with them and the grandchildren. We also have a place in the mountains and like to ride through the backcountry, looking for animals.

I took flying lessons on the GI bill and flew my own plane for 35 years. I enjoy growing flowers. I also read the paper backwards and forwards before I go to work. I still work, because I don't want to sit in front of the television all day.

Advice to Younger Generations

The most important thing is to set a list of values and plot a course. Life is a set of goals. Set a goal and when you accomplish one, set another. Don't set goals so high that you can't accomplish them. Otherwise you get into a mode of not finishing what you start. Set shorter goals that you can achieve.

Be *content*. If you are content you won't be envious of the fact that other people have more or can do more than you. Accept that life isn't fair—never has been and never will be. There will always be people who have more than you. If you let that frustrate you, you'll be frustrated all your life. People sometimes lament what they can't control. Be content with your own capacities in life and with yourself. Like yourself.

Derive satisfaction and pleasure from what you do, and not from what other people think, because they often forget the good you do.

We all have failures, but we can prevent many failures by thinking about our actions beforehand and committing to finish what we start.

Karl and Georgia Nielson

Karl Neilson, top left.

At home in Mesa, AZ

Chapter 34

Colonel Thomas McCoy Fields
Iwo Jima

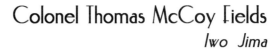

COL Tom Fields lives with his wife Patricia (Patty) in their modern brick "dream home" in College Heights Estates, in Maryland. At 5'9", spry and very friendly in manner, he possesses a certain spunk—a crisp, gutsy grit and determination.

As a college student, Tom was an All-American distance runner, and was named outstanding student-athlete. In WWII, he was in combat on Guadalcanal, Vella Lavella, Bougainville, and Iwo Jima.

Iwo Jima was considered a vital airbase from which B-29 bombers could attack Japan. The largest force of Marines ever to fight under a single command conquered the island after 36 days of grueling combat.

Following a career in the Marines, which included service in the Vietnam and Korean wars, Tom returned to the University of Maryland and for 20 years raised funds for athletic scholarships. He and Patty raised two daughters and two sons.

On May 12, 1918, I was born five miles outside of Carthage, North Carolina, where 300 people lived—it was sheer country. I was the oldest of three boys. In those days in the South, it was pretty poor; we had no electricity. I was six years old before I saw a loaf of store-bought bread. You took your own grain down to the mill and they ground it, and we ate biscuits and corn bread. We lived on a small-time farm, with a cow and a couple of mules. Practically everything we ate, we raised ourselves. I split wood for fuel and cooking, plowed with the mule, and was a water boy. I also gathered sticks of tobacco and hung them to cure. My father owned an old-fashioned sawmill, snaking logs out of the woods with mules.

When I was six, we moved into town, and then to Memphis, Tennessee. Dad had taken a job as a salesman for the Buckeye Traction Ditcher Company, which installed pipelines to pump gas and oil across the country. In 1932, we moved to Maryland where I went to high school and college. But, we still went back to North Carolina to spend the summers working on my grandparents' farm, and kept the connection there.

My parents were very good people. My father was gone much of the week, so I guess my mother gets a lot of the credit for raising us. We were always close. Dad was a six-footer, a good baseball player. He encouraged us to play ball. Everybody liked him. He set a good example for us. I remember once, somebody had been disrespectful to an official. He told us, "Everybody can't be a good athlete, but everyone can be a good sport." I've never forgotten that. My mother was a dear, warm lady who raised us well. In helping with homework, she was a whiz at English. She diagrammed sentences, which made a big impression on us.

Back then, children were to be seen and not heard. You didn't run your mouth at the table. Today my grandchildren come and call all the shots. It's a different world, but as a kid it was, "Yes, ma'am," and you opened doors for ladies. When my parents said do something, we did it. We went to church on Sunday. When I was three or four years old, I ran off to play in the creek when I wasn't supposed to. The creek was full of snakes. An old farmer saw me, puts me on his mule, and brought me home. My mother, you would have thought she was an Olympic high jump champion. She went up in the elm tree and broke off a switch and I got switched. So did my dog, because she thought the dog was smarter than I was, I guess.

In high school, I caddied at the golf course and delivered circulars for the movies. Delivering circulars gained us a free pass to Saturday movies, which cost twenty-five cents. Caddying earned seventy-five cents for 18 holes, plus a twenty-five cents tip, if you did a good job. Ice cream cones were a nickel, so that was a lot of money.

As a runner in high school, I'd beaten just about everyone on the East Coast in the half-mile and mile. On the university track team, we went to the Penn Relays in 1940 unheralded. We came out in the college medley and blew out the competition. We got a beautiful new watch for winning, which was something, because I had never owned a watch. The next day, we won the four-mile relay.

I worked to support myself and hitchhiked to campus. (In fact, I didn't own my first car until after the war—a used Studebaker). It was a busy, busy life, with very little time for a social life. I weighed about 140 pounds then, and had a heartbeat of 45. I enrolled in Army ROTC so that I could enter the war as an officer. After graduating in 1942, I entered the Marine Corps and became a parachutist. I'm told that the University of Maryland provided more Marine Corps officers than any other school. I'd seen them at ball games on campus with beautiful girls and was impressed.

In February of 1945, I began the assault of Iwo Jima as a rifle company commander. Iwo Jima was the bloodiest battle any of us had seen. Many said it was the bloodiest battle in the history of the Marine Corps. My company, Dog Company *[D Company, 2nd Battalion, 26th Marine Regiment]*, landed with 224 troops. Thirty-six days later, only 24 men were left. (That was the official count. I still think only seventeen were left, if you don't count some replacements that got mixed in.) I was one of only two officers left of the 21 in my battalion's three rifle companies who landed on the first day. By the fourth day ashore, the battalion commander and most of his staff had been killed or wounded, and by about that time only two officers were left in my company. By the eighth day, I moved up to replace the battalion executive officer. As highly trained as we were, we took a terrible beating. The island was only 4.5 miles long and 2.5 miles wide at its widest place. There was no place to hide—the volcanic island had been bombed out and there was little vegetation. Every square inch had been zeroed in by the Japanese. They could drop an artillery or mortar round in your pocket. They had 14 miles of tunnels and hundreds of reinforced concrete positions. There were about 21,000 Japanese against 70,000 marines. Perhaps as many as 26,000 Marines were casualties.

On board the ship to come home, I got the survivors of my company together and said, "I'm gonna write a letter to the next of kin of every Marine that was killed in Company D, and I'm going to need your help. I'll help write up citations, but let's sit here and talk." There were so many stories of bravery and individual initiative. They thought they were just doing their job. We did not decorate enough people.

PTSD Symptoms?

I remember the awesome price we paid—those fine young men that I had trained and led, and so many died, but I had none of those symptoms. I didn't know a single one that came home and went bad. Our second platoon corpsman treated 40 guys, killed or wounded. He was in a hole with a man who got shot in the head. The next day, a young Marine, dying from shrapnel, asked him, "Where is God?" He said, "God isn't here." At one point he sat down and cried a little. Then he bounced back and didn't miss a lick of work. He retired as a police captain. Robert H. Davis *[See Chapter 36]* was the tallest Marine in the company. An artillery shell landed right in the hole and blew off his legs. He showed up at a reunion standing tall and erect. I asked him why he didn't bleed to death. He said, "No problem; that shell cauterized my legs." He had a lovely wife and a successful career. No one felt entitled because of what they did in the war.

Colonel Thomas McCoy Fields

What Helped You Cope?

We had hard Marine Corps training that pulled no punches. We knew it was going to be tough. If you're a leader, it's easier because you have to set the example and keep things moving. One Marine told me, "You insisted that we know every weapon in the company, because you had seen many cases where the machine gunner went down and a rifleman had to take over. And you insisted that we be in good physical condition." Well, I had been a coach and I knew how to keep them in condition without overdoing it. But he said, "The best thing you did for us is that you had us psychologically prepared for combat. When the lieutenant went down, the sergeant unhesitatingly jumped forward. When he went down, the corporal. And when he went down, an 18-year-old PFC unhesitatingly moved straight forward and did the job."

My job was to motivate people to fight. Sometimes we had the John Wayne type that just wanted to charge up the hill. I had to get them some realism. I'd say, "Did it ever occur to you that the Japs want to kill you? Did you ever think of that? You have to shoot better, creep and crawl better, be smarter, play the game cagey." I tried to teach realism. If the first day, your best buddy loses his intestines, be ready for very tough stuff. Expect that. How many 18-year-olds have seen a dead person, even in a casket? Some are going to get hurt. You always think it's not going to be you, but you have to be prepared to see your buddy get it. If you go in there thinking you are going to get it, you won't be very effective.

Athletics helped me a lot, very strenuous stuff. Distance running teaches you to put forth the absolute maximum effort. I could outrun anyone in the Marine Corps, the record shows, from a half mile up to five miles. My conditioning was a big help. I didn't tire out as quickly.

When you volunteer for the Marines or Rangers, you start with the advantage of being motivated, knowing you'll have hard work. Then hard training builds up confidence. And like I say, don't tell your people that they're dumb. It undermines confidence under pressure. Build their confidence, don't tear it down. Get them mentally prepared. Exude confidence. My job as a leader was not to be tough on the troops, but to get the troops prepared to be tough on the enemy.

CALM UNDER PRESSURE

I had so much to do that I didn't have time to think how bad things were. I don't remember experiencing the fear at all. Twice in a two-day period, I almost had my head taken off by anti-tank shells that whizzed by me, but you can't fret about being hurt. You do your job. When you started forward, you never knew what would happen. Your training was behind you. You knew what you had to do. Worrying doesn't help things a bit.

I don't remember the hate stuff. But it was our job to win the war. They started the war and were inhumane, like on Guadalcanal, where they did horrible things. We tried to take prisoners. We told the enemy that we were all honorable warriors. Surrender and you'll be treated nicely.

RATIONAL THOUGHT PROCESSES

Seeing the big picture helped us through mistakes. Ira Hayes was the American Indian who helped put the flag up on Iwo Jima. He was a good Marine. When training in the States, he went to town in San Diego to drink beer and got apprehended by the shore patrol. I called the whole platoon in and said, "Is this the way you're gonna fight? You let the shore patrol get the Chief. In combat, you have to look out for each other. I restricted them for a week and made a big deal of taking care of each other." Later Ira Hayes said, "They don't make lieutenants like you anymore." I said, "Chief, they don't make PFCs like you anymore, either."

SOCIAL SUPPORT

I was single at the time, which is not a bad way to be if you're fighting a war. I wrote my mother once a week, and she wrote often to keep me posted on the home front. My younger brothers were in Europe at the Bulge, and we'd write each other.

Mutual respect was a big thing. We had great pride in our company. If we were playing softball against another company, you'd have thought it was WWIII. I felt close to my men. I was kind of their father figure. I'd been a head coach of cross country and an assistant track coach at the university. Having been a competitive athlete gave me an advantage in dealing with young people. After boot camp, it was more of a family feeling. I had a lot of respect for those guys. We still see each other at reunions. All the guys were 18, yet today we're great friends. It surprised me to hear them say I was a great role model. That got to me a little bit. One man in the company, whose brother had been killed carrying out orders, gave me a big bear hug and said it was an honor being in my company *[See Luther Crabtree, Chapter 35]*.

I married Patty in 1951. I was 34. I love my wife very much. She has been a great service wife. It probably helped that her father had been in the Navy. She helped me in every way, all through my career.

COMFORTABLE WITH EMOTIONS

I never had any trouble with my emotions. I had the ability to say, when shells were coming in, "Well, getting excited and jumping around just makes things worse." I really didn't feel the fear, I can say that in all honesty. Maybe I wasn't smart enough to fully understand the situation. If there are things over which you have absolutely no control, it does no good to get emotional. If there's something you can change, you do it. But if you're in a hole with artillery coming in, there's not a thing you can do to influence that.

SELF-ESTEEM

I was confident, heck, yes. We were well trained, well led, enthusiastic, and eager to go. I figured I was the leader of 243 Marines. There was no way they'd see me carrying on in a bad manner. I wanted to do as well as I could and set a good example for them, and that would reflect nicely down the line. I thought that I had value and so did they.

ACTIVE, ADAPTIVE COPING

The old rifle company spirit convinced us that we could kick ass and do whatever we needed to. As a commander, I was always aware that I had responsibility in life and death situations. I just tried to do my best. People are always watching you, and you're setting the example. It never occurred to us that we'd lose. You know you're going to win, even though there's a great cost. We never thought we weren't going to take the island. Never thought about pulling off the island.

SPIRITUAL AND PHILOSOPHICAL STRENGTHS

God

I was a believer. I always tried to support the chaplain and encouraged the guys to go to services. I do think more guys are believers when the bullets are flying. I'd say my prayers and pray for the outfit.

Meaning & Purpose

I believed in our cause. Japan started the war and we had to finish it. Every night I thought of what would happen if the Japanese won the war. No doubt a lot of heads would roll. They had to be beaten. We knew of the torture at Guadalcanal, for example. People in this country should not forget. Forty percent of the prisoners died.

It's important to me to inspire people. You have to build their confidence. Set a good example, and don't demean, but make them aware of reality.

Morality

I think you ought to abide by your commitments. If you're a married man, that's it. Live by the Ten Commandments. Don't lie or deceive. As a Marine officer and leader I had to set that example. As the leader, I would never put myself in the position of whoring or getting drunk. If you set the example, 50 to 75 years later, friends still look up to you. It means a lot when they remember me saying, "Make something of yourself."

Love

I felt very close to my men and very responsible for them. It is almost like family. We're still in contact. On my birthday a few days ago, several called to wish me a happy birthday. Every year wives send me letters informing me of someone's passing. I go to funerals.

A bunch of us get together once a year. No one uses bad language or gets drunk. We just sit there and talk about our buddies. There is a great bond between warriors. Many returned and married their high school sweethearts. They're all a part of it now. It makes you feel good to get letters saying, "We love you very much."

At 26 years old, I was like a father figure to them. One of my men came home—he had been our flame thrower—and became a college president. He said, "You always told us, 'When the war is over, go home and make something of yourself.'"

Optimism

It never entered our heads that we wouldn't win. We prepared ourselves to win, and we fought to win.

Humor

I always liked humor. You gotta stay a little loose. If something funny comes along, that's good. You have to know what's important and what isn't. Some people get upset over things that aren't important. It was always something with those guys. As I mentioned, when Bob Davis lost both his legs from an artillery round, he said, "No problem. I lost hardly no blood at all. The heat cauterized them."

Our company clerk made Radar Riley look like a small timer, and he was funny as heck. He'd brag to everybody, because he fired expert with the rifle at boot camp. When he had to move up to the line, seven or eight Japanese were flushed out and ran in front of him. He missed them all. To this day, we're on his case for that.

Long View of Suffering

Every time you go through an operation you learn something. I learned about leadership and I learned an appreciation of life. You remember so many guys who did such great, heroic things.

Maintaining Balanced Living

I've stayed very active. I just passed my ECG with flying colors. I have a treadmill in the basement and generally use it regularly. As a child, if I went to the store, I ran. I think that helped me to lead a long life. My wife is a gourmet cook. She loves to cook every night. She makes a lot of salads. We eat well and smart. I've usually been in bed by 10:00 p.m. and up at 6:00 a.m. In my career, I found that life was easier when you got to the office early.

I never got too much into alcohol. I've tried to lead a good, decent life. I never smoked. I drank in moderation—socially once in awhile. I never saw a bottle of whisky in my house growing up.

For recreation, we try to get the family together frequently. We have seven grandchildren who are all in the area. I go to all of the University of Maryland football and basketball games. I have a lot of friends, old fraternity brothers; we've stuck together. And I spend a lot of time sorting and clipping memorabilia.

Advice to Younger Generations

I don't like being thought of as a hero. To me the real heroes were the young eighteen-year-olds who got out of the foxholes and went forward every day. As I've told our splendid young troops on several occasions, "If you are ever faced with the tough assignments that many of us faced, you will do *as well or better* than we did." The military today is the best it's ever been. The young Marines are sharp, intelligent, dedicated. They are all volunteers, extremely well trained. I tell them to think, "If those old guys did it, so can we." That's building their confidence, and they won't crack up. I never fail to pass that message on. I really believe that.

Whatever your job is, look at it as the most important job in your service. General Patton told this to his army before Africa. He told the truck drivers, "If you don't get the trucks up there, we're going to lose the war." That is a message for every troop.

Do your best. I was never an all "A" student, but I worked at it, and had a good life *because* I worked at it. It's not always the smartest guy that gets to be President of GM, but the one who works the hardest and gets the job done.

Probably the overall word for everything is leadership. Whatever action you're taking, if it has a positive effect on people, then it's good. Be fair and good about things. Do your best. Look out for the troops at whatever level. See that they get what they have coming. I took care of my troops, but I didn't coddle them.

Christmas, 1943, Bougainville. Tom is kneeling, second from the left.

After the war, Tom, right, receives the Bronze Star from Regimental Commander Colonel Graham.

Distance runner for the University of Maryland.

Tom and Patty marry, 1952.

Tom and Patty Fields of Hyattesville, MD.

Chapter 35

Luther Carl "Juke" Crabtree
Iwo Jima

Luther "Juke" Crabtree has a joyful expression and a twinkle in his eye, as he speaks from the heart. He and his wife Wilma ("Willie") live in a well-organized and cheery home in Columbus, Ohio. Four of the Crabtree brothers served in the military during the war—two in the Marines and two in the Navy. "Juke" served in Tom Field's Marine company on Iwo Jima. He was awarded the Silver Star for gallantry there.

I was born April 29, 1924, in the south end of Columbus, Ohio. I come from a family of ten kids. I was the third of six boys. Then the four girls were born, as things were starting to get a little bit better. We were very poor. The older boys worked during the Depression.

Dad did PWA work. Hundreds of men near home were cleaning drains and ditches with picks and shovels, working for practically nothing. Dad got $15 a week. When the Depression broke, in the late thirties, he worked for a concrete company, and was a supervisor when he retired. We had 40 acres of corn, fruit trees, a grape arbor, hogs, cows, and chickens to survive.

We were a very close-knit family. We fought among ourselves, but if anyone interfered with one or the other, they had the entire family to contend with. Dad kept us under control. Anytime we got into a squabble, he put us out in the grape arbor with boxing gloves. The one standing at the end was the winner. He also gave us chores. I intensely disliked taking Bossy, the old cow, to stake her in the southern part of the county every morning. I walked her about a mile to find good pasture. Then I'd carry water to her, then milk her in the evening. We had to sucker (pull off the small shoots at the bottom of the stalk) and weed the corn every day. Dad would take me and my buddies to do this during the day while he worked. We'd get five to seven of my buddies. We'd all weed until noon and then go swimming in the reservoir all afternoon. Sometimes we'd confiscate a watermelon for a picnic. My buddies came from what we called the Old Oklahoma edition—a very poor development of people, most of whom had migrated from West Virginia and Kentucky.

Dad was a great guy, an all-around good husband and father, a great provider. Ours was a very disciplined family, including the girls. He said something only one time, and expected it to be carried out. If Mom enlightened him about our behavior, he had a pocket knife and went to the fruit trees for a switch. He'd say, "Now, son, you're going to have to pay the consequences." When he was finished, we all knew who was boss. He was interested in all of the kids. He was a very hard worker. We learned that you didn't get something for nothing. You had to work for what you got. He was devoted to Mom and the entire family. He also kept close contact with his brothers and sisters, who all migrated to the same general area from Kentucky in the 1920s. We still have the old farm there. Every year I go there to take care of it with the grandkids, or go camping and hunting there with my son.

Mother was 100% homemaker. She was a fabulous cook. During the Depression, you had to make a little go a long way. I can see her now, with her little chunky hands, making pan after pan of the best biscuits you ever tasted. Potatoes and meat and gravy stuck to your ribs. She kept everybody under control. She was a great lady, highly religious. She was always smiling. I'll never know how, given all her trials and tribulations during the Depression.

We had no indoor plumbing. You used the privy in zero degree weather, which made you appreciate modern living. I've wondered if people today could survive those kinds of conditions.

We were all very interested in all kinds of sports when we weren't working. We attended the old Marion Township schools, south of Columbus. We were all in the same boat. We didn't know we were poor. All the guys met at the schoolyard and played football, basketball, softball, and baseball. Everyone was a good athlete. I was bused to Columbus South High School from 1938 until 1942, when I graduated. I told the principal that I needed to complete all academics by noon, so that I could go home and change my one good shirt and pair of trousers and hitch to work by 2:00 p.m. I worked 70 hours per week at the produce gardens and markets in south Columbus. I started at five cents an hour and got up to ten cents an hour. At the same time, I had a paper route. I delivered more than 100 papers over five miles on an old red wagon. Anyone who couldn't pay me with money I bartered for government commodities—butter, meat, potatoes, flour, lard. That was one way I helped the family. I also found golf balls at a little nine-hole golf course and sold them back to people with money.

On Sundays, when we weren't playing ball, we'd go to the movies. We'd see three cowboy movies and buy a candy bar, all for a dime. Sometimes there was a stage show with traveling stars, like Buck Jones.

There were two bedrooms for all ten kids. Dad built shelves in the earthen basement, and Mom canned 400 to 500 quarts of fruit that we'd picked—blackberries, cherries, apples, peaches. A pot bellied stove in the middle room provided the only heat. It would get red hot. You kept moving your body around it, like a rotisserie. It seemed to be colder back then. We hurried to get into bed. There were always at least three kids in each bed. If you got in the middle, you got your brothers' body heat. There was absolutely no insulation. Many times I remember a half inch to an inch of frost on the inside of the walls. That's one of the reasons we became survivors. The Marines wasn't that tough by comparison. There was a mighty big table in the kitchen, which was the largest room in the house. We all could smell the food. We knew we'd better be there for supper or we wouldn't get to eat. For breakfast, Mother made pans of biscuits, gravy, eggs, and bacon or sausage, which we made from our hogs. We all ate together. Mom and Dad went to church regularly. I went to church and sat in the back a lot of the time.

We never knew vacations and were never away from home until I reported for the Marines with my older brother Harold ("Tiny") and our buddies. Four of us went to the old post office to enlist in December of 1942. My buddies flunked the test, and we met new buddies. We all went through boot camp in San Diego in the same platoon and all of us decided to be Marine paratroopers. We jumped in the same plane. Early in 1944, we all went into the 5th Division, then we went overseas together, and hit Iwo together—nine of us from Ohio. My brother and three of my buddies were killed there. Others were injured, but survived.

Everything was fascinating on the train to San Diego for boot camp, which lasted January and February 1943. Marine Corps training was extremely easy because we had been through so much worse in everyday life. After boot camp, we completed paratroop training in March 1943, and got additional training at Camp Elliott, near San Diego.

In January of 1944, we were training at Camp Pendleton. In March of 1944, we went from the paratroop tent camp to the main camp with the 5th Division. There had been four parachute battalions in our regiment. The Commandant broke up these four paratroop battalions and three or four raider battalions thinking that all Marines are equally qualified. All of these were absorbed into the new 5th Division, which was needed for what lay ahead. Absorbing these units also spread out the experience. Captain Tom Fields became our D Company commander in March of 1944. He'd already been overseas with a Marine paratrooper battalion on several islands in the South Pacific.

In June or July we went to the big island of Hawaii to train. Captain Fields had us run twenty miles a day. The next February we hit Iwo.

I first saw the island about four or five a.m. on February 19, 1945. I was mesmerized, as I watched the bombardment of the island from the deck. I couldn't believe what I saw—thousands of ships in every direction. About 6:00 a.m., we had steak and eggs for our going away breakfast. At about 9:00 a.m., we got notice to go over the side into the landing crafts. We were in the water for three or four hours. I was too anxious to get sea sick. I was in the landing craft with my assault squad. We had a bazooka team and a flame thrower. I was the demolition man.

In the early afternoon, we went into the beach. The hardest thing was to get on the beach. The guy piloting the LCVP (landing craft, vehicle and personnel, called a Higgins boat) dropped us 10-20 yards from the beach. With my heavy explosives, fortunately the water wasn't over our heads. We waded the rest of the way in. You can't describe the beach. It was a mess. Bodies were everywhere—floating, on the beach, on the terrace up the beach. There were abandoned landing crafts. It was absolute chaos from one end of the beach to the other. As long as I live, I'll remember the chaos. Everybody screaming and yelling, and nobody knowing what to do. We landed on Red Beach 2, near the base of Mt. Suribachi. We had to get up terraces 10 to 15 yards high. You'd crawl three feet and go back two.

Late in the afternoon, our assignment was to cross the neck of the island. The 28th Regiment had hit earlier, to cut across the neck and turn left and take Suribachi. My battalion was to cross the island and set up on the west coast. There was no such thing as the front lines. You were getting shot at from all directions. We got across at about 5:00 p.m. and were ordered to dig in. It was loose black sand, nothing but volcanic ash, but with guys getting shot all around, you could accomplish anything. We had two-man foxholes by nightfall. Flares were shot to illuminate Japanese, who were trying to infiltrate. We were taking a lot of fire from Suribachi primarily. General Kuribayashi allowed us to get on the island, although every inch of the island was zeroed in and well fortified. Then he opened up. All night long and all the next day, we were in the same position. We didn't move until the 21st. We started up the west coast of the island, in the thick of things pretty much every day. With every movement, we were taking a great deal of fire from various parts of the island. They were looking down our throats. Even if you took one pillbox, there were five others in the vicinity. In my assault squad of 15, we lost every man except me and one buddy from Maine.

The remaining days, all you kept in mind was: Try not to overexpose yourself; don't take any risks—which was impossible. Try to keep a canteen of water. Make sure you have faith and trust in the person in your foxhole. There was little or no sleep because of the infiltration. You were always exposed every minute. You never ran in straight lines. You hit the deck three or four times in order to move ten yards.

At night, you'd try to get K or C rations, if possible. I'd dig a little hole in my foxhole and try to heat up C-rations. You tried to find time to eat. You never had water to shave. You were always wondering who was hit, how many guys were still in the outfit, if you'd be assaulting for the next attack.

My brother Tiny (Harold) was killed on February 26th by machine gun fire. I had to walk past him to complete my mission. Later, I returned and, with a friend and two other volunteers, crawled to him to recover his body. The company commander laid down a smoke screen because the Japanese machine guns still had the area covered. That night I slept beside his body and talked to him.

When we got to the Northern half of the island the terrain was much more difficult. It was one ridge after another; one gully after another in between the ridges. There were hundreds and hundreds of pillboxes and caves at the base or dug into the ridges. Every day I was called up to eliminate pillboxes or caves, and to call up flame-thrower tanks to eliminate whatever was holding up the advance. I often wondered why I didn't see more dead Japanese. One day, working around a cliff, it felt spongy from the blood from the dead who had been buried during the night. Others were taken into the tunnels and caves that networked through the entire island. I wouldn't go into caves out of curiosity. Many who did were killed by booby traps or by Japanese soldiers waiting to shoot. The only exception was General Kuribayashi's command headquarters and hospital cave, which had little rooms off the main tunnel, each with two or three beds in the wall.

The pillboxes had dead spaces. Through training you knew where they were. So we could work up to them with satchel charges and our flame-thrower. I was available every day. Conservatively, I probably blew up over 200 installations—pillboxes, caves, tunnels, concrete foxholes. On a cliff, there might be 10 or 15 caves built in. They'd throw grenades as we worked our way up to the caves.

As you advanced, the Japanese would pop out behind you, because of the underground tunnels. Even as we left the island on March 26th, there was a banzai charge by several hundred and a great number of the Air Force pilots were killed. We didn't even know there were that many Japanese still alive.

We had the highest respect for the Navajo Code Talkers. They performed exceptionally well at our company. *[See Chapter 37]*

A few days before we left, we dedicated the 5th Division cemetery. We had over 200 guys in D Company initially. By March 26th only about 16 guys remained.

After one month, we came back to the same damned *(he said, "excuse me" with a laugh)* tent and the same tent camp in Hawaii, to await replacements. As we pulled into Pearl Harbor in April, the flags were at half mast, for FDR had died. We had seven days of R&R in Honolulu. There was only one high rise at the time. Families took us in and fed us.

We were informed that we'd be the assault division for the invasion of the main islands of Japan. Truckload after truckload of replacements came in. They were green—too young or too old. After a few days at Iwo, I'd become the squad leader. I decided to be more selective in who joined the assault squad. I wanted to know where the person was from, if he'd been athletic, if I felt he'd be able to take the stress and demands of the assault squad, if he'd look you in the eye. One of the questions I asked each guy, almost humorously, as he got off the truck was if he drank beer. If he said no, I'd confiscate his allotment and barter for things we needed. Then we went into training.

We had daily training in the boondocks with the new guys. The more we trained, the more skeptical I became of what we had to look forward to, hitting Japan with ill-trained, inexperienced young men in their late teens or 35- to 40-year-olds. This worried me. In combat, you must react; you can't over-think or ask questions. But these older fellows had families, and the young kids didn't know what they were getting into. Nevertheless, we continued training until the dropping of the atomic bombs. Then we were sent to Japan to the southernmost island for occupation. I stayed there until the last week of December, blowing up installations all up and down the coast up to Nagasaki. I became even more concerned, when I saw that the Japanese had every type of weapon and armament you could imagine in those caves. They were ready for the invasion, even in the small fishing villages that I visited and checked out. If we'd gone in there, it would have been a slaughter on both sides. Even the civilians had been indoctrinated to kill. Thank God for the bombs.

I met my wife in the summer of 1942. In the area I grew up in, there was a large athletic field. Every Sunday in the fall our amateur, semi-pro football team, one of the best in central Ohio, met all comers. These were tough kids. One Sunday, our center's girlfriend brought my future wife to our game. We met. She and the center's girlfriend had a farewell party for us. We corresponded until my first liberty, when we enjoyed a week or so of movies and big bands in Columbus. We continued to correspond. When I came back, we were even closer, together on a daily basis.

I'd made up my mind in the Marines that one of my goals was to be a teacher and coach. When I got back, one of the first calls I received was from the state auditor of Ohio. He sponsored a National Fast Pitch Professional Softball team. I was a first baseman. We traveled all over the Midwest from the end of January 1946 until August of 1946.

I told him I had decided to go to Ohio State University to get into the education field. I went year-round, and graduated after three years in 1949. I then taught and coached for four years. I was head baseball and basketball coach. After our kids came along, I got out of teaching for fifteen years and worked for one of the largest retail food chains in the country, working in merchandising management. Then I went back to teaching. I retired in 1986.

We married in August of 1946. We've been together 55 years, almost 56. We have two children—daughter Jacque and son Ted, who is a teacher and coach. Both live in Columbus. We have three surviving grandchildren.

PTSD Symptoms?

I had no symptoms at all. In my personal opinion, those are the guys I wouldn't want to be in the foxhole with. I never had any problems whatsoever. When I got back, I didn't go around bragging about my exploits. I didn't discuss it with people for 50 years. I didn't feel a need to bring it up or talk or even think about it, until 1995, when the phone began to ring on a constant basis for the 50th anniversary of Iwo. The Defense Department wanted to make a big deal of it. Newspapers and television and radio stations called me for interviews. I was inducted into the Ohio Military Hall of Fame. I concluded that maybe I was wrong to turn down interviews. The younger generations need to know what happened and why they enjoy what they enjoy today. So I began talking to high school groups and joined the American Legion and VFW. I came out of my shell and became more vocal.

What Helped You Cope?

I think I'm a strong person. Being in the Marine Corps, I was able to learn a lot of things as far as dedication, right from wrong, and getting the job done. There's a great deal that you will learn in the Marines that can become a part of everyday life. There are strong individuals who can overcome a lot of things they have to face in life.

By the time I went into the Marine Corps, I was already a survivor. From my earliest childhood, I was strengthened by not having a silver spoon in my mouth, by having to grub for everything I got—nothing was given to us. Being with a strong family, knowing I had to take care of myself in every shape and form on a daily basis, helped me.

On liberty, you could tell the men who'd had a relatively easy life and those who had had a difficult one. The ones who had had a difficult life and had to work for everything they got tended to gravitate toward each other and stay with each other. The ones who had the most difficult time in the Marine Corps did not know how to fend for themselves. For example, one buddy was the meanest character in the group, continually getting in fights and trouble on liberty, a real pain to be with. Everyone thought he'd be great to be with in combat. In combat, he was useless, the biggest wimp in the group. He wouldn't leave the foxhole. He was somewhere else when you needed help. He was tough when there wasn't a reason to be tough, but hiding when you had to rely on him. People who'd survived tough times carried themselves better, were true Marines, gentlemanly. They didn't have to go around making an ass of themselves when on liberty. I had a tendency to hang out with the ones that presented and conducted themselves well. I never felt you had to show how tough you were. The Depression helped you to be tough *inside*. You could still be a gentleman on the outside.

CALM UNDER PRESSURE

I knew there were people counting on me to do my job. If you are well trained to perform a certain way, you will perform that way under stress or demand. When I looked around me on Iwo, and knew people were counting on me and if I didn't perform there would be many who'd suffer or lose their lives, I almost felt that I had to do my job. I didn't want to let my buddies down. In my situation, the whole company would be held up in their advance if I didn't perform. Even in civilian life that applies. If you have a family, you know they're counting on you. I always felt that if you have a job to do, you do it. When you are with guys on a daily basis for years, you know pretty much who'll perform and who wont.

I didn't want to get killed. I knew that, if I wasn't focused 100%, I could be injured or killed. Some of the guys I was with wrote books about technical details of the battle, but I couldn't have done that because I had tunnel vision. I didn't know or care what was going on to my left or right. All I knew was straight ahead. I just thought about doing my job. I told my foxhole mates to simply focus on our field of fire. Period. When you become a little scatterbrained is when you make a mistake. In combat, you can't make that mistake. Everyone—even in teaching—has to keep 100% focused on their part of the job.

Until I got into combat, I had light regard for the enemy, because I didn't know any better. But from what I determined at Iwo, they were excellent fighters, well trained, well led. I had the greatest respect for the Japanese that I fought and for those I saw on the home islands. They were very dedicated, hard-working people. It was quite evident to me that we had defeated a very formidable foe. They were highly disciplined. It was only the lack of some things that caused their downfall: lack of water, ammunition, and food. We had the means to overcome them. They merely ran out of food, water, and armament. They were as good at fighting as the Marines that fought them.

On August 22, 1945, going into Japan, I had some concern and anger in my soul, and periodically do even now, for losing my brother. But generally speaking, they are just another group of people trying to survive.

RATIONAL THOUGHT PROCESSES

During the chaos, I just thought to dig a little deeper. I was concerned, trying to survive. I knew the Japanese were trying to prevent our advance. They had a job to do, as we did, like a football game. It was just a matter of which person had the greatest desire to come out the victor. I looked at it with an everyday viewpoint, without any negativity. I never thought of the war as something that I couldn't stand. Again, because from the very first day I arrived at San Diego in December, 1942, and stepped off the troop train and the sergeant started yelling and screaming at me to run and line up, the Marines ingrained, psychologically speaking, into you that you were a Marine. Marines were different. We'd react. We didn't think. We were better trained and could do it better than anyone. We knew we could do our job. On liberty, people looked at us in a different way.

I made a lot of mistakes. I don't know anybody who doesn't. I've always been taught that you learn from mistakes. If I make one, I first determine why, and second what I can do to eliminate mistakes and improve myself. So you use mistakes to become better. In the Marines, if I did something that wasn't quite right, and I knew it, I did everything I possibly could to make sure I didn't repeat it. Otherwise you stagnate.

When others messed up, I treated it the same way. I think, "Don't worry about it. I won't rant and rave. You made a mistake. Now, you're going to improve by knowing the mistake and not making it again." I tried to be calm and kind. I didn't think anyone learned by ranting and raving. By the same token, you make sure that the individual knows he made a mistake and expands his abilities through the mistake. If you ignore mistakes, you're compounding the problem. Woody Hayes [*the legendary Ohio State football coach*] was demanding, loud, rambunctious. Jim Tressel is also demanding in a different way—quiet and calm. I, personally, would rather play for the latter.

SOCIAL SUPPORT

Social support—family and friends—was the prime, main ingredient. You see movies of mail call. You would not believe how much receiving mail meant to every guy in the outfit. We had a tendency to share our thoughts and good news from home. Everyone was close-knit. We were able to talk about girlfriends or what was transpiring back home. That was one of the things that brought us closer together.

My girlfriend wrote about every day. My father wrote Tiny one day and me the next and we shared. It increased our spirits. You had to have that kind of bond. You knew you'd be returning to civilian life and wanted to maintain that contact. You couldn't be 100% Marine or 100% civilian. You had to keep contact with both. On a seven-day leave in 1943, we came home to Columbus and got together with military buddies and girlfriends. That did so much for us.

A week after I got out of the service, the phone rang. I was invited to the home of my flame-thrower buddy who had died at Iwo. Bill had been their only child. The parents cried. It was difficult. I stayed as long as I could, about a week. About two weeks later, the parents called again. They said they wanted me to have my buddy's new Plymouth convertible. They had given him the car for his graduation present, just before he left for the service. They wanted me to have it because we had been close friends. I had it for a lot of years. What I'm saying is that you have to stay close and keep in mind the civilian aspects of your life, even when you're in the service.

One thing I learned from Iwo was not to get too close to anybody, so close that you can't forget it when you see them mangled or in agony. I know that sounds hard and cruel. On the 26th of February, as I was working my way up to eliminate a pillbox that was holding up my brother's squad, I saw my brother lying in a pool of blood. It has a dire effect on you to see that happen to people you were so close to. I concluded that I would not let that happen again with anybody that was joining the outfit for the assault on Japan. You see how abruptly friendships are gone, so you can't expect friendships to last permanently. Those who came home, we have a permanent close bond. And we'd do anything, anything, for each other. We talk about that at our reunions. You're glad for your close friends, but you have to be able to give them up.

COMFORTABLE WITH EMOTIONS

I try to keep myself on an even keel. I don't get too high. I learned that you don't really gain anything from being too high or too low. If you get too high you fall, and of course people who get too low get depressed. When I went to my family doctor and found my PSA had jumped dramatically because of prostate cancer I didn't get down. I said, "OK, fine, now what do we do to whip it? Now let's develop a plan." And we did. For the last couple of years it's been practically non-existent. When I go to a funeral, I don't shed tears. I guess the only time I get a little excited is when Ohio State plays and wins (laughing).

In combat, I knew I was facing severe hazards, but I don't think I had any great fear. I knew I could be injured, but I didn't dwell on it. My greatest fear was the effect that my brother's death would have on my parents. That's why I wrote them a letter from Iwo that they would hear traumatic news, but to be brave, and face it, and not worry over me. I'd be fine. I've always felt that if you compound your problems and allow fears to enter, it effects your performance. So I tried to keep emotions out of my performance.

The only time the violence of Iwo really hit me was when I was NCO, in charge of the 26th Marines, 5th Division grave dedication. Each regiment had a group representing them. I looked down at the cemetery, and for the couple of hours before we left the island, we went among the rows of crosses and saw the namees of all my buddies that we were leaving behind. I sure shed a tear. I prayed at my brother's cross and those of all my buddies in Dog Company. And there were a lot of them. That was a lasting impression that will always stay with me as long as I live. It is hard to explain what you had to endure, when you were kneeling and praying and shedding tears and saying goodbye. Even now, when I think about it, I become emotional, because we left a lot of guys there.

SELF-ESTEEM

I went into the Marine Corps because I thought it was the #1 organization in the U.S. services. I felt it was the best in every respect. I liked the uniform, the training, the respect we got. I thought this was great. In any aspect of life you want to be with and perform with the best. The Marines is tops in every way. That's why I went into the Marines. I'm still a Marine. I was more than confident from my training and early life.

One of the prime factors for my going into the Marines was that I felt I could contribute; I went into education and coaching because I felt I could contribute to young people. I think self-esteem plays highly in the picture. Without it, you won't do the job. I think I had confidence to do well, but I also tried to work throughout my life to have self-esteem. Self-esteem, without trying to do well, doesn't mean anything. I felt I was a highly capable coach. I've been invited back to various school reunions. When I came back to education and took a real good look at it, I concluded that I didn't want to coach anymore, even though I was a good coach. I wanted to contribute more to education and society. I came to the conclusion that my calling was in special education working with special kids. I became certified. For over 15 years I had one of the top special education classes in the Columbus school system, and, almost on a weekly basis, I get phone calls from my kids. I was happy with what I was doing, knowing I was contributing to the welfare of those people, that I helped the greater proportion become better people, better able to face life. You have to be a special person to work with a child with special needs. You must get to their inner feelings and thinking. You have to make them realize they're not different, and are capable of doing anything at their level. I wouldn't have been as content as I was in the last years of my teaching if I hadn't worked with them.

ACTIVE, ADAPTIVE COPING

I never had a great deal of respect for someone who is passive. You can't rely on such people. I've said often, "Believe me, I am not the hero in the family. The hero was my brother, who didn't come back—the ones who paid the ultimate sacrifice, because they were doing their job. They were not in the foxhole hiding, or forty miles back, but right up there on the front lines, giving us the opportunity to advance and eliminating the problem." I just kept doing my job to the best of my ability. I didn't fall back. When you think about it, it was just plain luck that I survived.

As I mentioned before, I've always felt and attempted to keep an even keel. My experiences have taught me that this is not only the best way, but about the only way. If you get too high you can come down pretty hard. Too low and you get depressed. When I go to any kind of event as a spectator, I'm always interested to see someone sitting there as if they'd rather be elsewhere. I wonder why they came. On the other hand, if I see someone making an exhibition of himself, I wonder about him. I think it's better to try to maintain the even keel. But you have to actively cultivate this and persevere. It doesn't just happen.

In special needs, to be a good instructor you have to work on an individual basis, accept people's limits, and be flexible. You have to get the entire family involved. You determine the youngster's maximum capability at their level of achievement. You make and implement an individual plan for each student. All youngsters are educable to their level of achievement. You won't get a rocket scientist from a developmentally disadvantaged kid, but that doesn't mean that they can't perform and contribute to society, develop self-esteem, and feel that they're capable.

SPIRITUAL AND PHILOSOPHICAL STRENGTHS

God

I prayed a lot in the foxhole. Believe me, when I approached pillboxes and caves and directed the fire of flame-thrower tanks, I did an awful lot of praying. I think it carried me through. But I don't believe you have to be fanatical, or a weekly churchgoer, to be religious. I believe in God and think you need to get close to God to resolve a lot of your problems. I think He can help you. But you have to help yourself. There's a lot of truth to "God helps those who help themselves." He carried me through on Iwo. There wasn't an hour or a day that went by that I didn't ask him for guidance. When you approach a pillbox or cave and you can almost feel the shrapnel and bullets whizzing by, you have to know deep down in your heart that you have some guidance. I think of God as being a part of my life; that unknown ingredient you have to believe in. Eventually, everyone will ask guidance from God and begin to turn in that direction. I still pray and try to live a good life. I think there's a hereafter and eventually I'll see the guys and my family.

Meaning & Purpose

The main goal was to do my job, continue to survive, get off the island, and get back to my family. Even then, I knew what direction I wanted to go. I wanted to marry my girlfriend and be in coaching and education and could only do that if I survived. We wanted a daughter and son and that's what we had. I still want to survive.

I had a happy life prior to the war, but it was so contained. My grandpa was a conductor on the old trolley in Columbus. I was a teenager before I ever got on with him and went from one end of Columbus to another. We lived in a very secluded area, but we had a roof over our heads and food. WWII was a just war. Since then, with other wars, we've had occasions to wonder, but WWII was definitely just; one we were forced into. We went in to win. We fought for survival. Germany and Japan were headed for world expansion. I went in to preserve the type of life we enjoy— freedoms, free movement, democratic government. We had a lot going for us in the '40s. So many others are trying to get into the U.S. now, so we must have something going for us. I've often wondered what would have happened if we'd lost the war.

Morality

My dad instilled morality in every one of his kids very early in life. When I went into the Marines, I knew the difference between right and wrong and tried to my best ability to stay out of trouble.

The Marines instilled in me 100% to do the right thing. If you know it isn't right, don't do it. I think I have the highest morality from early family training and from my time in the Marines, and I tried to instill that into all I did in education. I didn't look the other way when something wrong was done, and did something about it. Looking the other way only compounds the problem.

Something is right if the action is accepted by the greater percentage of the population. Specifically, honesty is right; dishonesty is wrong. Stealing is wrong, regardless of the monetary amount. If it doesn't belong to you and you keep it, that's wrong. If you attempt to find out whom it belongs to, that's right. The slightest inclination of adultery is wrong; having the greatest fidelity is right. I absolutely 100% feel it's important to be true to your wife, completely; 49% isn't going to feed the bulldog. When you take those vows, they have to mean something. I'm concerned about divorces. I would never, under any circumstances, give any thought to marrying anyone who had already had an affair prior to marriage. I can't buy living together before marriage. You have to take the girlfriend's entire family into account. You have to have respect for your girlfriend, fiancé, or future wife. All of your actions have to be directed that way. I tried and still feel the best way is the old-fashioned way. We need to go back to the old-fashioned values. There isn't anything wrong with opening a door, being courteous, and saying thank you. I wouldn't think to eat a meal my wife prepares without saying, "Thanks, that was excellent. I appreciate it." You have to have respect and admiration for the individual you're going to marry. If you don't, don't get married. It won't last long. That includes being chaste.

In the service, you didn't have a worry in the world. There wasn't an instance of someone taking anything that didn't belong to him. You never thought of anything that would reflect dishonesty. We didn't use drugs or even think about it. People then had different values. I could leave a billfold on my bunk for two days, and it wouldn't be disturbed.

Love

We sure were like family. You get so close in the service. We lived together on an hourly basis. We looked out for each other, took care of each other, relied on one another. If someone went on liberty and had a problem, we helped each other. That's part of being a Marine. Even more so in combat. You know that the guy in your foxhole you can rely on and trust. You know he has your good at heart and vice versa in everything you do. It is still that way. There isn't anything I wouldn't do for the guys who came back. At reunions we don't shake hands, we hug each other. We're a band of brothers. We want to know how everyone is doing and how the family is. When you are that close that's what you think about.

Regarding Captain Fields, we were probably the most fortunate Marines in the Marine Corps. There isn't one Marine who was with Tom Fields who wouldn't do anything he asked us to do. He was the epitome of a leader. He had his men at heart every second. He died when they died. He laughed when they laughed. If someone was in the brig on liberty, he was the first one there to get him out. He made sure we looked out for each other. There was not any commander I've met that I would trade for Tom Fields—he was #1 in everybody's book. He wasn't unseen; he was right up there with you in battle. When the company commander was there with you, it gave you the feeling that maybe everything is OK. He didn't stay back at the command post. He was right there from foxhole to foxhole. He told the guys what was going on. He was a leader in the highest sense of the word. I'd do anything for Tom Fields.

Optimism

I'm 100% optimistic. You can't survive this life, if you're any other way. Wouldn't life be miserable if we were negative about everything? I try to be as optimistic as I possibly can. I always expect that you can win in competition. If I had a player that didn't think, going into the game, that he could win, he didn't play. I prefer not to associate with people who go into life looking at the negative aspect all the time. Not that I never felt negative or concerned at times with the country's trends, but I'm still optimistic that we'll work our problems out. I would have jumped out of an airplane with any parachute my buddies packed. I believed it would open.

Humor

This is a real necessity in modern-day life. I would hate to think that anybody could lead a good, happy life, one you'd look forward to, without humor. Things are so sober and trying now. There are so many problems. We've gotten away from laughter and humor. I would hope I've been the type of individual who has had it as part of my everyday make-up. I'd hate to be around individuals who couldn't laugh at themselves.

Humor tends to alleviate the problems you have to overcome. In the war we had a lot of fun, almost on a daily basis. Some of the guys were a little more loose than others. No matter how trying the situation, they'd keep everyone loose. On the daily twenty-mile jaunts in the paratroopers a few kept humor going, the guys laughing.

We pulled some good ones. When the paratroopers were on pass in a hotel in Los Angeles, we sprayed a fire hose from our window on cars and people ten stories below.

Just about ready to jump out of plane, a guy says, "Hey, Juke, Tiny didn't hook you up. Don't jump yet." Or, "Don't jump yet, your parachute doesn't looked like it's packed just right."

On Iwo, we had eaten C or K rations at every meal. Toward the end of the battle, we pulled off the front lines 100 yards. I went over to the Seabees who were building the airstrip. They always had the best food. We pounded on the mess hall door. The cook said, "What do you want?" I said, "I'm tired of eating C and K rations. I came over here to eat your good cooking." The cook rattled off a disgusting menu. C rations sounded better. Then he said he was just kidding, come on in. We ate high off the hog.

Long View of Suffering

I thought the Marines was easy. I suffered to a degree, when guys were injured or killed. But you can't hang on to that when you know you can't do anything about it. You have a job to do. These conditions were a part of my expectations and I accepted it. The next day was a new day. Even with Tiny, I suffered to a degree, but I always figured that the only way I'd survive was to look at each day as a new day. They guy next to me is gone and I can't do anything about it. I did that on an hourly basis. You make your own problems, if you can't adapt and go on and do the best job you can do. Even if it's only me alone surviving, I'd do my job. I adapted if I didn't have a flame-thrower one day.

The war made me better in one way. If there's one thing, I'm unusually organized. My wife says I'm the most organized person she's known. Friends say that too. If anybody moves something from where it's supposed to be, I raise nine kinds of hell. I make sure my basement and garage are organized. I learned it in the Marines. The first thing I learned in battle is how chaotic and disorganized everything was. There was no organization whatsoever. It was ingrained in my mind: you can't win if you're not organized.

Maintaining Balanced Living

I'm an outdoor enthusiast. I've done lots of hunting and fishing. I've enjoyed walking and lots of gardening. Lately my knees and back have gone out. It irritates me that I can't still do some things, but if you accept it, you're ahead of the game. I still hunt— turkey, deer and squirrel, although I'm slowed down. I've been going to Canada in June for 30 to 40 years to go fishing with a group of guys.

Believe me, I can lie down to sleep and nothing bothers me. I get eight to ten hours, from about 10:30 to 7:30. I eat three meals—lots of fruits and vegetables, probably too many fried foods from childhood.

I never smoked except for a little while after the war, but it was too expensive so I quit. I have one or two beers a week lately.

I used to play a lot of golf and competitive sports, but now mostly enjoy spectatoritis. I do water aerobics for my arthritis. I enjoy lots of reading, and go over newspapers thoroughly. We talk or visit with the kids almost on a daily basis.

Advice to Younger Generations

When I talk to groups of young people, I tell them to realize what the past generation has done to make their life better. Appreciate the old-fashioned values and traditions that this country and the past generation stood for. Incorporate them into your daily lives. Consider what you can do to contribute to the future. Realize how much we owe to others. Don't have a selfish outlook. Don't be a taker; be more of a giver. Don't expect things to be handed to you.

Develop good relationships on the job.

If you are going into the service, give your all. If you are married and worried about not coming back to family, you can't give your all. I saw too many guys crack, worried over wife and baby, and afraid of getting killed. Realize you're not going in for a picnic, but you have a job to do and the only way you can do it is if you are 100% committed.

Luther ("Juke") Crabtree, left, with brother Harold ("Tiny").

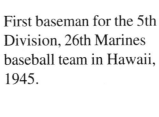

First baseman for the 5th Division, 26th Marines baseball team in Hawaii, 1945.

Juke and Willie Crabtree, Columbus, OH.

Chapter 36

Robert Davis
Bougainville and Iwo Jima

Robert Davis is fit and tall, over six feet tall. Robert lost his legs at Iwo Jima, serving with Tom Fields and Juke Crabtree, although it is difficult to detect that he walks on artificial legs. He and his wife Ercell live in Broken Arrow, Oklahoma, in a beautiful home with a pool, which he uses almost daily. Says his wife, Ercell: "He's been tested and tried and looks on the lighter side. He's never complained. He doesn't have time to complain. He stands real tall and faces the day, whatever it brings. He's a very, very strong man."

Jennings, Oklahoma, a real little town that today has a population of five hundred, is where I was born in January of 1925. I was the oldest of three children, having two younger sisters. My dad was an oilfield man from a little town in Arkansas, working on the pipeline for Shell Oil Company. He was a bit of an alcoholic. I grew up trying to defend my mother. So I didn't have too much respect for him until later years, when he dried up. My mother was a wonderful woman, an old hen who took care of her chickens, very loving. She was a strong Baptist. She always had us go to church and Sunday school.

I liked any type of sports—especially football and wrestling. Dad wouldn't let me play football anymore after I broke an arm. As dirt poor people, there wasn't a lot of recreation aside from watching the oil company baseball leagues. In my teens, I was asked to join the Cushing Refinery men's team. I usually played first base, because I was tall. I used to caddy for fifty cents for eighteen holes. In wintertime we had the course to ourselves, so we learned to play golf. I worked at a supermarket and also drove a milk truck on a little delivery route.

When I was half way through senior year of high school, Pearl Harbor was struck. About 20 of us left high school and enlisted in Oklahoma City. I went to San Diego, California, for boot training, and then Camp Pendleton.

My first trip was to Bougainville, near Australia. That's where I met Tom Fields *[See Chapter 34]*. I went as a replacement for the 1st Parachute Battalion. After the Marines secured the beachhead, we turned it over to the Army. They lost the line and we came back in to reinforce them. There was tough fighting in the jungle for about two months. The Japanese were hard to move out, but as an 18-year-old you didn't think much about it.

We came back to Camp Pendleton in 1944 and joined the new 5th Divison—the raiders and paratroops made up the backbone—in D Company, 26th Marine Regiment. Then it was on to Hawaii to train, and to Iwo Jima on February 19, 1945. I was scared. You're always scared. You see a lot of men getting killed. I was there almost from the beginning to the end. On March 13, the night before I was to go back, I got hit. It was like a bad dream. A lot of things I've forgotten about. They flew me out to Guam, to Hawaii, and then to Mare Island Hospital in California. Recuperation took about a year. I received artificial legs. I was discharged in 1946.

I attended a watchmaker school in Denver and became a jeweler. I was a jeweler in Tulsa for many years, until retiring in 1993. My first wife was my high school sweetheart. We had three children, who are still here in Tulsa. She died in 1990. I met Ercell ten years ago.

PTSD Symptoms?

I probably went through a year or two of trying to forget what I'd been through and readjust. I didn't avoid people or drink to cover the pain, though.

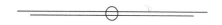

What Helped You Cope?

I had good friends and I stayed busy. I think that athletics was a big help. You always wanted to win at whatever you did and not quit.

Growing up poor in the Depression, you didn't expect too much. My dad was a superintendent, so I never knew hunger or went without shoes or clothes. But by the time he got home with the paycheck, it was pretty skinny. He sobered up after he buried two of his drinking buddies. He got to be decent enough about 1946.

CALM UNDER PRESSURE

You were trained to do what you had to do. It was good training. I never saw anyone break down. A couple started to cry, but stayed put and did their job. Nobody wanted to be a coward, so you always put your best foot forward.

You got irritated at the Japanese and wanted to do them before they did you. We were taught to hate them a little bit, and after you saw what they did to your friends, it wasn't hard to do. But the killing wasn't personal—the motivation was both duty and that hate. When I first got out of the service, I despised Japanese products. That feeling finally went away.

RATIONAL THOUGHT PROCESSES

I think I was positive in my thinking. I never thought negatively or that I couldn't take things. I just focused on my job. When I made mistakes, I passed it off as a bad goof and tried not to repeat it. When others messed up, I didn't hold it against them. One fellow's rifle went off in training and a colonel knocked him down and hit him. I thought that was unnecessary and felt sorry for him. I was never a good student, so with my kids I was more than lenient. I spanked my son only once. I was never hard-nosed with my children. I was fifteen when I had my first bike, so I gave them bikes early. I remembered things from when I was a poor kid. I was kind, and tried to be understanding.

SOCIAL SUPPORT

Friends and family were very important during the war. My family was always full of loving kindness. My mother wrote often. My high school sweetheart and I wrote at least once a week.

When you eat and sleep together, you get pretty close to your buddies. I had numerous close friends, usually ex-paratroopers. One of my close buddies pulled me off the line when I was wounded and got me back to the aid station. You'd share your histories. You got very close, staying together month after month. You didn't want to be a coward and disappoint your buddies in any shape or form. I felt a great loyalty to them.

COMFORTABLE WITH EMOTIONS

Any man who said he wasn't scared when shot at is lying or out of his mind. My outlet, once in battle, was to fire a few rounds, even if in the air. You needed to turn your energy loose somewhere. Plus, we were always moving, not sitting still. So physical activity was helpful.

SELF-ESTEEM

I was probably a little on the cocky side. They teach you as a Marine to "go get 'em." I was very confident about my training. We had a lot of practice, to include amphibious landing. In rough seas you could get hurt, so we got a lot of extra training. I thought that my company was the best. We had pride and espirit, knowing that they put the Marines right up front in the thick of things.

ACTIVE, CREATIVE COPING

I don't ever want to be passive. I like to be active. We didn't fight our orders; we tried to follow them. For example, we had to move if we could, whenever we thought the Japanese knew where we were, or they'd get you. Each day you had to go forward. Retreat was not in the book for the Marine Corps.

SPIRITUAL AND PHILOSOPHICAL STRENGTHS

God

I grew up believing in God. My mother was a strong believer and it rubbed off. I saw God as loving and kind. The first thing you say when you get hit is "God help me." I prayed daily. Often I read the New Testament in the dark.

Meaning & Purpose

War was a big adventure when you were 18. After Pearl Harbor, it was a just war. No way did I doubt the cause. We were fighting for our country and our country means freedom. I didn't ever think the enemy would win.

During that time, all I ever thought about was making a good living and supporting my family. I hoped to have my own family some day. I wanted to have children and send them to college, and they all did finish college.

Morality

You have to have a sense of high morals to survive anyplace, to be a good upstanding citizen and honest.

Love

You feel your buddies are closer than your brother. I had great respect for them. I carried one little badly wounded corporal on my back to get help. He was already dead when I got to the aid station, but you always helped people who were hurt. After I was carried on a stretcher to the field hospital, I told the medics to take care of others who were worse off than I. I try not to miss my reunions, especially in recent years. It's always a good feeling. We went to one in California and were standing overlooking the ocean. A man came out and told us that we were on private property. I said, "I'm very sorry, sir, we're just a bunch of old Marines remembering." He told us to stay as long as we wanted.

Optimism

I'm an optimist. Negative feelings are not good. You have to look for something better. When I lost my legs, I went through a period of feeling sorry for myself. I had to get rid of that, if I was going to get well. At Mare Hospital, most of the people were amputees. Many were worse off than I was. We had a lot of companionship and we helped each other not to feel sorry for ourselves. The best feeling you can get is to see someone use his hardware well. Some even roller-skated or skied. This gave your courage a lift. You got wheeled in but you had to walk out. I knew I would walk again. I had that cocky feeling. I was thinking that I wanted to play golf again.

Humor

If you can laugh about it, you can overcome it. In the hospital, there was a shortage of wheelchairs. Three of us wanted to go to the telephone exchange building at the bottom of the hill. So we piggy backed, putting one on the back and one on my lap. Going down the hill we lost control and smashed through the door. We were lucky we didn't get hurt too badly. Afterwards we laughed.

If you can believe, the VFW donated a car. Six of us used it to sneak off and go into town. Since we were double amputees, one guy got on the floor doing the brakes and the accelerator. Another guy was steering. That's a ridiculous story, but it's true. We also teased each other to keep up morale.

Long View of Suffering

Watching my dad made me stronger. I learned that I didn't want to be like him, that's for sure. You have to get stronger, if you're going to survive. You gather character in the service. I learned that you don't want to be too cocky or cock sure. You can get knocked down. That happened to me.

Maintaining Balanced Living

I was very active until recently. I golfed five days a week. I liked to fish and hunt with my son and friends. I've usually slept eight hours, from 10:00 p.m. to 6:00 a.m. We eat regularly, three meals a day. We try to keep it healthy and nutritious. I'm trying to be more of a vegetarian lately.

I smoked for 20 years, before I got smart enough to quit. I have a drink, one or sometimes two a day, but I can do without it. Sometimes I drink nothing, and don't drink to excess.

We've liked to play cards socially. We have friends to dinner at the house.

I had a stroke recently, and that has been difficult. I keep fighting and hoping for a miracle that I'll improve. My faith helps. We worship every Sunday.

Advice to Younger Generations

Stay physically and mentally healthy, and stay away from drugs and alcohol. Your faith in God has a lot to do with staying mentally healthy. Stay religious. You get strength through your beliefs—strength to get well and to avoid destructive behavior.

Robert and Ercell Davis of Broken Arrow, OK.

Chapter 37

Dr. Samuel William Billison
Navajo Code Talker

It is generally regarded by American and Japanese historians alike, that the Navajo Code Talkers saved the lives of thousands of Marines and profoundly affected the outcome of the war in the South Pacific. The Code Talkers developed a code that permitted the rapid translation of critical battlefield communications from English to Navajo and back to English. The process typically took seconds or minutes, compared to the hours taken using traditional codes, and was highly accurate. At the time of the war, the complex Navajo language was unwritten and was spoken by virtually no one outside of the Navajo Nation. Unless spoken from birth, it was very difficult to attain fluency in the language. A code within a code, it was never broken by the Japanese. The code's alphabet used several words for each letter. For example, for the letter A, Code Talkers might use either the Navajo word for ant (wol-la-chee), apple(be-la-sana) or axe (tse-nill). For military words without a Navajo equivalent, figurative equivalents were devised. For example, the word for humming bird (da-he-thi-hi) represented a fighter plane, while the word for tortoise (chay-da-gahi) represented a tank. No other oral code in military history had been unbroken. Even untrained captured Navajos could not decipher the code.

Beginning as a pilot project of 29 Navajo volunteers in the spring of 1942, the project expanded to more than 500 Code Talkers by the end of the war. The code was used in almost every South Pacific campaign in which the Marines participated, from Guadalcanal to Iwo Jima and Okinawa. Navajos were praised as outstanding Marines — loyal, intelligent, clean, responsive, and professional.

The Navajo call themselves Diné Bikéyah, people of the land. The beautiful Navajo tribal lands cover the corners of Arizona, New Mexico, and Utah, spreading over an area roughly the size of West Virginia. The Navajo Reservation is the home of the largest Indian tribe in North America. Navajo roughly translates as "tillers of the earth."

Dr. Samuel Billison is one of 88 delegates to the Navajo Nation Council, the sophisticated legislative body that is similar in function to the U.S. Senate. I met him in the Council House, a stone edifice that reminds one of Congress. Of a warm and friendly demeanor, he lives with his wife Patsy in Window Rock, Arizona, the capitol of the Navajo Nation. He presently serves as President of the Navajo Code Talkers Association.

I was born in a hogan between Kinlichee and Ganado, Arizona, on the Navajo reservation. At that time there was no hospital. A midwife and medicine man helped with the delivery. My birth date of March 14, 1925, is approximate, since we kept time according to dances to cure sicknesses in the winter months.

We lived isolated and in poverty. There were no conveniences: lights, running water, vehicles, or toys. We made our own toys out of thread spools. We'd put them together, run wires, and then put soap on it and wind it, and it went by itself. Nearby, were four or five hogans in which my relatives lived — grandparents, aunts and uncles, and cousins. I played in arroyos behind the hogans. When I could walk, I started to herd sheep. My grandfather had lots of sheep, three corrals of them. Sometimes, we'd go to the mountains to herd sheep.

I was a little boy when my father left my mother. I lived then with my mother and two sisters. Mother wove rugs for income. She took very good care of us.

The family was very close. We played with all my aunts' children. We made like we were horses with tails on our backs and ran races. My sister Mary outran all of us. In the wintertime, we played a shoe game with two teams. Each team tried to guess which of four shoes was hiding a little ball, by tapping the shoes with a stick. We'd sing certain songs as we played the game. It was a happy childhood. We didn't know about any problems, and I worried about nothing. We had horse races every Sundays—regular horses, wild horses, and wagon races, and there would be age groups, so that when I got old enough, I would race against other kids and my uncles would race each other.

My mother's father and three uncles were all medicine men, who participated in healing ceremonials. Sometimes my mother would take me to a sing. Some lasted a day, others up to nine days. I learned a lot of different songs. The ceremonials were conducted by season—summer and winter. There would be singing and prayer to cure different types of sicknesses. Medicine men were highly respected. When they came by horseback or wagon, we had to straighten up and Mother started cooking. There was no fooling around. Grandfather would tell us what we should and shouldn't do. He always brought something to my mother that was earned from a sing. There was no cash exchanged for this service, but corn pollen, buckskins, wedding baskets, clothing material, and sometimes a live sheep, horse, or cow. In those days, all medicine men would come for a sing, to help. During the day, they would go away from the ceremonial place and play cards in a ditch. My grandfather used to ask me to run to the trading post for pork and beans. They'd eat and play cards all day, and sing all night.

There was very little junk food. A lot of our food was made from corn, such as different types of bread. We also planted pumpkin and fruits and put these in a dugout, a ground cellar, which served like a refrigerator. For horses, we put alfalfa and hay up on a loft to preserve it, because the growing season was so short. We'd get up at 4:00 or 5:00 a.m. and were told to run for our health, even in the winter snow. My sister Mary would run a mile and back. Breakfast was tortillas and bacon. We'd sit around in a circle and dip bread in the grease. My mother would give assignments to my sisters, such as weaving, and I'd herd sheep. We'd often visit with aunts and uncles, and they would often come to visit us. By the clan system, people always helped each other with cooking and groceries and such. We'd also visit after a sing.

At four or five years of age, I started to attend St. Michael's, a Catholic boarding school near Window Rock, and attended during winter months until I finished the eighth grade in 1938. The sisters were good to us, but very strict. We couldn't speak Navajo. When I started school, I had a Navajo name. A sister, whose last name was Billison, gave me my name. Navajos were taught not to look into people's eyes, to look down. A sister held up my chin to get me to look at her as I spoke. It was difficult to talk with your chin held up. She asked me what my name was, and I said in Navajo that I didn't know. It came out sounding like Billison, which might have been part of how I got my name. Boarding school was a good experience. It was very rigid, like military school with companies. We marched to church, the dining room, and school. We drilled. We wore a uniform with a canvas-like striped shirt and Levi pants. It was a good education, the best school. I played basketball, on a team named Mickey Mouse. We had Mickey Mouse on our shirts. I also played saxophone in the band from fifth grade on up, and was really good by the eighth grade.

I then attended ninth through twelfth grade in a Bureau of Indian Affairs boarding school in Albuquerque, New Mexico. We studied academics in the morning and trades in the afternoon—carpentry, silver smithing, agriculture, masonry. I played football, baseball, and basketball. I graduated in May of 1943. On May 10, I enlisted in the Marines, and was sent to San Diego for boot camp. At the end of basic, there were two Navajos in the platoon. An officer called us aside and said, "Hey, Chief, are you an Indian?" I said, "No, I'm a Navajo." He asked me if I spoke Navajo and English. We were sent to a special program at Camp Pendleton, California. There were many Navajos studying the code there and I started studying and got real interested in it. It was very difficult and many didn't pass, some having to take the test two or three times. Everything was Top Secret right from the start. There could be no notes—everything was memorized. We couldn't talk about it outside of class. The code had already been developed, but we made some refinements to it. We were also trained in regular communications— semaphores, panels for airplanes, blinkers for ships, and Morse code. There was a lot of field training, practice landings, and practice in sending and receiving messages. The first group of 29 code talkers developed the code in 1942 and sent messages among the 1st and 2nd Marine Divisions, beginning with Guadalcanal. The code was refined and used by the 3rd Marine Division, which landed at Guam. I was training with the 4th Division, and just before I was sent overseas, the 5th Marine Division was organized. They asked for volunteers for a new unit, an elite amphibious reconnaissance company, which took the place of the famous Carlson Raiders in the South Pacific. They would be sent in three days before D-Day to reconnoiter. Six or eight of us volunteered. We were taken to a special training camp near San Clemente, where the Marine Raiders trained. There was lots of training near the ocean and on islands, including practice landings. We shipped to Hawaii for more training.

In December, 1944, we pulled out. We thought we were headed for Saipan, but instead went to Iwo Jima. Iwo Jima was needed as a base for fighters supporting the B-29s bombing Japan. It would also provide a place for damaged bombers to land, upon their return from Japan. On February 19, 1945, we landed on Iwo Jima. Half of our company went in before D-Day. The 5th Division took Mt. Suribachi and the airstrip. The 4th took a second airstrip. And the 3rd was supposed to be in standby, but in two or three days had to go in because it was pretty rough. Although the island had been thoroughly shelled, it didn't seem to impair the effectiveness of the Japanese, who were dug in their tunnels, which were lined with cement blocks.

They didn't want Code Talkers going in before D-Day for security reasons. Seven or eight code talkers stayed aboard the command ship with the generals, admirals, and Secretary of War Forrester. Messages were constantly coming in and going out. For 2½ days we didn't sleep. Every time someone told us to go below to get some sleep, we'd be asked to return for some more messages.

The first day saw the biggest casualties. The volcanic sand was knee deep. You had to crawl. Bodies were still on the shore when we left the ship to go ashore with the Recon Company. We were always on the front lines. In the Marine Corps, on small islands, there were really no rear echelons. Only the headquarters was a little bit back. Code Talkers were assigned to infantry, tanks, artillery, headquarters, ships, and in some cases airplanes. There were Navajo communications going in all directions. It took 26 days to secure that island.

Throughout the Pacific Campaign, 13 code talkers were killed. Others were wounded and some died later. There were many Congressional Medal of Honor recipients at Iwo Jima among the Marines. In 2000, the President awarded special Congressional Gold Medals to the original 29 Code Talkers. The rest of us received Silver Medals.

We pulled out on April 1, 1945. The same day, the 1st, 2nd, and 6th Marine Divisions landed on Okinawa with the Army. We were told that we were being shipped back to Hawaii to prepare for the invasion of Japan in November. Halfway back to Hawaii, on April 12, 1945, we heard on the radio that President Roosevelt had died. We felt deep pain. You could have heard a pin drop. Marines were crying. We thought a lot of FDR. He was our Commander in Chief. We were sick that he passed away.

In August, the atomic bomb was dropped on Hiroshima. Shortly thereafter, one was dropped on Nagasaki, and we knew the war would end. It did and we didn't have to land in Japan. Many Marines were discharged on the basis of points for being married, having children, length of service, time overseas, and combat. In October, I landed on an island in southern Japan for occupation. The Japanese had fled to the mountains, and our job was to tell them the war was over and try to get them to return to their town and normal living. While there, I played on the Marine basketball team. In 1946, I returned to San Diego to be discharged, then visited friends and family for two or three months.

When discharged, most of the Code Talkers were PFCs. We never understood why we weren't promoted. Someone told us that having no rank or specialty indication might help protect us if captured by the Japanese. At any rate, we were promoted to corporal upon discharge.

My objective was to use the GI bill and go to school. Since school didn't start for a few months, I worked for the Marine Depot at Barstow, California, for the summer.

I attended Bacone Junior College in Oklahoma. The first year, it was an all-Indian school, and the second year, it was opened to everyone. A former high school principal, who used to counsel me, had become a good friend. He got me a small scholarship to play football, baseball, and basketball. There I earned my associates degree.

An aptitude test I'd taken in the Marines indicated that I'd be suited for law, so, at East Central State in Oklahoma, I finished pre-law and education courses. I had enough credits to be a teacher, and graduated with a bachelors degree in government and history. I then attended Oklahoma University fall, winter, spring, and summer without a break to get a masters degree in City School Administration. After graduating I served as principal, teacher, and coach of various sports in schools in Oklahoma and Texas. In 1957, I attended as much of law school as my scholarship from the Navajo Nation would permit. I returned to Window Rock and worked myself up to assistant Director of Community Services, which managed construction, education, health, welfare, communication, police, and other services. I then became Director of the newly established Public Services Division for the Navajo Nation. In 1959 I was encouraged to run for the Tribal Council and was elected. I served four years and was on the education committee and was the chairperson of the police committee. It was during this time that I met my wife Patsy. She worked for a Navajo utility agency that I had oversight of. Losing the election for Chairman (now called the President) of the Tribal Council, I returned to serve on the Public Services Division, and then served as Head of the new Division of Education. Senator Barry Goldwater got me a job with the Governor of Arizona to oversee the Neighborhood Youth Corps for all non-Navajo Indian Reservations in Arizona.

In the fall of 1968, I went to the University of Arizona to get my doctorate. Subsequent jobs included principal of an Indian boarding school in Kinlichee, Arizona, superintendent over eleven elementary schools, establishment of the Department of Education for the Navajo tribe, establishment of a college prep school for gifted students, and consultant to different schools to improve education and leaning conditions.

PTSD Symptoms?

After the war, I suffered from tuberculosis that was determined to be war-related and spent a year in the hospital. However, I did not really suffer from psychological symptoms.

What Helped You Cope?

Poverty taught me to survive with very little food to eat and very little comfort. We slept on sheep skin and it was cold. We had to pull together as a family. Relatives around us wanted each other to be happy and to progress. Several times, as we were eating, my mother would tell me, "I want you to go to school to improve your living conditions. I don't want you to ever raise your children like this. Go to school, so you can earn enough money to raise your children so they're better off then we are." So, when things got rough at school, I dug in.

Upon returning from the war, a ceremonial that was conducted by medicine men and my family helped me clean my mind of bad things and reduced dreams. It included prayer, songs, dances from night to daylight, and herbal medicine.

CALM UNDER PRESSURE

Combat wasn't pleasant. Bullets were flying all around, and you didn't want to get in the way. But the Marines had very good training to the extent that you're not afraid of anything. You feel like you're part of a team. You protect each other and work together with one goal: to fight and defeat the enemy. I was never scared. I never had time to be.

At home, medicine men and family were praying for me, having prayer meetings and ceremonials. It gave me strength. I wore paraphernalia around my neck—sometimes an arrowhead or buckskin with medicine inside, or corn pollen. I prayed to the earth and sun and put corn pollen on the ground and up to the sun. All those are protection. Protective song and prayer kept me safer.

If you thought about the way the Japanese raped people and killed children it could lead to hatred, but if you just fought, you only thought of them as the enemy that we needed to defeat.

RATIONAL THOUGHT PROCESSES

Once, we thought we had cleared an area. Then, a sniper shot one of our men. I thought we shouldn't have been there, but you don't blame anybody. People get killed and you feel bad and can't help it, but you just have to go on. Even if someone needs help, and you're running, you have to keep going on the attack. Thereafter, I've felt that way about mistakes. In coaching and raising children, you know that they'll learn by mistakes and then do better. Sometimes you correct them nicely. Sometimes under pressure we yell—I had had five boys and each felt my belt and they respect that. That was a Navajo philosophy, to be strict. If you don't teach them right, it's not the children's fault. I was kind most of the time. Even after a spanking, I'd talk to them nicely and explain why they got spanked. They knew ahead of time what the consequences would be. I was usually gentle and patient with the kids.

SOCIAL SUPPORT

This is vital for morale. It kept us going. Even before going overseas, a box of cookies made me think that people still thought of me and knew me. I didn't have a girlfriend, but letters from the family helped. In basic, you got to know guys real close. I continually made more friends. I definitely felt a unit espirit de corps, which is a main emphasis in the Marines. We all felt respected as individuals.

COMFORTABLE WITH EMOTIONS

I think I was comfortable with my emotions. I was happy. I really liked the Corps and the training. I enjoyed the whole thing. I did what I was trained for. I always tell people if you have a job, live it and enjoy it. If you don't enjoy it, it will eventually affect your mind, body, and soul. Always think about the brighter things and keep smiling and laughing. Don't get negative.

I only got afraid when I'd dream. I'd dream that I fell and reached bottom, or someone was trying to kill me, or I was walking a narrow ledge, and was afraid to cross it. But other people made it, and I eventually made up my mind to go across.

SELF-ESTEEM

I felt like I was secure, with a good organization, well trained, and I knew my job.

I wanted to be a person of worth. Despite the way the government sometimes treated the Navajos, Native Americans, by percentage, are always the first to enlist. People asked me why I wanted to fight for the U.S., considering the government's mistreatment. In many treaties, there were provisions that the Navajo would not bear arms and fight anymore. However, our Council passed two resolutions authorizing young Navajos to fight for the U.S. We are a sovereign nation and the resolutions freed people to fight. All of us still feel that the U.S. is Mother Earth. This is why we don't want any foreign country to take over the U.S. This is why we defend it. I say that this is why I fight for the U.S. We're under a democratic government. I'm glad to live in the U.S. I'm proud to be an American Indian and also a member of the Marine Corps.

ACTIVE, CREATIVE COPING

I always think that if you have a complaint, you should come up with a positive alternative. Let's do it this way and not complain. I say this on the Council or the Education Committee.

Code school was difficult, but I wanted to finish. I thought of a way to organize code words, either as things of the air (such as birds, representing airplanes), things of the ground, or things of the sea (such as fish, representing ships). I'd remember what my mother told me and persevere when things got rough.

SPIRITUAL AND PHILOSOPHICAL STRENGTHS

God

I was in a dual situation. I believe in and practice the Navajo traditional philosophy and tried to follow the mores of the people. Outside of the reservation, I am a Catholic and go to church. I do believe in God. When things got rough, I'd pray to God in English, and in Navajo to the Holy People. We believe in the Holy People. Way, way back, they gave us the language, different prayers, ceremonies for different needs, and rules of behavior. We're losing some of this. All Native American Indian languages are powerful, sacred, and beautiful. I tell younger generations that they should continue to learn their languages and cultures, to live and enjoy them.

Every morning I'd pray. A person needs some kind of belief that there is a supernatural power, regardless of the name you call it. You can't do it alone.

Corn pollen is blessed in a ceremonial. You put some on the tongue and the top of the head, some on the ground and to the sun. You pray in the meantime for self, family, people, leaders, the world, the universe, human beings, creatures—every living thing. To Navajos these creatures are sacred. I did this whenever I thought of it. Prayer was a foundation—to know that your family was praying for you and you're praying for them.

Meaning & Purpose

I knew I was fighting to protect my country. I had the goal of getting a good education, as my mother taught me, which helped me to persist through difficult times. I was recently asked to speak to young soldiers in Germany and Kosovo. I told them that you train for a purpose. You have to believe in your purpose. Even though you're away from home, you have a reason for being there. We all went through it. I enjoyed it.

Morality

The Catholic Church teaches morality and commandments. The family teaches how you should act and respond to people. I always remembered these teachings and did the best I could. This gave me strength physically and mentally, and happiness inside. If you are moral, you feel you are an asset. Morality to me means you tell the truth, help people, guide others in the right direction, are true to your wife, don't get others into trouble, don't lie, and don't promise people something you can't do.

Love

I tried to help people in code school if they made mistakes. During the war, you help people for safety; there's a feeling of trusteeship.

In teaching school, you know that kids and parents have a love and respect for you, for what you say, and how you treat them. Likewise, I felt love and respect for them. One principal told me not to trust a boy. I'd take him to the gym. He had a fine shot. I hired him as a manager in the athletic department. My belief is that if you give a person some responsibility, you don't have to worry about him. He became the best manager and basketball player. He later got a track scholarship. He never stole anything. When you divert someone in a positive direction like this, it makes you feel good.

In junior high school football, the principal said, don't use this kid on the team. He was an Anglo from the bad side of town. I made him the quarterback. He really gave us a good team. We lost only one game by a mistake. He improved his grades, relationships with others, and was a good kid in school. To change someone to become a better citizen by caring makes me happy.

Optimism

Sometimes I think I'm from Missouri. You have to show me. But I feel good about a lot of things. I feel optimistic about people's potential.

Humor

Humor is definitely important. I have a lot of it in my speeches. It wakes people up and gets them in the mood to listen and feel interested..

During the war, a Code Talker would say, "Did you hear Tokyo Rose singing?" Another would answer, "Yes, she was at a squaw dance." Or, "After we finish this battle, so and so wants to go out and hunt wild goats and have stew."

Long View of Suffering

I always say I'd be willing to go back and do everything again. We still feel the U.S. is the country of the Native American Indians. Without my combat experience, I'd probably just be a sheepherder in the boondocks without an education. My family had no money and the tribe had no scholarships.

My wartime experience taught me the idea that the country is made up of a mixture of nationalities. In the service you meet, associate with, and fight with all nationalities, and begin to understand their backgrounds—Jews, Mexican, Italians, Irish, different tribes. It helped me to associate with different types of people under different circumstances and learn how to interrelate better.

Maintaining Balanced Living

Playing sports in school, the coach said tobacco and soda pop were not good for your health. So I used neither and didn't drink. From the service, I learned to drink beer and smoke a little, but I've never drank or smoked habitually. Maybe an occasional cigar or drink.

My wife and I used to walk every morning until recently. Now the only distances I walk are in parades. I have eaten three meals regularly—traditional Navajo stews, corn or fry bread, roast mutton, etc. I've cut down on amounts now. I don't want a potbelly. I've averaged about six or seven hours of sleep a night.

For recreation, I enjoy reading the paper and mail. I listen to Navajo radio and follow college football and Major League baseball on television. I've coached a lot of little league baseball, and volunteered to teach courses at St. Michael's when my boys were going through it. Patsy and I go to visit relatives. We enjoyed going to the boys' games and now go to the grandchildren's games.

Advice to Younger Generations

If you are an Indian, learn your native culture and language.

All young kids, stay in school. Continue on to higher education if you can. It will help you to secure a successful way of living, and to be happy, and to raise a good family.

Be an asset and good citizen to your community. Always help parents and grandparents, and, if possible, join the Marines.

Dr. Samuel and Patsy Billison outside their home in Window Rock, AZ

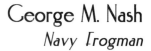

Chapter 38

George M. Nash
Navy Frogman

Robust and direct, 5'11" George M. Nash served in the Pacific Theater with the Navy Underwater Demolition Teams (UDTs). His UDT #7 earned the Navy Unit Citation. He presently serves on the Board of Directors of the UDT-SEAL Museum in Fort Pierce, Florida, and has served in virtually every position at the Museum from president to secretary treasurer. He often lectures about the roles of the Navy Frogmen during the war. He and his wife Joan live in Vero Beach, Florida, and have four children. Says Joan, "I'm blessed. He's my best friend. He's an honest man. You always know where you stand. He's always learning."

I was born in Albuquerque, New Mexico, September 12, 1920, but was raised in Brooklyn, New York, by my mother and grandparents, from the time I was two. I have a sister who is two years younger. My neighborhood was middle class, mostly white American Protestant, although we were Catholic. People were scratching to make a living. Most families owned their houses, which weren't very large. There were no extremes and no violence.

During the Depression, I thought everything was great. Only later in life did I realize that the people raising me were going through some very difficult times. They never discussed their problems with us. We had food, clothing, and a warm place to stay. I thought the rest of the world lived as we did. We had no outside entertainment. Our family got together for holidays, period. We learned to entertain ourselves. For recreation, I roller-skated and played sandlot football and baseball, and ball on the street. We got along as a family without any major arguments to speak of.

I went to Boys High School and Brooklyn Polytechnic Institute, an engineering college. In high school, I worked for the local butcher shop, earning enough to take care of minor things, like traveling by subway to high school, which cost a nickel. I graduated from high school in 1939. I went to work for a defense contractor, which had a contract to build or modify five-inch 38 caliber gun mounts for the Navy. Since I had some engineering background at the time, I became one of the young engineers.

In 1943, I applied for and received an appointment to the U.S. Merchant Marine Academy, but I also joined the Navy at the same time, and was called up. I went to Navy boot camp at Camp Peary, Virginia. They requested volunteers to join a combat demolition outfit. During the extensive initiation program, we concentrated very heavily on physical training for a month. I was then sent to the Naval Combat Demolition Training Base at Ft. Pierce, Florida, for further training in beach reconnaissance, beach demolition, small boat handling, swimming, the use of explosives and firearms, and all aspects needed to become a Navy Combat Demolition Unit (NCDU). I graduated as part of NCDU #83, although I didn't see combat with that unit. The units were sent either to the Atlantic or the Pacific Theaters of Operations. I was sent to the Pacific. Those in the Atlantic participated in the operations in North Africa, southern France, and the beaches at Normandy, where we had a very high casualty rate.

I was sent to Maui, Hawaii, where I ran the drone boat program. A drone boat was an LCPR (landing craft, personnel, ramped), that was radio controlled and loaded with explosives. We could head it toward a beach without a crew aboard. It didn't work, because the salt spray and atmospheric conditions were detrimental to the crude radio system— the housing was not waterproofed. So the program failed. Later, the Navy did put together a workable system with radar beacons, gyro-controlled rudders, and crystal control radios. They brought in some of these newer boats to work with. However, after the experience at Kwajalein, where the original system had failed, the Navy still wasn't convinced.

I left the drone boat unit and went to Underwater Demolition Team #7. They realized that the small NCDUs were not the best configuration for the Pacific. So they broke the NCDUs into larger UDTs consisting of four platoons of 20 men each and 10 to 12 in the headquarters unit. I joined UDT #7 as a replacement, but I knew all the fellows from Ft. Pierce.

Our UDT team went to Okinawa by way of the Philippines. Leyte, in the Philippines, was the staging area for Okinawa. We went aboard an attack personnel destroyer (APD), about 335 feet long, which was a destroyer converted to carry an assault team of about 100 men. We went with the fleet to various engagements. When we got to the engagement, we'd leave the APD by one of the four assault boats, and go toward the beach three to four days before the assault began. We would recon the beach and build a hydrographic survey map, indicating the nautical conditions—the depth of the water, currents, locations of obstacles, and so forth. Then, we would eliminate obstructions. Later, we might go in as guides with the first wave. This was all done because of what we learned at the island of Tarawa. When Marines went ashore without UDTs, the landing craft hit reefs. Marines had to then walk across 300 yards of reef to get to the beach. With 70-pound loads, men would hit potholes 10 or 12 feet deep. They drowned by the hundreds. Thereafter, the Navy always sent in UDTs first.

At Okinawa, the assault boat paralleled the beach and dropped a pair of men every 50 yards. We found obstructions and removed them or cut a channel in the coral and marked the channel with buoys. The obstacles that we blew up were mostly pilings. We had no scuba equipment like they have today, just a mask and flippers. Our protection, as we worked, was a cruiser or destroyer standing off shore firing over our heads.

The invasion of Okinawa took place on April 1, 1945. I did my job over a period of a several weeks on several beaches at various times prior to the invasion. At Okinawa, we discovered a major problem. We were so close to Japan that we were constantly harassed by kamikaze aircraft. They would come in at us by the hundreds. I've seen anti-aircraft fire from the ships so thick that it blocked out the sun. We were losing 1¼ ships a day to kamikaze attacks off Okinawa. During those attacks, our APD was bombed by a Japanese aircraft. One bomb was dropped aft (behind) about 50 yards or so, and another went 50 yards in front.

We didn't lose one man on the beach. We had our shells firing over the top of us, but we always feared short fuses, friendly shells that would fall short. Plus, we were getting machine gun fire from the beach, and we could see the bullets hitting the water.

On April 9, my APD got picked off by a shore battery, as it was screening mine sweepers. We took about eight shots on the port side. We lost about 20% of our team, either from death or from all variety of wounds—from losing both legs or arms, the whole gamut. I was in the washroom on the APD cleaning up after the beach and I heard the shots and immediately walked out of the washroom area and saw the gunfire in the companionway. I fell to my knees from the blast, got up, and walked to the starboard side of the ship. We all knew we were in trouble. I went back to take a look at that washroom. A shell had landed in it. There was a big gaping hole in the deck and every fixture on the wall was gone.

After Okinawa, we went down to the western Carolines, east of the Philippines, spending several weeks at anchorage at Ulithi Atoll. I went back to Brooklyn on 30-day leave in July of 1945. The Navy gave us air travel, the works, wherever we went. I met my wife while home on leave. I was introduced to her by my cousin. We married in 1947, and we have been together ever since.

I had to report back August 1 to the West Coast. We loaded on a brand new APD, headed to Pearl Harbor. We had no supplies, but were completely re-outfitted, including new uniforms, shoes, weapons, munitions, and so on at Pearl Harbor. We were scheduled to be part of the invasion of Japan. We arrived in Japan, September 4, 1945. The treaty had been signed two days before. We did a recon of a beach 185 miles north of Tokyo prior to putting troops ashore. We paddled to shore, a team of five, in a rubber boat with a submachine gun. I was left with the boat. A crowd of Japanese people surrounded me. I reached for my submachine gun, but it was not there. It had been lost in the surf. That was fortunate, because, if I had used it, I could well have been a casualty myself. The crowd broke up when the team returned. Shortly thereafter, we were sent back to the states and were decommissioned.

I went back to Brooklyn Polytechnic and to work. I worked for Sperry Gyro as senior draftsman in the instrument division. Then I went to work at Grumman as an engineer. I retired and came to Florida. I was in Florida only one week when Piper Aircraft asked me to work as assistant chief engineer for electrical and avionics systems. After another enjoyable ten years, I retired at seventy.

PTSD Symptoms?

I've seen people break down, but I never reached that point. By breaking down, I mean literally going to their bunk and shedding tears. I don't say I couldn't, but I never did. My wife tells me that I had nightmares when we were first married, and they lasted for about a year or two, depending upon what was happening at the time. Today they are gone. I didn't ever think about it anymore. I think I'm well adjusted.

In the very beginning, when you first go into combat, the adrenaline is really pumping. As the war drags on, every time you go into a combat situation or hear the general quarters alarm (precautions for coming under attack when the ship is most vulnerable—we'd get this once we entered combat areas every hour before sunrise and every hour before sunset), it gets a little bit less. As I got near the end, I realized I wasn't as driven as before. After awhile, you begin to feel the pressure.

What Helped You Cope?

I think I was a fairly well-adjusted person. I think I'd have to fall back on the way I was raised. I had religious beliefs. I was raised to understand that responsibilities came first, before privileges. Young people didn't demand things, like cars. You knew that you had to earn what you got. You recognized other people's property.

CALM UNDER PRESSURE

I had a responsible task to do, and was going to do it. To say "I can't do it" was not even an option. I had obligations to my team members and I expected them to have responsibility to me, too. As a group, we got along and we did what was assigned to us.

I disliked the enemy for their unfairness toward us, but I didn't hate. People in countries follow their political leaders, whose agendas may not be wise.

RATIONAL THOUGHT PROCESSES

When the APD was hit, I was friendly with the 1st lieutenant who was in the ship's company, not a team member. After I left the washroom, I went to ask him if I could help. He asked if I minded taking some tools down to after-steering (where the rudders are driven from). I knew that after I started, I could be trapped below, but said to myself, "Am I a man or a chicken? I'm going to do this." So I did.

When people make mistakes, you can't go nuts. You have to accept that people have opinions, rights, and thoughts. You can't blame them. They didn't know. I have to forgive them for that.

SOCIAL SUPPORT

In our team, we got along real well. Even to this day we do. I talked today to the man who last commanded the team. One of the fellows, whom I got along very well with, had his 80th birthday party in Kansas City, Missouri. I went to the party. In the teams, one thing was required. You must be a team player, not a Rambo. Every one of the team, plus all the officers, trained together. It makes a big difference. At Ft. Pierce we only had one weekend off in ten weeks. It was the training that built those bonds. At the end, at Hell Week, we were given a complex military problem to solve. We stayed at it until it was completed. It might have taken 24 to 36 hours to complete it, including hauling boats through the swamps.

We had long bull sessions with people on the teams, talking about things at home. One fellow I was very friendly with came from Missouri out of the railroad world. He was a great storyteller.

My family wrote to me. I had an extreme interest in my family. I also appreciated the letters from my future wife.

COMFORTABLE WITH EMOTIONS

Regardless of what people said, you have feelings. I felt strong fear at times, but only during short periods of time, when we were bombed or actually in contact with the enemy. The most harried times were when the enemy was firing at us in our small boats or on the APD. At the time, I didn't think too much about it. It bothered you, if someone were dropping bombs on you, realizing you could be in trouble. You might look for a safe place to be, but that didn't exist. You just hoped the danger would go away as fast as possible. I realized, near the end, that I felt I'd had enough, but we didn't talk much about it. We talked among ourselves about a lot of things, but not so much to relieve our own anxiety. My family had no idea what I was doing until a few years ago. I couldn't see burdening them. I have made an extensive write up of my experiences, but that was later.

SELF-ESTEEM

I don't remember thinking about things like that. I felt comfortable with who I was. We did feel confident. After a while we thought we were invincible. The Navy's attitude toward us was different from the usual sailor. We went aboard the ship as a team. We had free roam of the ship. I spent a lot of time in the engine room and on the bridge, watching the operations of the ship at all times. The ship had its own crew and they thought we were just passengers, until we got to the engagement. Then there was a completely different attitude towards us. One day, I asked one of the crew if he wanted to come with us on a mission, and he said I was out of my mind.

ACTIVE, CREATIVE COPING

On a mission, we got up at four or five, had breakfast, and the officers would give us the mission. We'd get into our boats and head into shore. We were all ready to go. That's the way it was. In the Navy at that time, there was a tremendous division between the officers and the enlisted men, but in the demolition teams, officers put their lives on the line just as much as we did and at the same time. We were all going to be together, we all trained together, so we had a different relationship. We were closer. The same story with our buddies. When you went on a swim (mission), you buddy's life depended on you and vice versa. It didn't make any difference whether he was just a plain seaman in grade or the lieutenant in charge of the platoon. Rank didn't matter.

The rest of the Navy wasn't always sure what to make of us. In training, they instilled in us the attitude that we were better than others. We had a tremendous attrition rate when we started out. Men fell like flies, because of the extensive training and the realization of what they were going to have to do. At the chow line in the mess hall at Camp Peary, we were always put at the head of the line. In Ft. Pierce, one Navy guy came to town and heard the explosions going on. Somebody asked what was going on out there, and his comment was, "That's those idiots from demolitions practicing."

After our ship was hit, we were in Ulithi Atoll at anchorage for a short period of time, a few weeks or maybe a month. As a favor to the Navy base, we widened a channel. We were put ashore and quartered on the island of Asor. The Navy base personnel on the island resented us and wished we'd go away, and the officers on our team were denied the right to go to the officers club, because of the attitude of our officers and men. Even our own Admiral Kauffman (the father of the demolition teams, then a lieutenant commander) said, "You people are the motliest group I've seen in a long time." To this, one of the team officers said, "Yes, but we got the job done." And we did. We didn't always dress in the right uniform or follow all the rules, but we had the attitude that we'd complete our assigned missions.

SPIRITUAL AND PHILOSOPHICAL STRENGTHS

God

I believed in God, and believed that He could do anything for me and was protective, not vindictive. I think of Him as a pure spirit. Heaven is the desire of the human spirit to be associated with that supreme spirit. Hell is lack of association with that spirit. I was raised by a strict Irish Catholic family. I went to church every Sunday. I still go to church.

Meaning & Purpose

I felt that we had been attacked by the Japanese, and we were defending ourselves. Today I feel that too many are making decisions of a political nature, who have never seen shots fired in anger. When you see people mangled and killed, you have a different opinion of the reasons to go to war. War isn't easy. The cause must be just and the forces well supported.

Morality

In the Philippines, I was going to go ashore, looking for drinks—typical of sailors. I went and got some rice from the cook and put it in a pillowcase and went ashore with some of the other team members to trade. We couldn't find anything, but we went into a hut. A team member went over to a shelf and was going to take something. I saw the look of the people living there and said, "Jimmy, leave that alone. Don't touch it. You're not going to take it." Finally, Jimmy agreed with me and we left. I didn't think it right to abuse the people who couldn't fight back. If people can't fight back, leave them alone.

The moral code we have today is very lax. I don't think it's a desirable one. I think the one we had back fifty or seventy-five years ago was far superior. We practiced more respect toward other people's property. Honesty was important.

Morality, to me, means being faithful to your wife. When you marry, there ought to be a commitment. I think divorce is the worst thing in the world, and unsettling for the children. I was absolutely faithful to my wife and family. I believe we were far better off when the family structure was much stronger. I think we were better off when mothers took care of the home and children and set an example for them.

Love

Because we were a small unit of volunteers, we knew everyone in the unit intimately, liked each other, and would do anything for each other. We started out from raw recruits to the level of being team members in combat.

Optimism

One thing about war: You know exactly what's going on in your particular area, which may be, say, a quarter mile wide. But you don't know what's going on in an adjacent sector, and you're always trying to find out. We were hopeful that everything was going well and we'd get back home soon. I saw the operation from Pearl Harbor to Japan. When we started up the island chains and one after another we were knocking off the Japanese bases, I realized we were going to win. I didn't know when. I never considered going into Japan, although I knew near the end that we would. They were planning on very heavy losses there.

I've probably been an optimist most of my life. I want to live as long as I possibly can. I look forward to seeing family—my children, my sister, and other family members. I don't want to die tomorrow, but I do look ahead—I'd like to see and talk with some of my ancestors who have passed on.

Humor

I always liked a good laugh or joke. We always used to joke around. I'm more of a serious person, not good at telling jokes, but I'm reasonably quick to laugh.

Long View of SufferingSuffering

I was more adventuresome at that time and volunteered for a challenging organization. So I don't know that I would say that I would have chosen to miss the experience. The war wasn't horrible, but a very, very good life experience—everything we did: our associations with one another and other people, accomplishing our job without complaint, what we were taught. Once it was over, it was over. I had to get back to my life, earning a living and establishing my own family, living a middle class lifestyle.

Maintaining Balanced Living

I walk before breakfast every morning, and I walk again every afternoon— a total of a few miles in about forty minutes. I go to the gym twice a week. Until recently I was in a group that walked three-miles regularly. I eat three meals a day, and try to stay away from excesses. We eat normally, meat, vegetables, and fruit. My primary physician, a black man, is a cardiologist. My heart rate is about 60 and my blood pressure is about 120/60. He has never told me to take anything out of my diet. When I was younger I averaged six or seven hours of sleep. Today I get eight or nine. I retire now at about 10:00 or 11:00.

I never smoked cigarettes. Cigars, but not in over 40 years. I was a light drinker, but stopped altogether six years ago.

My wife and I are best friends and we go everywhere and do everything together. For recreation, I like to travel. Since the war, I've traveled as a tourist in Europe, the Middle East, China, Australia, New Zealand, and other places. I enjoy photography and reading about foreign affairs and politics. I spend a lot of time at the UDT-SEALS Museum, once a week or more. I give lectures to various groups like the Daughters of the American Revolution.

Advice to Younger Generations

Duty, honor, and country. That says it all.
Be committed to family, your friends, and your associates.
Avoid avarice. It's good to be satisfied with what you have and to work as hard as you can to sustain your goals. Enjoy your work.

Underwater Demolition Team #7 in Maui

George and Joan Nash, Vero Beach, FL

Chapter 39

Frank Albert Tinker
Pilot in Japanese Prison Camps

Drive through a spectacular rock canyon, and you arrive at Sunsites, Arizona, and the patio home of Frank and Nancy Tinker. A slim six-footer, Mr. Tinker was an Air Force bomber pilot who endured more than twenty months in Japanese prison camps. During this time he became acquainted with two well-known POWs: Louis Zamperini, a famous Olympic runner, and Major Gregory "Pappy" Boyington, the commander of the famous Black Sheep squadron. Mr. Tinker is a cultured man of broad interests. We sat at a patio table, overlooking the golf range, the distant mountains, and his garden of tomatoes, beans, and squash. We listened to the wind chimes and the birds as we spoke. Frank and Nancy Tinker raised two daughters and a son.

I was born into a family of four children on October 19, 1920, a long time ago, in Lapeer, Michigan, in the thumb district of Michigan. I was the second child. I had an older brother and two younger sisters.

My grandfather was a doctor, so we all lived with them in an old mansion. It was difficult, though, because we had no money. Granddad, being a doctor, was paid off in potatoes and apples and whatnot. Dad was not all that well. He fortunately had a job as a chief electrical engineer for a Detroit Edison company. So we had stress, but no real starvation. Looking back, it was very difficult for the adults. I feel very sorry for the parents at that stage. There was just no money available, period. Milk was ten cents a quart. You'd give potatoes away. Dad had steady work, although the head executive (Sam Insull) left the country with all the money. Like the Enron scandal, it was the biggest scandal of the time. So from the time I was 12 to 18 years old, we lived on the edge of things. I never felt poor, because we were living in relatively good, comfortable circumstances with granddad being a doctor and the town mayor, yet everyone felt tight. No matter what your profession, everyone felt out of money.

My grandfather graduated from the University of Michigan, back when a medical degree was a two-year degree. Dad graduated from an electrical college, also with a two-year degree. So we did have the capacity to learn. Grandmother was a musician, so I was given a piano in my early life. We had cherry, nut, and apple trees in the back yard. In the springtime I'd sit in a tree fighting the robins off, and picking cherries. We made wonderful cherry pies.

My grandfather was a typical crusty country doctor. He didn't take nonsense. Downstairs there was a crank telephone. Once, he picked up the receiver once and said, "Who the hell cares what you think!" Bang. That was the end of it—the shortest conversations on record. It was a rich, wasteful son, refusing to pay his father's bill, who had called.

Dad was not in good health all his life and suffered as a result. Mom was a country girl, a teacher. They got along well. We had a very normal household. Grandmother was the pillar of the Presbyterian Church. Grandfather didn't attend. Mom was much the same as grandmother, except that she was Episcopal, and Dad didn't attend.

Granddad taught me the game of golf. I caddied for him all of my young life. Dad was immersed in the scientific fields. I recall he won a prize once in a scientific magazine for figuring out a simple way to measure the voltage drop in a five-phase circuit over distance. He was considered a genius in the town. By himself, he made the first airplane flown in that area. After the war, Dad's good friend Mal Vosburgh, now gone, was one of JFK's scientific advisors. Mal had been asked if you could provide propulsion in space with light. Dad and Mal covered the floor with equations. Dad had been working on the same thing, and said that yes you can, by shining light on an ionized surface. They've just now started to use this concept of ion propulsion. With that sort of a background, science was not particularly new to me.

Academics came easy. I skipped my first two grades of elementary school because Mom taught us to read. I graduated high school as I was just turning 16.

Home was very pleasant for me, although, looking back I can see all the stresses going on underground. My grandparents didn't get along, but it was more of a joke. In a way, I had an ideal boyhood in Michigan.

I was in athletics in high school—football, baseball, basketball, tennis, the whole load. I was involved in music all the time. I sang and played the piano, although I never took a piano lesson. I simply sat down and started playing. Then I got books—Mozart, Beethoven, etc. I was encouraged and helped by a fine fellow in town who had studied under the last student of Franz Liszt. He helped me with the nuances of the Liszt rhapsodies.

In high school, I was busy all the time with sports and piano. I had a job in a local store, but I trapped muskrats after school or on weekends in the winter and made more money selling the furs than from jobs.

I graduated high school during the worst of the Depression, in 1937. I attended the University of Michigan at great sacrifice from my granddad, even though the tuition was minimal, $75 a semester. I lived just off campus for $50 a month for room and board. I started in pre-med, then shifted to liberal arts. I wrote for the *Michigan Daily* and a couple of other newspapers. I have a letter from my English teacher, saying that I was the best reporter material that he had in his classes. I tried out for the Michigan basketball team, but wasn't big enough or good enough. I sang for the university glee club and recorded Brahms Alto Rhapsody with a soloist; I think it was Marian Anderson.

I wanted to see if I could sing professionally, so I hitched to Curtis Institute in Philadelphia. I stayed at a YMCA. I sang for an elite group but didn't make it. So the next year I went to Julliard with grandpa's backing, and spent a semester and a half. I had a good time with a little room on Riverside Drive. I tried out at Madison Square Garden for the chorus of the Aquacade, part of the World's Fair at Flushing, Long Island, but couldn't swim. Billy Rose was running it. My instructor at Julliard said I could sing, but not grand opera so we shouldn't waste our money. So I returned to finish college at the University of Michigan. Now the war was brewing.

I went to Canada to join the Royal Canadian Air Force. There was a long delay. The Naval ROTC at the University of Michigan said I had to fix a deviated septum in order to be accepted. The university hospital surgically corrected it. Then the Navy said that fixing that problem was no longer necessary.

I signed up with the Army Air Force, leaving in October 1941. Only one in ten applicants made it. You needed to be 21, have two years of college, and be unmarried. I completed primary training at Hicks Field, Ft. Worth Texas. It was rough. We trained on the BT-19. Basic training was at San Angelo, Texas. We trained on the BT-14. Here the war started. Advanced training was at Brooks Field, San Antonio, Texas, with training on the AT-6. I was commissioned a second lieutenant in April 1942.

My first assignment was at Denver Colorado as a photo pilot. I asked to go to a B-24 outfit in Wendover, Utah, near the Nevada border. I trained as a pilot, and checked out as an aircraft commander. Then I went to New Mexico for basic training in bombing and navigation. Final training was in Topeka, Kansas, for long range bombing and navigation.

We shipped out in the fall of 1942. The word was that we were going to the campaign in Alaska, so they issued us fur jackets. At the last minute they said we were going to Hawaii, so we landed there with our fur jackets and parkas. We flew long distance patrols from Wheeler Field, Oahu, 600 to 800 miles, looking for suspicious boats and whatnot.

From Hawaii, in the summer of 1943, we began long range bombing in the South Pacific, hitting the Gilbert, Marshall, and other islands. It was a poorly run campaign, as far as I was concerned. We were bombed when we were on the ground at an intermediate base. We suffered severe losses on the ground, but only a few hits in the air.

We came back to Hawaii to regroup. I got into an argument with the commander over the tactical value of bombing some potash island, and was proven right later on. I asked to leave, if he didn't mind. I transferred to dive bombers, and was sent to Canton to attack possible movements of the Japanese fleet. I was there four to five months in the late summer and fall of 1943.

They got their act together and started a big campaign across the Central Pacific. First, we hit the Gilbert Islands (including Tarawa, where the Marines suffered so many losses) and the Marshall Islands. Our job was to reduce the outer islands of the Marshalls. We bombed them while the fleet approached Kwajalein, the main island of the Marshalls.

I was leading the last echelon in a bombing run over Jaluit, the capitol of the Marshall Islands at the time. You could have gotten out and walked on the flak. They killed my gunner and ruined the aircraft. I dove, unleashed my bombs, and bailed out at about 1200 feet. I floated down right in the middle of them. I saw the tracers as they fired at me as I parachuted. I was captured on December 23, 1943. They beat me with stalks and interrogated me. I lied like a trooper. I tried giving only name, rank, and serial number, but that didn't work out at all. I stayed alive by giving false information and repeating unclassified headlines from the Honolulu newspaper. This bought time.

I succeeded in spite of my personality. My interrogator spoke poor English and pretended to appreciate my correcting him. The Japanese pilots wanted to meet me. We had a nice round table discussion about baseball. As a result, I was sent with the wounded Japanese on an old motor launch to the main island of Kwajalein. I was thrown into a compound, in a four by six cell with a hole in the floor for personal use. Next to me was Lieutenant Fred Garrett, who was shot down along with his commanding officer, Lieutenant Colonel Art Walker. I was between these two guys. Garrett had been shot in the ankle, and maggots had set into his foot. So they dragged him off and lopped of his leg without anesthetic. I had to go in and tend to him. They had done a terrible suturing job. The Japanese guard now and then beat on his amputation to hear him howl. On the other side, Walker had a broken back and was in terrible pain. I saw and was told about other captives—18 from the Navy, Marine raiding parties who'd been left behind, and miscellaneous who had somehow fallen into their hands. They beheaded the 18, I was told, and sent the three of us to Japan, because we were officers and recent captives. They thought we could provide intelligence about the approaching invasion fleet, which the earlier captives didn't have. We were there only a few weeks.

We three were shipped to Ofuna, Japan, in January or February of 1944. This is a beautiful little village that is now a film center of that area. There was a secret interrogation camp run by the Japanese navy, way up in the hills. It was run by a little old warrant officer who had been pressed back into the service to head the camp. Every morning his orderlies brought him his shined shoes and paper. He'd sit under the arbor and read the paper as he drank his tea. My friend Louis Zamperini (Zampo) would sneak up and steal the paper when he fell asleep. We'd read it and replace it. What a comedy that was. One of our guys, an Australian lieutenant named Lempriere, could read Japanese.

They were rough about the interrogation. They made us understand that we either answered the questions or we'd be shot, an idle threat. We lied or claimed ignorance about the fleet invasion or gave common knowledge. So the interrogation was mostly a joke. They gave up on us after a short time.

Rations were soup now and then and rice twice a day. Once in a while we'd get fish. I was losing weight. I weighed 165-170 pounds when I was shot down, and was now at about 100 pounds. They kept us there until summer of 1944.

Marine Ace "Pappy" Boyington showed up in camp at Ofuna. He won the Medal of Honor and wrote the book *Baa Baa Black Sheep*. He was a stout, square-jawed, rough-tough guy. He was being sequestered. I talked to him through the walls in the latrine and asked him how the war was going. He said, "Look, I don't know you guys. You might be plants." A set of Japanese admirals interrogated him. Lempriere interpreted and told us, "I don't believe this man. He was wounded, beaten, and in rags. He goes over and sits on the desk of the admirals and says, 'Look, you guys are stingy. I haven't had a cigarette since I got here.' They were amazed and got him cigarettes. He said, 'I'm going to lie and you know it. Let's be frank. If you want to hear answers, I'll give them to you, but I'm going to give you the greatest story you ever heard.'" He was downright rude to them. He could have been executed, but he wasn't.

We were transferred to Omuri, an artificial island in the Tokyo Bay near Yokosuka, Japan. We were there until the winter of 1944. Shortly after Christmas, we were taken by train to Naoetsu, near Nagano where the winter Olympics were recently held. It is very snowy there. The snow comes across from Siberia and covers up the first story of the houses. I finished out the war there.

We met the Bird *[infamous camp administrator Watanabe Mitsuhiro]* in Omuri. He made life miserable for us. He was truly fanatical and psychotic. We were so relieved when we learned that we were leaving Omuri, and be damned if he didn't transfer with us to Naoetsu. He was war criminal #26 on MacArthur's list. He beat me up time and again for no good reason—if you didn't salute, or something like that. He hit me with the butt of the rifle, or banged me over my head with his metal helmet. Usually he hit me with his fist. He'd stand you at attention for long periods of time in the cold and kick you. He was unbalanced mentally, so we never knew what he might do. We were afraid that he'd draw his sword and then be committed to use it. He told us that we'd all be killed if Japan were invaded. You had to mollify him. Luckily, we had a couple of people who were born diplomats who probably kept us from getting executed. They'd talk to him. One captain from the Philippines, named Samson, was an artillery officer who'd been through the death march at Bataan. He had come on a ship with other prisoners. The Japanese would lower a bucket of rice into the hull. He stood astride the bucket, fought off the POWs, and doled out a cup to each man. He was that kind of a guy. Samson took off his glasses when he knew he was going to get beaten up. After the Bird beat the hell out of him, he'd say, "OK, that's over. Let's settle down and talk." He saved lots of us from severe injury.

Lempriere was a certified genius if I ever saw one. He was a middle-aged man who seemed to own half of Australia. He spoke fluent Japanese. I believe that he had been an intelligence agent and that he would have been executed had the Japanese known it. He had been in Japan before the war and knew people of substance there, including the royal family. He owned property in Tasmania, Australia, and donated it to raise war orphans. I met him in Manhattan after the war and found him to be a fabulous character. He knew the in-crowd in Europe, and spoke many languages. There was another genius there from West Point, named Bill Harris. His father, a Brigadier General, was a commander of Marine aviation. Harris and Lempriere would get together on the cold benches and discuss medieval history and talk about things most people never heard of. Lempriere could mollify the Japanese because he knew them and could explain things to them. He looked like an old man and he'd bow to them, and they hesitated to beat on him. In Japan, usually you don't beat up little old men.

Most POWs had nothing to do but walk around. Zampo made friends with the guards. He was very personal. He tried to trot around the compound. In the Olympics he had run like a thoroughbred, but here it was pitiful in a way to watch. You could see he was struggling to run because he felt one should stay in condition. We became very good friends. In fact, I may owe my life to him. At Omuri, I got jaundice very bad, but we had learned you could cure many diseases with food. For example, you could cure dysentery and diarrhea with cheese, so we got cheese out of the Red Cross boxes and gave it to the medics. You could also cure jaundice with sugar. Zampo had made friends with the Royal Scots, who were with us in the same barracks. They were a bunch of happy thieves and brigands who had been given the choice of serving in the Royal Scots or going to prison. They'd been captured at Hong Kong and Singapore. They went out to work everyday and as a result came back loaded with everything from smoked salmon to sugar. They'd tie their pants at the bottom, then take a hollow piece of bamboo with a razor sharp end and stick it into a sack of sugar. They'd carry the sugar back in their pants legs. Zampo went across the barracks and said we had a man who was dying and we needed sugar. Well, sugar was worth its weight in gold, but they gave him a cupful. In two days I was well.

Some of the guards were more lenient. If you had a Christian guard, you were in good shape. They were kinder. They would confess under the table that they were Christian. We only had two or three, but they were outstanding. They made a pretense of being tough, but were much different. The rest of them would beat you up just because you were American. At Naoetsu, I was in lineups where the guard would sell opportunities to the soldiers to beat us with sticks. You learned to roll with the punches. We all had beriberi, amebic dysentery, hepatitis—100%, there was no getting away from it. We had a lot of fatalities, mainly from starvation and despondency. If you lost your joie de vivre, you were done for. The native Filipinos and prisoners from that region were not accustomed to the cold. They died like flies.

The approximately one hundred of us who were left alive were liberated in August of 1945, when the armistice was signed. The guards didn't tell us about it so that we wouldn't become unruly, but we knew from the pipeline. I'm alive because they used the atomic bomb, and because the Emperor told his people to endure the occupation. When the armistice had been declared but we were still technically at war, a brave Navy lieutenant commander got on a cruiser, landed unannounced at the Niigata air base just north of Naoetsu, and said, "Take me to your leader." He told the commander of the area to get a train to evacuate prisoners to Tokyo and a waiting hospital ship. That Navy officer, named Harold Stassen, later became governor of Minnesota and a perennial candidate for the presidency.

The train came about September 1, 1945. The USS *Missouri* was in the harbor. We got on a hospital ship, the *Benevolence*. We were deloused, medicated, and given new uniforms. We took a DC 6 to Manila, where we stuffed ourselves. A week later we boarded a troop ship to San Francisco. During the two-week trip, we had access to the galley, and went through the chow line two to three times each meal. I got back up to 180 pounds.

In the hospital in San Francisco, I ran into Lieutenant Garrett and LTC Walker from the prison in Kwajalein. They had operated on Garrett's stump and sewed it up properly. Walker and I became well acquainted. When we tried to leave the grounds, the guard at the gate said, "Sorry!" Walker replied, "Look, lad, better shots than you have tried it. If you think it's important enough go right ahead, but we're going to walk out this gate and go into town for a good time. We'll be back in a couple of hours." We just walked past. The guard presented arms and didn't say a thing. Walker later became personnel officer for the Strategic Air Command.

I was then sent to Hines General Hospital near Chicago. On leave in Mexico, I met Nancy Coe, who was vacationing from Milwaukee. She had spent the war as an interpreter for the Labor Department. Mexico was sending thousands of workers to help in the fields in the Midwest. We married in Lapeer, Michigan, in August 1946.

We went to the West Coast, where Zampo arranged a movie test for me at Universal International. No soap, of course. We then came to Phoenix, Arizona, where our first child was born. I was a radio program director for a couple of radio stations. One night, a drunk driver fractured my skull and put me in the hospital. When I got out, we didn't have much money. Colonel Walker was stationed at a nearby air base and said, "Come back in the Air Force." So in 1948, I became an intelligence officer. But I ended up back as a pilot of B-29s and B-50s for two years.

In the meantime, I had passed the exam for the State Department, to be a Foreign Service Officer. It was a four-day test that was very difficult. Only about 50 out of 10,000 passed and were accepted. Earlier, in 1951, I was assigned by the Air Force to Japan, which was unusual. Some Marines had been returned to Japan, looked up their old guards, and beat them severely. I asked to be returned from Japan to join the State Department and began a career as a Foreign Service Officer. From 1952 until 1955 we were in Toronto, where I quickly realized I was not cut out to be a diplomat.

I wanted to write and had been doing so quietly for years. In Toronto, I met an editor *of MacLean's Magazine*, the *Saturday Evening Post* of Canada. As I left, I wrote an article blasting the anti-American sentiments of Canadian media. They got more mail regarding that article than they'd received in ten years, I was told, and 60% were in my favor. I wound up in *Time* magazine—a short tut-tut piece.

Coming back to Arizona in 1955, I helped Pappy Boyington with his book briefly. I wrote articles for the *New York Times* on Tucson's desert museum, on hunting for *Field and Stream* and *Outdoor Life*, and on many subjects for *Popular Mechanics*.

In 1956, I took a job flying two flights a week from Oklahoma City, carrying high priority goods to Air Force bases. We moved to Oklahoma City and were later transferred to Ogden, Utah, and raised our kids there for 14 years. In the meantime I was writing, like mad, articles on western history, hunting and fishing, aviation, nuclear medicine, and other topics, for *Popular Mechanics, Field and Stream, Denver Post*, and women's magazines

Back in Tucson in 1969, I did contract flying for the Forest Service and Intermountain Aviation, supporting exploration for oil in Alaska. I continued writing, and retired in 1985.

PTSD Symptoms?

I didn't have PTSD symptoms. I had a disability interview six months ago for my wounds. The psychiatrists who interviewed me for PTSD said, "The man has a superior ability to recover; he's as normal as apple pie." When I first came back, my wife said I was on edge, fairly nervous. I felt very responsible for my wife and youngster. We didn't have much money, so I probably was irritable. But as time went on, we've had success and fun, and I've felt very placid.

I felt like a celebrity when I came back. I was giving talks. I look back on it dispassionately. I'm a separate person from what happened then.

Memories never kept me awake. One factor was that I kept so active. I had other concerns right off the bat, so I had no time to worry about the past. I have written about the war experience. One article was about the food situation. As any Buddhist knows, when you fast, your mind becomes super active. It expands consciousness. You can remember things.

What Helped You Cope?

Going back to Japan in 1951 was a catharsis. I set up a small intelligence operation. The Japanese were very cordial and nice and I got along well and dropped some hatred. The Bird was still on MacArthur's list of wanted criminals. I located the Japanese police file on him. I went with my interpreter to confront his mother and we got along quite well. She apologized for his behavior. She didn't realize he wasn't really dead. She showed me the altar to honor her dead son. She put food in front of it every morning. Apparently, he had let her believe that he was dead.

Athletic competition helps you know not to wilt when you lose. Music helped a lot, too.

The Depression was strengthening. Not having money (both in the Depression and in Japan), you learned you won't starve, that you can survive on little. So you don't worry too much about finances. Nancy and I have been on the edge several times, but were never really depressed. You can always get a job. Finances are the number one cause of worry, because happiness and success today are equated with how much money you make. Well, that's an awful way to think. Absconding with millions of dollars at Enron isn't success. You're successful because you can do what you like to do and do it well, not because of money.

In the camps, your mind becomes very sharp, very clear. Memory was crystal clear because of the diet. Although it was cruel, we basically had the same diet as the civilians, which was nothing. I thought about pleasant memories, good things. I very seldom dwelt on the bad things that happened. You think back on good girl friends and family. I had a remarkable family behind me to look back upon.

Those who survived *in* the camps had to have a certain savoir-faire. Post-war survival is one thing, but *during* the war you needed this. I associated with such remarkable people on my own level—a very high level of POWs who operated on a very high intellectual level. You feed off each other and survive as a result. I'll never forget the conversations I had and overheard. I'll never forget Samson, who was a tower of strength without knowing it. A poet from San Francisco who later taught poetry at a university, Dave Kirk, felt very deeply. Such people almost made the POW experience worthwhile. They were wonderful people.

CALM UNDER PRESSURE

With a music background, I may have been fairly emotional, but it just seemed to me that the camp situation was cut and dried. We were there and had to put up with it as best we could. You got furious at the brutality, but you fed off each other. If one or two others helped maintain the calm and were leaders, you automatically copied them. Samson was such an example that we watched and copied him. He was so calm and matter of fact. "So I'll get beat up. So what?" You see him, and you take it. Tough. Some people today go off their rockers when they know they're going to get mugged.

As a pilot you learned time and again to face crises in which you simply have to control yourself. We were selected to be sure we weren't too excited in the cockpit. If one engine is out, you have another. Don't worry about it. We're going to land. This is the difference between a seasoned combat pilot and some civilian pilots. We could hear flak above the roar of the engine, so we knew it was pretty close. By both seasoning and nature we were not excitable. The Tinkers came to this county in 1630 from England on the sister ship of the Mayflower. We had a history of being engineers and doctors. Genetically, we may have been pretty unflappable for the most part.

Before I was captured, the Japanese were simply competitors. It was not personal. I was not very moved toward them one way or the other. When I got caught and was so poorly treated, my opinion changed. I saw how they mistreated animals and later learned how they treated their wives, and would follow any order to remain in the fold, including things like the Rape of Nanking. I resented my treatment. The people were 100% behind the military and obedient to authority. They were worse to the Chinese, but bad enough toward me. I became furious and told my captors several times they wouldn't get away with what they were doing. In Omuri, there had been a number of incidents with the Bird. One day, we were told to clean up for an honorable visitor. It was a Swiss ambassador representing the Red Cross. We knew we'd get bashed if we said too much. He came to Lempriere, whom he knew. Lempriere broke into French and told him exactly what was happening. The ambassador scolded the Bird and told him that after the war they would have to answer for what they were doing. We were disillusioned toward the Japanese. You realize it's a temporary hatred. As a pilot, you had a competition. You had a compound, building, or factory to hit, The fact that the target has people in it is incidental. At the time, I felt that I'd never cotton to these people. Later, when I went back to Japan, I realized that there were Japanese whom I became acquainted with that I liked—for instance, the interpreter and girls who waited on us, and others whom I'd meet one-to-one. My generation might be bitter toward a generation, but not toward the entire group. I'm not bitter still, so much as suspicious of the culture. Because of the limited quarters, they developed a tradition—a commonality, which is the antithesis to American individuality. Everything goes to the group. Many POWs return to Japan and enjoy the visit. Zampo went back and forgave his captors. Others meet former Japanese adversaries at Pearl Harbor. The hatred subsides but the indignation about some things remains. At the end of the war some people were hating the Japanese. But you mellow out over the years. You have to. You can't live with that sort of thing. Day after day, we were humiliated. You must have a good capacity for forgetting.

RATIONAL THOUGHT PROCESSES

Everyone was despondent at times, but I've never been black despondent. I'm sorry about things I haven't accomplished in life, but am not despondent.

When someone messed up in the aircraft and violated the discipline of aviation, for example, coming apart when we lost an engine, you'd correct him and express your indignation, but it didn't eat into your soul. I was mad, but there's a difference between being mad and despondent. You come close to being despondent when you lose a loved one. But it's remarkable how quickly you recover, even from the loss of a loved one, such as parents. You're sorry to see them go, but you can accept it when it's their time to go. It's more difficult when you lose a younger person, justifiably so.

I never thought things were so awful that I couldn't take it. You never really gave up as a POW. Your despondency was translated to anger at being kept there. There's a certain point at which you feel you've done everything you can to survive, at which point you turn to a divine being if you are so inclined and say, "Lord, I've done all I can, now it's in Your hands." After I was shot down, I supposed I was scheduled for execution. After beating me up thoroughly, they threw me into a closet. I was leaning against the wall, bleeding all over the place, my nose had been broken and a few other things. I thought, "This is as low as it gets. I can't get out of this. Lord, it's up to You."

SOCIAL SUPPORT

We got no letters. Support came through memories of family and from friends. The friends you have are very significant. If I'd been alone or with a bunch of louts, without relief through conversation, I might not have made it. Friendship enlarged your intellectual arenas. As I mentioned, Zampo brought that sugar that probably saved my life.

You don't bond unless you admire people. Those who were intellectual were also compassionate. A good intellectual sees all sides of situations. There is a cognizance of humanity about them.

You automatically connected when a word or phrase indicated that you were on the same wavelength. You listened to Lempriere. It was obvious that he was intelligent enough to be a lay minister. He had the *Book of Common Prayer* with him. He officiated at the funerals we had. It was obvious that he was a giant in this field. If you used a Shakespearean or biblical phrase, people knew you were of a particular character or education. It was a common meeting ground that made automatic friends. Growing up, I'd read a lot on my own and at school.

COMFORTABLE WITH EMOTIONS

I'm surely comfortable with my emotions. I'm not smug, but I'm not upset when I do become upset. It will pass. I don't brood or cherish a disaffection or insult. If I were mad at a co-pilot I let him know and usually it's done. You get it out or it oozes out of your system over a period of time. If you don't let your anger toward a person go—forgive or settle a score—you become prisoner of that person. This is from Shakespeare and it's a very good line.

At the time, I assumed combat was like a football game. I assumed nothing bad would happen to us. I felt consternation, and once in awhile I felt terrified for a moment.

Pilots are notorious about joking about their fear in the air because it reduces it to a joke so it doesn't fester. A brash friend of mine named Thoresen flew with me in Utah. We hit a bad standing wave and the aircraft fell out of the sky. He dropped to his knees, in a joke, I thought. He said, "Lord, Lord, get me down out of this and I'll be your true blue servant for evermore." After that he was True Blue Thoresen. I think he was half joking and half terrified. We made a joke out of it. I knew a bomber pilot flying over Germany, a real wit. After a frightening experience, he said, "Lord, does gas have lumps?" Bob Hope got a lot of material from the Air Force. Humor reduced the fear quickly. You wouldn't last long in flying if you were addicted to fear—fear that persists rather than a momentary alarm. So you settled your fear quickly. For insecurity, such as the worry of not making enough money, you have to just do something.

SELF-ESTEEM

I was very proud to be an Air Force officer and pilot. I was sure I could handle my aircraft and myself. Although it sounds silly to say it, my self-esteem was reinforced by the beautiful gal I was going with.

ACTIVE, CREATIVE COPING

As a POW you think about getting out as the ultimate revenge, as a gesture of freedom. Otherwise you'd be ashamed of yourself for doing nothing about it. Bill Harris had a plan to commandeer a wooden boat and ride out to sea and contact a submarine. It was suicidal. Since we couldn't realistically escape, I'd fantasize about life back home, hunting pheasants, going out with girlfriends.

After the war, I kept busy and occupied my mind, not just my body. Getting married gave me responsibility to keep my mind off things.

If you are creative you will be eternally prodded and never completely satisfied. Creativity stimulated my mind. I still have ideas about writing semi-fictional stories about the POW experience, aviation, and so forth.

SPIRITUAL AND PHILOSOPHICAL STRENGTHS

God

I think of God as the all-powerful being, the overall motivator of the universe. There is certainly a moral component. God is good, not evil. I don't think of God as a personal protector or defender for an individual who gets himself into trouble.

Meaning & Purpose

No doubt about it, in the camps you lived day by day. A French philosopher, Alain, said something very resonant and important: "Men are often happier than they wish." Even in the worst of circumstances, we always looked forward to the next meal, the next day, perhaps eventually being released." Our only purpose was survival from day to day and week to week, a momentary thing. If we survived, all we wanted to do was get out if we possibly could and go back and pick up from the past and do what we did, like hunting or seeing old friends. We had no idea of what was going on outside.

The war was a competition, but once I was imprisoned and met the opponent, I thought that the war was a very fine thing. I thought how horrible it would be if the Japanese ever got control of our country. They were so sure of themselves that they said they were selling California real estate on the Japanese stock exchange.

Morality

I've tried to be moral. A person who does what he thinks is right is a more pleasant person to be with and will be better able to cope. Treating human beings as friends covers the whole thing. Honesty is the prime morality. Don't lie to people or impinge on their space wrongly. I don't know how people can do thievery. Walking away with someone's money, knowing that it will be a hardship on someone else, takes indifference to social structure. There was very little thievery in camp. I never thought about stealing from buddies. It is foolish to get involved in sexual immorality. Fidelity is certainly good.

Love

I felt love for family and friends. In the camps, I tried to help others when possible, but there wasn't much we could do for each other. In a material way, I'd give away cigarettes or give cheese from the Red Cross package to the medics. I also tried to give consolation. There were so many people who were down that you'd try to cheer them up or divert their attention. We'd share recipes or recall old times. Zampo was a master at helping. On the train to Naoetsu, the Japanese gave us a cigarette but no matches. We didn't smoke so we gave ours away. Then Zampo took a shoelace and a stick and made a fire to light the cigarettes.

Living near the border, I recently had a Mexican immigrant show up at my house. The poor guy was just like you and me. He'd reached the end of his rope and had no water. So I made some calls for him and got him in contact with his employer who wired him some money so he could get a bus ticket. He was a decent individual. He became a person. It would have been very difficult to throw him out.

Optimism

I was very optimistic in a vague sort of way. I knew instinctively that somehow, sometime, we were going to get out of this damned thing. Thinking that we might survive until tomorrow and the anticipation of getting out was a bright light every day. After the war I was naturally optimistic that things would flow.

Humor

We frequently joked about our circumstances and the Japanese. They were comical even when they were being cruel and detestable. We thought what a ridiculous bunch of people they were. We laughed at our own predicament. We'd look at teach other, emaciated and dirty, fighting for a grain of rice, and you couldn't help but laugh.

We used the Japanese language to create jokes. If something was not going right, we'd say the Japanese word for *What is this?* (Nan-ei!) to other Americans and the Japanese dissolved in laughter.

We put on theater that was very subtle. In Japanese theater, everything was black and white. When we used subtleties and the Japanese caught on, they appreciated it. In Omuri, we put on "Desert Song." A man portrayed a female part and they got that. When on the good side of our guards, we burlesqued their actions (but never the officers or the Bird). The Japanese do not mimic themselves, but we did. We'd pretend to drag a rifle like one of the guards. Or we'd pretend to hit a POW as the guard would hit him. Here were these Americans mocking them. They'd realize it was ridiculous and eventually they would laugh. If someone limped, we'd walk behind him and limp to make fun of him. They also thought it was great when we made fun of each other.

The Bird asked us if we had rice. We said, "Sure, we do, at every meal." He was trying to say, "Do you have lice?" but couldn't, the "R" not being part of the Japanese vocabulary.

We were all food fiends. We had bets as to when the war would end. Chuck Bransfield was a Naval aviator and an heir to the Miller High Life Brewery. He bet a barrel of chocolate covered peanuts that the war would end before Christmas. Lo and behold, after the war some received such peanuts, delivered to their homes. He was a real wit. I also had a bet with a doctor for $500 and he sent it to me via Samson.

The British who were captured in Hong Kong brought along their instruments. When we put on "Desert Song" in Omuri, I sang the male lead. It was great and lifted our spirits very much. The Japanese thought that was amazing. They wanted to broadcast it, but we said that would be inappropriate.

I sang to troops in the barracks from the middle of the compound. The guys appreciated it. Pappy Boyington mentioned it in his book. I didn't realize he'd been so affected by it. We'd been asked to entertain the troops, and I thought it was only right to do my part. I sang melodic songs, like "Someday I'll Find You," "Drink to Me Only with Thine Eyes," and a bunch of songs from "Oklahoma."

Long View of Suffering

I gained the perspective that having gone through the prison camps, nothing could be worse. Since I made it through this, I'll be fine. After the war I could look at things that were going to happen more placidly. Things like running out of money didn't make the impression that they might have, had I not gone through these things. I didn't feel that we were really suffering in the prison camps. It was just something that happened, tough luck.

The worst part was when I first was captured and beaten and threatened with execution. I felt hopeless. That was the low point. The best part, next to the euphoria of being freed, was the Red Cross boxes. I got 1½ boxes the whole time in two years. The others were confiscated by the Japanese as war booty. One of the highlights was that a box came at Christmas time. Here was a chocolate bar. It tasted so unbelievable. You had forgotten how things tasted.

The experience helped me appreciate little things today. I know I appreciate food more. For the last three to four months, we were down to dried ferns and Korean millet without seasoning or vegetables to speak of. You don't know hunger until you've been hungry for two years. I saw another POW walking along the road on a work detail. He picked up a dead sparrow, de-feathered it, and put it in his mouth. That's hunger.

Maintaining Balanced Living

I've never had any addictions. I never smoked. If you sing you can't smoke. If you're flying you can't really smoke. Cigarettes were included in the Red Cross boxes. I gave mine away. I didn't drink to excess. After getting bombed twice when I was fairly young, I decided this was not the way to go. I occasionally have a rum and coke with lime, or a beer with food.

I can eat like a horse and still weigh 175 pounds. I've always had a good appetite. I like unusual foods. I cook Chinese, Hungarian, and whatnot. I make my own bread and soup, and retained Japanese recipes. *[For lunch we enjoyed his wonderful vichyssoise and homemade bread on the patio, served by Mrs. Tinker. Mr. Tinker told me not to pinch the waitress.]* My family has always been thin. I eat at least three meals a day and snacks—healthy food, very seldom get into junk. Lots of fruits and vegetables.

I get lots of exercise, but not through a formal exercise program. We hike a lot and spend a lot of time outdoors. I play golf, and can still play the course out behind the house near par. I used to play tennis. Nancy swims.

I usually slept from eleven to seven, but now I find I can get by with less sleep.

I like to listen to classical music. We both read quite a bit. We still travel often. We're headed for Oregon soon. I have two daughters in Phoenix. We email and they come to visit with care packages frequently. We like to go to restaurants for good food.

Advice to Younger Generations

Be grateful to your country without being chauvinistic about it. We've gotten a lot, now give back in some way, whether it's through the service, helping people, or improving the environment.

Be sensible about drugs.

As I get older, I think you have to have some means of income. Solidify your position. Get at least a small income.

Broaden your educational horizons, so that you have an appreciation of the arts and literature. Have an outdoor sport. Be a well-rounded person.

On leave in Mexico, 1946

Frank and Nancy Tinker,
Pearce Sunsites, AZ

Chapter 40

Byron Stanley Harris
Abandon Ship!

Byron Harris was a Marine gunner on the third USS Houston, *of which he painted a beautiful picture that hangs in his home. The 2nd USS* Houston *was sunk in February of 1942 as it courageously attacked the invading Japanese armada off of Java. The storied third USS* Houston *was launched in June of 1943 and would become part of the most formidable armada ever assembled. After his ship was struck by a torpedo, Harris was ordered to abandon ship.*

His wife Martha says: "He's straight as an arrow, honest to the nth degree. He is a good provider, easy going, quiet, and rarely riled. His feet are well planted." He has valiantly battled Parkinson's Disease for twelve years.

I was born November 6, 1924, in Frederick County, Virginia. I grew up poor, on a farm, in the same house I was born in. I had an older brother and older half sister (My mother's first husband had died in an industrial accident).

Mother ran the farm while Dad sold insurance. She worked our one horse in the garden and milked the cows. I hoed weeds, helped plant, and put hay in the barn.

Dad was born and raised in Tennessee. His father disappeared. I never knew what happened to my grandfather. Dad was 34 when he met my mother. They married in 1917. He gave her a ride in his Model T. Dad never spanked me, but he talked to me. He had rules. You didn't slam doors. He was quiet. He expected us to obey. My dad seemed more like a grandfather. He was in his forties when I was born. He was a fine man. Nobody living in that part of the country would say a word against him. We'd sell vegetables in town on the street. He'd always give people more than they paid for. That's the way he lived, giving people an extra measure.

Mother was very loving. She loved life, was joyful. She broadened my mouth a few times, she said. We teased her about being stout, and she said she was just big boned. We said, "Bones don't jiggle when you laugh," and she did love to laugh.

I worked 10-hour days on a nearby farm for fifty cents a day plowing and working a team of horses. I worked all summer to buy a bike for $21.88. A truck brought it in a crate. Dad made me finish shelling bushels of beans first. Then, I was in such a hurry to put it together that the handlebars weren't tight, and I ran it into a post. It didn't hurt the bike, but it beat the tar out of me.

For other jobs, I picked strawberries in the summer and picked apples in the fall for three cents a bushel. I also worked at a filling station 89 hours in a week for sixteen bucks. We didn't talk about the Depression. We just thought of it as the way things were supposed to be. There was no plumbing in the house. Only one room of the six was heated, the kitchen, which is where we all lived most of the time. I hated getting out in the snow. Our neighborhood was all woods then. Today, there are expensive houses all around.

In high school I was on the rifle team, and usually took first place in our meets. I played trombone in the band. The band played at summer community picnics. I met my wife after one of those picnics. She was 13. I was 15. I rode my bike nine miles to see her, asked her what she wanted to do, and she said, "Let's go bike riding." We also went to movies sometimes.

WORLD WAR II SURVIVORS - LESSONS IN RESILIENCE

I caddied one summer part-time. For fun, I made a little four-hole course on our farm in the cow pasture, and made five or six more holes on my neighbor's. I also went squirrel hunting, and walked a dirt road to a swimming hole three miles away. You were dirtier when you got back than when you started.

It was hard work, and we wanted to leave the farm, but we had a good life, and in retrospect, I'd prefer that life to the life of a boy today.

I graduated high school in 1941. I won a scholarship to Strayer's Business College in Washington, D.C., and enrolled in September. I was attending when the war broke out in December. All the men in college dropped out and joined the service. I joined the Marine Corps and went to boot camp at Parris Island, South Carolina, until May of 1942. I went to the naval air station in Jacksonville, Florida, for a year. I applied for sea duty and was assigned to the third USS *Houston*, a light cruiser, at Norfolk Navy Yard, where I was the gunner on a 20mm four-man crew anti-aircraft gun. I fired the gun that was on the main deck, port side.

Our shake down cruise went to Trinidad in February of 1944. Then we went through the Panama Canal and arrived in Pearl Harbor on May 6, 1944. We joined Admiral Spruance's Fifth Fleet. We took part in the invasion of the Marianas, including the bombardment of Guam and Tinian. The concussion of the big guns, that would go off right over our heads, deafened me in one ear. The Marianas Turkey Shoot, June 19, 1944, was the biggest carrier engagement of the war. Over 400 Japanese planes were destroyed by American planes and antiaircraft fire in a matter of hours. The Japanese fleet tried to outrun us back to Japan, but our carrier planes and subs sank three carriers and damaged others.

We bombarded Okinawa on October 10, 1944. We joined Admiral Halsey's Third Fleet off the coast of Formosa, now Taiwan, to strike the powerful base there with five carriers. The *Houston* downed eight low-flying aircraft near Formosa. The Japanese were sending planes from Formosa to attack us. We were the closest U.S. ship to Japan, only 60 miles due east of Formosa. Our ship was torpedoed by a Japanese plane on October 14, 1944. We were dead in the water and listing badly. We got the order to abandon ship. I did so with a good many others. I went down a steel ladder off the side of the ship. Then they decided to try to save the ship. It was torpedoed a second time two days after they got it under tow, but it still stayed afloat. The remaining crew downed the torpedo plane. I wasn't on the ship then.

I was in the water from about 7:00 p.m. until just before daylight the next morning. I had no life raft for the first eight hours. It was very cold and wet and dark. The Navy destroyers dropped depth charges on Japanese submarines, or else we'd probably have been eaten by sharks. There were ten to twelve-foot waves covered with oil. The fact that the water was in turmoil saved our lives because everyone was shooting at each other and there were explosions. It was like being in a foxhole half the time. Once or twice ships came near, but no one heard our whistles or hollering.

We drifted about 40 miles from the *Houston*. My buddy Bill Redd and I had gone overboard together. We were hanging on to each other in the water and watching the ship disappear by the light of the Japanese parachute flares. We finally came upon an eight-man life raft with a lone sailor in it, screaming and crying, completely gone. We crawled on it and he quieted down. Then we started pulling others in. A lot were hurt. We moved them to the center and then we got out of the raft to hold on from the outside, because many weren't able to hold on. Eventually we had 33 men in the raft.

Eventually, we were picked up by the destroyer USS *Grayson*. Our life jackets got saturated after eight hours, and I'd already been in the water nine hours. When the *Grayson* came upon our raft, they reversed engines. That upset the raft and drew us in the water. My life jacket pulled me down. I was under so long I lost consciousness. I woke up lying on someone's bunk on the *Grayson*. My oily clothes had been pulled off.

I learned that one of my best friends, who was from Richmond, Virginia, abandoned ship and was picked up by another ship, the *Santa Fe*. He went up to help the 20mm gun crew. They shot down a Japanese plane, which crashed on the side of the ship and burned my buddy to death.

A Marine gunnery sergeant couldn't swim. They'd brought another ship alongside the *Houston* to rescue the men but the water was too rough and the ships were banging together. He panicked and jumped off the ship before he was ordered. He fell into the water between the ships and was crushed. He and my buddy from Richmond were the only Marines we lost, along with about fifty-seven sailors. Before leaving the ship, I was supposed to be on the starboard side at number two gun—the abandon ship station. A Navy officer told us to go to the other side because the main deck was awash. I had had exactly the same dream a month or two before we were hit

I was transferred to the cruiser *Birmingham*, then to an old tanker and brought back to Pearl Harbor. I came back to California and got married December 1, 1944, in Virginia while on a thirty-day leave. Then I went back to the Treasure Island Navy Base in California. For two months, I worked on the night shift loading mail sacks for the railroad to make extra money. They sent us back to Pearl Harbor and the *Houston*. This was one of the hardest things to do. There was still a lot of damage and bodies were still in closed-off compartments. We took the *Houston* back to the U.S., where it was put into dry dock. We had to clean those compartments. The smell was terrible.

I was discharged in September of 1945 and intended to go back to college to be an accountant at Strayer in D.C., but we had a son on the way who was born in December of 1945. So I came home and painted my dad's barn, and painted and wired his house for electricity. I fixed up the old school house where I'd gone to first grade. They'd closed it and now my aunt owned it. We moved in with borrowed furniture and made it our first home. It had no water or inside plumbing. I became the first and only policeman at the time in the little village of Stephens City, Virginia, about three miles away. I later became a Virginia state trooper for five years. After that, I was a field claimsman for an insurance company for eight years, then I went to Richmond for five more years, as an office manager for the company. In 1964 we decided to move to Ft. Pierce, Florida, where I worked for the post office until I retired in 1986.

PTSD Symptoms?

I had nightmares for several years about the bulkhead being on fire, but no major difficulties otherwise.

What Helped You Cope?

CALM UNDER PRESSURE

My wife says I've always been calm, a deliberate type person, even when dating. When I was a state trooper, the county clerk told Martha, when she was working there, that no one was better on the stand.

I never had any personal thoughts or animosity toward the enemy. It was just an airplane. We didn't think of the consequences of shooting it down. They put us in a tight spot and our job was to stay alive and stay afloat. We concentrated on our weapons, knowing we only had a few seconds to fire. They'd pass by no more than fifty feet above us.

In the water, I had a dogged determination to live. There was no panic among the thirty-three men who were with me on the life raft when we were picked up. We weren't as scared as we should have been. We floated away from our ships in a five-knot current toward Formosa. We kept busy trying to keep our heads above water. I felt sad about the guys that died, but we just pressed on.

RATIONAL THOUGHT PROCESSES

Once a Japanese plane came straight over me. My biggest regret was that, just as that happened, my loader had pulled a magazine off, thinking I was getting low on ammunition. I asked him why in the world he had to do that. I could have blown his tail straight off. You don't get many shots like that. He was right, though. Things like that just happen.

In the water, we took the attitude that we had a rough time and would get through it. It never occurred to me that I wouldn't get out of there, one way or the other. The temptation to let go and give up didn't occur. My mind and body were working toward the same goal: get out of here and get your feet on dry land. It's a miracle that as many of us were picked up as were. We were scattered all over the ocean, but didn't lose a single Marine from drifting away. A lot of these boys were from strong farmer stock and had a strong work ethic and determination.

There was no widespread complaining or grumbling about being on the ship. We'd asked for sea duty and took it as it came. We all made mistakes, but I never lost faith in any of my men. They performed as well as possible.

SOCIAL SUPPORT

Martha and I were engaged. We wrote every day or two, even though we didn't get all of the letters, or sometimes they'd arrive weeks late. Every now and then the mail would be sent to us from another ship on a line with a pulley. Once the line broke and the sacks with the mail went to the bottom. Everyone was so disappointed. Her letters were so important. They made me wish she was here or I was there. My mother also wrote faithfully.

I chummed around with the same group of Marine friends. My friends were very important. To have no friends would have been terrible. Bill Redd, my buddy that I went overboard with, and I stayed friends for years before he died. We'd been friends ever since I went aboard. We visited back and forth. It was important to be in the water and in the life raft beside a friend.

My gun team was very close. We were friends as well as teammates. It seems like a lot of the men repressed the war memories. But as we matured and put the war behind us, the desire to get together again grew. We started going to reunions in 1980, and have kept up with each other.

COMFORTABLE WITH EMOTIONS

I got afraid sometimes, but I didn't get shaking afraid. Aboard ship, when asleep, you could be blown out of your bunk or torpedoed at any time, but I never felt great fear to the point that I couldn't perform my duties. When we were torpedoed, the ship went up 20 feet and then dropped down. My spotter had his earphones on. He said, "We took a fish." I was strapped in my gun. It nearly took the straps off. As soon as it hit the ship started listing. That was the time of my greatest fear. We just took fears as part of the game. Now, I talk more about what happened than I did during the war, such as with old buddies. My brother was in the Army Air Force, and as long as he lived, would never speak about what he did.

SELF-ESTEEM

My self-esteem was very good. I liked who I was and felt that I had something to contribute. I was probably one of the youngest sergeants in the Marine Corps. I made it aboard ship when I was 19. I wondered why I hadn't made it sooner.

ACTIVE, CREATIVE COPING

I got promoted quickly, because I was conscientious. I had a good relationship with all the people I dealt with, whether they were equal, above, or below me in rank. I never had any trouble with anyone, except one. I took part in everything that went on. I did what I was asked to do to the best of my ability. I knew that if I didn't, I wouldn't survive to tell about it.

There was one incident. The gunnery sergeant had rank over me. I didn't care much for him. I took a pop at him and was confined for three weeks, while Martha was up in New York visiting me toward the war's end. This was in March when the ship got back to the Brooklyn Navy Yard. My crew was supposed to go to work at one o'clock like everybody else. He told me to get my crew to work sooner. I told him my men would be there when they were supposed to be. He raised his arm to hit me, and that's when I hit him. I'd do it again, only harder. There aren't too many people I disliked, but he was one of them. My wife was there by herself at 19 in New York.

On the raft, we pulled many people out of the water. We pulled the Marine commander out. He got in and sat in the middle and tried to organize a paddle detail, but it didn't work. He told us to paddle with our hands against the current. I figured the best thing was to rest and keep ourselves alive, rather than wear ourselves out. There were no ships in sight. We just ignored him.

As a state trooper, everything—my car and uniform— had to be perfect, as things had been in the service. And people who were driving around had to drive perfectly *(laughing)*.

SPIRITUAL AND PHILOSOPHICAL STRENGTHS

God

I have always believed in God. I think of God as all-powerful. I think He let's us make decisions and lets things happen that He could prevent. God has never done anything mean. We can do anything we want to, but we pay the price for wrong choices. If the window is stuck open or shut, I don't think he is the one holding it. These things just happen. It's just part of an imperfect world, with imperfect people. It scares me when I hear people say that there is no God.

As a child in my family we went very regularly to church, unless there was snow or a farm emergency. I went to services on board ship. And I now attend regularly, health permitting.

Meaning & Purpose

We wanted to do all we could to get the war done and get back in one piece. It was a very patriotic time. After the Japanese attack, enlisting was the thing to do. When I told my dad I was joining the Marines, he said it was a tough outfit. I said I knew that and would go if he'd sign the paper. I was only seventeen.

Morality

A sense of morality is a great strength and a pretty good-sized job. We need to live a life so that when you walk down the street people don't point a finger for what you're doing wrong. What we considered right and wrong then, seems different from today. A little smooching is okay, but not doing what married people do, even when you're engaged. Being faithful to your wife is the thing to do. I've always been honest on my income tax; if anything has ever been wrong, it's been a mistake, not intentional. You're honest or you're not. I sure don't believe in stealing.

Says Martha, " He's always been straight lined. He didn't bend the rules playing golf, driving, or whatever."

Love

I'd help my fellow Marine, even if I didn't know him. I got along with all the guys. Love is very important, especially for your family. My last sister just died, so no one in my immediate family is left. Martha and I were engaged when she was seventeen, before shipping to the Pacific. On leave, after the *Houston* was torpedoed, we married. I loved the heck out of all my family.

Optimism

I take things as they come. I'm not a serious pessimist, but I try to anticipate what could go wrong. I try to have two of everything, like hearing aids or riding mowers. My wife says it's a wonder I don't have two wives. My faith gives me hope. I'd be very disappointed when I die, if things don't turn out right.

Humor

I am known as a dry humorist in my Sunday school class. *(When his wife started singing his praises, he quipped, "Say much more and I'll think I'm dead.")*. I have a picture of a friend and me on leave in New York, after we traded ties with the civilians. We were celebrating our return to the states and we ended up wearing polka dot ties. To get back on to base we had to conceal our ties with our handkerchiefs. We pretended we were blowing our noses.

Maintaining Balanced Living

Although I haven't had a formal exercise regimen, I loved golf and walked when I played, gardened, planted all the big trees around the house, and painted the house outside and inside. I have a very great affection for fishing. I went on week-long float trips in the Virginia wilderness. I built a homemade raft of inner tubes and plywood with a buddy who was in the Battle of the Bulge. I've surf fished a lot in Florida. Martha would beach comb when I fished.

I usually had jobs with shift work. I'd get a total of eight hours of sleep—five or six hours at a time, plus a two or three-hour nap. We've usually had balanced meals—meat, a starch, a green vegetable and a salad. Growing up, we ate farmers' meals—hearty, but not health conscious, until people became aware of healthy eating.

I was a sporadic drinker, never regularly or to excess. Maybe I'd have a cocktail at a party or before dinner. It has never caused a problem between us. I smoked in the Marines a bit, and thereafter intermittently and lightly. I really didn't like cigarettes, and haven't smoked in fifteen years.

In the '80s, I played a big bass with friends in a musical group just for fun. My wife and I liked to travel. We've been to every state in the union, except two, and to Canada, Mexico, Panama, and Europe. We've been very active in our church.

Advice to Younger Generations

Tough it out. Make a rule that everything you do is being done the best you can do.

Be upright. If you have a penny in your pocket that belongs to the company or to someone else, get it out of there. Don't go to bed with it.

Don't try drugs. It's imperative to have a clear mind under pressure.

Byron and Martha Harris

Byron and Martha at their Ft. Pierce, Florida, home

Chapter 41

Brigadier General Oscar Esko Davis
Serving in Three Wars

At 5'9" retired General Oscar Esko Davis was a career Army officer who saw combat in three wars. In WWII, he served in the Pacific Theater. In demeanor, he is quiet, resolved, and self-possessed. Wife Patty says, "I feel lucky to have had Oscar. We've been really happy. He has a terrific sense of humor." Daughter Candace says, "My father was the wind beneath my wings, like the song says." Oscar and Patty have four children.

I was born in Tucson, Arizona, July 18, 1918. My middle name, Esko, was the name of my uncle, an early-day WWI pilot. I was the oldest. I had a younger sister and brother. Tucson was a desert town, a wonderful place. When I was growing up, 70% of Tucson's 25,000 residents were Mexican. A lot of my playmates were Mexicans, great people.

My mother had come from Milwaukee with her parents for her father's health. My father had come from Little Rock, Arkansas. He used to ride horses into town to court my mother.

I was a Boy Scout. I went to the YMCA, initially to learn to swim, because there wasn't much water in Tucson. This was the athletic hub for grade school kids. I played basketball there and went to summer camps in the mountains. My mother sent me to Page Military Academy in Los Angeles for the 5th and 6th grades, because she was afraid I wasn't getting a good education.

From sixth grade until college I worked for a florist, making bouquets and driving the truck. I started at twenty-five cents and hour and later doubled that. I was lucky to get a job. Most kids couldn't. Everyone was in the same boat in the Depression. We didn't have a lot of money, but I didn't realize we weren't very rich.

I had chores around the house, like keeping the yard up and going to the store. In those days, we had neighborhood stores. My mother would phone her favorite butcher and I'd go to pick up the meat for the meals. Of course, the kids were so spread out that I thought I did more than anybody. My brother was only eleven years old when I got married. I kidded him that we were going to use him for the flower girl. That really upset him and he never forgave me.

I always liked horses and ranching. An uncle had a ranch. A lot of summers, he'd let me go and work there. I enjoyed going out with the cowboys. He fed me, but didn't pay me. I also liked to hunt blue quail with my father.

Dad was a real estate broker. I had a great feeling for my father. He had very high morals. He was strict in many ways and lenient in others. He never got on me for bending a fender or for big things, but pounded me on little things. For example, one time I referred to my mother as "the old lady," a term I'd heard someone use. I didn't think that was derogatory, but Dad scared me to death and I never used that expression again. He put ladies on a pedestal and believed you should always be a gentleman. He was such a wonderful guy and a good man, but at times he'd explode and shout and scare us. I think I inherited that. I've tried to curb my temper for a lot of years, and think I have.

Mother was a wonderful person. We'd take our problems to her. She was very supportive always and very loyal to her family. She was kind of quiet, but a tiger in protecting her children. She sacrificed a lot for the family. I was fortunate to have such good parents. We were a close knit family. We lived next door to my mother's parents. As a family, picnics were a big thing. Sometimes, we'd go to the desert for picnics.

As far as we were concerned, the Depression hit mostly around 1935 to 1937. We were never short of food. There were a lot of things I couldn't do, like go to a show, which cost money, but everyone was in the same boat. I probably played too much sports and neglected my studies. I was kind of small, and in high school mostly ran track—broad jump and dashes. I competed in college as well. My claim to fame in college was that I competed against Jackie Robinson in a dual track meet between UCLA and the University of Arizona. Robinson was an all-around star at UCLA. His events in track were the 100 yard dash and the broad jump. He won the 100 yard dash in 9.6 seconds during our meet, close to a world record. He took one broad jump and won that with a world class type of jump. Then he went to play in a baseball game against USC. The rest of us jumped all day trying to catch up. I jumped my best jump ever, but was still a couple of feet short.

The University of Arizona, where I attended college, was a land grant college, and you were required to take ROTC for two years. If you wanted to get a commission, then you had to take ROTC for the last two years. Well, to show how, sometimes, frivolous decisions affect your life: the university was a cavalry ROTC school. I learned that you could draw horses for weekend dates, if you took the advanced ROTC. So I enrolled in that and graduated in 1941 with my commission and orders for the 1st Cavalry Division. 1941 was quite a year. I went on maneuvers in Louisiana and we were pushed to exhaustion. We tested the use of horses and found that the cavalry probably couldn't exist in war. After maneuvers, I was married to my wonderful wife, Jeannette (Patty), of now 61 years. We met at the university and went together the last two years. She's the best thing that ever happened to me. I'd planned to go to law school, but then Pearl Harbor changed my thinking.

I was shuffled around in the cavalry and realized that it probably wouldn't be a factor in the war, and so I applied for parachute school in 1943. I was kept at Fort Benning, Georgia, as an instructor, but all my friends were going overseas and I wanted to join them. So I joined the 541st Parachute Infantry Regiment and went to the Philippines as replacements for the depleted 11th Airborne Division. We chased Japanese remnants in Luzon for a month or two, then went to Okinawa for a week, prior to moving into Japan for occupation. There was a tragic incident in my battalion during our short stay in Okinawa. Although the island was securely in U.S. hands, there were still Japanese hiding in caves and we were told to avoid the caves. One of my lieutenants was real curious and went into one and got shot in the head. I observed a lot of destruction when we landed in Japan, but the Japanese were very industrious and were cleaning up quickly. I was greatly surprised by the attitude of the Japanese. General MacArthur kept the Emperor in place and used him. When the Emperor said that they wouldn't fight, they didn't. In general the people were docile and receptive to our requests. It was hard to believe, because they had been such ferocious fighters. They readily turned in all their weapons, including stacks of samurai swords. I've heard criticism of Truman's decision to use the atomic bomb, but I also understand that probably one million on each side would have been lost in an invasion. They'd have fought to the death. My regimental commander suggested I apply for a regular Army commission. I liked the life and so I did.

I fought in Korea with the 45th Division, a fine Oklahoma National Guard unit. Initially, I commanded a battalion, one of the first ones to replace a Thai outfit. They had used frozen Chinese soldiers as sandbags. Toward the spring, the dead soldiers started to smell terrible, so we had to bury the Chinese. I went right from Pork Chop hill, where we got beat up, to Old Baldy. I lost a lot of good men trying to occupy those hills as outposts.

In Vietnam, I was the senior liaison officer with I Force V, coordinating the operations of Korean units with the Americans. Then I was deputy to Gen. S. H. Matheson, who'd been with the Band of Brothers in WWII. Matheson commanded the 1st Brigade, a separate brigade of the 101st Airborne Division before the rest of the division arrived in Vietnam. He was country smart, brilliant in tactics, and concerned for his men—one of the best leaders I ever worked for. I had a break in assignments to Vietnam in 1967—I was returned to the United States to take helicopter training prior to joining the 1st Cavalry Division. I was with the 1st Cavalry Division during the Tet Offensive and on several occasions flew under fire into the walled city of Hue. On one occasion, it was to set up a fire coordination center, and on another trip, it was to take General Abrams to speak to Major General Troung, the Vietnamese commander of the 1st Viet Airborne Division, in charge of allied forces holding onto the northeast portion of Hue. The rest of the city was in enemy hands.

After retiring from the Army in 1972, I managed a bank on the post of Fort Bragg for two years. This was not my cup of tea. I found a very challenging job in Israel, as a camp commander for an engineering company, building airfields for the Israelis in accordance with President Carter's Camp David Accord. When this venture was completed I returned to the United States and pursued the game of golf.

PTSD Symptoms?

I had occasional nightmares, maybe after I overate, but that decreased over a year or two and then stopped. This was mostly after Korea. I also had to adjust my language. In the woods, around men in combat, you learn to swear. I have been working on that ever since. Otherwise, I wasn't bothered by PTSD symptoms.

What Helped You Cope?

Some personalities handle stressful situations better than others. Some people are more sensitive than others. It's tough sometimes. I think about people killed around me and I remember them in dreams once in awhile, but that's it.

CALM UNDER PRESSURE

I stayed calm mostly because I felt a responsibility. If you command, your troops depend on you. I can't let these guys down, so I force myself to stay calm and think.

I regarded combat mostly as a mission to get territory or capture the enemy. I wanted to protect my men and myself. I wasn't enjoying the killing, absolutely not. Very few people enjoy that. The toughest thing for me occurred when I was 12. I was with a cowboy on my uncle's ranch hunting for deer just for meat, not fun. I broke the deer's leg with a rifle shot. We finally caught up to the deer. He made me cut his throat. Today, I'd never shoot a deer. I don't like to hunt or kill things. In combat, you get so excited you do things to save lives and don't think about it.

RATIONAL THOUGHT PROCESSES

Regarding mistakes, most people try their best. Sometimes mistakes are made, but you try to avoid mistakes. If a mistake is serious and caused by negligence, you must hold people accountable. Otherwise, you try to learn from mistakes and correct them.

Once, the sergeant in charge of a parachute maintenance unit improperly packed a parachute. A man was killed as a result. The sergeant had been outstanding for years, but it got by him. It was hard to do, but I had to have him tried. It was very difficult. He was usually very careful. I hated to do it, but he served time for negligence. I felt sympathy, but there was no doubt whose fault it was.

I almost did a terrible thing one time. I was training at Ft. Campbell, getting the men used to facing tanks. I had them dig foxholes in the sandy soil, then guided tanks over the holes so that their tracks straddled the holes, not thinking that the weight of the tanks would collapse the holes. We dug the soldiers out of the holes, and thank the Lord they were okay. I said I'd never make that mistake again. I'll think it through better in the future. Thereafter, I was especially careful in training. I wanted to teach the soldiers without getting anyone hurt.

I was a fairly hard disciplinarian with my children. I don't know if I've ever spanked. They usually went to Patty, who was so sweet and understanding, to cushion the blow before she got to me. I tried to be reasonable. My son had long hair at one point. I told him he looked like a clown. He explained that he looked at me and my dad and wanted to enjoy his hair while he had it. I understood. My daughter Candace was independent, like me, and we clashed, although now we are best of friends. Once she slammed the door in anger and I told her to go back and close it right. It took her five attempts, and by that time we were both laughing. But she never slammed it again. I have become softer as I've gotten older, more understanding. I used to be black and white as a lieutenant; less so as I got to be a parent.

SOCIAL SUPPORT

I was fortunate. I always had great support from my wife, parents, and friends. They'd do anything for me. My wife wrote me in all three wars. In WWII, we wrote every day that we could. In Korea and Vietnam I'd come in and make a tape recording to send to her nearly every day.

I really loved cigars at one point. Dad went out of his way to ship my favorite kind to me.

I felt close to buddies, both officers and some enlisted men. In particular, Paul Huff was my command sergeant major and the first airborne Medal of Honor winner in WWII (Sicily). He was a country boy from Tennessee. In Sicily, he got behind a group of Germans and started picking them off. They thought he was an entire unit and 27 of them surrendered to him. We were friends. He was loyal. We'd do anything for each other. For example, when my daughter's car broke down one night near where he was living, he went out and got her and took her to his house and got her car fixed. He was that kind of a friend.

In Korea, a buddy, a tough fullback at Tennessee who played in the Rose Bowl, was a good guy to have around when artillery was coming in. He wasn't afraid and calmed me down. He'd been hit in the head and had a plate in his head, and maybe didn't know any better.

COMFORTABLE WITH EMOTIONS

I'm fairly emotional. I can get emotional about friends and family. I've outlived a lot of my friends. Just thinking of them I get choked up.

(Laughing) I think everyone is afraid in combat. A lot of people are stupid and do dangerous things. I've never tried to be stupid. As an officer you didn't admit to others or show you were afraid. For some reason I started to get afraid once, when doing parachute jumping at night. There was considerable turbulence. But I didn't dare show it. I had men in the plane. Concern for my soldiers helped to allay my own fears.

It's always good to talk about your concerns. In Korea I was going from one command post to another one night. I thought I saw a Chinese or North Korean moving out there. I jumped into a hole with a GI in it. I said, "Did you see anything out there?" He said, "No, Major, out here at night you see a lot of things you think are coming at you." I said, "Ok, buddy." Humor helped. I did used humor a lot.

I didn't tell my wife much, other than to say we had a tough time in a particular area, because I didn't want to worry her.

SELF-ESTEEM

Oh, yes, I liked who I was. I think I prepared myself well. I worked hard at being an officer. I really saw the need to know more. The more you know about what you're doing the more confident you are. I learned and worked hard at my career.

ACTIVE, CREATIVE COPING

I didn't dare relax too much. I probably slept less than anyone in my unit. I tried to be on top of situations as much as I could, to stay ahead. Until they have had a lot of experience, soldiers are lazy. You have to get them to dig in, even if they are tired or cold. In Korea, a lot of our guys got too comfortable in their sleeping bags to get out and fight in raids and they were killed. Cooks can get tired and lazy and you have to kick them to get food to soldiers on the lines, but then they have a sense of accomplishment.

SPIRITUAL AND PHILOSOPHICAL STRENGTHS

God

I believed in God. Most people in combat want to believe in something. I can remember thinking, "God, if you get me out of this situation, I'll do better." I relied on Him when times got tough, and relied on myself most of the other times. I prayed. My mother sent me to church when I was a youth. I went fairly regularly. We had a real fine, strong youth counselor who took us on hikes. I go to church every Sunday now.

Meaning & Purpose

Three things that happened in my life are frozen in time in my mind: Pearl Harbor, the assassination of Kennedy, and 9/11. Most people can tell you exactly where they were and what they were doing when those startling events occurred. Pearl Harbor gave us a purpose to fight. I felt a real need to do something about it. What worried me most was Vietnam. The longer I was there, the more I saw how rotten their government was. It bothered me that the South Vietnamese didn't have the same spirit and incentives to fight as the North. They didn't feel the loyalty to the government that the NVA did. They didn't seem to have a sense of purpose or know they were fighting for a better life. They weren't fighting for democracy, because they didn't have democracy. And we didn't have our own country's backing. In WWII, we had that loyalty to our government. I was fighting for democracy and the country was behind us.

Morality

Morality is extremely important. I always felt that American soldiers basically were wonderful soldiers. They didn't want to let their buddies down and did heroic things. There were very few in any outfit that I felt ashamed of. One man, on a patrol in Vietnam, raped a civilian. I got that SOB tried.

I was very proud of the way most Americans conducted themselves. I was against mistreatment of civilians and wouldn't allow it. I always corrected the use of derogatory terms for the enemy and explained that they were good people, just a little different than we are in their way of life.

Morality covers honesty, being comfortable with what you do, following your conscience. My mother built my character. She told people that I was always honest, that I'd never take a coin from her purse. Once I did and felt so bad I said I'd never do that again. Her faith in me led me to want to live up to that. You don't lie to get yourself out of trouble.

To be moral is to let people know what you expect and back your people up. You can't fool the people who work for you—they'll pick out phonies in a minute. Don't pretend to care, if you are a self-promoter who won't support them.

I've always felt lucky to be married to the lady that is my wife. There are plenty of gals I've looked at and said, "Wow," but I couldn't be unfaithful.

Love

Love, comraderie, brotherhood—that's what really kept me in the service. I got so much joy out of the association I had. I'd never trade that for anything. Friendship is the richest thing you can have. I'm outliving a lot of my friends but I still keep contact with my old buddies. We still meet and socialize with old Army friends in various parts of the country. One of my buddies, Butch Kendrick, who lives nearby, has been with me in jump school, Japan, Europe, and stateside assignments. He is like a brother, a joy to be around. We get together in a group of Old Soldiers for dinners each quarter. *[See Chapter 29]*

Optimism

I want to think that everything is going to be better. I just want to believe that. I want to believe I'm going to succeed in whatever I do or I won't undertake the project.

Humor

I like people with a good sense of humor. I like to be around them. It's a joy to laugh and enjoy somebody's company. I didn't like to work for or be around sour pusses.

When I think of humor, I think of a person who gets joy out of life, who isn't so serious that he doesn't see the light side. I can see humor in people's mannerisms and things they do. I look at friends, trying to be so serious and they are really not. I can see humor in that. I laugh a lot. I'm glad I do.

Long View of Suffering

In combat, you talk about bonding. A tough situation bonds together people from different backgrounds. You get really close. That's happened to me many times.

Living through a hell of a challenge, you gain some strength. You're bound to acquire knowledge, experience, and confidence.

Maintaining Balanced Living

I've exercised all of my life. I love athletics. In the airborne we ran ourselves to death and did countless pushups. Every morning I exercised at home and with my unit—calisthenics and running. I belong to a top-of-the-art health club and have a specialized daily program. I've been a golf nut.

I've always gotten up early. I usually slept from 11:00 or 12:00 to 6:00 while in the service. Six or seven hours were plenty. Lately I'll get seven or eight hours of sleep.

I've always liked breakfast, a light lunch and dinner. I eat lightly now. I try to eat balanced meals—fruits, grains, vegetables.

I never smoked cigarettes. I started cigars in the Army and smoked them until 15 years ago, when the doctor scared me. I like a drink with my wife every night.

I enjoy everything with my wife. We've traveled frequently, played golf, socialized, did many things. I read when I can. Each Friday I go out to lunch with friends..

Advice to Younger Generations

Have concern for your fellow man. Friends and friendship are extremely important. We used to be close in the Army. We were thrown together and did everything together: lived, socialized, trained, worked, played, and we were proud of our units. We took care of each other. We didn't have social service agencies helping military families. We looked after each other. We were a family. That's missing today.

You'd better be happy with what you're doing or you can't be a success. I looked forward to every day in the service. Each day had a varied challenge. If they hadn't kicked me out, I'd still be in the Army. I loved what I was doing.

Knowledge is power. Get educated.

In ROTC at the University of Arizona, 1941

At Ft. Benning, GA, following the Korean War. Davis is front row, third from right. To his left is Butch Kendrick with whom he still eats breakfast every Saturday.

Preparing to jump with his son, Waddy, right, on his son's qualifying jump, 1969

General Oscar and Patty Davis

Chapter 42

Epilogue
Portrait of Resilience

Taken together, the stories of these remarkable survivors shed great light on resilience and permit us to paint a portrait of the resilient individual. As we explore this portrait, I will add my impressions from these interviews, interviews not included in this book, and other research.

DEVELOPMENT

Resilience is, in one sense, a confidence that develops from experiences such as hard work, challenging training, athletic competition, self-reliance, making due with little, learning to work with others, and the realization that all people are in the same boat in life. Generally, this confidence was developed prior to immersion into combat. As a general rule, resilience tends to develop over the life span, not in a moment.

Although there were a few exceptions, most resilient survivors enjoyed the security and stabilizing influence of close-knit families—"close-knit" being used repeatedly to describe their families. The divorce rate among their parents was low, but most of those whose parents did divorce had the security of at least one stable adult figure or role model in their lives. Discipline and the teaching of values (such as honesty, responsibility, and respect for property and people) were evident. While pre-war life was hard for many of the survivors, there was the sense that it was also happy and worth returning to.

PHYSICAL PREPARATION AND HABITS

These resilient survivors understood the mind/body connection and have taken exceptionally good care of their bodies. This care has undoubtedly contributed to their longevity and sound mental health. Over their adult lives they have averaged 7.6 hours of sleep nightly, more than one half-hour more than American adults presently get. Almost all had and still have exercise programs. None were sedentary. One commented that his wife made him give up skate boarding for his 81st birthday. All ate three meals a day, save one who ate two. None were smoking at the time of the interview. Half had never smoked despite the availability of tobacco during the war years. More than half either never drank alcohol, or had quit. Most of the rest would be described today as light drinkers.

BALANCED LIVING

In addition to healthy living, the survivors also have lived balanced lives with varied interests, ranging from hobbies to reading, traveling, service to meaningful causes, athletics, worship, and entertainment. Many of these interests were shared with their spouses. One mentioned that his beloved wife loved bridge, but she did not want it said on her tombstone that she *only* played bridge. So she designed a bridge marathon program that has earned over $350,000 for the rehabilitation of hospitalized children over the years. We might speculate that varied interests provide healthy distraction from traumatic experiences.

SOMETHING DEEPER

It became evident that these survivors—and perhaps this is the essence of resilience—felt great love: They loved life, their country, their families, their friends, God, freedom, and principles more than pleasure. They were not burdened by hatred or lasting bitterness. One who had been tortured sadistically by his captors returned to Japan. There he located his former captors, forgave them, and embraced them. Releasing bitterness facilitated his healing. A German prisoner of war, who saw 90% of his comrades die from starvation in the Russian prison camps, counsels younger generations to not let wrongs embitter them, but to overcome bitterness and not judge. It appeared that great love enabled these survivors to endure and overcome hardship courageously.

CALM UNDER PRESSURE

These survivors had the extraordinary ability to calmly focus under pressure—perhaps because they had a *reason* to perform, be it to protect their comrades, their countries, or their futures, or to set a strong leadership example. Again, their judgement was not clouded by negative thoughts, malice, or impulsiveness. Some people today think that combatants need to be motivated by hatred toward the enemy. It would appear that duty and principle are far more effective motivators, and result in far fewer psychological casualties.

RATIONAL THOUGHT PROCESS

This group of survivors was remarkably free of the common thought distortions that underlie PTSD, depression, problem anger, anxiety, and other mental disorders. Although the desire for excellence was palpable, demanding perfection or holding unrealistic expectations of self or others was rare. The faults of self and others were generally accepted, with little dwelling on mistakes. There was little name-calling or judging ("How could I judge when I was scared, too?"), which tend to promote intense anger or disappointment. Also infrequently observed were catastrophizing ("This is too awful to bear!") and blaming, which tend to leave one feeling powerless. Instead, frequent expressions of appreciation and gratitude—for pay, meals, friendship, freedom, and the like—overshadowed the expected grousing.

COMFORT WITH EMOTIONS

Resilient people tend to be comfortable with the full range of emotions, and can regulate negative emotions. They do not deny or avoid unpleasant emotions, for anesthetizing these also tends to numb the ability to experience positive emotions. Instead, they acknowledge emotions such as fear or grief without shame, express them (or suppress them until the time is appropriate to do so), and then move on. It was noteworthy that many in the veterans had written their own accounts of their WWII experiences. They seemed to understand that feelings are normal, and that it is better to talk about distressing events and emotions than to keep them bottled up. This is consistent with considerable research indicating that verbalizing traumatic memories improves both the mood and the immune system.

SELF-ESTEEM

There is general agreement that self-dislike is a risk factor for PTSD, depression, and other stress-related mental disorders. Conversely, wholesome self-esteem is central to sound mental health and coping. I have defined self-esteem as being a realistic, appreciative opinion of oneself. That is, one with self-esteem sees one's strengths and weaknesses accurately, and still accepts oneself (i.e., feels favorably toward oneself despite one's faults). Those with self-esteem are secure in their inner worth and dignity, feel quietly glad to be who they are, and are motivated to grow and develop in satisfying ways. They do not need to be arrogant or superior, nor do they feel inferior to others or less worthwhile as people.

With this secure foundation of worth, they know that they can meaningfully contribute in their own unique ways.

Self-dislike was absent in all of these survivors. As already mentioned, this group of survivors had developed a strong and realistic sense of self-confidence in the crucible of experience. While this confidence occasionally bordered on youthful cockiness, it was tempered by humility and respect for others. They had a sense of wholesome pride— not the arrogance that says "I am better than I really am or I am better than you as a person," but the quiet and deep sense of satisfaction gained from living well. There was little self-aggrandizement or an inflated, unrealistic sense of self. Indeed, many seemed reluctant to sound boastful. Others used a charming self-deprecating humor to remind themselves and others that each person has limits and still has much to learn. Because of their inner security, they enjoyed the pursuit of excellence, without being joylessly driven toward unrealistic, perfectionistic demands. In short, these survivors seemed "comfortable in their own skins," but their healthy self-regard did not exceed their empathy for others or their concern for principles and the common good.

ACTIVE, FLEXIBLE COPING

There was no quit or passivity in this group of survivors, as symbolized by the many who day after day went forward and did their best. Pride prevented quit. These individuals were characterized by determination, perseverance, courage, and the will to overcome adversity.

When confronting obstacles, these survivors were creative improvisers. Some POWs created theatrical productions to lift spirits. One POW occupied his mind by making a book of recipes and stories out of discarded cigarette paper, an ornately carved box from wood scraps, and a leather pouch. Other POWs created escape fantasies when escape was impossible. On the battlefield, when one plan was thwarted, innovations were often tried.

After the war, an active approach to life (including physical activity) seemed to facilitate recovery and reintegration into normal, healthy living.

SPIRITUAL AND PHILOSOPHICAL STRENGTHS

One's deepest attitudes undoubtedly influence one's ability to cope in profound ways. All of those interviewed had a belief in God, save one respectful agnostic. Most perceived God as being kind and loving, not vindictive. Although it was not unusual to hear survivors wonder why so much suffering is allowed, many prayed frequently, and still find comfort from worship, prayer, and belief in an afterlife.

What deep satisfaction ensues from knowing we are fulfilling a meaningful purpose! The Holocaust survivor Viktor Frankl has noted that a sense of meaning in one's life can help one survive even the worst conditions. Certainly, these survivors' engagement in a meaningful cause enabled them to persist and endure. Without exception, they were clear about why they were fighting, be it to protect their loved ones, their brothers in arms, their country, or the world from tyranny. Most also wanted to return to family and live a fruitful life.

This was an extremely moral group. In addition to mentioning chaste courtships and marital fidelity, they also frequently related morality to honesty, treating others with respect, refusing to steal from buddies, and refusing to mistreat enemy POWs or civilians. They understood the relationship between morality and inner peace, self-confidence, self-respect, leadership, and trusting relationships. One is reminded of Winslow Homer's observation that with integrity, "All is lovely outside my house, and inside my house and myself." Traumatic exposure can strip the soul bare; it is good to like what we see. Perhaps moral pride is an important component of survivor's pride.

Frankl also noted love's essential role in survival. As mentioned previously, these survivors loved deeply. The bonds forged with family and comrades who became like family were frequently cited as important factors in sustaining their ability to carry on. Indeed, in the prison camps and on the front lines, those bonds were often literally life saving. Sometimes these bonds were described as love, sometimes as brotherhood, camaraderie, respect, or friendship.

Optimism might be regarded as the attitudinal foundation for active coping. The realistic optimist assumes that with effort things can be better. As one on Iwo Jima said, "The only way I'd survive was to look at each day as a new day and adapt." While defeat occasionally was mentioned in understandable circumstances, this was a fundamentally optimistic group who believed they would prevail and return to a bright future.

Every survivor felt that humor was essential to lighten things up and ease tension. Humor came in many forms: playful pranks, laughter, good-natured ribbing, nicknames, and noting the ridiculous. It is a testament to the strength of human nature that humor can surface even in the direst circumstances. Humor bonds and reminds us that we are deeper and better than the chaos around us.

Finally, these survivors were able to take the long view of suffering. That is, they could endure suffering, seeing beyond its capacity to defeat and dispirit. Indeed, suffering was perceived as something that revealed strengths and caused strengths to be developed. Sometimes what was revealed was the strength to bounce back after being vulnerable, or to control a temper whose expression would invite torture from prison guards. Suffering led to memories of friendships, to appreciation of life and good leadership, to the development of character and a work ethic, to the discovery of a new purpose in life, to respect for others for what they could do under pressure, to the belief that good can overcome bad, and to perspective (e.g., a traffic jam is not WWII). As Frankl (1959, pp. 76-81) wrote: "There is purpose in bearing suffering with high moral behavior; only a few keep their full inner liberty (in prison camps), yet suffering permits the exercise of moral strength, or spiritual greatness... Only the men who allowed their inner hold on their moral and spiritual selves to subside eventually fell victim to the camp's degenerating influences...Don't overlook the opportunities to make something positive of camp life...one could make a victory of those experiences, turning life into an inner triumph."

Resilience, then, characterizes people at their best. It enables people to endure and rebound from adversity, and to function effectively, sometimes extraordinarily, under duress. And having solidified these strengths under fire, resilience then promotes growth across the lifespan. Like most personality traits, it seems that people start out life with different levels of resilience, but resilience can be cultivated. These profiles of resilient survivors certainly suggest what is possible. My impression is that the survivors in this book would feel deep satisfaction in knowing that their stories have in some way benefited others, encouraging each of us to become ever more resilient.

Appendices

Appendix I

Key Dates

General

October, 1929	U.S. stock market crashes, beginning the Great Depression
September 18, 1931	Japan invades Manchuria
November 8, 1932	Franklin D. Roosevelt elected as President
January 31, 1933	Adolf Hitler named Chancellor of Germany
March to June, 1933	Congress creates Civilian Conservation Corps (for 17-25 year olds, who get room, board, medical care and $30/month, most of which is sent home to families); Tennessee Valley Authority, Federal Deposit Insurance Corporation. (In October of this year Einstein arrives in U.S. as refugee from Germany; in 1939 he urges FDR to begin atomic weapons research)
1935	Executive orders create Works Progress Administration (renamed Works Projects Administration in 1939, formed to build hospitals, schools, airports, highways and parks) and Rural Electrification Administration (to bring electricity to rural areas)
July 7, 1937	Japan invades China
October 16, 1940	U.S. draft begins
April 12, 1945	FDR dies

European Theater*

August 23, 1939	Soviet-German Non-Aggression pact signed
September 1, 1939	Germany invades Poland. Two days later Great Britain and France declare war on Germany. Sixteen days later Soviet Union invades Poland.
May 10, 1940	Winston Churchill replaces Neville Chamberlain as Prime Minister of Britain. Three days later he promises Britain "blood, toil, tears and sweat."
July-October, 1940	Battle of Britain (Luftwaffe bombing campaign)
June 22, 1941	Germany invades U.S.S.R.
December 7, 1941	Japan attacks Pearl Harbor, killing 2433 Americans. U.S. declares war on Japan next day. Italy and Germany declare war on U.S. December 11, 1941.
January 20, 1942	Germany adopts a "final solution" policy that would result in the death of 6 million Jews
June 12, 1942	First U.S. air combat mission. B-24's based in Egypt raid Ploesti, Romania, oil fields.

August 17, 1942	U.S. Eighth Air Force makes first raid on European target in France
November 8-11, 1942	Operation Torch. Allies land in North Africa.
May 12, 1943	Axis forces in North Africa surrender (More than 11,000 Americans killed or wounded in Tunisia Campaign)
July 1943	Combined bomber offensive against German industry begins
July 9-August 17, 1943	Operation Husky, Sicily Campaign
August 1, 1943	Operation Tidal Wave. U.S. B-24s bomb Ploesti, Romania, losing 54 planes, 55 seriously damaged
September 3, 1943	Allies land on Italy; Italian army surrenders shortly thereafter
September 9-19, 1943	Battle of Salerno, U.S. Fifth Army
January 22-May 24, 1944	Battle of Anzio, U.S. Fifth Army. Approximately 5500 Americans killed, 15,000 wounded.
January 22-September 9, 1944	Rome-Arno Campaign. Approximately 11,000 Americans killed, 28,000 wounded.
March 6, 1944	Berlin Raid results in loss of 69 U.S. bombers and 11 fighters
April 5-mid-August, 1944	U.S. Fifteenth Air force bombers raid Ploesti, losing more than 200 planes
May 18, 1944	Monte Cassino falls after four-month battle
June 4, 1944	U.S. Fifth Army enters Rome
June 6, 1944	Operation Overlord, Normandy Invasion (D-Day)
July 25, 1944	Operation Cobra, U.S. Third Army breaks out of St. Lo
August 15, 1944	Operation Dragoon. Allies land on southern coast of France.
September 15, 1944-March 21, 1945	Rhineland Campaign
September 17-November 28, 1944	Operation Market Garden. 82nd and 101st Airborne Divisions land in Holland.
October 4-21, 1944	Battle of Aachen
November 2-December 15, 1944	Battle of Huertgen Forest
December 3, 1944	95th Division captures first bunkers on Siegfried Line
December 16, 1944 to January 25, 1945	Battle of the Bulge, last German offensive of significance

December 26, 1944	Bastogne. U.S. Third Army armored column reaches surrounded U.S. soldiers.
February 9, 1945	Colmar Pocket liquidated
February 13, 1945	U.S. First Army crosses Rhine
March 7, 1945	Bridge at Remagen crossed
March 9, 1945	U.S. First and Third Armies meet and encircle ten German divisions
April 25, 1945	U.S. and Soviet forces link up near Torgau on Elbe River
April 30, 1945	Hitler commits suicide in Berlin
May 7, 1945	V-E Day, Germany surrenders at Reims. Total estimated casualties in Army, Air Force, and Navy: 183,342 killed in action, 478,819 wounded in action, and 151,920 evacuated due to combat exhaustion.

Pacific Theater

December 7, 1941	Japan attacks Pearl Harbor
April 9, 1942	75,000 emaciated U.S. and Filipino soldiers surrender following three-month Battle of Bataan. The next day begins the infamous trek of over sixty miles known as the Bataan Death March. Only 54,000 reach the prison camps, where 40% of U.S. prisoners eventually die vs. 1% in Germany.
April 18, 1942	Colonel James Doolittle leads sixteen B-25 bombers on raid on Tokyo.
June 4, 1942	In Battle of Midway, three American carriers destroy/cripple four of Japan's five great carriers and a smaller carrier, while losing the carrier USS *Yorktown*. Many feel this was the turning point in the war in the Pacific.
August 7, 1942	Operation Watchtower. 1st Marine Division lands at Guadalcanal in Solomon Islands. America's first counteroffensive.
October 23-25, 1944	Battle of Leyte Gulf
January 9, 1945	Americans land on Luzon, Philippiines
February 19, 1945	Marines land on Iwo Jima
April 1, 1945	U.S. invades Okinawa
August 6, 1945	U.S. drops atomic bomb on Hiroshima
August 9, 1945	US. Drops atomic bomb on Nagasaki
August 15, 1945	V-J Day
September 2, 1945	Peace treaty signed on USS *Missouri* in Tokyo Bay ends WWII

*Adapted from "A GI's Combat Chronology: Europe, 1941-1945," VFW Magazine, May 1995, 26-33.

Appendix II

References and Further Reading

Ambrose, Stephen E. (1992). *Band of Brothers*. New York: Touchstone.

Ambrose, Stephen E. (1994). *D-Day: June 6, 1944: The Climactic Battle of World War II*. New York. Simon & Schuster.

Aanenson, Quentin C. (1994). *A Fighter Pilot's Story*. Video produced in association with WETA-TV, Washington, D.C.

Dockery, Kevin. (2001). *Navy SEALS: A History of the Early Years*. New York: Berkley.

Downs, John W. (1966). *The Life Story of John Winston Downs*. Unpublished autobiography.

Dunham, Russell E., with D. R. Wilson. (1981). *Episode on Hill 616: The Story of Congressional Medal of Honor Recipient Russell E. Dunham and his 400 Days in Combat During WWII*. Alton, IL: Crossroads Communications.

Dunn, Benjamin. (1979). *The Bamboo Express*. Chicago: Adams Press. (Revised printing Murphysburo, IL: Jackson Printing and Publishing)

Frankl, Viktor E. (1959). *Man's Search for Meaning: An Introduction to Logotherapy*. Boston: Beacon.

Hickman, Don R. (2000). *No Regrets: The Autobiography of Brigadier General Don Rue Hickman, U.S. Army*. Unpublished autobiography.

McClain, Sally. (2001). *Navajo Weapon: The Navajo Code Talkers*. Tucson, AZ: Rio Nuevo.

Miller, John Grider. (1985). *The Battle to Save the Houston: October 1944 to March 1945*. Annapolis, MD: U.S. Naval Institute.

Newcomb, Richard F. (1965). *Iwo Jima: The Dramatic Account of the Epic Battle that Turned the Tide of World War II*. New York: Henry Holt.

Opdyke, Irene Gut, with Jennifer Armstrong. (2001). *In My Hands: Memories of a Holocaust Rescuer*. New York: Anchor.

Robinson, Leonard L. (2003). *Forgotten Men*. Victoria, Columbia: Trafford Printing.

Smith, Charlene E. M. (1999). *Tuskegee Airman: The Biography of Charles E. McGee*. Boston: Braden Publishing.

Sledge, E. B. (1981). *With the Old Breed at Peleliu and Okinawa*. New York: Oxford University Press.

About the Author

Glenn R. Schiraldi

Glenn R. Schiraldi, Ph.D., has served on the stress management faculties at the Pentagon, The International Critical Incident Stress Foundation, and the University of Maryland, where he received the Outstanding Teaching Award in the College of Health and Human Performance for teaching excellence. He is the author of various articles and books on human mental and physical health. His books on stress-related topics include: *The Post-Traumatic Stress Disorder Sourcebook: A Guide to Healing, Recovery & Growth; WWII Survivors: Lessons in Resilience; The Self-Esteem Workbook; Conquer Anxiety, Worry & Nervous Fatigue: A Guide to Greater Peace; The Anger Management Source Book; Ten Simple Solutions to Build Self-Esteem; Hope and Help for Depression: A Practical Guide;* and *Facts to Relax By: A Guide to Relaxation and Stress Reduction.* Glenn's writing excellence has been recognized by various scholarly and popular sources, including the *Washington Post, American Journal of Health Promotion,* the *Mind/Body Health Review,* and the *International Stress and Tension Control Society Newsletter.*

While serving at the Pentagon, he helped to design and implement a series of prototype courses in stress management for the Department of the Army—including hostility/anger management and communication skills. For the International Critical Incident Stress Foundation he designed and presents resilience training to prevent post-traumatic stress disorder (PTSD) in high-risk groups (military, police, firefighters and other emergency responders). Serving at the University of Maryland since 1980, he has pioneered a number of mind/body courses, which have taught skills to a wide range of adults to prevent stress-related mental and physical illness. His recent research indicates that multiple mental health indicators can be favorably impacted by a semester's course. He has trained clinicians in the U.S. and Canada on treating PTSD and teaching self-esteem skills. Because of his expertise in practical skill building to prevent mental illness, he was invited to join the Board of Directors, Depression and Related Affective Disorders Association, a Johns Hopkins University, Department of Psychiatry, cooperative. He also serves on the editorial board of the *International Journal of Emergency Mental Health* and on the ABC News Post-Traumatic Stress Disorder working group.

He is a graduate of the U.S. Military Academy, West Point, and is a Vietnam-era veteran. He holds graduate degrees from BYU (Summa Cum Laude) and the University of Maryland. His research interests at the University of Maryland center on personality and stress, including resilience, post-traumatic stress, self-esteem, depression, anger/hostility, and anxiety.

Photo Credits

Front Cover photos, from left to right: Courtesy National Archives, photo no. 146. "Back to a Coast Guard assault transport comes this Marine after two days and nights of Hell on the beach of Eniwetok in the Marshall Islands. His face is grimey with coral dust but the light of battle stays in his eyes." February 1944. 26-G-3394.

Courtesy National Archives, photo no.194. "Jubilant American soldier hugs motherly English woman and victory smiles light the faces of happy service men and civilians at Piccadilly Circus, London, celebrating Germany's unconditional surrender." Pfc. Melvin Weiss, England, May 7, 1945. 111-SC-205398.

Courtesy National Archives, photo no. 200. "These Jewish children are on their way to Palestine after having been released from the Buchenwald Concentration Camp. The girl on the left is from Poland, the boy in the center from Latvia, and the girl on right from Hungary." T4c. J. E. Myers, June 5, 1945. 111-SC-207907.

Courtesy National Archives, photo no.121. "Happy 2nd Lt. William Robertson and Lt. Alexander Sylvashko, Russian Army, shown in front of sign [East Meets West] symbolizing the historic meeting of the Russian and American Armies, near Torgau, Germany." Pfc. William E. Poulson, April 25, 1945. 111-SC-205228.

Back Cover, top right: Courtesy National Archives, photo no. 88. "Two bewildered old ladies stand amid the leveled ruins of the almshouse which was Home; until Jerry dropped his bombs. Total war knows no bounds. Almshouse bombed Feb. 10, Newbury, Berks., England." Naccarata, February 11, 1943. 111-SC-178801.

Back Cover photos, from left to right: Courtesy National Archives, photo no. 131. "This picture, captured from the Japanese, shows American prisoners using improvised litters to carry those of their comrades who, from the lack of food or water on the march from Bataan, fell along the road." Philippines, May 1942. 208-AA-288BB-2. *(This photo also appears on page 1 inside the book)*

Courtesy National Archives, photo no. 156. "Flag raising on Iwo Jima." Joe Rosenthal, Associated Press, February 23, 1945. 80-G-413988. *(This photo also appears on page 237 inside the book)*

Courtesy National Archives, photo no. 105. "American troops of the 28th Infantry Division march down the Champs Elysees, Paris, in the `Victory' Parade." Poinsett, August 29, 1944. 111-SC-193197. *(This photo also appears on page 41 inside the book)*

Courtesy National Archives, photo no. 202. "F4U's and F6F's fly in formation during surrender ceremonies; Tokyo, Japan. USS MISSOURI left foreground." September 2, 1945. 80-G-421130. *(This photo also appears on page 343 inside the book)*

Page 339: Courtesy National Archives, photo no. *176.* "Gaunt allied prisoners of war at Aomori camp near Yokohama cheer rescuers from U.S. Navy. Waving flags of the United States, Great Britain and Holland." Japan, August 29, 1945. 80-G-490444.

Page 342, from left to right: Courtesy National Archives, photo no. *53.* "In an underground surgery room, behind the front lines on Bougainville, an American Army doctor operates on a U.S. soldier wounded by a Japanese sniper." December 13, 1943. 111-SC-187247.

Courtesy National Archives, photo no. *56.* "The crew of the USS SOUTH DAKOTA stands with bowed heads, while Chaplain N. D. Lindner reads the benediction held in honor of fellow shipmates killed in the air action off Guam on June 19, 1944." July 1, 1944. 80-G-238322.

Courtesy National Archives, photo no. *97.* "From Coast Guard-manned "sea-horse" landing craft, American troops leap forward to storm a North African beach during final amphibious maneuvers." James D. Rose, Jr., ca. 1944. 26-G-2326.

Courtesy National Archives, photo no. *40.* "Marine Pfc. Douglas Lightheart (right) cradles his 30-cal. machine gun in his lap, while he and his buddy Pfc. Gerald Churchby take time out for a cigarette, while mopping up the enemy on Peleliu Is." Cpl. H. H. Clements, September 14, 1944. 127-N-97628.

Photos of the WWII Survivors and their families that appear in this book are the property of the survivors with all rights returned to them.